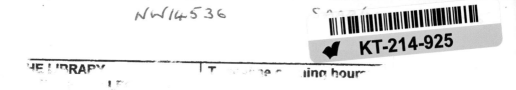
COGNITION IN CHILDREN

WITHDRAWN

Cognition in Children

Usha Goswami

Institute of Child Health
University College, London

Psychology Press
a member of the Taylor & Francis group

Reprinted 1998

Psychology Press Ltd, Publishers
27 Church Road
Hove
East Sussex, BN3 2FA
UK

British Library Cataloguing in Publication Data

A catalogue record for this book is available from the British Library
ISBN 0-86377-824-0 (hbk)
ISBN 0-86377-825-9 (pbk)

ISSN 1368-4566 (Developmental Psychology: A Modular Course)

Front cover illustration:
Baby at Play, by Thomas Eakins/John Hay Whitney Collection.
©1997 Board of Trustees, National Gallery of Art, Washington.

Cover design by Joyce Chester
Printed and bound in the UK by TJ International (Padstow) Ltd.

For Elisabeth Irene Goswami

Acknowledgements

This book was largely written while I was on sabbatical leave at the Department of Psychology, University of Wuerzburg, and The Psychological Institute of the Eberhard-Karls University, Tuebingen. I would like to thank these institutes and also my two hosts, Professor Wolfgang Schneider and Professor Fritz Wilkening, for so generously providing all the facilities and support that I needed during my stay. I would also like to thank Wolfgang and Fritz, and Sabina Pauen, Beate Sodian, and Claudia Roebers, for many useful discussions during the course of my writing. Sabina Pauen and Karen Freeman deserve special mention for patiently reading through a number of draft chapters and providing me with valuable feedback, and many valuable comments were also made by my reviewers George Butterworth, Peter Bryant, Alan Slater, and Henry Wellman. Louise Dalton also merits a special mention for her invaluable library work in England. I thank the Alexander von Humboldt Foundation Research Fellowship scheme for making my stay in Germany possible. Finally, I would like to thank my dear husband Mark Thomson for his love and support, and for his continual enthusiasm for my work.

USHA GOSWAMI
London, August 1997

Contents

Series preface

Developmental psychology is an exciting and a fast-moving subject. Great strides are being taken in understanding the origins of people's behaviour in early childhood and in accounting for the dramatic and often varied ways in which children's behaviour changes as they grow older. The main aim of *Developmental Psychology: A Modular Course* is to provide an up-to-date and flexible account of the subject.

Different people come to development psychology for different reasons – some because they want to know about its clinical and educational implications, others because they are interested in the origins of human behaviour, others because they are concerned with a particular period of childhood, such as the pre-school period, or adolescence. The series is designed to satisfy all such needs. It will consist of a set of books, each of which gives an account of psychological theories about children and of the research that is being done to test these theories. In different combinations they will answer the more specific questions that different people want answered by developmental psychologists.

The texts will suit a broad audience, including teachers and other interested professionals, undergraduates studying psychology, and A-level psychology students. The topics covered include reviews of research on children's intellectual and emotional development, as well as coverage of practical topics, such as learning to read and learning about mathematics. Aspects of abnormal development will also be considered.

Peter Bryant
George Butterworth

Foreword

Foetuses have surprisingly active lives. Ultrasonic scanning studies reveal that, by the fifteenth gestational week, the foetus has at least 15 distinctly different movement patterns at its command, including a yawn-and-stretch pattern and a "stepping" movement that enables it to change its position completely in the womb (via rotation) within two seconds (de Vries, Visser, & Prechtl, 1984). We also know that foetuses have some form of cognitive life (Hepper, 1992). Research has shown that memory for the mother's voice is developed while the baby is in the womb (see Chapter 1), and there is also evidence for foetal learning of particular pieces of music (such as the theme tune of the soap opera *Neighbours*, Hepper, 1988). Learning and memory are fundamental cognitive skills. However, there is little evidence for more sophisticated cognitive activity in the foetus, such as reasoning or problem solving. The full spectrum of cognitive skills only emerge when the infant enters the everyday world of people and objects, when vision becomes possible, and when auditory input is no longer mediated by amniotic fluid. In fact, the infant brain doubles in size during the first year of life.

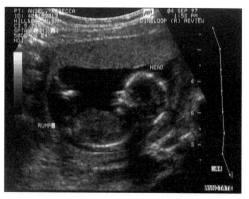

TRIP/H. ROGERS

The "what" and "why" of children's cognition

The study of cognition in children has traditionally focused around two major questions. The first is the apparently simple question of *what develops*. This question can be investigated by observing changes in children's cognitive abilities over time, and by defining certain principles of logical thought and then tracking the development of these principles with experimental tests. Information about *what develops* provides data for the second major question in cognitive developmental psychology, the less simple question of *why* development pursues its observed course. This question requires us to develop causal explanations for observed cognitive changes.

Domain-general vs. domain-specific accounts of cognition in children

Two alternative (although not mutually exclusive) explanatory systems have been developed to account for changes in children's cognition. The first theoretical account is based on the idea that key logical developments are applied across all cognitive domains. This is a "domain-general" explanation of cognitive development. Domains can be thought of as the set of representations sustaining specific areas of knowledge (Karmiloff-Smith, 1994). Whether a child is attempting to understand why another child is upset (the "domain" of psychological causation), why animals usually have babies that look like them (the "domain" of biology), or why objects fall when they are insufficiently supported (the "domain" of physical reasoning), domain-general accounts postulate that certain logical developments, such as the ability to make deductive inferences, are applied to the acquisition of all of these understandings.

The second theoretical account postulates that the development of logical thought is piecemeal, occurring at different time points in different domains. According to this view, logical development is "domain-specific". For example, deductive inferences may appear in the domain of physical causality long before they appear in the domain of psychological causality. The reason may be that a rich and principled understanding of the physical world is acquired before a rich and principled understanding of the psychological world (the latter is often called a "theory of mind"). Domain-specific accounts of cognitive development demonstrate the importance of the *knowledge base* in children's cognition.

The importance of the knowledge base in cognitive development explains why the two explanatory systems that have developed to account for changes in children's cognition are not mutually exclusive. While the ability to make deductive inferences *per se* may be a domain-general development, the use of this kind of reasoning may be domain-specific, because children may need sufficient *knowledge* in order to use their deductive abilities in different domains. Other factors may also affect the pattern of cognitive development. These include the richness of the child's environment, the maturation of certain cognitive structures such as the frontal cortex, and the quality of the support and teaching that a child receives at home and in school.

As we will see in this book, the knowledge base expands exponentially during infancy and childhood. The amount of knowledge that children acquire about their everyday worlds increases at a terrific rate, with a causally coherent body of knowledge about the physical world developing during the first year of life, and rich and principled knowledge about categories and kinds being available as early as the third year. Some very basic cognitive mechanisms play a key role in acquiring these rich bodies of knowledge. Learning, memory, and perception function well in the neonate, and "higher" cognitive processes such as reasoning and problem solving can be demonstrated by 6 months. However, perhaps the most fundamental process in cognitive development is the apparently innate bias found in the human infant to learn about causal relations and to acquire causal explanations.

The causal bias

This simple causal bias bestows an enormous amount of information on the infant and the young child. Anyone with a child of their own or a young sibling is familiar with the constant tendency of young children to ask for causal information ("Why is the sky blue? How does the telephone call know which house to go to? How come the moon is big and orange now but other times it's little and white?", see for example Callanan & Oakes, 1992; Hood & Bloom, 1979). This relentless questioning is not just a device that children employ to keep a conversation going. Instead, causal questions such as these have an important developmental function. Children's bias towards seeking causal information gives them the ability to explain, predict, and eventually even to control events within their everyday worlds. This causal bias acts to organise early memory, it underlies conceptual development, it helps the child to understand the physical world, and it acts as a pacesetter for logical thought.

Furthermore, children's causal questions demonstrate that abilities such as deductive reasoning are present from an early age. Here is an example of everyday deductive reasoning at work, taken from an interchange that took place at the child's bedtime (Callanan & Oakes, 1992, pp. 221–2):

> *Child* (age 4;2) to *Mother*: "Why does Daddy, James [big brother] and me have blue eyes, and you have green eyes?"
>
> *Mother* : [*Told her she got her eyes from Daddy. Then said goodnight and left the room.*]

Child : [calls her mother back five minutes later] "I like Pee Wee Herman [a comedian] and I have blue eyes. Daddy likes Pee Wee Herman and he has blue eyes. James likes Pee Wee Herman and he has blue eyes. If you liked Pee Wee Herman you could get blue eyes too."

Mother : Told child that God gave her this colour and they couldn't be changed.]

Child : "Could you try to like Pee Wee Herman so we could see if your eyes turn blue?"

The logical deductions here are impressive. The little girl reasons that X (liking Pee Wee Herman) implies Y (having blue eyes) in three cases out of three, and that X' (not liking Pee Wee Herman) implies Y' (not having blue eyes) in one case out of one. This covariation information appears persuasive, and so she forms a causal hypothesis (liking Pee Wee Herman determines eye colour). She then thinks of a way to test her hypothesis (change X' into X, and see if Y' changes to Y). This exchange incorporates the knowledge that causes and their effects should systematically covary, and illustrates that young children are capable of deductive logic and hypothesis testing—even at the tender age of 4!

Causal reasoning is an example of a mechanism that seems to be *both* domain-general and domain-specific. Children make causal inferences in different domains at different points in development, for example using causal inferences to learn about the physical world before they use causal inferences in the biological domain. However, physical knowledge develops much earlier than biological knowledge, partly because the world of objects and events becomes familiar to the young infant long before the world of plants and animals. The ability to make causal inferences thus appears to be domain-general, emerging at different times in different domains according to the growth of domain-specific knowledge.

Innate vs. acquired accounts of cognition in children

A related theoretical issue to that of domain-specific versus domain-general explanations of cognitive development is that of nature versus nurture. Should the underlying causes of development be explained in terms of a rich genetic endowment of complex behavioural abilities, or in terms of a rich experience of the environment?

The metaphor of the mind of the infant as a blank slate has long been discredited, and so the "nature versus nurture" debate may appear no longer relevant to developmental psychology. However, recent research demonstrating the relevant sophistication of infant cognition has led to a renaissance of strong nativist views—a kind of "genetic determinism". Yet as pointed out by Turkewitz (1995), genes cannot "code" psychological traits in any fixed or hard-wired fashion. Genes get turned on and off as a result of the operation of other genes, and contribute to the formation of gene products. Thus knowing whether a particular ability is present at or near birth does not help us to understand its developmental source, being instead a starting point for the investigation of causes and consequences. The real question for developmental psychology is how genes and environment *interact* to produce development. We need to ask questions about how the characteristics and limitations of infant motor, sensory, perceptual, and cognitive functioning produce modes of responding to the environment that help to shape the development of adult cognitive functions.

Qualitative vs. quantitative accounts of developmental change

A rather different explanatory system for characterising cognitive development can be found in the work of Jean Piaget. Piaget's theoretical framework for explaining children's cognition has dominated the field of cognitive-developmental psychology. Piaget saw cognitive development as a *qualitative* process, involving the emergence of new modes of thinking as revolutions occurred in the structure of thought. Such a qualitative explanation of cognitive development is at first sight at odds with the *quantitative* nature of much developmental change, which involves the piecemeal and gradual acquisition of strategies and knowledge. The theoretical debate concerning the qualitative versus quantitative nature of developmental change is, like the debates concerning nature versus nurture and domain-specificity versus domain-generality, more apparent than real. Both kinds of explanation have a role to play in explaining cognitive development.

Piaget's stage theory

Piaget's explanation of cognitive development was qualitative in nature because it was a stage theory. Piaget argued for three major stages in cognitive development, the *sensory-motor* stage, during which cognition was based on action; the stage of *concrete operations*, during which cognition was based on the symbolic understanding of concrete objects and the relations between them, and the stage of *formal operations*, during which cognition was characterised by hypothesis testing and scientific thought. However, Piaget also allowed for quantitative change. The main causal mechanism underlying the fundamental cognitive restructuring found with the onset of a new stage was the quest for cognitive equilibrium, which depended on the complementary processes of *accommodation* and *assimilation*. These processes were gradual and incremental, accommodation acting to gradually change childrens concepts ("cognitive schemes") to fit reality, and assimilation acting to interpret experience in terms of current cognitive schemes.

We can illustrate the cognitive functioning of children during the three stages by considering an example of a key cognitive achievement at each stage. A key achievement during the stage of sensory-motor cognition was the concept of "object permanence"—the understanding that objects continue to exist when they are out of view. According to Piaget, the attainment of a cognitive representation of the object was acquired gradually over the first 18 months of life. Very young infants could not differentiate between objects and their own actions, and even infants as old as 12 months believed that the existence of objects was tied to action and spatial location. The latter belief was demonstrated by the "A-not-B" search error found in infants aged from 8 to 12 months. Infants who make A-not-B errors persist in searching at a previously successful location (A) even when the object that they seek has been moved to a new location (B) in full view of the infant. Piaget suggested that the infant believed that the object could be re-created at location A by the action of searching there for it. Full object permanence was only achieved when infants could find objects wherever they were hidden, even if the act of hiding occurred out of view of the infant.

A key achievement of the concrete operational stage was the understanding of transitivity—the ability to organise entities into an ordinal sequence via the use of logical inferences based on the relations between them. Transitivity was one of the particular group of logical "operations" or concepts that marked the onset of the concrete operational stage of logical thought. Most children acquired these logical concepts at the ages of around 6 to 7 years. For example, a typical transitive inference problem of the form "If Tom is bigger than Edward, and Edward is bigger than John, who is bigger, Tom or John?" could not be solved by younger children. Younger children were thought to be unable to use mental logic to combine the premise information and work out that Tom was bigger—at least, when the premises were presented successively, as in Piaget's transitive inference tasks.

Finally, a key achievement of the formal operational stage was the ability to reason by analogy. The formal operational stage was marked by the ability to take the results of concrete operations, such as the nature of the relations between objects, and to reason about their logical relationships. This kind of cognition became available around the age of 11 to 12 years. Analogies involve the recognition of relational similarity, as in the Piagetian example "Bicycle is to handlebars as ship is to rudder" (the similar relation here being "steering mechanism"). The construction of possible relations *between* the relations between objects was thought to be a higher-order form of reasoning, characteristic of the final stage of logical development, and so analogies were a prime example of formal operational thought.

The organisation of this book

As we will see, Piaget's claims concerning object permanence and transitive inferences have been the focus of considerable debate in the field of children's cognition. If infants lack object permanence, they must live in a constant "snapshot world" of the here and now, and if children cannot make transitive inferences they will have difficulties with several basic mathematical concepts such as ordinal relations and measuring. Piaget's claims about the late onset of analogical reasoning have also been questioned. We will leave discussion of these debates until the final chapters in this book. We will begin by examining the remarkable extent of the cognitive skills that have been revealed by more recent research post-Piaget.

The early chapters in this book will focus on the question of "what develops" in children's cognition rather than on the question of "why". We will examine "what develops" in areas such as learning, memory, problem solving, reasoning, conceptual development, and causal reasoning. Although we will return to the question of "why" children's cognition pursues its observed course in the final chapter, the explanatory systems or theories used to explain what develops vary greatly, and will not be treated in any depth, with the exception of Piaget's theory. This book will focus more on the different kinds of knowledge that children acquire, and on how this acquisition is achieved. This is because while findings from a given experimental study ("what develops") are generally fixed, the interpretation of what particular findings mean ("why") is fluid. This is one of the most exciting aspects of research. Developmental theories can be thought of as organising the information about development that has been gathered by researchers studying "what develops". Some of the experiments that will be discussed have alternative interpretations, and every student interested in children's cognition is invited to develop their own ideas about what the different studies mean (preferably along with some ideas about how to find out whether the studies are right or not!). Once a clearer picture of the expanding knowledge base is available, a clearer understanding of the appropriate explanatory frameworks for the "why" of cognitive development should be possible.

The aim of this book is to provide a selective, but hopefully representative, review of some of the most interesting current work in cognitive development, grouped around themes that are familiar from discussions of cognition in adults. However, it is not possible to cover all aspects of children's cognition in one volume. Some important aspects of children's cognition are major topics in their own right, and are the subject of separate volumes in this series. These topics include linguistic development and the relationship between language and thought; the understanding of psychological causality and the minds of others ("theory of mind"); the importance of cultural transmission and cultural tools for cognitive development, including the ideas of Vygotsky; the effects of schooling on cognitive development and the development of reading and mathematical cognition; and a consideration of abnormalities in cognitive development. Some of the topics that are included in this volume but only discussed briefly, such as infant perceptual development, are also the subject of separate volumes in the series.

Cognition in infancy: Basic cognitive processes 1

Cognition can be defined as the set of processes that enable us to gain information about our environments—processes such as learning, memory, reasoning, and problem solving. Information processing is not an end in itself, however, as the goal of cognition is to give us *control* over our environment. A degree of control enables us to manipulate the environment to serve our needs and desires. This requires *understanding*—in order to have control, we need knowledge about *causation*. Cognitive development in a broad sense is thus the development of the set of processes that enable us to gain knowledge about causation.

The fundamental processes of cognitive development are learning, memory, perception, and attention. According to many theories, without some form of *memory*, infants would live in a constant world of the "here and now". In order to remember, babies must *learn* what is familiar. A cognitive system cannot display memory without simultaneously displaying learning. At the same time, learning and memory in infants and neonates would be impossible if infants lacked adequate perceptual skills and adequate attentional mechanisms. Although there are some important immaturities in the visual system at birth (see Atkinson & Braddick, 1989), recent research has shown that the visual and auditory perceptual abilities of babies are much more sophisticated than was once supposed. In fact, recent research has revealed that surprisingly young babies have active cognitive lives.

Memory and learning

Memory is a good place to begin to study infant cognition. Memory is a cognitive process that begins to function within the womb, indicating that learning is also functional before birth. Evidence that babies begin storing memories while they are still in the womb comes from an ingenious study by DeCaspar and Fifer (1980), who tested babies' memory approximately 12 hours after they had been born.

Neonate memory for the mother's voice

It is known that infants can hear noises from inside the womb during at least the third trimester onwards (6–9 months). One sound that they hear a lot is their mother's voice. She may be talking to other people during her daily routines, talking on the telephone, or even talking to the infant in her womb. If infants can *remember* the sound of their mother's voice, then they should be able to distinguish her voice from the voice of a female stranger. In order to see whether infants were able to do this, DeCaspar and Fifer first measured how strongly infants sucked on a dummy in the absence of any auditory stimulus. They then introduced two tape recordings, one of the infant's mother reading a story, and one of a strange woman reading the same story. For some infants, every time their suck rate increased compared to baseline, they were rewarded with the tape of their mother's voice. Every time their suck rate fell below the baseline measure, they heard the tape of the voice of the stranger. For other infants, the contingencies were reversed. A low suck rate relative to baseline was rewarded with their mother's voice, and a high suck rate relative to baseline was rewarded with the voice of the stranger.

Both groups of infants rapidly learned to suck at the appropriate rate to hear their mother's voice. This shows that they remembered the sound of their own mother's voice, and that it was a familiar and comforting stimulus. Even more impressive, they could remember the contingency in a second test session given on the following day. Babies who had learned to suck strongly to hear their mother began by sucking strongly on the dummy, and those who had learned to suck slowly began by sucking slowly. The experimenters, however, had reversed the contingencies. Babies who had learned to suck strongly for their mother's voice were now meant to suck slowly, and babies who had learned to suck slowly were now meant to suck strongly. Around 80% of the babies learned to reverse their suck rate. This is good evidence for learning and memory in these extremely young babies. In fact, the ability to reverse a learned rule is considered to be a strong test of cognition in animals, and so the rapid learning found in these babies shows that day-old babies are at least as cognitively sophisticated as rats and pigeons, and are more cognitively sophisticated than goldfish, who cannot learn rule reversals even after thousands of trials!

Neonate memory for familiar stories

In order to provide a strong test of the idea that memory for the mother's voice does indeed occur via learning *in utero*, rather than from very rapid learning during the first few hours after birth, DeCaspar and

Spence (1986) conducted a further study in which mothers read three stories onto a tape. The mothers then selected one of the three stories and read it every day during the last six weeks of their pregnancies. Following birth, the infants' baseline suck rates were established, and the infants were then rewarded for sucking either above or below baseline by their mother's voice reading the familiar story. If sucking fell to baseline, the infants heard their mother's voice reading an unfamiliar story. DeCaspar and Spence found that the infants consistently sucked at the rate that was appropriate to produce the familiar story. Interestingly, a second group of infants showed the same pattern of preferences when tested with another mother's voice reading the stories. DeCaspar and Spence argued that the target stories were preferred because the infants had heard them before birth. The babies had apparently learned something about the acoustic cues specifying a particular target passage as foetuses, and could recognise these cues even when a strange female voice was reading the story.

Memory for objects

Although the sound of one's mother's voice could be argued to be an unusually salient stimulus, infant memory for more mundane objects and events is also impressive. For example, Bushnell, McCutcheon, Sinclair, and Tweedie (1984) studied infants' memory for pictures of simple shapes such as red triangles and blue crosses, which were mounted on wooden paddles. The infants were aged 3 and 7 weeks. Memory for a simple stimulus such as a yellow circle was first developed by asking the infants' mothers to present the stimulus daily for a two-week period. The mothers were encouraged to show their babies the stimulus "actively" for two 15-minute sessions per day. The babies were then visited at home by an experimenter, who showed them the habituating stimulus and also a random selection of the other stimuli, varying in either colour, shape, or colour *and* shape. The aim was to test the infants' memories for these different aspects of the stimuli. For example, to test colour memory, the baby might be shown a red circle rather than a yellow circle. To test memory for shape, the baby might be shown a yellow square instead of a yellow circle, and so on. Bushnell et al. found that the infants retained information about every aspect of the stimuli that they had been shown—shape, colour, and size.

Cornell (1979) used pictures of groups of such stimuli to study recognition memory in infants aged from 5 to 6 months. In addition to pictures of patterns of geometric forms (see Fig. 1.1), he also used photographs of human faces. The babies were first shown two identical pictures from Set 1 side-by-side, followed by two identical pictures from Set 2, followed by two identical pictures from Set 3 (the photographs of human faces), and were allowed to study each set for a period of up to 20 seconds. Two days later they were shown the pictures again, first in a brief "reminder" phase in which each previously studied picture was presented on its own, and then for a recognition phase in which the familiar picture from each set was paired with an unfamiliar picture from the same set. Recognition memory was assumed if the infants devoted more looking time to the novel picture in each pair.

Cornell found a novelty preference across all the sets of stimuli that he used. Even though two days had passed since the infants saw the pictures, they remembered those that were familiar and thus preferred to look at the novel pictures in the recognition phase of the experiment. Their recognition memory was not due to the brief reminder cue, as a control group who received the "reminder" phase of the experiment without the initial study phase did not show a novelty response during the recognition test. Given that the stimuli were fairly abstract (except for the faces) and were presented for a relatively short period of time

FIG. 1.1.
The stimulus sets used by Cornell (1979) to study recognition memory in infants. Reproduced by permission of Academic Press Inc.

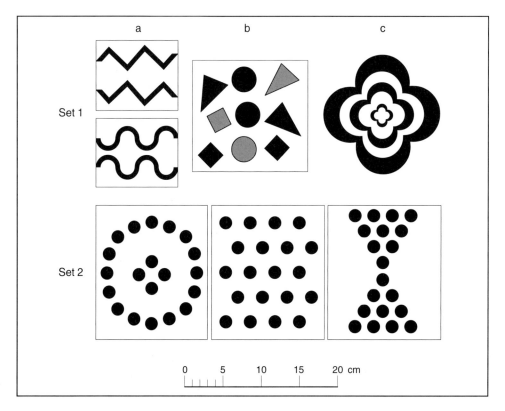

in the initial study phase, their retention over a two-day period is good evidence for well developed recognition memory in young infants.

Memory for events

Some striking studies carried out by Clifton, Perris and their colleagues have shown that 6-month-olds can also retain memories for events, and do so over very long time periods. For example, in one such study, 6½-month-olds were able to retain a memory of a single event that had occurred once until they were 2½ years of age (Perris, Myers, & Clifton, 1990).

Perris et al. (1990) demonstrated this by bringing some infants who had taken part in an experiment in their laboratory as 6-month-olds back to the laboratory at 2½ and retesting them. During the infancy experiment the babies had been required to reach both in the dark and in the light for a Big Bird finger puppet that made a rattle noise (the experiment was about the localisation of sounds). The reaching session had taken about 20 minutes. Two years later, the children were brought back to the same laboratory room and met the same female experimenter, who said that they would play some games. She showed them five plastic toys, including the Big Bird puppet, and asked which toy they thought would be part of the game. She then told them that Big Bird made a sound in the game, and asked them to guess which one it was out of a rattle noise, a bell, and a clicker. Finally, the children played a game in the dark, which was to reach accurately to one of five possible locations for the sounding puppet. After five uninstructed dark trials, during which no information about what to do was given, the children were given five more trials in which they were told to "catch the noisy Big Bird in the dark". A group of control children who had not experienced the procedure as infants were also tested.

Perris et al. found that the experimental group showed little *explicit* recall of their experiences as infants. They were no more likely than the control group to select Big Bird as the toy who would be part of the game, or to choose the rattle noise over the bell and the clicker. However, they showed a clear degree of *implicit* recall, as measured by their behaviour during the game in the dark. They were more likely to reach out towards the sound than the children in the control group in the first five trials, and they also reached more accurately. If they were given a reminder of their early experience, by hearing the sound of the rattle for three seconds half an hour before the test in the dark, then they were especially likely to show the reaching behaviour. Again, this was not true of the control group. Finally, the children who had experienced the auditory localisation task as infants were much less likely to become distressed by the darkness during the testing than the children who had not experienced the auditory localisation task as infants. Nine of the latter children (out of 16) asked to leave before completing the uninstructed trials, compared to only two children in the experimental group. Children who had experienced reaching in the dark as infants thus showed evidence of remembering that event two years later in a number of different ways. Similar results were reported in a study by Myers, Clifton, and Clarkson (1987), who showed that children who were almost 3 years old also retained memories of the laboratory and the auditory localisation testing procedures that they had encountered as infants. These children had had 15–19 exposures to the experimental procedures as infants, however, and so their memory is in some sense less surprising than that demonstrated in the experiment by Perris et al.

Memory for causal events

Event memory can also be studied by teaching infants a causal *contingency* between a response and a reward, as in De Casper and Fifer's work. This technique of using learned causal relationships between the production of a response and the delivery of a reward has been extended to older infants by Rovee-Collier and her colleagues (e.g. Rovee-Collier et al., 1980). In their pioneering studies, the conditioned response was kicking, and the reward was the activation of an attractive mobile hanging over the infant's crib. The contingency was that kicking activated the mobile. Activation of the mobile occurred via a ribbon that was tied to the infant's ankle. As kicking comes naturally to young infants, the kicking response is present whether the mobile is there or not. The important point about Rovee-Collier's paradigm is that the infant must *learn* that kicking makes the mobile start to work. Memory for this cause–effect relation was measured by returning the infants to the same crib after some time had passed, and seeing how much they kicked in the presence of the mobile.

For example, in a typical experiment, the infant is visited at home (see Rovee-Collier & Hayne, 1987, for a review). An attractive mobile is erected on the side of their crib, and a second empty mobile stand is also erected (see Fig. 1.2). The ribbon is first tied to this empty stand, to measure the baseline kick rate in the absence of reinforcement with the mobile. After approximately three minutes, the ribbon is attached to the correct mobile stand, and the infant is allowed to kick for about nine minutes for the reward of activating the mobile. The ribbon is then moved back to the empty stand for a final three-minute period. The difference in kick rate between this second three-minute period and the

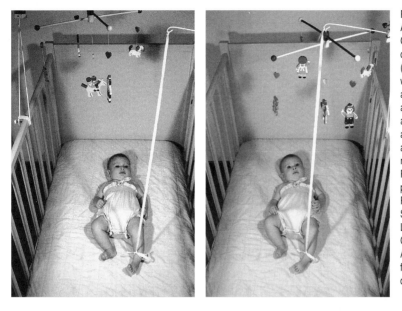

FIG. 1.2.
An infant in Rovee-Collier's causal contingency paradigm (A) during baseline, when kicking cannot activate the mobile, and (B) during acquisition, when the ankle ribbon is attached to the mobile.
Reprinted with permission from Rovee-Collier, Sullivan, Enright, Lucas and Fagan. Copyright (1980) American Association for the Advancement of Science.

initial baseline period provides a measure of the infant's short-term retention of the contingency. The infant is then visited a second time some days after the original learning phase, and the ribbon is again tied to the empty stand. Long-term retention of the cause–effect relation is measured by comparing kicking in the absence of reinforcement during this second visit with the original baseline kick rate.

Rovee-Collier and her colleagues have found that 3-month-old infants show little forgetting of the mobile contingency over periods ranging from two to eight days. By 14 days, however, forgetting of the contingency appears to be complete. Furthermore, as the time between the learning and test periods increases, the infants forget the specific details of the training mobile (its colours and shapes), and respond as strongly to a novel mobile as to the original. Twenty-four hours after learning, the infants remember the objects on the mobile, and will not respond to mobiles containing more than one novel object. By four days, however, they will respond to a novel five-object mobile. This suggests that infants, like older children and adults, gradually forget the physical characteristics or attributes of what they have learned, retaining only the gist of, or the associations between, specific attributes and the context of learning.

Interestingly, at the same time as memory for the mobile itself declines, memory for the surrounding context (e.g. the pattern on the crib bumper) becomes more important in reactivating the infant's memory of the contingency. Infants show perfect retention of the contingency at 24 hours, whatever the pattern on the crib bumper. By seven days, infants who have been trained with a distinctive crib bumper show apparently complete forgetting if they receive a different crib bumper at test, while infants who receive the distinctive crib bumper at test remember the contingency. The different cues on the crib bumper, such as its colours and the particular shapes in its pattern, appear to be forgotten at different rates (Rovee-Collier, Schechter, Shyi, & Shields, 1992). It is difficult to escape the conclusion that details of the learning context, such as details of the pattern on a distinctive crib bumper, are acting to *cue* recall.

If the crib bumper indeed provides an appropriate "reminder" cue for recall, then we can examine whether "forgotten" memories become accessible again when appropriate retrieval cues are provided. Rovee-Collier and her colleagues have developed a *reactivation* paradigm to study this question. The retrieval cue that they have studied most intensively is a *reminder* of the mobile contingency, namely showing the infants the moving mobile for three minutes prior to measuring kick rate. During the reminder phase, the mobile is activated by a hidden experimenter pulling on the ribbon, and the infants are prevented from kicking by a special seat that also precludes "on-the-spot" learning. The infants are then retested in the crib procedure 24 hours after the reminding event. With a reminder, 3-month-old infants demonstrate completely intact memories for the mobile contingency 14 and 28 days after the training event; 2-month-old infants show excellent memories after a 14-day delay, but only a third of this age group show intact memory after 28 days. By 6 months of age, the retention period is at least three weeks (Rovee-Collier, 1993). Thus very young infants can develop long-term memories for causal events, and memory retrieval appears to be governed by the same kind of cues that determine retrieval in adults.

Another way of examining infants' long-term memory for causal events is to use delayed imitation, a technique pioneered by Meltzoff in his studies of learning (see Chapter 2). Mandler and McDonough (1995) used delayed imitation to examine 11-month-old infants' retention of causal events over a three-month period. The events were two-step action sequences, namely "make a rattle" (by pushing a button into a box with a slot, which then rattled when shaken), and "make a rocking horse" (by attaching a horse with magnetic feet to a magnetised rocker). Imitation of the events was measured on the following day (24-hour retention period), and three months later. On each occasion the infants were simply presented with the materials (the horse, the rocker), and were then observed. To check that the older infants were not simply more likely to discover the sequences without having seen them being modelled, a control group of 14-month-old infants were also given the materials at the three-month follow-up.

Mandler and McDonough found that recall was good at both the 24-hour and the three-month retention intervals, and that there was little forgetting over the three-month period. In contrast, retention of non-causal events (e.g. "put a hat on the bunny, and feed him a carrot"), was poorer than that of causal events at 24 hours, and non-existent after the three-month interval. Mandler argues that retaining causal relations is one of the major ways of organising material that is to be remembered in a coherent and meaningful fashion. The importance of causal relations for memory development is covered more fully in Chapter 5.

Procedural vs. declarative memories?

It is notable that all of the studies just discussed have measured infant memory in terms of the infants' *behaviour*. Rovee-Collier measured the amount of kicking that was produced to the mobile, Mandler the number of action sequences that were reproduced with the props, and Clifton children's reaching behaviour in the auditory localisation paradigm. This raises the question of whether these memories are somehow different in *kind* to the type of memory in which we bring some aspect of the past to conscious awareness (e.g. Mandler, 1990). Is infant memory an active remembrance of things past, or is it more akin to a conditioned response of the type studied in animals?

In fact, it is widely accepted in cognitive psychology that there are *two* types of memory system in humans. One is automatic in operation, and is not accessible to verbal report. This kind of memory is usually called implicit or procedural memory. The second involves bringing the past to mind, and thinking about it. This kind of memory is usually called explicit or declarative memory. Only the latter involves information that has been encoded in such a way as to be accessible to consciousness. Infants are generally assumed not to encode explicit or declarative memories until they become verbally competent, a phenomenon that has been called "infantile amnesia". This is discussed more fully in Chapter 5. The development of implicit and explicit memories are also discussed more fully in that chapter.

Perception and attention

As noted earlier, recent research has shown that the visual and auditory perceptual abilities of babies are much more sophisticated than was once supposed. In this section, we focus on visual perceptual abilities.

However, similar sophistication is found in the auditory domain. We have already seen that the auditory perceptual system is functioning during the third trimester of pregnancy, to a degree that enables neonates to discriminate a familiar story from an unfamiliar one. Infants are also able to group or organise auditory stimuli into patterns, perceiving temporal rhythms and melodies when played a series of discrete notes (Mehler & Bertoncini, 1979). They can locate sounds in space, turning their heads in the direction of preferred sounds (Clarkson, Clifton, & Morrongiello, 1985); and they can inter-relate perceptual information from more than one modality (this is discussed further later). A large variety of studies, only some of which can be mentioned here, show that the perceptual world of even the very young infant appears to be organised into objects and their relation-ships.

Adequate attentional mechanisms also appear to be available shortly after birth. However, it is not clear whether these mechanisms are under the infant's volitional control. It can be very difficult to attract an infant's attention, particularly to a stationary visual stimulus, as many infant experimenters will tell you! At one point it was believed that infants were passive in their selection of visual stimuli. The idea was that attention to certain stimuli was obligatory, and that visual "capture" by these stimuli controlled infant attention (e.g. Stechler & Latz, 1966). For example, 1-month-old infants can have great difficulty in disengaging from one stimulus in order to make an eye movement to another location, and may end up bursting into tears! (Johnson, 1997). By 3 months of age, however, infants appear to have more control over their eye movements.

One way to study when attentional mechanisms in infants come under volitional control is to study their *expectations* of visual events. The visual world of the baby is an active one, characterised by a dynamic flow of perceptual events over which the babies themselves have no control. In order to deal with this dynamic flow of events, infants need to develop expectations of predictable visual events, around which they can then organise their behaviour (Haith, Hazan, & Goodman, 1988). The development of visual expectancies requires the volitional control of visual attention.

Attention in infancy

In order to find out whether babies as young as 3½ months of age can develop visual expectations, Haith and his colleagues devised a paradigm that involved showing babies a series of stimuli to the left and to the right of their centre of gaze. In Haith et al. (1988), the stimuli used included pictures of chequerboards, bullseyes, and schematic faces in different colours (the kind of stimuli used by Fantz, 1961, to examine visual perception in babies, see later). Sixty stimuli were used in all. Thirty of these were presented in a left–right alternating sequence, which was thus predictable, and the remaining 30 were presented in a random left–right order. The movements of the babies' eyes were observed during both the predictable and the random presentation sequences. Haith et al. argued that, if the infants could detect the alternation rule governing the appearance of the predictable stimuli, then they should develop expectations of the left–right alternation, and should make anticipatory eye movements to the location of the next slide. Such eye movements should be less common during the random presentation sequences. This was exactly what happened. The infants showed more anticipatory fixations to the predictable (alternating) sequence than to the unpredictable (random) sequence of pictures, and also showed enhanced reaction times, meaning that they were developing expectations for the visual events quite rapidly. This shows that, at least by the age of 3½ months, babies can control their own perceptual (attentional) activity.

Using a somewhat different task, Gilmore and Johnson (1995) have shown that, by the age of 6 months, infants can also control their visual attention over delays of at least three to five seconds. Gilmore and Johnson's paradigm involved showing the infants an attractive geometric display presented on the central screen of an array of three computer screens. This encouraged fixation to the centre (see Fig. 1.3). Once the infants were reliably looking at this fixation point, a blue

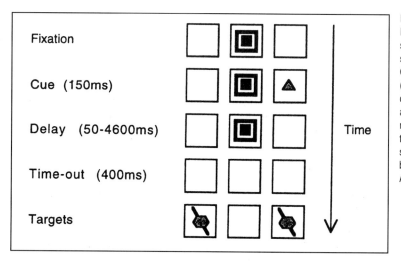

FIG. 1.3. Example of one of the stimulus presentation sequences used by Gilmore and Johnson (1995) to study infant control of visual attention. Each box represents one of the three computer screens. Reproduced by permission of Academic Press Inc.

triangle ("cue stimulus") was flashed briefly either to the left screen or to the right screen in the array. The central fixation point then stayed on for a set time period of between one and five seconds, after which all three screens went dark for 400 milliseconds. Two rotating, multi-coloured cogwheel shapes (which were highly attractive to the infant) then appeared, one on the left screen and one on the right screen. The experimenters scored whether the infants showed a preference for looking at the cued location during the delay period, prior to the onset of the cogwheel targets.

Gilmore and Johnson found strong preferences for the cued location at each of the three different time intervals that they studied, which were 0.6 seconds, 3 seconds, and 5 seconds. They argued that this showed that the infants were maintaining a representation of the spatial location of the cue, and were using it to plan their eye movements several seconds later. In a follow-up study, Gilmore and Johnson cued the eventual left or right location of the target stimulus by presenting different geometric displays at the central fixation point, and omitting the blue triangle. For example, if the centre-screen stimulus was a pattern made up of four shifting light- and dark-blue circles, then the target would appear on the right three or five seconds later, whereas if the centre-screen stimulus was a pattern made up of small red and yellow squares which spiralled around each other, then the target would appear on the left three or five seconds later. The infants quickly learned this contingency, and again showed strong preferences to look to the cued location. Gilmore and Johnson argue that their expectation paradigm shows the early operation of "working memory" in the infant. Working memory is a short-term storage system for holding information, and its development is discussed further in Chapter 5.

Visual preference and habituation

The existence of visual preferences in infancy provides a useful index of infants' perceptual abilities as well as of their attentional skills. Suppose that we want to discover whether an infant can make a simple visual discrimination between a cross and a circle. One way to find out is to show the infant a picture of a cross and a picture of a circle, and to see which shape the infant prefers to look at. The existence of a preference would imply that the infant can *distinguish* between the different forms. The "visual preference" technique was first used by Fantz (1961), who found that 7-month-old infants showed *no* preference between a cross and a circle. Instead, they looked at both shapes for an equal amount of time (see Fig.1.4).

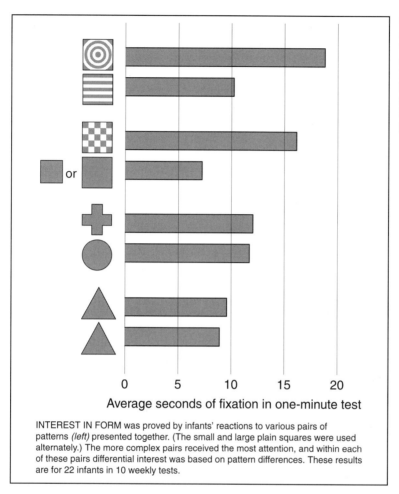

FIG. 1.4.
Examples of the visual preference stimuli adapted from Fantz (1961) to study infant form perception, showing average looking time for each stimulus.

0   5   10   15   20
Average seconds of fixation in one-minute test

INTEREST IN FORM was proved by infants' reactions to various pairs of patterns *(left)* presented together. (The small and large plain squares were used alternately.) The more complex pairs received the most attention, and within each of these pairs differential interest was based on pattern differences. These results are for 22 infants in 10 weekly tests.

A "no preference" result in the visual preference paradigm is difficult to interpret. It could mean that the infants were unable to distinguish between the two shapes being tested. Alternatively, it could mean that they found both shapes equally interesting (or equally dull!) to look at. One way to find out whether infants can in fact distinguish two equally preferred visual stimuli is to use the *habituation* paradigm. This has now become one of the most widely used techniques in research with infants.

In simple habituation studies, the infant is shown one stimulus, such as a circle, on repeated occasions. Typically, the infant's interest is at first caught by the novel stimulus, and a lot of time is spent in looking at it. Following repeated exposures of the same stimulus, the infant's looking time decreases. This is quite understandable—seeing the same old circle again and again is not that exciting. Once looking time to the stimulus has fallen to half of the initial level, the old stimulus is removed and a new stimulus is introduced—such as a cross. This is a novel stimulus, so if infants can distinguish between the cross and the circle, renewed looking to the cross should be observed. Renewed looking to a novel stimulus is called "dishabituation". When dishabituation occurs, we know that the cross is perceived as a novel stimulus, and this tells us that infants can distinguish between a cross and a circle.

Research with neonates by Slater and his colleagues has shown that infants can indeed discriminate a cross from a circle (Slater, Morison, & Rose, 1983). In Slater et al.'s experiment, the cross and the circle were *both* presented during the dishabituation phase, thereby combining the habituation method with the preference technique. Slater et al. showed that when the cross and the circle were presented after habituation to the circle, then the cross was preferred. When the cross and the circle were presented after habituation to the cross, then the circle was preferred. As neonates in a habituation paradigm can distinguish a cross from a circle, we can conclude that the absence of a preference in 7-month-old infants in Fantz's experiments did not arise out of an inability to distinguish between crosses and circles.

Rudimentary categorisation

Another way to use habituation is to vary the stimuli that the infant sees during the *habituation* phase of the experiment. The variation of exemplars during habituation requires the infants to *categorise* what they are being shown in some way in order to remember it. At test, we can present the infants with a *new* exemplar of the familiar category that they haven't seen before, as well as a new exemplar from a contrasting category. If the infants have formed a representation of the familiar category, then they should prefer to look at the exemplar from the new category, even though both shapes presented at test are novel stimuli.

In order to present two novel stimuli at test, Slater and Morison (1987, described in Slater, 1989) used this technique with 3- and 5-month old babies. During the habituation phase of their study, they showed the babies a variety of types of circle (or of squares, triangles , or crosses—see Fig. 1.5) that differed in their lower-level features. For example, a circle might be formed from a solid line or from a set of smaller circles. At test, they showed the "circle" babies a new exemplar of a circle, and an exemplar of another shape, such as a cross. The infants preferred to look at the novel shape (the cross). This suggests

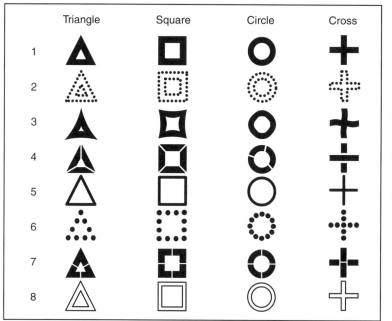

FIG. 1.5.
The different exemplars of triangles, squares, circles, and crosses used during habituation by Slater and Morison (1987, cited in Slater & Bremner, 1989). Copyright © Giunti Gruppo Editoriale, Firenze, Italy. Adapted with permission.

that the babies had formed a "prototype" or generalised representation of the familiar shape, to which they appeared to be comparing all subsequently presented stimuli. The ability to form prototypes plays an important role in retaining information in memory, in conceptual development, and in categorisation, as we will see in later chapters.

Cross-modal perception in infancy

As well as the ability to form perceptual prototypes, the ability to match perceptual information across modalities (cross-modal perception) is also present early in life. Infants seem to be able to connect visual informaton with tactile information, and auditory information with visual information, soon after birth.

Linking vision and touch. One of the most striking demonstrations of infants' ability to make cross-modal connections between vision and touch comes from an experiment by Meltzoff and Borton (1979). They gave 1-month-old infants one of two dummies to suck that had different textures. The surface of one of the dummies was smooth, whereas the other had a nubbled surface (see Fig. 1.6). The infants did not see the dummy as it was inserted into their mouths, and so in the first phase of the experiment their experience of the dummy was purely

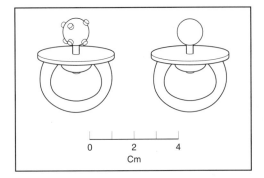

FIG. 1.6.
The two dummies
used to study inter
modal connections
between vision and
touch by Meltzoff and
Borton (1979).
Reprinted with
permission from
Nature, 282,
© 1979 Macmillan
Magazines Ltd.

tactile. In the second phase of the experiment, the infants were shown enlarged pictures of both dummies, and the experimenters measured which visual stimulus the infants preferred to look at. They found that the majority of the babies preferred to look at the dummy that they had just been sucking. The babies who had sucked on the nubbled dummy looked most at this picture, and the babies who had sucked on the smooth dummy looked most at this picture. This preference for congruence suggests an understanding of cross-modal equivalence.

Linking vision and audition. Infants also appear to be able to make links between the auditory and visual modalities soon after birth. For example, Spelke (1976) showed 4-month-old infants simultaneous films of two rhythmic events; a woman playing "peek-a-boo", and a baton hitting a wooden block. At the same time, the soundtrack appropriate to one of the events was played from a loudspeaker located between the two screens. Spelke found that the infants preferred to look at the visual event that matched the auditory soundtrack. Again, this preference for *congruence* across modalities suggests an understanding of cross-modal equivalence. Dodd (1979) has found similar results in experiments that required infants to match voices to films of faces reading nursery rhymes. When the soundtrack was played "out of sync" with the mouth movements of the reader, the infants got fussy. They preferred to look at faces whose mouths were moving in time with the words in the nursery rhyme. Adults also get fussy when they experience this phenomenon—think of being in the cinema when the soundtrack is out of time with the actors. Clearly, we have a strong perceptual preference for *congruence* across different perceptual modalities, and this preference is present from early in life.

Imitation. A final example of cross-modal equivalence in babies comes from evidence that neonates can imitate the facial and manual gestures of adults. For example, Meltzoff and Moore (1983) have shown that babies aged from 1 hour to 3 days can imitate gestures like tongue protrusion and mouth opening after watching an adult produce the same gestures (see Fig. 1.7). In Meltzoff and Moore's experiment, the babies were supported in a seat in a darkened room. A light came on for 20 seconds, illuminating an adult's face. The adult demonstrated a

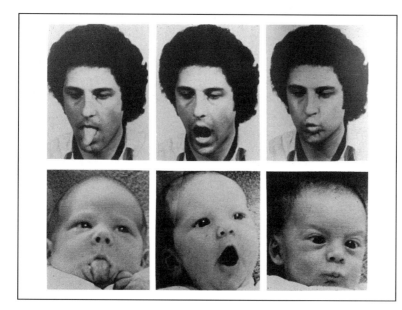

FIG. 1.7.
Babies imitating Meltzoff demonstrating tongue protrusion, mouth opening, and lip pursing.
Reprinted with permission from Meltzoff and Moore (1977). Copyright © (1977) American Association for the Advancement of Science.

gesture such as tongue protrusion for the entire 20-second period, and the light was extinguished. The babies were then filmed in the dark for the next 20 seconds. Following this imitation period, another gesture was modelled by the adult, and so on. An experimenter who was "blind" to the experiment later scored the behaviour of the baby in each 20-second segment of video. Significantly more tongue protrusion was scored in periods following modelling of tongue protrusion, and significantly more mouth opening was scored in periods following modelling of mouth opening. The conclusion that the babies were imitating the adults seems inescapable, although initially it proved controversial (e.g. Hayes & Watson, 1981; McKenzie & Over, 1983).

More recently, a number of other experimenters have confirmed Meltzoff and Moore's findings, using a variety of different gestures and testing babies from a variety of different countries. For example, Vintner (1986) investigated whether newborn Italian babies could imitate tongue protrusion and hand opening–closing. She contrasted imitation in two conditions; an "active" condition in which the gesture was continuously modelled for a 25-second period, and a "static" condition in which a protruding tongue or an open hand was maintained for 25 seconds. Vintner found imitation behaviour in the "active" group only, even though the babies in the "static" condition spent a lot of time looking at the experimenter. She suggested that movement may be a fundamental property for eliciting imitative responses at birth.

One reason for the controversy generated by the early reports of imitation in babies was that Meltzoff and Moore argued that successful imitation necessitated representational capacity. It is simple to demonstrate that a number of cognitive skills are required for successful imitation to take place. At a minimum, the infants need to (i) represent the action of the adult, (ii) retain this representation during the period that the adult is invisible in the dark, and (iii) work out how to reproduce the gesture using their own facial musculature. In 1983, the idea that neonates might have a representational system that allowed them to match their own body transformations to those of others was seen as rather incredible. Now it seems almost self-evident! Issues relating to representation in infancy are discussed more fully in Chapter 2.

Links between measures of early learning, memory, perception, attention and later intelligence

If the capacities for learning, memory, perception, and attention found in infancy are indeed the building blocks of cognition, then it should be possible to find continuity between measures of these skills in infancy and later individual differences in cognitive development. Two such measures have been the focus of recent investigations of this continuity hypothesis. These measures are speed of habituation and visual recognition memory. Both measures reflect basic information-processing capacity, involving all of the capacities outlined earlier. The idea is that if early learning, memory, perception, and attention are related to later cognitive processing, then speed of habituation and visual recognition memory should be predictive of later individual differences in intelligence.

Speed of habituation and individual differences

The notion that there should be a relationship between the *speed of habituation* in infancy and later differences in intelligence has been proposed by a number of authors (e.g. Fagan, 1984). The argument goes something like this. A baby who is relatively quick to habituate to a stimulus might be relatively fast at processing information, and therefore capable of learning that something is familiar in only a few trials. Another baby may take three times as long to habituate to the same stimulus, requiring many more trials to accurately and completely encode a stimulus in memory. As a young child, this second baby may still be slower at processing information, and will therefore be slower and perhaps less efficient at performing a variety of cognitive tasks that contribute to standardised measures of intelligence. However, it is important to be clear that speed of habituation is *not* the same thing as having a low attention span. Children who are easily distracted and move quickly from one activity to another may have an "attention deficit disorder" (ADD), and ADD children usually *under-perform* in various intellectual tasks. These children are unlikely to be fast habituaters, although so far no-one has studied the connection between attention deficit disorder and habituation in infancy directly.

In order to examine whether individual differences in habituation are associated with later individual differences in intelligence, Bornstein and Sigman (1986) conducted a "meta-analysis" of available studies. The meta-analysis included studies that related decrements in attention (habituation or total fixation time) to later intelligence measures, and also studies that related recovery of attention (novelty preference and response to novelty) to later intelligence. They found that attention scores correlated on average 0.44 with follow-up studies conducted at 2–3 years, 0.48 with follow-up studies conducted at 4–5 years, and 0.56 with follow-up studies conducted at 6 years or more. This suggests significant continuity between early habituation measures and later IQ.

One of the longest-running longitudinal studies of the relationship between speed of habituation and individual differences is that of Sigman and her colleagues, who have been following the same cohort of nearly 100 children since they were born, for over 12 years. For example, Sigman, Cohen, Beckwith, and Parmelee (1986) reported data from a group of 93 of the infants who were tested as neonates. These babies were tested again at 4 months, and were then followed up when they were 8 years old. Two-thirds of the group ($N = 61$) had English-speaking backgrounds, and the rest came from varied language backgrounds (the study was conducted at a large hospital in California). As neonates, the infants were shown a single 2 x 2 chequer-board for three 1-minute trials, and at 4 months they were shown pairs of chequerboards of varying complexity (2 x 2, 6 x 6, 12 x 12, 24 x 24) for eight trials. Two measures of visual attention were taken: a measure of total fixation time, and a habituation measure of the percentage decrement in looking time across trials.

When the children were revisited as 8-year-olds, they were given the revised version of the Wechsler Intelligence Scale for Children (the WISC-R). This test measures IQ by combining performance scores on a number of verbal and non-verbal measures (e.g. verbal fluency, picture completion, block design, memory span). Sigman et al. found that the neonate measure of total fixation time predicted IQ at 8 years for the whole group ($r = -.36$), while the neonate habituation measure predicted IQ at 8 years for the children from varied language backgrounds only ($r = -.42$). The measures taken at 4 months did not add to the associations between the neonate measures and later IQ. Sigman et al. concluded that infants who spent a long time looking at the stimuli at 0 and 4 months performed less well on the intellectual assessments given in childhood. It seems as though infants who take a long time to process an unchanging stimulus as neonates are less intelligent later in life (although the actual magnitude of the differences found is not given in the paper). Similar relationships were found when a smaller sub-group of the sample ($N = 67$) were seen again as 12-year-olds (Sigman et al., 1991). In addition, more efficient processing of stimuli as a neonate (looking for a lesser amount of time) was related to performance on a test of analogical reasoning at age 12 (e.g. *bread* is to *food* as *water* is to *beverage*).

Visual recognition memory and individual differences

Another candidate for a learning measure that should predict later IQ is visual recognition memory. Recognition memory differs from habituation in that the familiarisation period allowed for learning is extremely brief, but also requires the infant to encode a stimulus, to recognise it as familiar, and to recognise an alternative stimulus as novel. These are all basic information-processing requirements that could be related to intelligence. Fagan (1984) used a visual preference paradigm similar to that of Cornell (1979, discussed earlier) to test this hypothesis. He measured looking preference for a novel visual stimulus (a face) over an already experienced visual stimulus (a different face of the same sex) in a group of 7-month-old babies, and then tested the same group when they were 3 and 5 years of age. The median amount of time that each infant spent looking at the novel stimulus rather than the familiar stimulus formed the dependent measure. Fagan found stable correlations of around 0.42 between the novelty preference measures taken at 7 months and performance on the PPVT (Peabody Picture Vocabulary Test, a measure of verbal ability) at 3 and 5 years. Surprisingly, however, the novelty preference measures were not related to visual recognition memory *itself* at 5 years.

In Fagan's view, however, this failure to find a specific connection between visual recognition memory at 7 months and visual recognition memory at 5 years is not surprising at all. Fagan suggests that visual novelty preference measures in infancy are picking up something of *general* importance for later cognition, for example encoding abilities, the ability to detect invariant features, or categorisation abilities. As recognition memory becomes a highly automatic process with development, later visual recognition memory measures are no longer measuring encoding or categorisation abilities. Fagan's idea that early visual recognition memory is a general rather than a specific measure has received support from a study by DiLalla et al. (1990) who showed that Fagan's novelty preference measure was a significant predictor of IQ at 3 years as measured by the Stanford–Binet intelligence test. Fagan's second claim, namely that later recognition memory is an automatised process that has little to do with intelligence, appears to receive support from the different developmental trajectories of implicit vs. explicit memory (discussed in Chapter 5). Whereas implicit memory ("memory without awareness") appears to undergo little development after the age of around 3–4 years, explicit memory continues to develop into adulthood. Implicit memory is usually measured by tasks similar to the visual recognition task, as we will see later.

In another long-running longitudinal study of the relationship between visual recognition memory and individual differences in cognitive development, Rose and Feldman (1995) studied the relationship between visual recognition memory and visual attention and later intelligence as measured by the WISC-R at 11 years of age. They found that the infancy measure that best predicted IQ at age 11 was visual recognition memory, with a correlation of 0.41. A total of 90 infants took part in the study, 50 of whom were pre-term. The pre-term infants were included as a group at risk (pre-term infants tend to score on average about 10 points lower on later IQ tests compared to full-term infants). Rose and Feldman found that the predictive strength of the visual recognition memory measure was very similar for both groups. In addition to overall IQ infant visual recognition memory predicted performance on two abilities at age 11, after controlling for IQ. These abilities were memory (measured via a speeded task) and perceptual speed. As Rose and Feldman point out, the relationship with perceptual speed may mean that *processing speed* is the common thread underlying cognitive continuity from infancy. The importance of processing speed for cognitive development has also been highlighted by Anderson (1991).

Finally, we can ask which is the *better* index of early information processing; habituation or visual recognition memory. The difference between these two measures may be more apparent than real, however. In a recent meta-analysis of studies of infant habituation vs. recognition memory as predictors of later IQ, McCall and Carriger (1993) found that the two measures were *equivalent* in their predictive powers. The predictive raw correlations with IQ were essentially the same for both measures, each measure showing correlations of around 0.45 with later intelligence. McCall and Carriger suggested that, rather than providing an index of information processing in terms of encoding, discrimination etc., both visual recognition memory and habituation derived their predictive power from their ability to provide an index of individual differences in the ability to *inhibit* responding to stimuli that have been seen before. Inhibition as an important cognitive process is only just beginning to receive attention in the field of children's cognition (e.g. Dempster, 1991), and is discussed further in Chapters 2 and 5.

Summary

We began this chapter by considering learning and memory within the womb, and ended it by finding that there is considerable continuity between measures of learning, memory, perception, and attention in infancy and later individual differences in cognitive development. Neonates demonstrate learning and memory of repeated salient auditory events experienced in utero, and babies as young as 3 weeks show learning and memory for simple objects. Three-month-olds can learn causal contingencies and retrieve them 28 days later when given the appropriate retrieval cues, while 6-month-olds can form event memories that can be retrieved two years later in the presence of the right reminders. These memories seem to be procedural rather than declarative in nature, as both learning and memory are demonstrated via infant *behaviour*. The relationship between such memories and bringing some aspect of the past to conscious awareness has yet to be determined.

Perceptual and attentional abilities are also impressive early in life. Neonates can discriminate between simple visual forms such as crosses and circles. Work with older infants suggests that the basis of these discriminations is fairly abstract perceptual information, as habituation also occurs to different exemplars of the same shape, novel exemplars being seen as familiar. Habituation at an abstract level suggests that rudimentary categorisation is occurring, with babies forming a generalised representation or "prototype" of a particular visual form. Infants can also match perceptual information across modalities, 1-month-olds being able to equate the textured surface of a dummy with its visual appearance, and 4-month-olds being able to match the sound and appearance of rhythmic events such as a drumbeat. Neonates even seem able to co-ordinate information across the visual and kinesthetic perceptual systems, as they can imitate facial gestures as early as an hour after birth. Successful imitation may demonstrate the existence of early representational capacities. Overall, therefore, the evidence for arguing that the basic building blocks of cognition are available at birth seems quite compelling.

Cognition in infancy: Higher cognitive processes 2

In the last chapter, we saw that the fundamental cognitive processes of learning, memory, perception, and attention are available from, and even before, birth. In this chapter, we will examine how these fundamental processes enable further cognitive skills to develop. For example, we can study how learning, memory, perception, and attention enable "higher" cognitive activities such as reasoning and problem solving. In order to discover this, we must first find out how infants represent information about the world around them.

Knowledge representation is fundamental to all higher cognitive processes. Both reasoning and problem solving require the manipulation of represented knowledge. Knowledge representation also entails *categorisation*, because if we were unable to impose categories on the perceptual world, then every percept, object, or event that occurred would be processed as if it were unique. This would produce an overwhelming amount of information. The ability to organise incoming information into categories is thus essential for cognitive activity. Furthermore, the categorisation of objects or events as similar enables a generalised representation or *prototype* to be formed for a class of objects or events, to which subsequently encountered stimuli can be compared. As young infants lack language, we cannot use activities such as labelling as a guide to infant prototypes and knowledge representation. Instead, we must investigate whether infants can use the *perceptual structure* of objects and events in the visual world as a basis for representing knowledge. If they can, then this would be an important step in enabling categorical or prototypical knowledge representation.

Moving into cognition: Perception-based knowledge representations

Representing the structure of object features: The extraction of prototypes

Although infants need to be able to categorise both objects and events as similar, the categorical representation of objects will be considered first. The ability to recognise that exemplars of the same object category are similar has been studied intensively in adult cognition, where one important theory of categorisation is prototype theory. This was first introduced by Eleanor Rosch (e.g. Rosch et al., 1976). She proposed that the use of prototypes or generalised representations of different objects enabled an organism to store maximal information about the world with the minimum cognitive effort.

We already know from Slater's work that infants can form prototypes of simple perceptual forms such as circles and crosses. When Slater and Morison (1987, described in Slater, 1989) showed infants a number of specific instances of a circle or a cross that differed in lower-level features, the infants abstracted the general category of circles or crosses to which these exemplars belonged. Can we assume that infants do the same with more complex stimuli? One way to find out is to use habituation studies.

For example, suppose that you showed babies a number of pictures of different stuffed animals. You might show them a picture of a stuffed frog, a picture of a stuffed donkey, a picture of a stuffed alligator, a picture of a stuffed bear, and so on. Although these exemplars would differ in numerous features, the infants may be able to abstract a category like "stuffed animals" from seeing these different instances, in which case they should eventually habituate to these changing exemplars. By the time they saw their fifteenth stuffed animal, even if it was a novel stuffed octopus, they might find the "stuffed animals" category rather *too* familiar, and show habituation of looking.

Cohen and Caputo (1978) carried out a habituation experiment that was very similar to the one just described. They used three different groups of babies, all aged 7 months. The first group saw the same stuffed animal on each trial of the habituation phase of the experiment. The second group saw a different stuffed animal on each trial, and the third group saw a set of totally unrelated objects (e.g. a toy car, a ball, a stuffed animal, a telephone). At test, the infants were shown a novel stuffed animal and a rattle. The first group showed dishabituation to both the novel stuffed animal and the rattle. The second group showed dishabituation to the rattle only, and the third group (who in any case had shown little habituation) showed no dishabituation. This pattern of results is shown in Fig. 2.1. Cohen and Caputo argued that the second group of infants had abstracted a category of "stuffed animals".

Processing inter-relations between features: The differentiation of prototypes

In order to argue that the infants were abstracting a prototypical "stuffed animal" from all of these instances, we would need evidence

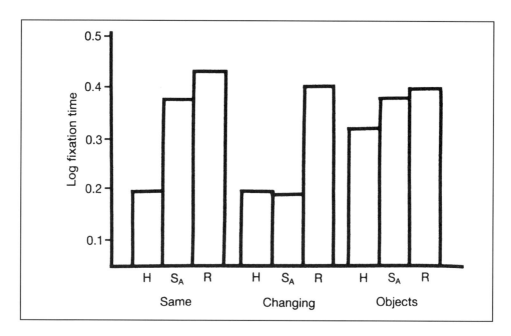

FIG. 2.1.
Looking time on the
last habituation trial
(H) and the first
dishabituation trials
with the novel stuffed
animal (SA) and the
rattle (R) in Cohen
and Caputo's (1978)
experiment with three
groups of babies;
those shown the
same stuffed animal
(Same), those shown
different stuffed
animals (Changing),
and those shown
totally unrelated
objects (Objects).
From Cohen (1988).
Reprinted by
permisson of Oxford
University Press.

that they were attending to the *interrelations* between the different features of each stuffed animal, rather than habituating to a single recurring feature, such as the eyes. If infants can code the perceptual structure of objects in terms of the correlational structure between different features, then this would be good evidence for representation on the basis of perceptual prototypes. In fact, Rosch et al. (1976) argued that humans divide the world into objects and categories on just such a correlational basis (see also Chapter 3). Certain features in the world tend to co-occur, and this co-occurrence gives rise to a correlational structure which specifies natural categories such as trees, birds, flowers, and dogs. For example, birds are distinguished from dogs partly because feathers and wings occur together, whereas fur and wings do not. According to Rosch, this process of noticing co-occurrences between sets of features results in a generalised representation of a prototypical bird, a prototypical dog and so on, and it has been argued that these prototypes provide the basis for *conceptual* representation.

Younger and Cohen (1983) examined whether infants were able to attend to the interrelations between features as required by prototype theory. They designed a habituation study based on "cartoon animals" to study this question (see Fig. 2.2). The cartoon animals could vary in five attributes: shape of body, shape of tail, shape of feet, shape of ears, and shape of legs. There were three different forms of each attribute (e.g. the feet could be webbed feet, paws, or hooves). During the habituation phase of the experiment, the babies were shown animals in which three critical features varied. Two of them varied together, and the third did not. For example, long legs might always occur with short necks, but tails could be any shape. Following habituation, the babies were shown three different cartoon animals. One was an animal whose critical features maintained the correlation. The second was an animal whose critical features violated the correlation. The third was an animal with completely different features. Younger and Cohen found that 10-month-old babies showed dishabituation to the second and third animals, but not to the first. This result suggested that the babies were sensitive to the relationship between the different critical features. They had formed a prototype of an animal with a short neck and long legs.

One way to test whether the infants really were coding the correlational structure between the different features is to show different

FIG. 2.2. Examples of the cartoon animals used by Younger and Cohen (1983). Reprinted by permission.

infants different sets of correlations between features, and then see whether they form different prototypes. Younger (1985) devised an ingenious method to enable such a test. She reasoned that if babies were shown cartoon animals in which all possible lengths of necks and legs could co-occur, then they should form a prototype of the *average* animal. As the different features would be uncorrelated with each other, the infants should abstract a prototypical animal with an average-length neck and average-length legs. However, if they were shown animals in which neck and leg length covaried in two clusters, for example long legs and short necks and vice versa, then they should form two different prototypes. One would be of animals with long legs and short necks, and one of animals with short legs and long necks.

In order to test her hypothesis, Younger used cartoon animals whose leg and neck lengths could have one of five values (e.g. 1 = short and 5 = long, see Fig. 2.3). Infants in a *broad* condition saw animals in which all possible lengths co-occurred except for length 3 (the average value), and infants in a *narrow* condition saw animals in which short legs went with long necks and vice versa. At test, she found that the infants in the broad group preferred to look at cartoon animals with either very short legs and very long necks, or very long legs and very short necks. In contrast, the infants in the narrow group preferred to look at cartoon animals whose legs and necks were of average length (3, 3). This suggests that the infants in the broad group found the average familiar, even though they had never seen those particular attributes before. They had abstracted a prototypical animal with an average-length neck and average-length legs. The infants in the narrow group had

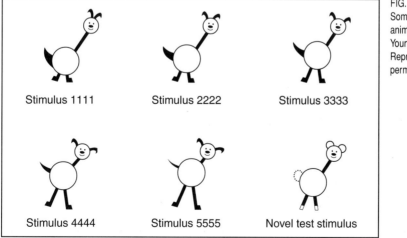

Stimulus 1111   Stimulus 2222   Stimulus 3333

Stimulus 4444   Stimulus 5555   Novel test stimulus

FIG. 2.3.
Some of the cartoon animals used by Younger (1985). Reproduced with permission.

formed *two* prototypes, and thus found the average animal novel. Younger (1990) went on to demonstrate that babies were also sensitive to correlational structure when stimuli that were based on features taken from real animals ("natural kinds") rather than cartoon animals were used.

The use of more natural categories and real features to study prototype formation is important, as the correlational structure of objects in the real world is quite complex. Recently, developmental psychologists have begun to study whether infants can form prototypes of natural kinds, such as cats, horses, zebras, and giraffes. For example, Eimas and Quinn (1994) habituated 3- and 4-month-old infants to coloured photographs of horses, using 12 different photographs. Following habituation, the infants were given three different kinds of test trial in a looking preference paradigm: a novel horse paired with a cat, a novel horse paired with a zebra, and a novel horse paired with a giraffe. The infants reliably preferred to look at the photograph of the new animal on each type of test trial, showing that they could distinguish between horses, zebras, giraffes, and cats. A second group of infants were habituated to coloured photographs of cats. They could distinguish cats from horses and tigers, but not from lionesses. Research such as this shows that the information-processing systems of young infants can cope with the natural featural variation found among exemplars of real species, and can form categorical representations of those species which are perceptually based.

Why couldn't these young babies distinguish lionesses from cats? Eimas and Quinn argued from their data that the categorical representation of horses may be more *exclusive* than that of cats, as the "horse" prototype apparently excluded zebras, while the "cat" prototype *included* female lions. However, the pictures of cats and lionesses used in the experiment may have been more similar than the pictures of horses and zebras. The greater inclusivity of the "cat" prototype may thus have been a reflection of the particular pictorial stimuli that were used in the experiment. In the real world, other perceptual features such as relative size and movement patterns would differentiate cats from lionesses, and so babies would be supplied with richer perceptual information than was available in the laboratory. The very richness of the perceptual information provided by natural kinds and artifacts in the real world means that the ability to process interrelations between perceptual features gives infants a powerful information-gathering tool, which has a cognitive pay-off. The accretion of perceptually based knowledge must result eventually in *conceptual* categories (see Chapter 3 for a discussion of how this might occur).

Processing relations between objects

The evidence for prototype formation shows that infants can code the perceptual structure of discrete stimuli in terms of the relationships (covariations) between different features of these stimuli. However, if this ability to detect covariation were restricted to the static features of natural kinds and artifacts, then even though it would be very useful, its cognitive value would be relatively limited. The ability to detect regularities between perceptual *events* would markedly increase the cognitive value of this mechanism.

Events in the visual world are usually described by *relations* between objects (such as football *collides with* goalpost, child *pushes* friend). The ability to detect structural regularities in these relations would confer much greater cognitive power, as events in the visual world are frequently *causal* in nature. The detection of regularities in causal relations like *collide, push,* and *supports* between different objects (such as football collides with goalpost, car collides with garage door, bird collides with window) may be an important mechanism in knowledge representation and thus eventually in conceptual development. Similarly, other types of relations, such as spatial relations (*above* and *below*) and quantitative relations (*more than* and *less than*) may also be detected. One way of measuring infants' ability to process and represent spatial, numerical, and causal relations is to introduce *violations* of typical regularities in the relations between objects, which then result in physically "impossible" events. For example, an object with no visible means of support can remain stationary in mid-air instead of falling to the ground. The experimental investigation of infants' ability to detect such violations has provided developmental psychologists with an important way of measuring infants' ability to process relations between events.

Representing spatial relations.   One way to test whether infants are sensitive to spatial relations is to use habituation. For example, if an infant is shown a variety of stimuli that are all exemplars of the same spatial relation, and if the infant shows habituation to these stimuli, then the infant must be sensitive to relational information. If the infant is then shown an example of a *new* spatial relation, dishabituation should occur. This method was used in a recent experiment by Quinn (1994). He familiarised 3-month-old infants to the spatial relations *above* and *below*. This was achieved by showing half of the infants repeated presentations of a black horizontal bar with a dot above it in four different positions, and half of the infants a black horizontal bar with a dot below it in four different positions. These patterns provided exemplars of the spatial relation *above* and the spatial relation *below* respectively. At test, the infants were shown a novel exemplar of the familiar relation (a dot in a new position above or below the bar, depending on the habituation condition), and an exemplar of the unfamiliar relation (a dot on the other side of the bar). Both groups showed a visual preference for the *unfamiliar* relation. This finding suggests that infants can categorise perceptual structure on the basis of spatial relations.

Experiments based on the spatial relations between dots and lines may appear to provide rather impoverished tests of relational processing and representation. However, there is evidence that infants show the same abilities with far more complex stimuli. For example, Baillargeon and her colleagues investigated whether infants of $5^{1}/_{2}$ months realised that a tall rabbit should be partially visible when it passed behind a low wall. During the habituation phase of the experiment, the infants saw a display of a tall painted "wall" (Baillargeon & Graber, 1987). A rabbit appeared at one end of the wall, passed along behind it, and reappeared at the other end. This "habituating" rabbit could either be tall or short, but as both the tall and the short rabbit were too small to be visible when they were behind the wall, the infants watched the rabbits disappear and reappear as they moved from left to right. At test, the mid-section of the wall was lowered. The wall now had two tall ends and a short middle (see Fig. 2.4). The short rabbit could still pass behind the entire length of the wall without being

FIG. 2.4.
The habituation and test displays in the tall and short rabbit experiment devised by Baillargeon and Graber (1987). Reproduced with permission.

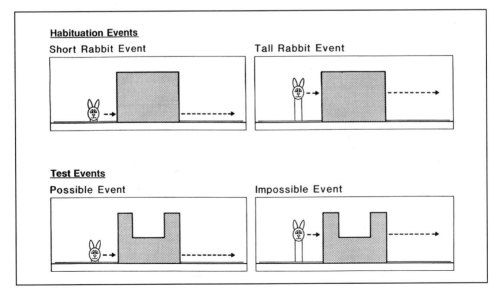

visible, but the tall rabbit could not. The tall rabbit's head would appear as it passed behind the middle section of the wall.

Both groups of infants then again watched the habituating rabbit (tall or short) passing behind the wall. In fact, they saw the *same* event to which they had been habituated. For the "small rabbit" group, the failure of the rabbit to appear in the mid-section of the apparatus was perfectly acceptable in terms of the spatial relations between the wall and the rabbit, and accordingly there was no dishabituation. For the "tall rabbit" group, the test event was not acceptable in terms of the spatial relations between the wall and the rabbit—in fact, it was physically impossible. The tall rabbit's head should have appeared behind the mid-section of the wall, but it did not—just as in the habituating event. Baillargeon and Graber found that the babies in the "tall rabbit" group spent much longer staring at the experimental apparatus than the babies in the "short rabbit" group. The infants' surprise at the non-appearance of the tall rabbit suggests that they had represented the spatial relations between the wall and the rabbit. Later work (Baillargeon & DeVos, 1991) has shown that 3½-month-old infants behave in the same way (this was demonstrated in a modified version of the experiment which used a tall and a short carrot). Thus very young babies appear to be able to represent spatial relations.

Baillargeon and her colleagues have also used habituation to measure infants' *memory* for spatial locations. This is a strong test of representation, as the infants must retain the spatial relations defining location *over time*. In one experiment, Baillargeon and Graber (1988) showed infants a display that had two possible locations in which a toy could be placed, A and B. The two locations were marked by identical mats. As the infants watched the display, an attractive object was placed at location A (in fact, the object used was a plastic styrofoam cup with matches stuck into its sides, an object that the infants found far more visually interesting than the toys that were used when the experimenters tried to pilot the experiment!). Two screens were then slid in front of the two locations, hiding the mats. As the infants continued to watch the display, a hand wearing a silver glove and a bracelet of bells appeared, and the fingers danced around—this was also visually interesting, and was designed to keep the infants attending to the display. The hand then reached behind the screen at location B, and retrieved the styrofoam cup.

Of course, this retrieval was an "impossible" event. Location B had been visibly empty when the screens slid in front of the mats, and the styrofoam cup should only have been retrievable at location A. Baillargeon and Graber argued that if the babies could remember the location of the object during the delay, then they would be perturbed at this event, and should show increased looking at the display. This was exactly what they found. The babies were extremely surprised at the impossible retrieval, and looked at the display for a long time. Increased looking time did not occur in a control event, which was a "possible" event. In this event, the hand retrieved the cup from behind the correct screen, and the infants were not particularly interested. The fact that their attention was caught only when the cup was retrieved from the wrong spatial location suggests that they were able to represent the location of the cup even when it was out of view. Baillargeon, De Vos, and Graber (1989) went on to demonstrate that 8-month-old infants could retain these spatial memories for up to 70 seconds. So "out of sight" is not necessarily "out of mind" for the infant.

A different test of spatial learning and memory was devised by McKenzie, Day, and Ihsen (1984). They seated 6- to 8-month-old babies behind a kind of semi-circular "newsdesk" (see Fig. 2.5). The babies sat on their mothers' laps in a central position (like a "newsreader"), enabling them to scan the entire desk. The shape of the desk meant that there were a number of different locations at which events could occur, both to the left and to the right of the babies. The location at which an

event was about to occur was always marked by a white ball. The events were visually exciting to the babies—an adult appeared from behind the desk and began playing "peek-a-boo".

McKenzie et al. found that the babies quickly learned to anticipate an event at the spatial location marked by the white ball. As the white ball could either appear to the right or to the left of the midline, the babies could not have learned a specific motor response, such as turning their heads to the right. Instead, they were learning to *predict* the spatial location of the visual events by using the white ball. McKenzie et al. argued that this showed that babies did not always code spatial position in memory *egocentrically*, with respect to a motor response based on their own position in space. When given the appropriate opportunity, they could also code spatial location in memory *allocentrically*, with respect to a salient landmark such as the white ball. The representation of spatial relations in 8-month-olds thus involves landmark cues, just as it does in adults.

Representing occlusion relations. Baillargeon's experiments also indicate that infants have some understanding of occlusion relations. When an object is partially occluded by a second object, we as adults believe that the hidden portion of the first object still exists. Even when one object totally occludes another, we assume that the hidden object continues to exist and to occupy the same location in space behind the occluder. Thus perceptual events can also provide knowledge about the continued existence of objects when they are out of view.

Babies seem to make similar assumptions about the existence of occluded objects to those of adults. One of the most ingenious demonstrations of their belief in "object permanence" comes from an experiment by Baillargeon, Spelke, and Wasserman (1985). Baillargeon et al. habituated 5-month-old babies to a display in which a screen continually rotated through 180° towards and away from the baby, like a drawbridge (see Fig. 2.6). Following habituation, a box was placed in the path of the screen at the far end of the apparatus. As the screen began its 180° rotation, it gradually occluded the box. When it reached 90°, the entire box was hidden from view. For babies who were shown a "possible event", the screen continued to rotate until it had passed through 120°, at which point it came to rest, apparently having made contact with the box. For babies who were shown an "impossible event", the screen continued to rotate until it had passed through the full 180° rotation. In the physically "impossible" condition, the box had apparently caused no obstruction to the path of the screen's movement. Although the 180° rotation was the familiar (habituating) event, the

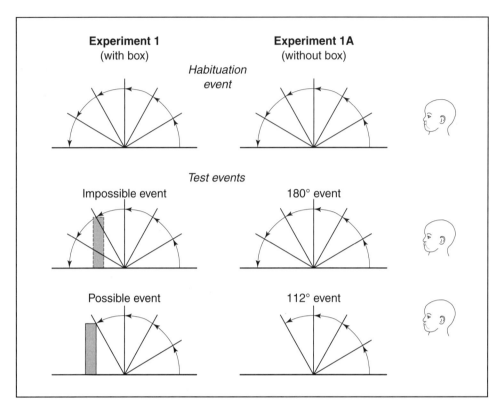

Experiment 1
(with box)

Experiment 1A
(without box)

Habituation event

Test events

Impossible event

Possible event

180° event

112° event

FIG. 2.6.
Diagram of the
habituation and test
events in the rotating
screen paradigm
devised by
Baillargeon et al.
(1985).
Reproduced with kind
permission of
Elsevier Science.

babies in the impossible condition spent much longer staring at the experimental display than the babies in the possible condition (who were seeing a novel event). This finding suggests that the babies had represented the box as continuing to exist, even when it was occluded by the screen. They were surprised because the screen could pass through an apparently solid object.

In later work, Baillargeon has shown that babies as young as 3¹/₂ months of age are surprised when the screen passes through the box, particularly if they are "fast habituators" (Baillargeon, 1987a). She has also shown that infants can represent some of the physical and spatial properties of the occluded objects, such as whether an object is compressible or not (e.g. a sponge vs. a wooden block, see Fig. 2.7), and whether it is taller or shorter than the height of the screen (e.g. a wooden box measuring 20 x 15 x 4 cm standing upright vs. lying flat; Baillargeon, 1987b). These experiments suggest that not only can young infants represent the existence of hidden objects, they can also represent some of the specific properties of the objects that are hidden. They can

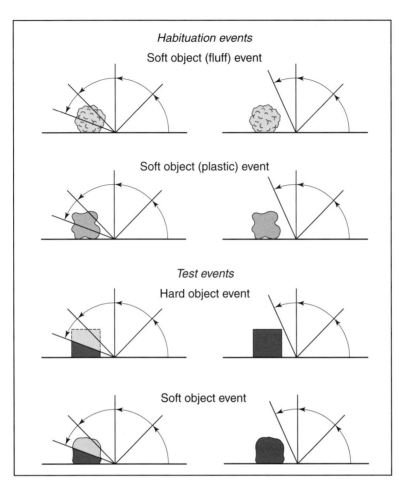

FIG. 2.7.
Diagram of the
habituation and test
events in the rotating
screen paradigm with
soft vs. hard objects
(Baillargeon, 1987b).
Reproduced with
permission.

Habituation events

Soft object (fluff) event

Soft object (plastic) event

Test events

Hard object event

Soft object event

then use these physical and spatial characteristics to make predictions about how the drawbridge should behave as it begins to rotate.

Despite the many variations of the "drawbridge" paradigm that Baillargeon has devised, her choice of a rotating screen to demonstrate infants' belief in object permanence has proved to be a controversial one. For example, it has been argued that the perceptual structure of events in the "drawbridge" paradigm leads the infants to form a strong expectation that the drawbridge should stop, an expectation that does not necessitate a representation of the occluded object. Rather, the representation that the child constructs of the *initial* display is argued to be sufficient for the child to expect the drawbridge to stop. This criticism is arguably weakened by the demonstration that infants' expectations about the behaviour of the drawbridge differ depending on the nature of the object that is hidden (e.g. Baillargeon, 1987b). Furthermore, the series of drawbridge studies that Baillargeon and her colleagues have conducted is only one piece of evidence that babies represent hidden objects as continuing to exist. A different paradigm, also devised by Baillargeon (1986), tests the same understanding, and does not seem vulnerable to an "expectation" criticism at all.

This paradigm was based on a toy car and a ramp. During the initial phase of the experiment, 6½-month-old infants were shown a display in which a toy car was poised at the top of a ramp. A track for the car ran down the ramp and along the base of the apparatus. When the infants were attending to the apparatus, the middle section of the track was hidden by lowering a screen, and the habituation phase of the experiment began. The car ran down the ramp, passed behind the screen, and reappeared at the end of the apparatus. Following habituation to repeated presentations of this event, the screen was raised and a box was placed either *on* the car's track, or behind it. The screen was then lowered again, hiding the box, and the car began its journey. The apparatus used is shown in Fig. 2.8.

FIG. 2.8.
Depiction of the habituation and test events in the car on the ramp paradigm devised by Baillargeon (1986). Reproduced with kind permission of Elsevier Science.

All the babies then saw exactly the same set of events as during the habituation phase of the experiment. For babies in the "possible" condition, the box was behind the track and out of the car's path, and so the reappearance of the car was not surprising. For babies in the

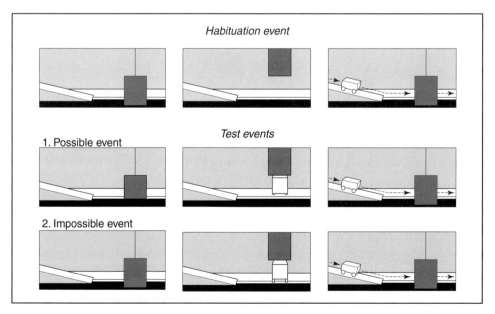

Habituation event

1. Possible event

Test events

2. Impossible event

"impossible" condition, however, the box was *on* the track, directly in the path of the car—and yet the car *still* reappeared in the familiar way! The babies in the impossible condition spent much longer staring at the apparatus than the babies in the possible condition. The only explanation was that they had represented the box as continuing to exist and as therefore blocking the car's path, and so they were surprised at the reappearance of the car. Baillargeon and DeVos (1991) later demonstrated that babies as young as $3^{1}/_{2}$ months of age were surprised to see the car reappear when they knew that a hidden object (a Mickey Mouse doll) was blocking its path.

However, although babies as young as 3 months seem to make similar assumptions to adults concerning the continued *existence* of occluded objects, it has recently been suggested that infants are unable to set up representations of numerically distinct occluded objects until the end of the first year. On the basis of a series of experiments using an occlusion paradigm with two perceptually distinct objects, a toy elephant and a toy truck, Xu and Carey (1996) have suggested that infants have a fairly generalised representation of objects until the age of at least 10 months. They argue that infants do not represent the identity of *individual* objects until slightly later in development.

Xu and Carey's basic paradigm contrasted two occlusion conditions, a *property-kind* condition and a *spatio-temporal* condition (see Fig. 2.9). In the property-kind condition, the infant was shown a single screen. A toy truck was brought out from the right side of the screen and returned behind it. A toy kitten was then brought out from the left side of the screen, and returned behind it. These successive events were repeated three more times. This set of repetitions comprised the habituating event. At test, the screen was removed to reveal either one object or two objects. Xu and Carey reasoned that infants who could set up representations of numerically distinct objects should find the single object outcome surprising, and so look longer at the single object than at two objects. In the spatio-temporal condition, the same sequence of successive emergences of the truck and kitten was preceded by a single trial in which the two toys were brought out *simultaneously* from behind the screen, one to each side. Infants in this condition were again expected to find the single object outcome surprising. Finally, a *baseline* condition assessed infants' intrinsic preference for looking at one object versus two objects in the absence of any occlusion events.

Xu and Carey found that infants looked longer at the two-object outcome in the baseline and property-kind conditions, but looked longer at the single-object outcome in the spatio-temporal condition. This basic finding was then replicated a number of times. Xu and

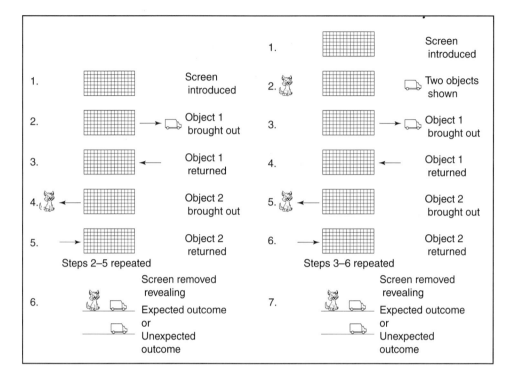

FIG. 2.9. Schematic representations of the property-kind condition (left) and the spatio-temporal condition (right) used in the experiments by Xu and Carey (1996). Reprinted by permission of Academic Press Inc.

Carey concluded that infants have an intrinsic preference for looking at two objects, and that this preference is overridden in the spatio-temporal condition but not in the property-kind condition. From this, they concluded that 10-month-old infants were unable to use the perceptual differences between the toy kitten and the toy truck to infer that there were two distinct objects behind the screen. This conclusion is somewhat at odds with some of the research discussed earlier, which suggested a rather detailed attention to the perceptual features of objects by infants younger than 10 months (e.g. Younger & Cohen, 1983). However, it is important to realise that Xu and Carey's claim is based on a negative result. There are many reasons why infants might fail to overcome their intrinsic preference for two objects in the property-kind condition, and an inability to use perceptual features to support object individuation and numerical identity is only one of them.

Representing quantitative relations. The perceptual structure of events in the visual world can also be used as a basis for representing relational knowledge about number. The understanding of relations such as "greater than" and "less than" are an important underpinning of our number system. Equally important is the understanding that a quantity remains the same unless something is added to it or taken away from it. Habituation studies have been used to show that babies can represent quantitative relations fairly early in life, and also some numerical relations.

For example, Cooper (1984) used a habituation paradigm in which infants were habituated to pairs of arrays of coloured squares. These arrays depicted either the relation "greater than" or the relation "less than". For the "greater than" relation the infants might be shown a pair made up of 4 squares in array 1 vs. 2 squares in array 2, then a pair of 4 squares in array 1 vs. 3 squares in array 2, and then 2 vs. 1 square (see Table 2.1). At test, the infants received either a reversed relation ("less than"; 3 squares in array 1 vs. 4 squares in array 2), an "equal" relation (2 vs. 2), or a novel exemplar of the same relation (3 vs. 2). At 10

TABLE 2.1
Examples of numerosity arrays used by Cooper (1984)

Condition	Numerosity of Array 1	Numerosity of Array 2	Trial Type
Less than:			
Habituation	3	4	
	2	4	
	1	2	
Test	3	4	Old
	2	3	New
	4	3	Reversed
	2	2	Equal
Greater than:			
Habituation	4	2	
	4	3	
	2	1	
Test	4	3	Old
	3	2	New
	3	4	Reversed
	2	2	Equal
Equal:			
Habituation	4	4	
	2	2	
	1	1	
Test	4	4	Old
	3	3	New
	2	4	Less than
	4	2	Greater than

months, the infants dishabituated to the "equal" relation only, showing that they could differentiate equality from inequality. By 14 months, the infants dishabituated to the "less than" relation as well, showing an appreciation of relational reversal. Similar paradigms have also been used with younger babies (e.g. Starkey & Cooper, 1980).

One of the most convincing demonstrations of an understanding of numerosity in infancy comes from some recent work by Wynn (1992). She studied the ability of 5-month-old babies to add and subtract small numbers, using an occlusion procedure. All babies first viewed an empty display area. Once they were attending, a hand appeared in their field of view and placed a Mickey Mouse doll in the display area. Next, a small screen rotated up from the floor of the apparatus, hiding the doll from view. The hand then reappeared and placed a second Mickey Mouse doll behind the screen. When the screen dropped, it either revealed two Mickey Mouse dolls (possible event) or a single Mickey Mouse doll (impossible event). This sequence of events is shown in Fig. 2.10. Wynn found that the babies looked significantly longer at the single Mickey Mouse doll, the impossible outcome. A group of babies who initially saw two Mickey Mouse dolls in the display area and then saw one being removed after the screen came up showed the opposite pattern: they looked significantly longer when the screen dropped to reveal two Mickey Mouse dolls (impossible event) than when it dropped to reveal a single Mickey Mouse doll (possible event). Wynn argued that this showed that the infants could compute the numerical results of simple arithmetical operations.

Support for her view comes from a replication of her study by Simon, Hespos, and Rochat (1995). Simon et al. pointed out that Wynn's results could be explained on the basis of violations of infants' knowledge about the physical world, rather than on the basis of an innate possession of arithmetical abilities. In the "impossible addition" condition, objects seen placed behind the screen ceased to exist, and in the "impossible subtraction" condition, objects that did not previously exist magically appeared. Simon et al. noted that this alone could explain increased looking time. However, if Wynn's results depended on the recognition of physically impossible outcomes regardless of arithmetic, then infants should also show increased looking time in "possible arithmetic" conditions in which the identity of Mickey Mouse was changed to someone else. Simon et al. therefore included "impossible identity" and "impossible identity and arithmetic" conditions in their replication of Wynn's study.

Rather than using Mickey Mouse dolls, however, Simon et al.'s "impossible identity" conditions involved a switch between the two

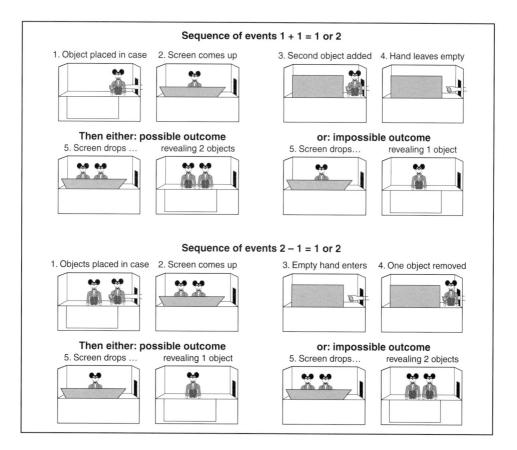

Sequence of events 1 + 1 = 1 or 2

1. Object placed in case　2. Screen comes up　3. Second object added　4. Hand leaves empty

Then either: possible outcome
5. Screen drops … 　 revealing 2 objects

or: impossible outcome
5. Screen drops… 　 revealing 1 object

Sequence of events 2 − 1 = 1 or 2

1. Objects placed in case　2. Screen comes up　3. Empty hand enters　4. One object removed

Then either: possible outcome
5. Screen drops … 　 revealing 1 object

or: impossible outcome
5. Screen drops… 　 revealing 2 objects

Sesame Street characters Ernie and Elmo. This is shown in Fig. 2.11. For example (impossible identity), if the infants saw a second Elmo doll being added to a first Elmo doll which was concealed by the screen, the screen would drop to reveal two dolls, Elmo and Ernie. Similarly, if the infants saw an Elmo doll being removed from behind a screen known to conceal two Elmo dolls, the screen would drop to reveal a single doll, Ernie. Both of these outcomes are arithmetically correct but physically impossible. In the arithmetically impossible conditions (1 + 1 = 1, 2—1 = 2), the identity of the dolls was also switched (Elmo + Elmo = Ernie, 2 Elmos—Elmo = Elmo + Ernie). Here the outcome was *both* arithmetically incorrect and physically impossible.

Simon et al. found that 5-month-olds in the "impossible identity" condition behaved just like the infants in the "possible arithmetic" condition used by Wynn, whereas the infants in the "impossible identity and arithmetic" condition behaved just like the infants in her

FIG. 2.10.
The addition and subtraction events used by Wynn (1992). Adapted from *Nature*, *358*, © 1992 Macmillan Magazines Ltd.

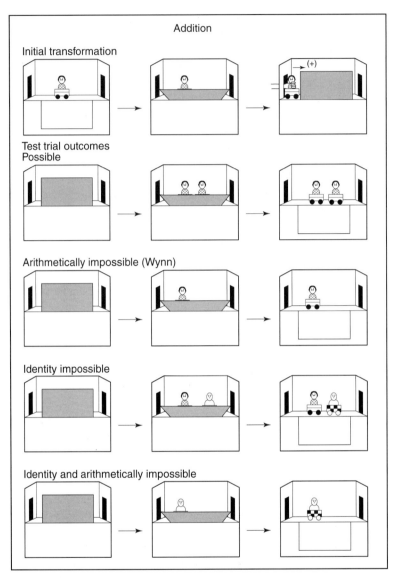

"impossible arithmetic" condition. The infants thus looked longer at arithmetically incorrect outcomes, but not at physically incorrect outcomes (a control condition had established that they *could* distinguish between Elmo and Ernie). Simon et al. argued that the spatio-temporal information in Wynn's set-up caused the infants to focus on the *number* of objects behind the screen rather than on their identity.

These findings are also consistent with the ideas of Xu and Carey (1996), discussed in the previous section.

There have even been reports of *cross-modal* understanding of number fairly early in life. Starkey, Spelke, and Gelman (1983) used a paradigm similar to that used by Spelke (1976, see Chapter 1) to examine whether infants equated three sounds with three objects, and two sounds with two objects. In their experiment, the infants were given a choice of two visual arrays, one of which contained two objects and the other three objects. The objects in the arrays were changed from trial to trial, but one array always contained *two*, and the other *three*. The infants also heard a soundtrack from a speaker placed in between the two arrays. The soundtrack was either repeated pairs of drumbeats, or repeated triples of drumbeats. Starkey et al. found that the infants preferred to look at arrays of two objects when they were listening to a pair of drumbeats, and at arrays of three objects when they were listening to triples of drumbeats. This preference for cross-modal *congruence* was also found in the cross-modal work discussed in Chapter 1. In order to recognise cross-modal congruence in Starkey et al.'s paradigm, the infants must have been representing the *numerosity* of the drumbeats. This striking result has proved difficult to replicate, however (Moore et al., 1987).

Representing causal relations. The preceding sections have already provided indirect evidence that infants can represent causal relations. Most of the experiments discussed in these sections involve causal relations *as well as* the relations of space, number, and occlusion, as in order for the physical violations discussed to be surprising, an understanding of cause–effect relations is necessary. For example, in the study based on the car running down the ramp, it is the expected *collision* between the car and the box that makes the reappearance of the car surprising. In the study with the rotating screen, it is the expected *contact* between the screen and the box that makes the continued rotation of the screen surprising. However, all of the causal events in these paradigms occur *out of view*. This means that we have to infer that, for example, the babies in the car experiment expected the car to collide with the box and thus to stop (they might have been surprised because the car appeared to be able to occupy the same space as the box, or because they expected the car to reappear shunting the box in front of it!). In order to assess infants' ability to represent causal events *directly*, we need to study causal events that occur *in full view* of the infant.

Collision events provide a useful set of events for such experiments. For example, when one billiard ball collides with another, the second ball is launched into motion. This is a pure example of a cause–effect relation, and Michotte (1963) showed that adults always have an impression of causality when they view "launching" events, even if they are watching patches of light moving on a wall. This impression of causality even in the absence of a mechanical connection was taken by Michotte to show that adults are subject to a perceptual *illusion* of causality, but it can also be taken to show that the perceptual system *assumes* cause–effect relations in the absence of contradictory evidence. Young infants appear to possess a similar perceptual mechanism that assumes causality. This mechanism is probably at the roots of their causal understanding.

The existence of this mechanism was shown in some experiments devised by Leslie and Keeble (1987), who were interested in 6-month-old infants' understanding of launching events. In a typical experiment, infants were shown one of two films. In one film, a red block moved towards a green block and then collided with it, directly setting the green block in motion. In the other film, the red block again moved towards the green block and made contact with it, but the green block only began to move after a delay of 0.5 seconds. Whereas the first launching event gave an impression of causality to watching adults, the second did not. Following habituation to one of the films (either direct launching or delayed launching), the infants were then shown the *same* film in reverse. Although the change in the spatio-temporal relations in the films was the same for both groups, the reversal of the "direct launching" film resulted in a *novel* causal event (green launches red). Leslie and Keeble argued that if the infants in the direct launching condition were perceiving a causal relation (red launches green), then they should show more dishabituation following reversal (green launches red) than the infants in the delayed launching condition.

This was exactly what they found. Leslie (1994) argued that this effect showed that the infants were interested in the *mechanical structure* of launching. In the "direct launching" film, there was a change in the mechanical roles of the two billiard balls. The "pusher" was now the "pushed". In the "delayed launching" film the billiard balls did not have roles, and so the roles could not be reversed. Leslie's description of the launching event in terms of mechanics entails a notion of *agency*, an idea that is discussed further later.

Another set of cause–effect relations that are commonly encountered in the physical world are the causal relations involved in support. Adults are well aware that if they put a mug of tea down on a table and the mug protrudes too far over the table's edge, then the tea will fall onto the floor. However, if only a small portion of the bottom surface of the mug is protruding over the edge of the table, then the mug will have adequate support and the tea can be consumed at leisure. Baillargeon, Needham, and DeVos (1992) investigated similar intuitions about support in young infants. They studied 6½-month-old infants' expectations about when a box would fall off a platform.

In Baillargeon et al.'s experiment the infants were shown a box sitting at the left-hand end of a long platform, and then watched as the finger of a gloved hand pushed the box along the platform until part of it was suspended over the right-hand edge (see Fig. 2.12). For some infants, the pushing continued until 85% of the bottom surface of the box protruded over the platform, and for others the pushing stopped when 30% of the bottom surface of the box protruded over the platform. In a control condition the same infants watched the box being pushed to the right-hand end of the platform, but the bottom surface of the box remained in full contact with the platform. The infants spent reliably longer looking at the apparatus in the 85% protrusion event than in the full-contact control event. This suggests that they expected the box to fall off the platform (the box was able to remain magically suspended

FIG. 2.12. Depiction of the familiarisation and test events in the box on a platform paradigm devised by Baillargeon et al. (1992). Panel (a) depicts the 85% protrusion event, and panel (b) the 30% protrusion event. Reproduced with permission.

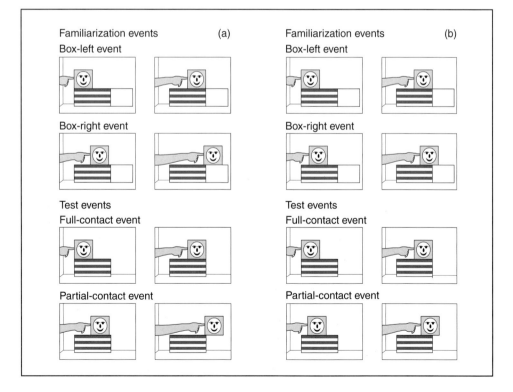

in mid-air via a hidden hand). The infants in the 30% protrusion event looked equally during the protrusion event and the control event. Baillargeon et al. argued that the infants were able to judge how much contact was required between the box and the platform in order for the box to be stable.

Interestingly, younger infants (5½- to 6-month-olds) appeared unable to make such fine judgements about support, looking equally at the 85% and 30% protrusion events compared to the full-contact control event. Baillargeon et al.'s interpretation of this finding was that younger infants perceive *any* amount of contact between objects to be sufficient to ensure stability. They operate with a simpler causal rule that *no contact = object falls*, and *partial contact = object is supported*, even when the partial contact is very partial indeed. In fact, Baillargeon argues that much physical causal reasoning develops according to this all-or-none pattern. Infants begin with representations that capture the essence of physical events (e.g. contact vs. no contact), and then gradually develop more elaborate representations that identify variables that are relevant to the events' outcomes (such as *degree* of support). Experience of the physical world has an important role to play in this developmental sequence. For example, at around 6 months of age most babies become "self-sitters". They are able to sit up with support, and for the first time they can be seated in high-chairs etc. in front of tables, and can deposit objects on surfaces and watch them fall off. Baillargeon has suggested that these experiences help infants to refine their understanding of the cause–effect relations underlying support. The idea that *specific* experiences of this kind help in the development of specific aspects of physical reasoning is an exciting topic for future research.

From representing causal relations to an understanding of agency. The ability to represent causal relations between objects may appear to be a simple extension of infants' ability to represent relational information in general, but attention to causality is actually a critical cognitive tool. Causal relations are particularly powerful relations for understanding the everyday world of objects and events. In later chapters, we will see how a sensitivity to causal relations underlies conceptual development, the development of memory, and logical development in general. A sensitivity to causal relations may also underlie the development of a notion of *agency*. Agency may be considered in terms of an understanding of mechanical agency or an understanding of human agency.

An analysis of the development of the understanding of *mechanical* agency has been put forward by Leslie (1994). Leslie argued that causal analyses of motion in infants serve the important purpose of generating mechanical *descriptions* of events. Such descriptions are more than a perceptual description of what has occurred, and so the perception of cause and effect cannot be said to be purely visual. Instead, this perception is the basis of a mechanism for understanding the mechanical properties of *agents*. Inanimate objects move in the real world as a result of the redistribution of energy, and these mechanical forces differ in important ways from animate sources of motion. Things that move on their own are agents, and things that move because of other things obey certain cause–effect, or mechanical, laws. Infants' interest in things that move helps them to sort out the source of different cause–effect relations in the physical world.

Recent evidence that infants make a distinction between mechanical forces and animate sources of motion comes from an experiment reported by Spelke, Phillips, and Woodward (1995). They compared 7-month-old infants' use of the principle of contact as a force that causes motion for inanimate objects versus people. The inanimate objects were meaningless patterned shapes 5' to 6' high, that were moved from behind by hidden people walking at a normal pace. The experiment was based on an occlusion paradigm (see Fig. 2.13). During habituation, the infants saw either a person or an inanimate object appear to one side of the display and move behind a central screen. A second object or

FIG. 2.13. Schematic depiction of the events used to study infants' understanding of the forceful contact principle by Spelke, Phillips and Woodward (1995). Copyright © John Wiley & Sons Ltd. Reproduced with permission.

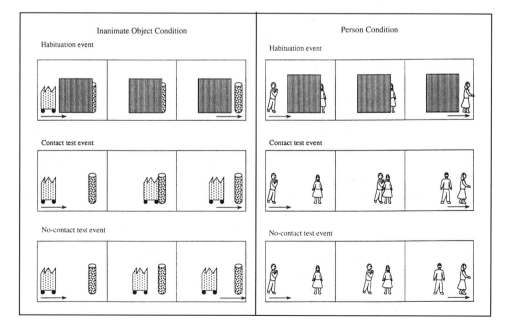

person then appeared from the other side of the screen and exited the display. These events were then repeated in reverse. The timing of the events was identical for objects and people, and for the objects it was consistent with the first object setting the second object in motion via contact behind the screen.

At test, the screen was removed and the infants saw either a contact event or a no-contact event. In the contact event, the two inanimate objects or people followed the same movement paths as in the habituation event, the second object or person moving once the first had made contact with it. In the no-contact event, the two objects or people never made contact, the first stopping a short distance from the second, which began moving after a suitable pause. Both events were then shown in reverse, and were repeated as long as the infants kept looking at them. If the infants were able to distinguish mechanical forces from animate sources of motion, then they should find the no-contact event more visually interesting for the inanimate objects, where the absence of contact should not cause motion. For the people, there should be no difference in the visual interest of the contact and the no-contact events, as people are agents who are capable of self-propelled motion. This was exactly what Spelke et al. found. A control condition established that there was no difference in the intrinsic attractiveness of the contact and no-contact events. Spelke et al. thus concluded that, at least by 7 months of age, infants do not apply the forceful contact principle to people. They reason *differently* about people and objects, appreciating that people are agents who can move on their own.

The development of an understanding of human agency has also been investigated in an elegant way by Meltzoff (1995). He showed that older infants can understand the causal *intentions* of others, which requires an understanding of humans' capacity for agency. In his experiment, Meltzoff showed 18-month-old infants an adult who demonstrated an intention to act in a certain way. However, the intention was never fulfilled. For example, the adult would try to put a string of beads into a cylindrical container, but the beads would keep falling outside the container rather than inside it. The adult would try to hang a loop of string over a hook, but would continually under- or over-shoot the target. A second group of infants saw the adult modelling the same actions, but in each case completing the entire action successfully. Both groups of infants then received the beads, string etc. to manipulate by themselves.

Meltzoff found that production of the target acts (putting the beads inside the container, hanging the loop of string over the hook etc.) was identical in these two groups of infants, even though one group had never actually seen the target acts being performed. A control group of babies who were given the same objects produced very few of the target acts, suggesting that the target acts were not in themselves a natural way in which to manipulate the objects. Meltzoff concluded that a psychological understanding of the intention of the human actor led the babies in the experimental group to produce the target acts. They were aware of the acts that the adult had intended to produce, even though the acts themselves had failed.

Interestingly, however, the babies did *not* behave in the same way when an inanimate device performed the same movements in space as the human hand. A new group of babies watched a pincer device performing slipping motions matched to those performed by the human hand when failing to complete one of the target acts. The aim was to see whether the babies would respond solely to the physics of the situation, or whether they had been responding previously to the human agent. Meltzoff found that, although the babies' attention was riveted by the mechanical device, they were much less likely to imitate the target acts when the inanimate object failed to demonstrate an intended act than when a human agent failed to demonstrate the same act. In fact, babies who watched the human failing were six times more likely to produce the target act than babies who watched the inanimate device failing.

Meltzoff argued that his results were suggestive of the existence of two *separable* causal frameworks by the age of 18 months, a physical causality for explaining the behaviour of things, and a psychological causality for explaining the behaviour of people. He suggested that infants represented the behaviour of people in a psychological framework that involved goals and purposeful intended acts, and not in terms of purely physical movements and motions.

Recent data from Gergely and his colleagues has shown that the attribution of agency on the basis of causal analyses of physical situations is even more sophisticated than Meltzoff supposed. In an innovative study designed to examine the beginnings of the understanding of agency, Gergely, Nadasdy, Csibra, and Biro (1995) have shown that 12-month-old infants can analyse the spatial behaviour of an agent in terms of its actions towards a goal, and will apply an "intentional stance" to this behaviour when it appears rational, thereby attributing a mental cause for the goal-directed behaviour. When there is no basis for attributing rationality to goal-directed spatial behaviour, then an intentional stance is not adopted.

In their experiment, Gergely et al. took as their starting point the fact that the prediction and explanation of the behaviour of agents requires the attribution of intentional states such as beliefs, goals, and desires as the mental causes of actions. This is the adoption of an "intentional stance". The adoption of an "intentional stance" towards agents entails an assumption of rationality—that the agent will adopt the most rational action in a particular situation to achieve his or her goal. To examine whether 12-month-old infants would generate expectations about the particular actions an assumed agent was likely to perform in a new situation to achieve a desired goal, Gergely et al. designed a visual habituation study in which a computer display gave an impression of agency to the behaviour of circles. The infants saw a display in which two circles, a large circle and a small circle, were separated by a tall rectangle (see Fig. 2.14). During the habituation event, each circle in turn expanded and then contracted twice. The small circle then began to move towards the large circle. When it reached the rectangular barrier it retreated, only to set out towards the large circle a second time, this time jumping over the rectangle and making contact with the large circle. Both circles then expanded and contracted twice more. Adult observers of this visual event described it as a mother (large circle) calling to her child (small circle) who ran towards her, only to be prevented by the barrier, which she then jumped over. The two then embraced.

FIG. 2.14. Schematic depiction of the habituation events shown to the rational approach group by Gergely et al. (1995), with (a) depicting the expansion and contraction events and the first approach, and (b) depicting the retreat, jump, and eventual contact. By permission of Oxford University Press.

Following habituation to this event, the infants saw the same two circles making the same sequence of movements, but this time without a barrier being present. In this "old action" event, there was no rational explanation of the retreat-and-jump action. In a "new action" event, the small circle simply took the shortest straight path to reach the large circle. Gergely et al. predicted that, if the infants were making an *intentional* causal analysis of the initial display, then they should spend

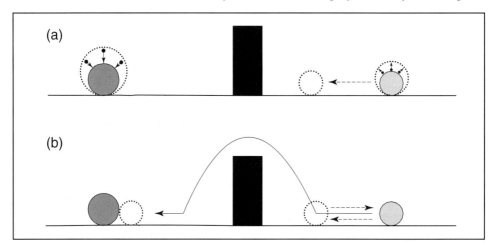

more time looking at the old action event than the new action event, because even though the former event was familiar it was no longer rational. This was exactly what they found. A control group who saw the same habituating events without the rectangle acting as a barrier (it was positioned to the side of the screen) showed equal dishabituation to the old and new action events. Gergely et al. argued that the control group had not considered the small circle to be a rational agent, as the behaviour of the small circle during the habituation event did not lead the infants to adopt an intentional stance towards it.

This intriguing result shows just how powerful the ability to represent causal relations between objects may be for the young infant. Causal analyses of the everyday world of objects and events appear to be able to supply information about the physical world of inanimate objects and *also* about the mental world of animate agents. Although this may lead to the eventual development of two separable causal frameworks, one for explaining the behaviour of objects and one for explaining the behaviour of people, the foundation of both frameworks appears to be the same. The attribution of causal mechanisms such as beliefs and desires seems to develop from the *same* source as the attribution of causal mechanisms such as collision and support— namely from a causal analysis of the spatial behaviour of objects.

Moving further into cognition: Meaning-based knowledge representations

The ways in which infants go beyond perceptual categorisation and representation of the relations between objects to form concepts and schemas (*meaning*-based knowledge representations) is not well understood. Meaning-based knowledge representations are defined in adult cognition as representations that encode what is significant about an event, omitting the unimportant perceptual details (e.g. Anderson, 1980). A *propositional* format represents the meaning of a sentence or an image in terms of key relations and nouns. For example, the sentence "Nixon gave a beautiful Cadillac to Brezhnev, who was the leader of the USSR" might be represented as (*Give*, Nixon, Cadillac, Brezhnev, Past; see Anderson, 1980). *Schemas* are complex units of knowledge that represent what is typically true of a *category*, for example *birds* (has wings, has beak, can fly ... etc.) or an *event*, such as *going to the doctor* (report to receptionist, wait a long time, enter surgery ... etc.). Schemas for events are also called *scripts*.

As infants are sometimes assumed to have categories that are purely sensory or perceptual in nature (based on the storage of structured perceptual information), the problem of conversion to a propositional or schematic format seems at first sight to be insuperable. However, infants' sensitivity to causal relations provides a possible means for going beyond the perceptual information given. After all, we have seen that infants store a remarkable amount of information that is not purely sensory in nature. For example, infants store information about launching events that goes beyond the perceptual characteristics of the events themselves to a notion of agency (Leslie, 1994). We have also seen (in Chapter 1) that infants can retain two-step causal event sequences like "make a rattle" over long periods of time (three months), whereas they lose their memories for two-step non-causal or arbitrary event sequences like "put a hat on the bunny and feed him a carrot" over the same period. Research such as this suggests that what is being represented and remembered is *not* the perceptual characteristics of the events themselves, but their causal structure or their meaning. This makes it unlikely that infants have to wait until they have acquired language to represent knowledge in a meaning-based fashion, as was once thought. In any case, such a proposal begs important questions, questions about what kind of cognitive structures underpin language acquisition. Infant representations in at least some domains are thus different from the sensory information given.

Image schemas

One theorist who has tackled the problem of what form such representations might take is Jean Mandler. Mandler (1988, 1992) has argued that one source of non-sensory conceptual activity in infancy is infants' representations of the *spatial* properties of objects and events. Her idea is that the perceptual analysis of spatial structure can lead to mental redescription in terms of "image schemas", which may be the precursors of concepts such as animacy, agency, and containment. Image schemas are analogical representations of the perceptual structure of the event, such as the spatial relations and the movements in space that characterise an event like *containment*. The formation of image-schemas involves the active abstraction of key information about such events, which is then recoded into a non-perceptual form that represents a meaning. These meanings are simple notions such as *up–down*, *part–whole*, and *link*. Mandler argues that this meaning-based knowledge is unlikely to be consciously accessible, requiring redescription again into imagery or words in order to become available to the infant cogniser.

As an example, the notion of *containment* may be represented by the image schemas shown in Fig. 2.15. Babies experience many different perceptual examples of containment relations. The frequent acts of eating and drinking involve a large number of containment relations (milk in bottle, milk out of bottle, cereal in bowl, cereal in spoon, cereal on floor etc.), and other containment-rich activities include having one's clothes changed, being put in and out of the pram or playpen, and spitting things out. Mandler's idea is that infants analyse the perceptual characteristics of all these events, abstract what is similar in terms of movements in space and spatial relations, and then create a containment image-schema that specifies the three crucial structural elements of *interior*, *exterior*, and *boundary*. The related image schemas for *going in* and *going out* are also shown in Fig. 2.15. Mandler suggests that these image-schemas are in effect conceptual primitives, or pre-verbal representations. They are unlikely to be propositional in nature. Instead, Mandler argues that image-schemas *facilitate* language acquisition.

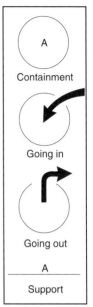

FIG. 2.15. Image schemas for containment, going in, going out, and support (Mandler, 1992). Reproduced with kind permission of Elsevier Science.

Specialised modules for certain information?

Leslie (1994) has argued that Mandler's ideas are somewhat at variance with his own notion, which is that there are specialised information-processing systems in the brain that provide the basis for cognitive development. According to Leslie's *domain-specificity* view, there are mechanisms in the brain that, by virtue of the position that they occupy in the overall organisation, receive inputs from particular classes of objects in the world and end up representing certain kinds of domain-specific information. One example is the mechanism that acquires the syntactic structure of natural language. Other proposed "modules" include *number* and *music*. In addition, Leslie proposes two core domains that he argues are central to infants' initial capacities for causal conceptual knowledge. These are *object mechanics* and *"theory of mind"*. In these two core domains, the central organising principle is the notion of cause and effect.

For example, infants' processing of the physical world seems to organise itself fairly rapidly around a core structure representing the arrangement of cohesive, solid, three-dimensional objects which are embedded in a series of mechanical relations such as *pushing, blocking, and support*. Leslie argues that this organised processing is the result of a specialised learning mechanism or module adapted by evolution to create conceptual knowledge of the physical world. In Leslie's view, the modular organisation of the brain *itself* allows the infant to acquire rapid and uniform knowledge about object mechanics (and also about psychological causality). A different way of describing this organised processing is to say that babies have rudimentary "theories", such as a "theory" of mechanics. As we will see in later chapters, the idea that babies and young children have emergent theories has also been used to explain cognitive development in the domains of biological knowledge and psychological knowledge.

The difference between Leslie's domain-specific processor which understands the *mechanics* of physical causal events and Mandler's notion of image schemas is that the latter are conceptualised in purely spatial terms. One assumption that is common to both theories, however, is that young infants have representations that go beyond the sensory or perceptual data and represent *meaning*. Both Leslie and Mandler argue that meaning-based knowledge representations are emerging in infants as young as 4 months of age.

The different types of meaning-based representations introduced here will be discussed further in later chapters. The relationship between spatial/mechanical analyses of movement and the animate/inanimate distinction that aids conceptual development is discussed further in Chapter 3. The evidence that even very young children are developing event schemas is discussed in the first chapter on memory development, Chapter 5.

Reasoning and problem solving

Two other hallmarks of cognitive activity are reasoning and problem solving. Defining reasoning and problem solving is not straightforward. One popular definition of reasoning is that it comprises those processes in information retrieval that depend on the *structure*, as opposed to the *content*, of organised memory (Rumelhart & Abramson, 1983). However, this definition leaves us with the problem of deciding which parts of organised memory are structural and which are content. According to Anderson (1980), reasoning and problem solving usually involve three ingredients. First, the reasoner wants to reach a desired end state, which usually involves attaining a specific goal. Second, a sequence of mental processes must be involved in reaching this end state. The involvement of a sequence of mental processes is intended to distinguish reasoning from goal-directed behaviour such as opening your mouth when you see a feeding bottle. Third, the mental processes involved should be cognitive rather than automatic. An automatic or routine sequence of behaviour, such as playing a "peek-a-boo" game, does not qualify as cognitive. Although we will only discuss a few examples of reasoning and problem solving in infancy in this chapter, recent experiments investigating infants' understanding of the physical world have produced many more. Useful reviews include Baillargeon (1995), and Spelke (1991).

The bear in the cup

One ingenious problem-solving experiment concerning the infant's understanding of the physical world investigated whether infants understand that, when they have seen a toy bear sitting under an inverted plastic cup, it is impossible to retrieve the *same* bear from a previously empty toy cage. Baillargeon, Graber, DeVos, and Black (1990) examined this question by showing infants a display in which an inverted clear plastic cup and a small bottomless cage were sitting side-by-side on a table, with the cage to the right of the cup. A toy bear was visible inside the inverted plastic cup, but the cage was empty. A screen was then raised so that the two containers were hidden from the infants' view.

As the infants watched, a hand appeared to the right of the screen, reached behind it, and reappeared holding the cage (see Fig. 2.16). The hand then reached behind the screen for a second time, and reappeared holding the toy bear. This was an impossible event, and the infants looked significantly longer at this event than at the same event in a control condition in which the bear was first shown to be inside the cage

FIG. 2.16. Depiction of the familiarisation and test events in the bear in the cup paradigm devised by Baillargeon et al. (1990). Copyright © 1990 by the American Psychological Association. Adapted with permission.

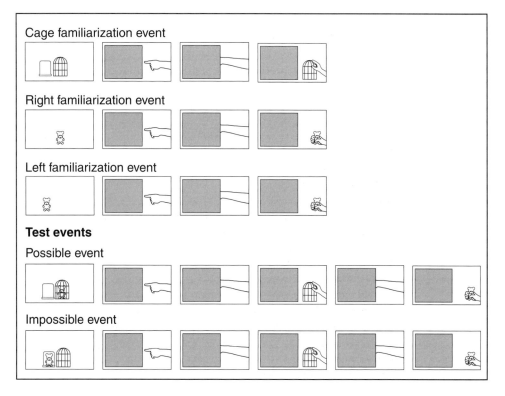

rather than inside the cup. In order to be surprised at the impossible event, the infants had to believe that the bear, cup, and cage continued to exist behind the screen, and also had to retain a representation of their locations once they were hidden by the screen. On the basis of these premises, they then had to *reason* that it was impossible to retrieve the bear from the empty cage.

The dog beneath the cloth

Another example of reasoning about physical events in infancy concerns infants' ability to judge the size of a hidden object (Baillargeon & DeVos, 1994). In Baillargeon and DeVos's "hidden object" studies, the infants' task was to work out the size of an object hidden beneath a cloth. In a typical experiment, the infants were first shown a lump covered by a soft, fluid cloth. This array was then occluded by a screen. As the infants watched the display, a hand reached behind the screen and first reappeared holding the cloth cover, then reached again and subsequently reappeared holding a very large toy dog. This toy dog was so big that, to an adult, it was obvious that it could not have been the object causing the original lump beneath the cloth. However, the infants (12^1/$_2$-month-olds) were not surprised by the impossibly large size of this "hidden" object.

Subsequent experiments showed that one reason that the infants were not surprised was that they found it difficult to retain a memory of the *absolute* size of the lump once it had been occluded by the screen. When Baillargeon and DeVos provided a second, identical protuberance under a cloth as a memory cue (this cloth remained visible when the screen concealed the target lump), then 12^1/$_2$-month-old infants were able to reason about the size of the hidden object. In this study, the infants were able to make a direct comparison between the very large toy dog that emerged from behind the screen and the memory cue lump as the hand reached first for the cloth and then for the toy dog (see Fig. 2.17). When they could make a *relational comparison*, the infants looked significantly longer at the emergence of the impossibly large toy dog than at the emergence of a smaller toy dog that was of a suitable size to have caused the original lump beneath the cloth. The infants were able to use the visible lump to reason about the size of the hidden object.

The rabbits behind the wall

How can we be certain that infants were indeed *reasoning* about the physical parameters of the situation in the paradigms just discussed? One way is to see whether they would stop being surprised at impossible physical events if the mechanisms behind the "tricks" were revealed.

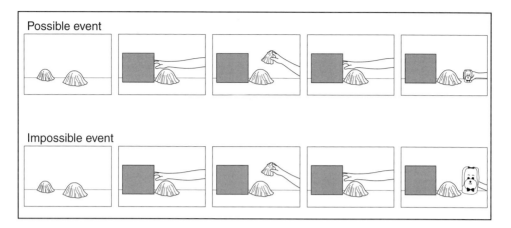

Possible event

Impossible event

This would be good evidence for problem-solving skills in infancy, as it would require a sequence of mental processes which are non-automatic.

One experiment in which the "trick" behind an impossible physical event was eventually revealed to the infants is the study by Baillargeon and Graber (1987) concerning spatial relations (discussed earlier). In this study, infants were habituated to either a tall or a short rabbit passing behind a wall. The mid-section of the wall was then lowered, and the impossible physical event was that the tall rabbit passed behind the short mid-section of the wall without the top half of his body becoming visible. This impossible event generated considerable surprise among 5½-month-old babies. The impossible event was actually produced by using *two* rabbits. In a follow-up study, Baillargeon and Graber showed a new group of infants how the "trick" had been produced. These "informed" infants received two pretest trials, during which first two tall rabbits and then two short rabbits were shown standing motionless at each side of the windowless screen. The experiment then proceeded as before. This time, neither group showed surprise when the rabbit failed to appear behind the short section of the wall, whether they had been habituated with the tall rabbit or the short rabbit. The infants had apparently used the infor-mation from the pretest trials to reason that the trick had been produced by using two rabbits.

The disappearance of the dishabituation effect in this experiment is particularly remarkable when it is remembered that the infants never saw the rabbits in motion during the pretest trials. They simply saw two short rabbits, and two tall rabbits. They then used this information to work out that while one rabbit disappeared behind the fence at the beginning of a habituation trial, a *second* rabbit reappeared at the other

FIG. 2.17. Depiction of the events used in the dog beneath the cloth experiment when a relational comparison was possible (Baillargeon & DeVos, 1994). Reproduced with kind permission of Elsevier Science. Reproduced with permission.

end. The infants were using the information about two rabbits to make sense of a surprising phenomenon. They were solving the problem of how an impossible event of this nature could have been produced.

The box suspended in mid-air

Recently, Baillargeon and her colleagues have also experimented with the effects of providing infants with information that enables them to work out the "trick" of how the suspended box remains in mid-air in the "violation-of-support" paradigm. As discussed earlier, Baillargeon, Needham, and DeVos (1992) investigated infants' intuitions about support by studying their expectations about when a box would fall off a platform. The infants in their study were reliably surprised that a box that was pushed along a platform until it was in contact with only 15% of its surface failed to fall to the ground. In work in progress, Baillargeon and her colleagues are studying the effects of a pretest trial in which the infants see the box sitting on the platform with the front panel of the box removed. A hand is clearly visible at the back of the box, gripping it firmly. If the infants can use this information to solve the problem of how the impossible event is contrived, then they should cease to find the impossible event (the box remaining suspended in the air when it is pushed off the platform) surprising. Preliminary results suggest that this is exactly what happens. The infants apparently reason that a hidden hand is holding the box in place, and fail to show increased looking time to the "impossible" event.

These experiments provide fairly convincing evidence of reasoning and problem-solving behaviour in young infants. All of the criteria set by Anderson (1980) for defining reasoning and problem-solving behaviour appear to be fulfilled. The *desired end state* is to generate an explanation for an impossible event, which is a specifically cognitive goal. This is achieved by a *sequence of mental processes*, requiring the combination of a number of premises that are represented in memory. These processes are *cognitive* rather than automatic, because the premises involve information that is not directly observable. Thus it is difficult to disagree with Baillargeon's conclusion that the infants in her experiments are engaging in a knowledge-based, conceptual analysis of the physical world.

Learning

Finally, certain kinds of learning are also hallmarks of cognitive activity. Although one way of defining learning is to say that it is the modification of behaviour in the light of experience, even simple organisms such as *aplysia* learn according to this definition. In fact, a number of different kinds of learning have been identified in work with animals. These include habituation, associative learning, social learning (e.g. by emulating others), and "insight" learning, when solutions to problems come "in a flash". In cognitive psychology, learning is usually measured in terms of what has been *remembered* as a result of learning, either via measures of *recognition* or via measures of *recall*. We will examine the more cognitive forms of learning here. These are learning by imitation and learning by analogy, neither of which is found in animals.

Learning by imitation

Learning by imitation can be defined as "B learns from A some part of the form of a behaviour" (Whiten & Ham, 1992, p.247). One example is learning the use of a novel tool by imitating the actions of another user with that tool. Most definitions of imitation require that something new is learned, and such learning has proved remarkably difficult to distinguish in animals, even though until quite recently the contrary was believed to be true. In fact, most psychologists now believe that learning by imitation is beyond the cognitive abilities of all animals, even animals like monkeys and chimpanzees, who are arguably the most human-like members of the animal kingdom (e.g. Tomasello, 1990; Visalberghi & Fragaszy, 1990). Tomasello has argued that humans differ profoundly from apes in their skills of imitation and imitative learning, because the ability to learn novel behaviours via imitation depends on the ability to understand the *intentions* of others.

Despite its cognitive sophistication, learning by imitation is present in human infants by the age of at least 9 months (Meltzoff, 1988a). As we saw earlier, older infants (18 months) can even imitate an adult who demonstrates an *intention* to act in a certain way, although the action is never completed, suggesting that imitation may indeed involve the ability to understand the intentions of others (Meltzoff, 1995). In fact, most of our knowledge about imitative learning in infants comes from the pioneering work of Meltzoff, who has expanded his early research on the imitation of adult facial gestures in a number of interesting ways. Many of his more recent experiments depend on the use of *deferred imitation* as a test of learning. Meltzoff's test is to see whether infants can reproduce a novel action that they have observed previously even if they were not allowed access to the critical materials at the time of learning. This is a strong test of imitation, as the ability to duplicate actions that have been absent from the perceptual field for some time makes it more likely that the infant is actively reconstructing what he or she has seen and therefore actively imitating. The involvement of "recall" rather than "recognition" memory in deferred imitation also makes it a useful test of memory (see the research by Mandler and her colleagues, discussed in Chapter 1).

In one of his first studies of deferred imitation, Meltzoff (1985) devised a paradigm suitable for 14-month-old infants based on the manipulation of a novel toy. The toy, which was specially constructed for the experiment, was a kind of wooden dumb-bell made up of two wooden blocks joined by a short length of rigid plastic tubing. The rigid tubing gave it the appearance of a single object. However, the wooden blocks could in fact be pulled apart, but only if sufficient pressure was applied. In the experiment, the experimenter sat opposite the baby at a small table, and produced the toy. In the *imitation* condition, he then pulled it apart three times in succession, using very definite movements. In the *control* condition, the experimenter moved the toy in a circle three times, pausing between each rotation. Each action (pulling vs. circling) lasted for the same amount of time. In the *baseline* condition, the experimenter simply gave the infant the toy to manipulate, without any behavioural modelling. In all three conditions, the infants were then sent home.

Twenty-four hours later the infants returned to the laboratory, sat down at the same table, and were given the toy to manipulate. The critical question was whether the infants in the imitation condition would be more likely to pull the toy apart than the infants in the baseline and the control conditions. This was exactly what happened. Of the babies in the imitation condition, 45% immediately pulled the toy apart themselves, compared to 7.5% of the control and baseline groups, whose data were added together. The babies in the imitation group were also much faster at producing the pulling-apart behaviour than any control babies who managed to do so.

In a later study, Meltzoff (1988b) expanded the novel modelled behaviours to six, and the delay before allowing imitation to one week. In addition to the dumb-bell used in the 1985 study (target act = pulling apart), 14-month-old babies were shown a flap with a hinge (target act = hinge folding), a box with a button (button pushing), a plastic egg filled with metal gravel (egg rattling), a bear suspended on a string (bear dancing), and a box with a panel (head touching of the panel, which then lit up). The control group observed six different modelled behaviours with these novel objects, and the baseline group observed no actions. Imitation was again measured in terms of the production of the target acts by each group. Meltzoff found that the infants in the imitation group produced significantly more of the target behaviours than the infants in the control group and the infants in the baseline group, who did not differ from each other. The infants in the imitation group were also significantly faster at producing the target acts. Once again, therefore, Meltzoff found clear evidence for learning by imitation, even after a delay of a week. The fact that six different novel behaviours had to be retained in memory makes this demonstration particularly impressive. In a related paper, Meltzoff (1988a) demonstrated retention of three novel acts by 9-month-olds over a delay of 24 hours, and more recently he has demonstrated deferred imitation in 14-month-olds over delays as long as two to four months. Learning by imitation appears to be an important and remarkably neglected area of infant cognition.

What if infants could learn not only by observing people acting on objects in real life, but by observing people acting on objects in films and videos? Given the ubiquity of the television in the modern home, this would expand infants' potential learning experiences by a huge degree. Meltzoff (1988c) has evidence that infants of 14 months of age can indeed learn novel actions from watching television. In his television study, the target action was again pulling apart (the dumb-bell), but this time the infants watched the experimenter model the action on a 22" television set and never saw him in person. The experimenter was filmed separately for each infant, enabling him to see their reactions on a video monitor so that he could wait until the infant was fixating on the dumb-bell before pulling it apart. The experimenter also gained the infant's attention if necessary by calling "Look", or "Can you see me?" to babies who did not immediately begin to watch the television (this was apparently quite rare). Following the demonstration of the pulling-apart action, the infants were sent home. Control and baseline groups were also tested, as in previous studies.

When the infants returned to the laboratory the following day, they were given the toy to manipulate. As in real TV viewing, the infants did not see the experimenter "live", but were handed the toy to manipulate by their parents, who followed instructions from the televised experimenter. Meltzoff again found that the imitation group were significantly more likely to produce the target behaviour than the control and baseline groups, just as in the "live" version of his study. Of the babies in the imitation group, 40% immediately pulled the dumb-bell apart, compared to 10% of control and baseline subjects. This demonstration of deferred imitation from the TV is a rather sobering one, as Meltzoff himself points out. If such young infants can reproduce behaviours that they see on TV and incorporate them into their own routines, then it is unlikely that TV viewing leaves older children unaffected. On the other hand, Meltzoff's demonstration is also an exciting one, as it means that TV can be used in a constructive way to enhance learning in target infant groups. Perhaps we should leave the last word to a toddler quoted by Meltzoff, who, on seeing his father pick up a bottle of beer, pointed to the bottle and exclaimed "Diet Pepsi, one less calorie!".

Learning by analogy

Learning by analogy involves finding certain correspondences between two events, situations, or domains of knowledge and then transferring knowledge from one to the other (e.g. Keane, 1988). So far, learning by analogy has only been demonstrated in one member of the animal kingdom, the highly unusual ape Sarah, who has learned a limited language (Gillan, Premack, & Woodruff, 1981). As put memorably by Winston (1980, p.1), in learning by analogy "we face a situation, we recall a similar situation, we match them up, we reason, and we learn". We may decide whether a dog has a heart by thinking about whether people have hearts (see Chapter 3), or we may solve a mathematical problem about the interaction of forces by using an analogy to a tug-of-war (see Chapter 4). Reasoning by analogy has usually been measured in children aged 3 years or older (see Goswami, 1992, for a review). Recent research, however, has shown that learning by analogy is available in infancy.

Chen and his colleagues devised a way of studying learning by analogy in infants as young as 10 months of age, following a procedure first developed by Brown (1990) for $1\frac{1}{2}$- to 2-year-olds. Brown's procedure depended on seeing whether toddlers could learn how to acquire attractive toys that were out of reach. Different objects (such as a variety of tools, some more effective than others) were provided as a *means* to a particular *end* (bringing the desired toy within grasping distance). The analogy was that the means-to-an-end solution that worked for getting one toy in fact worked for all of the problems given, even though the problems themselves appeared on the surface to be rather different. Brown and her colleagues used this paradigm to study analogical reasoning in children aged 17–36 months. Chen, Campbell, and Polley (1995) were able to extend it to infants.

In Chen et al.'s procedure, the infants came into the laboratory and were presented with an Ernie doll that was out of their reach. The Ernie doll was also behind a barrier (a box), and had a string attached to him that was lying on a cloth (see Fig. 2.18). In order to bring the doll within reach, the infants needed to learn to perform a series of actions. They had to remove the barrier, to pull on the cloth so that the string attached

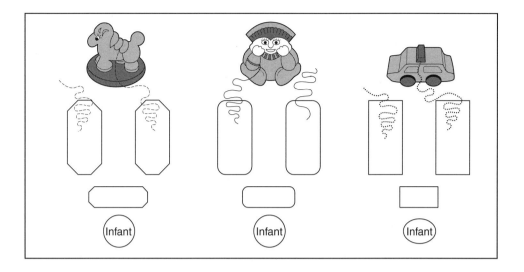

to the toy came within their grasp, and then to pull on the string itself so that they could reach Ernie. Following success on the first trial, two different toy problem scenarios were presented, each using identical tools (cloths, boxes, and strings). However, each problem appeared to be different from the problems that preceded it, as the cloths, boxes, and strings were always dissimilar to those encountered before. In addition, in each problem *two* strings and *two* cloths were provided, although only one pair could be used to reach the toy.

FIG. 2.18. Depiction of the problem scenarios used to study analogical reasoning in infants by Chen et al. (1997). Reproduced with permission.

Chen et al. tested infants aged 10 and 13 months in the Ernie paradigm. They found that although some of the older infants worked out the solution to reaching Ernie on their own, others needed their parents to model the solution to the first toy-acquisition problem for them. Once the solution to the first problem had been modelled, however, the 13-month-olds readily transferred an analogous solution to the second and third problems. The younger infants (10 months) needed more salient perceptual support in order for learning by analogy to occur. They only showed spontaneous evidence of using analogies when the perceptual similarity between the problems was increased (for example, by using the same goal toy, such as the Ernie doll, in all three problems).

Analogical reasoning may be a particularly important form of learning for cognitive development, as it involves reasoning about *relations*. As we will see throughout this book, a focus on relations, particularly *causal* relations, is very important in children's cognition. Analogies, especially analogies involving causal relations, may provide another critical cognitive tool for knowledge acquisition and representation and for conceptual development. More detailed treatment of the view that analogies play a fundamental role in cognitive development can be found in Carey (1985), Goswami (1992), and Halford (1993). The potential importance of analogical reasoning for cognitive development may also be indicated by Sigman et al.'s (1991) finding that information processing measured at birth predicts analogical reasoning measured in adolescence (as discussed in Chapter 1).

What babies can't do

So far, the case for claiming that the higher processes characteristic of adult cognition are active in infancy appears to be a fairly strong one. However, some surprising gaps have been documented in infants' cognitive abilities, gaps that have frequently been explained in terms of cognitive confusions (see also Chapter 8). More recent research has suggested that most of these gaps occur because of neural immaturities. Rather than reflecting cognitive confusions, they appear to reflect the relatively slow maturation of the frontal cortex, which is involved in the planning and monitoring of cognitive activity.

One definition of cognitive activity was considered earlier in this chapter, taken from Anderson's (1980) discussion of reasoning and problem-solving. Anderson noted that the characteristics of reasoning and problem-solving situations are that the reasoner wants to reach a desired end state, that a sequence of mental processes are involved in reaching this end state, and that the mental processes are cognitive rather than automatic. He pointed out that routine sequences of behaviour did *not* qualify as cognitive. When we examine the documented gaps in infants' cognitive abilities in some detail, it is interesting to note that most of them turn out to involve repetitive, or perseverative, behavioural routines.

Search errors in reaching

The best known of these gaps is a search error that emerges at around 9 months of age, the "A-not-B" error, which was first documented by Piaget (see Chapter 8 for theoretical detail). This search error occurs in simple hiding-and-finding tasks that involve more than one location. Imagine that an object is hidden at one location, location A, for a number of trials. The infants retrieve the object without difficulty. The hiding location is then moved to another location, location B. Although this switch in hiding location occurs in full view of the infants, the infants persist in searching at location A. This is the "A-not-B" error, and is shown in Fig. 2.19. Although the A-not-B error was originally

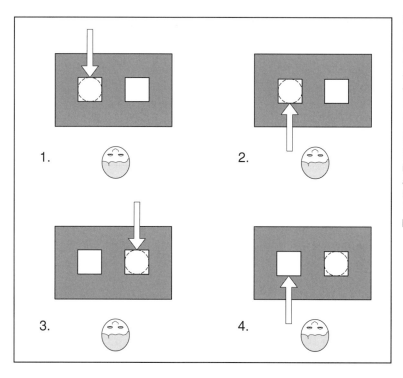

FIG. 2.19.
The sequence of events in the A-not-B error. The experimenter hides an object at location A (1), and the infant reaches successfully (2). The object is then hidden at location B (3), whereupon the infant again searches at A (4). From Bremner (1988). Reproduced with permission.

thought to stem from a cognitive confusion (see Chapter 8), a growing number of studies suggest that it may have a simpler neural explanation. The A-not-B error, and other surprising gaps in infant performance that depend on perseverative behaviours, may be due to immaturities in pre-frontal cortex.

The frontal cortex of the brain has a number of cognitive functions. Its central role is thought to be the planning and monitoring of action and cognitive activity. The frontal lobe is said to be the site of higher thought processes, abstract reasoning, and motor processing, and contains the primary motor cortex, which is involved in the planning and control of movements. Adult patients with lesions to frontal cortex exhibit a tendency to persist in certain motor actions. For example, if a frontal patient is asked to discover the rule (colour, shape, or number) for sorting a pack of cards (with feedback), the patient will do so very successfully. However, if the rule is then switched, for example from colour to shape, the patient is unable to sort the cards according to the new rule. Instead, the patient continues sorting the cards according to the rule that was previously correct (e.g. Milner, 1963).

Monkeys with frontal cortex lesions demonstrate similar *perseverative* behaviours. The classic test for prefrontal cortex function in non-human primates is "delayed reaching", which is essentially identical to the A-not-B task. In delayed reaching tasks, monkeys retrieve a desired object from one of two identical hiding wells after a short delay. The hiding location is varied randomly over trials. Monkeys with lesions to frontal cortex fail the delayed reaching task following delays as brief as 1–2 seconds, although they succeed if there is no delay (Diamond, 1988). Similarly, 9-month-old infants show perseverative searching in the A-not-B task following a delay of 1–2 seconds, but succeed if there is no delay. Older infants also show A-not-B errors if they are subjected to *longer* delays. In fact, the delay needed to produce the A-not-B error increases at an average rate of two seconds per month (Diamond, 1985). In addition 8- to 12-month-old infants fail the delayed reaching task following short delays (Diamond, 1991).

Diamond (and others) have suggested that babies who make "perseverative" errors such as continuing to search in location A when the object has been hidden in location B are doing so because of immaturities in frontal cortex. Her argument is that perseveration is a symptom and not an explanation of the problem faced by these infants when they are searching for desired objects. Their underlying problem is an inability to *inhibit* a predominant action tendency. The predominant action tendency in the A-not-B task is to search at A. When the hiding location is moved to B, infants find it difficult to inhibit their tendency to search at location A, and thus show perseverative errors. Infants even show these errors when the object is *in full view* at B, which seems to support this explanation (data from Butterworth, 1977). In the same way, frontal patients who are unable to sort a pack of cards according to a new rule are finding it difficult to inhibit their prepotent tendency to sort by the old rule. They may actually tell you this themselves. Some patients say, as they are sorting the cards by the old rule, "This is wrong, and this is wrong ... " (see Diamond, 1988).

Search errors in crawling

We will return to the role of inhibition in cognitive development in Chapter 5. For the time being, it is worth noting that infants show difficulties in inhibiting prepotent action tendencies in crawling as well as in reaching. Perseverative crawling has been observed both in studies using random switching of the location-to-be-crawled-to (analogous to the random switches in delayed reaching) and in studies requiring infants to crawl to a consistent location which is then switched following a series of successful trials (analogous to the A-not-B paradigm).

For example, Rieser, Doxey, McCarrell, & Brooks (1982) examined whether mobile 9-month-olds could crawl around a barrier to reach their mothers (see Fig. 2.20). The barrier went across the centre of the experimental room, and was too high for the infants to see over it. However, they could hear their mothers calling to them from the far side. Prior to being allowed to crawl to their mothers, the infants were carried around the apparatus, and were shown that the barrier was open at one end. On the first trial, 85% of the infants crawled successfully to their mothers. However, on subsequent trials 75% of the infants crawled to the *same* side as before, even though the "open" side of the barrier was then varied randomly. In fact, these infants crawled perseveratively to the same side on *every* trial, whether this led to success or failure, despite being shown the open end of the barrier on *each* trial. The infants seemed incapable of inhibiting the previously executed motor pattern. In a second study of infants aged from 9 to 25 months, Rieser et al. showed that the perseverative crawling response dropped out slowly with increasing age. Perseverative crawling was shown by 80% of the 9- and 13-month-olds, 44% of the 17- and 21-month-olds, but only 6% of the 25-month-olds.

McKenzie and Bigelow (1986) carried out a similar "detour crawling" task with 10-, 12- and 14-month-olds. However, instead of varying the open end of the barrier at random, they kept the open end of the barrier consistent across a series of trials and then changed it. The open path lay either to the right or to the left side of the barrier for four trials at a time. The crucial measure was the direction of crawl on the

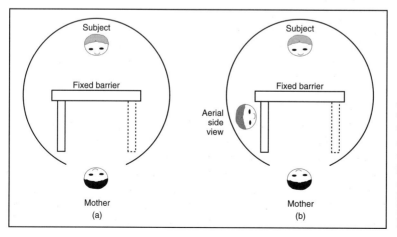

FIG. 2.20.
The experimental set-up used by Rieser et al. to study perseverative crawling, seen (a) from the viewpoint of the infant, and (b) depicting the aerial view shown to the infant. From Bremner (1988). Reprinted by permission of Blackwell Publishers Ltd.

fifth trial (which is similar to the first B trial in an A-not-B search task). McKenzie and Bigelow found that 75–80% of the younger babies showed perseveration of the now inappropriate motor response on the fifth trial, crawling to the same side as before. In contrast, only 25% of the 14-month-olds made a perseverative response. However, as the second block of four trials progressed, the younger babies, too, were able to learn to crawl to the correct side of the barrier. This suggests that the babies could learn to correct their perseverative errors. It would be interesting to measure the effect of imposing increased delays on infants of different ages in detour crawling tasks. With longer delays, perseverative crawling may be observed in later trials as well.

The observation that infants have difficulties in inhibiting prepotent motor tendencies in crawling as well as in reaching supports the view that the A-not-B search error does not arise from shortcomings in infants' understanding of where to search for objects that they have watched being hidden. Instead of reflecting a cognitive confusion, it seems to reflect a deficit in gaining control of one's behaviour so that one's behaviour can *reflect* what one is thinking (Diamond, 1988). The conclusion that knowledge representation, reasoning, problem solving, and learning are progressing well in infancy is therefore not undermined by errors such as the A-not-B error.

Summary

This chapter set out to examine knowledge representation, reasoning, and problem solving in infancy, and also examined those forms of learning that go beyond making simple associations. We found that knowledge representation begins with attention to the *perceptual* structure of objects and events, and that this knowledge in turn becomes *conceptual*. The perceptual prototypes of objects take on conceptual significance, and schemas develop that encode what is significant about events while omitting unimportant perceptual details.

Although the processes by which perceptual knowledge representations become conceptual is not well understood, a number of possible mechanisms can be identified. Mandler has argued that the mental redescription of the spatial properties of objects or events can lead to "image schemas" which represent non-sensory notions such as containment. Baillargeon has suggested that initial perceptually-based descriptions of concepts such as support, and core descriptions like "has contact", are gradually refined in the light of experience of the physical world into more elaborate representations that identify variables that are highly relevant to outcome, such as "degree of support". Leslie's idea is that, at least for causal analyses of motion, infants generate mechanical descriptions of events that go beyond a perceptual description of what has occurred, enabling them to understand the mechanical properties of agents. All of these mechanisms probably play their own roles in the shift from perceptually-based to meaning-based knowledge representations. As noted earlier, infant sensitivity to causal relations may have a particularly important role to play in enabling perceptually-based representations to become meaning-based. Gergely et al.'s demonstration that a causal analysis of the spatial behaviour of objects can lead infants to adopt an intentional stance is a particularly intriguing example of this.

Reasoning and problem solving are dependent on knowledge representations. We saw that reasoning and problem solving can be defined as requiring at least three ingredients. The first is a desired end state or specific goal, the second is that a sequence of mental processes are involved in reaching the goal, and the third is that these mental processes are cognitive and not automatic. A series of experiments by Baillargeon and others based on impossible physical events showed that young infants do indeed seem capable of reasoning and problem-solving behaviour. Baillargeon described the young subjects in her experiments as engaging in a knowledge-based, conceptual analysis of the physical world, and her experiments in which the "tricks" behind impossible physical events were subsequently revealed certainly support this contention. The infants' ability to work out how the impossible events were produced suggests that "higher" forms of cognition are also present as young as 5 months of age. Infants' capacities for learning by imitation and learning by analogy, cognitive skills almost universally absent in other species, also support the view that infant cognition is highly sophisticated. The ability to imitate an action seen only on a video is a particularly remarkable demonstration of this sophistication.

Finally, we considered what infants can't do. The conclusion reached was that cognitive operations that depend on a mature frontal cortex are absent in early infancy, during which time this neural system is still developing. Infants are poor at monitoring their cognitive activities, especially when these activities involve perseverative behavioural routines. Like frontal patients, infants find it difficult to inhibit predominant action tendencies. They find it difficult to stop themselves searching at a previously successful location or crawling along a previously travelled route. These "cognitive failures" demonstrate the intimate connection between cognitive activity and the underlying neural substrate. Our understanding of this intimate connection is still very preliminary, but experimental investigation of it is increasing via the "new" field of developmental cognitive neuroscience. Developmental cognitive neuroscience seems to be a very promising area for future work in infant cognition (Johnson, 1997).

Conceptual development 3

The research discussed in the last two chapters has shown that both fundamental and higher-order cognitive processes are well established by the end of the first year of life. Studies of perception, attention, learning, memory, knowledge representation, reasoning, and problem solving have all converged on the same conclusion, namely that most cognitive mechanisms are present very early, and that these mechanisms become increasingly active as infants become able to sit up on their own, to move around on their own, and of course, to speak and to comprehend language. In the rest of this book, we will examine how the cognitive processes present in infancy facilitate cognitive development during and beyond the first two years of life. We begin with conceptual development and categorisation.

Superordinate, subordinate, and "basic-level" categories

Categories have traditionally been treated as having a hierarchical structure. We can think of categories at a global or "superordinate" level, such as the category of furniture, at an intermediate level of different kinds of furniture, such as tables vs. chairs, and at a very detailed or "subordinate" level of individual kinds of tables or chairs, such as deckchairs vs. armchairs. Perceptual structure must be an important source of information about these different hierarchical levels. The attribute structure of the world provides a reasonable basis for the assignment of objects to particular categories. For example, most furniture shares perceptual features such as straight edges and angular lines, and most chairs share features such as seats and back supports. Perceptual structure is most helpful for categorisation at the so-called "basic level". At this basic level, we can both see *directly* what things are and have a *theory* (popularly supposed to derive from our prototypes) that tells us how they should be classified. The distinction between perception and conceptualisation is particularly difficult to draw at the "basic level" of categorisation.

Conceptual development is intimately linked to the ability to categorise. Neisser (1987, p.1) defines categorisation as the ability "to treat a set of things as somehow equivalent, to put them in the same pile, or call them by the same name, or respond to them in the same way". For example, a person may indicate the category "bird" by naming a robin, an eagle, a chicken, and an ostrich "bird", or may indicate the category "things that can be sat on" by sitting on a chair, a couch, a stool, and a tree stump (Mervis & Pani, 1980). As we saw earlier, categorisation is essential because the world consists of an infinite number of discriminably different stimuli, and each object or event cannot be treated as unique. Recognising novel objects or events as familiar because they belong to a known category enables us to know more about those objects or events than is possible just from looking. This means that categorising is not just another form of perceiving, even though perceptual and conceptual processes are intertwined. Categories also involve *beliefs* about the world.

The core developmental role of the "basic level"

The notion of a "basic level" of categorisation originated in the work of Rosch, who pointed out that many naturally occurring categories in the world can be distinguished by perceptual similarity. Rosch (Rosch & Mervis, 1975: Rosch et al., 1976) argued that at the so-called "basic level" of category abstraction, concepts such as "cat", "bird", "cow", "tree", and "car" were perceptually "given" by covariations in the constituent features of category members. According to this account, the world contains intrinsically separable things because features co-occur in regular ways. For example, feathers reliably co-occur with wings, with flight, and with light body weight, and this co-occurrence helps the child to distinguish the category "bird". Basic-level category exemplars are thought to have the greatest number of features in common with one another, and the fewest number of features in common with members of contrasting classes. For example, birds share more features in common with each other than they share with dogs.

Rosch further proposed that the basic level was the level of categorisation that offered the greatest *psychological* utility. She argued that at this level, an organism could obtain the most information about a category with the least cognitive effort. Her views have also been widely interpreted to imply that the most efficient means of storing conceptual information will be in terms of *prototypes*, or highly typical basic-level objects (Rosch herself argued that prototypes do not constitute a theory of representation for categories). In terms of conceptual *development*, it has been assumed that if children indeed categorise the world around them at the basic level, distinguishing between objects such as cats, birds, cows, trees, and cars, then this will result in the development of a conceptual system that codes categories by prototypes.

As we saw in Chapter 2, the perceptual abilities of infants are certainly sophisticated enough to respond to the featural co-occurrences that distinguish a prototypical category member (e.g. Eimas & Quinn, 1994; Younger & Cohen, 1983). However, the prototype effects demonstrated by these authors point to *perceptual* rather than conceptual categories. In order to provide evidence for basic-level *conceptual* categories, developmental psychologists need to demonstrate that these perceptual differences have *conceptual* significance for children. One way of investigating this has been to study sorting behaviour in pre-verbal children. If children reliably group objects by their basic-level category, for example by putting toy dogs with other toy dogs and toy cars with other toy cars, then this may imply conceptual significance, although of course there is a high degree of perceptual similarity in these groupings as well.

Sequential touching as a measure of basic-level categorisation

One way to examine sorting behaviour is to measure touching. Infants and children like to handle objects that interest them, but spontaneous grouping of objects is rarely seen prior to 18 months of age. However, sequential touching is often observed: children tend to touch objects from the same category in sequence more often than would be expected by chance, and this systematic touching behaviour gradually develops into systematic sorting. Children's tactile behaviour was used to measure emergent categorisation in a set of studies designed by Mandler and Bauer (1988). They used sequential touching to see whether there was any evidence that children would sort toys into basic-level categories.

The toys used in Mandler and Bauer's studies were (a) dogs vs. cars (a basic-level contrast), and (b) vehicles vs. animals (a superordinate-level contrast). In the basic-level task, the children were given a toy poodle, collie, bloodhound, and bulldog, and a toy sports car, sedan, station wagon, and Volkswagen beetle. Sequential touching of the cars or the dogs was taken as evidence for differentiation of these basic-level categories. In the superordinate-level task, the children were given a toy horse, spider, chicken, and fish, and a toy aeroplane, motorcycle, truck, and train engine. A set of kitchen things vs. bathroom things was also used (mug, spoon, plate, pan vs. soap, toothbrush, toothpaste, comb), to explore so-called "contextual categories". These were defined as categories of objects that are associated because they are found in the same place or are used in the same activities. The sequential touching behaviour of infants aged 12, 15, and 20 months who were faced with these pairs of categories was then measured, and any spontaneous grouping of the objects was also noted.

Mandler and Bauer found that the touching behaviour of the 12- and 15-month-old infants as a group indicated categorisation at the basic level only, as their touching was non-randomly sequential only for the dogs vs. cars. Sequential touching within the contextual and superordinate categories was only reliably non-random at 20 months. However, there were large individual differences within this overall pattern. For example, 25% of the 12-month-olds were responsive to the superordinate categories. In a second experiment, Mandler and Bauer compared sorting behaviour with basic-level categories when the objects came from either the *same* superordinate class or *different* superordinate classes. Objects from the same superordinate classes (animals) shared a high degree of within-category similarity while *minimising* between-category differences (e.g. dogs vs. horses), whereas objects from different superordinate classes (animals vs. vehicles) shared a high degree of within-category similarity while *maximising* between-category differences (e.g. dogs vs. cars). Only older children were tested (16- and 20-month-olds). The results showed that basic-level categories were clearly distinguished when animals were compared with vehicles, but not when animals were compared with animals. Mandler and Bauer argued that the role of superordinate classes in the development of categorisation may be greater than was previously supposed. In their studies, so-called "basic-level" sorting apparently occurred only when the basic level coincided with *different* superordinate categories.

Another way of describing these results, however, is to argue that the children's sorting behaviour reflected the differing amounts of *perceptual* similarity evident in the stimuli. The contrast between basic-level objects from the same or different superordinate categories does not hold perceptual similarity constant. For example, the distinction between dogs and cars is an easy one to make in terms of perceptual similarity, because dogs are more similar to each other than they are to cars (all dogs have heads, tails, four legs etc., whereas all cars have wheels, no legs, seats and so on). The distinction between dogs and horses is less easy to make in terms of perceptual similarity, as both dogs and horses have heads, tails, four legs, and so on, and so it is more difficult to differentiate between them (at least, when one is looking at *toy* dogs and horses!). Mandler and Bauer's result does not necessarily imply an inability to differentiate at the basic level within the same superordinate category.

Furthermore, features that suggest membership at the basic level also suggest membership at the superordinate level. For example, feathers suggest "animal" as well as "bird", "fur" suggests "animal" as well as "cat" (see Murphy, 1982). This is recognised in Rosch's theory, as she argues that perceptual similiarity *correlates with* structural similarity. The perceptual similarity between dogs and horses reflects a deeper underlying structural similarity, namely that both dogs and horses are natural kinds. Similarly, cars have wheels and no legs because they are artifacts, and are thus more perceptually similar to aeroplanes and trains, with whom they share a deeper underlying structural similarity. Of course, in the real world dogs and horses are easily distinguished at the basic level by a striking difference in size, texture of coat etc., distinctions that are not a feature of plastic toy animals. Both basic-level and superordinate concepts must originate in some sense from perceptual knowledge, as the evidence for perception-based knowledge representations discussed in Chapter 2 makes clear. The differing degrees of perceptual similarity between horses, dogs, and cars are an intrinsic part of Rosch's hypothesis.

The matching-to-sample task

Another way to look at category knowledge is to use a matching-to-sample task. In matching-to-sample tasks, children are given a sample or target object, and are asked to select the correct match for the target from a pair of alternatives (this task is often used with monkeys!). Bauer and Mandler (1989a) used a matching-to-sample task to contrast super-ordinate and basic-level matches in children aged 19, 25, and 31 months. The distinction between superordinate matches and basic-level matches was created by varying the objects in the choice pair. For example, triads like *bird*, different bird, nest or *toothbrush*, different toothbrush, toothpaste, enabled basic-level matches. Triads like *chair*, table, person, or *monkey*, bear, banana enabled superordinate matches (see Table 3.1). The children were told that they were going to play a "finding" game. The experimenter would indicate the target object (e.g. the toothbrush or the monkey), and then say "See this one? Can you find me another one just like this one? Can you show me the other one like this?".

Bauer and Mandler found that, although basic-level sorts were slightly easier overall, the children were highly successful at categorical sorting in both tasks at all ages. For the basic-level sorts, correct responses by age were 85% for the 19-month-olds, 94% for the

TABLE 3.1

Examples of triads of stimuli from Mandler and Bauer (1988)

Column 1	Column 2	Column 3
Bird	Nest	Bird
Toothbrush	Toothpaste	Toothbrush
Mug	Juice can	Glass
Brush	Mirror	Comb
Pear	Knife	Apple
Chair	Person	Table
Baby	Bottle	Adult
Flower	Vase	Plant
Bed	Pillow	Crib
Spoon	Plate	Measuring scoop
Coat	Umbrella	Sweatshirt
Pot	Spatula	Skillet
Hammer	Nail	Pliers
Wagon	Child	Trike
Monkey	Banana	Bear
Pail	Shovel	Flowerpot
Lion	Cage	Elephant
Shirt	Hanger	Pants
Sink	Soap	Bathtub

Basic-level triads comprised two non-identical objects from Column 1 and one object from Column 2. Superordinate-level triads comprised one object each from Columns 1, 2, and 3. The first three rows of stimuli formed the example triads.

25-month-olds, and 97% for the 31-month-olds. For the superordinate-level sorts, the figures were 91% correct for the 19-month-olds, 81% for the 25-month-olds, and 93% for the 31-month-olds. We can conclude that a sensitivity to *both* basic-level and superordinate-level categories exists by at least 19 months.

The core developmental role of the superordinate level?

More recently, Mandler and her colleagues have proposed that sensitivity to superordinate-level categories may *precede* sensitivity to basic-level categories, reversing the sequence of development proposed by Rosch. This provocative conclusion was based on a series of studies contrasting basic-level objects within the *same* superordinate categories, such as horses vs. dogs (e.g. Mandler, Bauer, & McDonough, 1991; Mandler & McDonough, 1993).

For example, Mandler et al. (1991) used the sequential touching technique to investigate basic-level distinctions between toy dogs and toy horses (which have a low degree of perceptual contrast), toy dogs and toy rabbits (which have a medium degree of perceptual contrast), and toy dogs and toy fish (which have a high degree of perceptual contrast) in 19-, 24-, and 31-month-olds. They found that only the 31-month-olds could differentiate the dogs from the horses with any degree of reliability ($P< .08$). For the medium degree of perceptual contrast (dogs vs. rabbits), both the 24- and 31-month-olds could reliably differentiate the animals, and for the high degree of perceptual contrast (dogs vs. fish), all groups could differentiate the animals reliably. All groups could also differentiate animals from vehicles (a superordinate-level contrast with high perceptual dissimilarity). From these data, Mandler et al. argued that categorisation proceeds from the differentiation of a global domain (such as animals) through successively finer distinctions until the basic level of abstraction is approximated. Again, however, sorting behaviour seems simply to be correlated with perceptual similarity, and may not imply the *absence* of conceptual distinctions as such.

Further negative evidence against the view that categorisation begins at the basic level and then differentiates upwards to the superordinate level and downwards to the subordinate level has been reported by Mandler and McDonough (1993), working with 7-, 9-, and 11-month-old infants. They again compared the basic-level contrasts of toy dogs vs. toy fish and toy dogs vs. toy rabbits, but this time they used an object examination task rather than the object manipulation task used in the studies with older children. In the object examination task, infants are given a series of objects from one category to examine manually, one at a time, until the objects are familiar. For example, they may be given a series of toy fish. Following familiarisation, they are given a novel exemplar from the familiar category (a new toy fish) and a novel exemplar from a new category (a toy dog) to manipulate in turn. If the infants show increased examination time for the object from the new category (dog) compared to the novel object from the familiar category (fish), then they are assumed to differentiate the two categories. Using this technique, Mandler and McDonough found no evidence that dogs were discriminated from fish, nor that dogs were discriminated from rabbits. However, animals were discriminated from vehicles (a superordinate-level contrast). On the basis of these data, Mandler and McDonough argued that infants have a fairly undifferentiated concept of animals that does not include basic-level information.

Further studies are needed to see whether their view is correct or not. The claim that the developing knowledge base is characterised by children making finer and finer distinctions among initially fairly global conceptions is based at the moment on a series of negative results. Negative results are those that fail to support the predictions made by the basic-level hypothesis, and are not necessarily positive evidence for the global conceptions hypothesis. Also, the data rely on the manipulation of *toys*. Toys vary in their prototypicality as category members, and are extremely perceptually impoverished as stimuli. Toys only preserve some of the features of the objects that they represent (such as overall appearance, number of legs, and number of eyes), and omit many others (such as relative size, smell, and texture of skin). These other features may make a key contribution to basic-level distinctions between, for example, dogs, horses, fish, and rabbits (real fish and real dogs look, feel, and smell very different!). The importance of using perceptually rich stimuli in studies of conceptual development has been pointed out by Jones and Smith (1993).

Child-basic categories vs. adult-basic categories

Another reason for the series of negative results reported by Mandler and her colleagues may be that what is basic for a child may differ from what is basic for an adult. The idea that "child-basic categories" can be distinguished from "adult-basic" categories has been proposed by Mervis and her colleagues (e.g. Mervis, 1987). Mervis pointed out that children may notice or emphasise different attributes of the same object than adults do, for example because of their different experiences and their different knowledge of the culturally appropriate functions of objects. They may thus form slightly different basic-level categories from adults, even though they are using the same process of grouping together objects with similar shapes, functions etc. Children's categories may thus be broader than, narrower than, or overlap with, the corresponding adult categories.

To illustrate her theory about "child-basic" categories, Mervis kept a detailed record of the development of her son Ari's first category, which was *duck*. The objects that he was first prepared to countenance as members of this category are shown in Fig. 3.1, which also shows the objects that he excluded. Ari's category boundaries were tested by giving him sets of four objects, and asking "Can Ari get the duckie?". Over time, Ari's duck category evolved to include first pictures of ducks, then the plastic duck rattle shown in Fig. 3.1, and finally the plush duck head rattle and the Donald Duck head. At this point, he began to spot instances of ducks that his mother failed to notice, such as a picture of a duck inner-tube in a magazine that she was reading and a swan soap-dish in a shop. The fact that Ari initially considered some toys to be ducks and not others is obviously important for the design of future studies of basic-level distinctions that rely on toys.

FIG. 3.1.
Examples of the objects included in and excluded from Ari's initial duck category. The top row depicts objects included immediately (plush mallard, carved grebe, porcelain snow goose, wind-up chicken). The second row depicts objects that were included as soon as they were available for testing (plush Canadian goose, swan, great blue heron, ostrich). The bottom row depicts objects initially excluded (plastic duck rattle, Donald Duck head, porcelain song bird, plush owl). From Mervis (1987). Reproduced with permission.

Beyond the role of perceptual similarity in categorisation

In the studies of categorisation at the basic, superordinate, and subordinate levels just discussed, a recurring factor in children's categorisation behaviour has been the degree of perceptual similarity between different category exemplars. As noted earlier, one reason for this is that perceptual similarity is correlated with structural similarity. Perceptual similarity can act as a guide to structural similarity, providing an indication that objects share deeper characteristics (such as the non-observable features shared by biological kinds: has a heart, has blood inside, and so on).

However, we can also study how children behave when perceptual similarity and conceptual similarity are *not* correlated. When perceptual similarity is pitted against category membership, children prove surprisingly adept at categorising on the basis of deeper structural characteristics. However, younger children perform better when language helps their intuitions about category membership (2-year-olds), whereas slightly older children do not (3-year-olds). This has been demonstrated in a series of experiments by Susan Gelman and her colleagues. They devised a picture-based technique which allowed category membership and category appearance to be independently manipulated (e.g. Gelman & Coley, 1990; Gelman & Markman, 1986, 1987).

For example, Gelman and Coley (1990) asked 2-year-old children questions about the properties of typical and atypical members of familiar categories like birds and dinosaurs. The children were shown pictures of birds and dinosaurs, and were asked questions such as "This is a bird. Does it live in a nest?", and "This is a dinosaur. Does it have big teeth?". Each category comparison was introduced by showing the children a target picture of a typical category member, such as a typical bird. The children were then asked one question about the target picture ("Does it live in a nest?"), and this picture remained in view during the presentation of the test pictures. Pictures of other category members and of the members of a contrasting category were then shown to the child one by one. The same question ("Does it live in a nest?") was asked for each picture in turn.

The key manipulation was that one of the members of the contrasting category looked highly similar to the target picture, and one of the members of the same category looked highly dissimilar to it (see Fig. 3.2). For example, for the bird category just mentioned, the highly dissimilar test picture was a *dodo* (atypical category member) and the highly similar test picture was a *bluebird* (typical category member). In the contrasting category of dinosaurs, the highly dissimilar test picture was a *stegosaurus* (typical category member) and the highly similar test picture was a *pterodactyl* (atypical category member). If the children answered the questions on the basis of overall appearance, then they should have judged that the bluebird and the pterodactyl both live in a nest, while the stegosaurus and the dodo do not. However, if they were sensitive to the deeper structural properties that specify category membership, then they should have judged that the bluebird and the dodo both live in a nest, while the stegosaurus and the pterodactyl do not.

Gelman and Coley found that the 2-year-olds correctly ascribed the different properties to the atypical category members only 42% of the time (dodo), compared to 76% for the typical category members (bluebird). The 42% level of responding was significantly *below* chance, suggesting that appearance does seem to control judgements about category membership in the absence of linguistic support in this age group. However, if category membership labels were provided during questioning, for example by saying "This is a bird/dinosaur. Does this

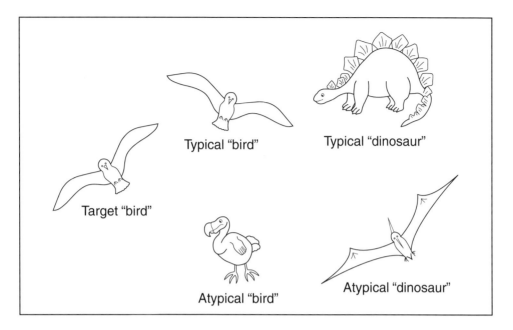

FIG. 3.2.
Examples of the
stimuli used to test the
"bird" category by
Gelman and Coley
(1990). Copyright ©
by the American
Psychological
Association.
Adapted with
permission.

bird/dinosaur say 'tweet tweet?'", then the 2-year-olds correctly
ascribed the different properties to the atypical category members 69%
of the time, and to the typical category members 74% of the time.
Adults given the same task succeeded even without labels. Of course,
this is unsurprising as all the atypical members were unfamiliar to the
children, but not to the adults. Nevertheless, Gelman and Coley's
experiment demonstrates clearly that, when children are provided
with category labels, category membership rather than perceptual
appearance guides inferences about the extension of category
properties.

In related work, S. Gelman and Markman (1986, 1987) have demonstrated that 3- and 4-year-olds succeed in a similar categorisation task,
even without labels. For example, in their work with 3-year-olds the
children were shown a picture of a target object, such as a *cat*, and were
told a new fact about it, such as that it "can see in the dark". They were
then shown pictures of four more animals (see Fig. 3.3), one that looked
like the target picture and was of the same category (another cat), one
that looked like the target picture but was of a different category (a
skunk), one that did not look like the target picture but was of the same
category (a cat with different colouring), and one that did not look like
the target picture and was of a different category (a dinosaur). The
children were asked in each case whether the animal shared the

property ascribed to the target picture ("can see in the dark"). Gelman and Markman found that the children consistently assigned properties on the basis of category membership rather than perceptual appearance. This finding suggests that 3–4-year-old children can use category information *alone* as a basis for drawing inductive inferences about biological kinds.

However, these findings should not be interpreted as evidence that category membership is *more important* than perceptual similarity in guiding inferences about the extension of category properties by the age of 3–4 years. This is because the perceptual stimuli in these experiments were line drawings, and so were fairly impoverished in perceptual terms. Jones and Smith (1993) have argued that perceptual and non-perceptual knowledge do not play distinct roles in our concepts but complementary ones, without a clear boundary between the two. The experimental work discussed so far appears to support this view. It seems that "Surface appearances, just like nonperceptual properties, support theoretical relations within and among different bits of knowledge" (Jones & Smith, 1993, p.126).

The role of language in conceptual development

The potentially critical role of language in conceptual development is clearly illustrated by the finding of Gelman and her colleagues that

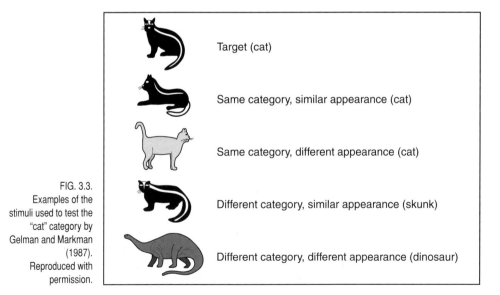

FIG. 3.3.
Examples of the stimuli used to test the "cat" category by Gelman and Markman (1987). Reproduced with permission.

Target (cat)

Same category, similar appearance (cat)

Same category, different appearance (cat)

Different category, similar appearance (skunk)

Different category, different appearance (dinosaur)

category membership labels promote accurate conceptual distinctions in 2-year-olds. In fact, there is a lot of experimental work on the relation between language and conceptual development. We will give only a brief flavour of the nature of this kind of research here. A key finding in such work with respect to conceptual development is that children seem to have *linguistic biases* that guide their conceptual organisation at the different hierarchical levels identified by Rosch.

Learning new words apparently teaches children about conceptual relations between objects and classes of objects. For example, names in natural language designate relations between basic-level objects and superordinate and subordinate relations. The provision of a common label like "animal" for multiple referents like dogs, horses, and fish acts *in itself* to classify these referents as members of the same superordinate class. In particular, work in language acquisition has shown that children interpret the introduction of novel *nouns* as highlighting super-ordinate categories, but the introduction of novel *adjectives* as highlighting subordinate categories.

One researcher whose studies have led to this conclusion is Waxman, whose experimental technique involves teaching children novel labels (Japanese words) for objects from familiar categories which have been sampled at different hierarchical levels. For example, Waxman (1990) taught 3-year-olds novel labels for superordinate categories like *animal*. Here the basic-level objects were photographs of dogs, cats, and horses, and the subordinate-level objects were photographs of collie dogs, Irish setters, and terriers. The children were shown some Japanese dolls, who were introduced as being unable to speak English and also as being "very picky" (choosy). Each doll only liked a certain kind of thing, and three examples of the thing that the doll liked were given by the experimenter. If the doll liked *animals*, the experimenter placed photographs of a dog, bird, and fish by the doll (superordinate level), and if the doll liked *dogs* then the experimenter placed photographs of a setter, a bulldog, and a poodle by the doll. The children were then given a variety of other photographs to assign to the dolls (e.g. *superordinate sort*: horse, elephant, duck, pig, mixed in with photographs of clothing and food; *basic-level sort*: photographs of four other varieties of dog mixed in with photographs of varieties of cats and horses).

Some of the children were given the sorting task in the context of novel nouns, and others were given the sorting task in the context of novel adjectives. For example, in the novel noun condition the experimenter would say "This doll likes only *suikahs*, and these are the *suikahs*". In the novel adjective condition, the experimenter would say

"This doll only wants *sukish* ones, and these are the ones that are *sukish*". Waxman found a striking cross-over effect in sorting behaviour, with the 3-year-olds in the novel noun condition classifying more pictures correctly at the superordinate than at the subordinate level (e.g. doing better with animals than with dogs), and the 3-year-olds in the novel adjective condition classifying more pictures correctly at the subordinate than at the superordinate level (e.g. doing better with dogs than with animals). This indicates that nouns are interpreted as indicating superordinate categories, and adjectives are interpreted as indicating subordinate categories. Note also that the perceptual cues were equivalent in both conditions, as the children were sorting the same sets of photographs.

Furthermore, classification at the basic level was close to ceiling in both conditions, with linguistic cues neither facilitating nor inhibiting performance. Waxman argued that, at non-basic levels, children used syntactic cues to aid the establishment of taxonomic classes. She also argued that children have a linguistic bias to behave like this, because they are sensitive to the powerful links between conceptual hierarchies and the language that we use to describe them. Novel labels can thus promote classification at precisely those levels that are most subject to cultural influence and variation—the non-basic levels.

The biological/non-biological distinction

As noted earlier, however, categories also involve *beliefs* about the world. At the same time as they are developing conceptual hierarchies *within* categories like animal and vehicle, children are also developing knowledge about some fundamental conceptual distinctions. One of the first and most important of these conceptual distinctions is that between animate and inanimate entities, which leads eventually to the development of biological knowledge. Biological entities engage in certain distinctive processes. They can often move on their own, they can grow taller, fatter, or (in some cases) change their colour or form, and they can inherit the characteristics of their forebears. They also share certain core properties, such as blood, bones, or cellulose. Non-biological entities do not engage in self-generated movement, and do not exhibit growth, metamorphosis, or inheritance, although they can also share certain core properties (e.g. they may be made of plastic). Infants and young children are aware of some of these differences between animates and inanimates at a surprisingly early age. This basic understanding of the animate–inanimate distinction is then enriched by the child's growing experience of the world. For example, plants are biological entities but they cannot move on their own in the way that animals can. Thus biological knowledge is more than an appreciation of animacy, but the distinction between animate and inanimate kinds is an important precursor of this knowledge.

Evidence from studies of biological movement

One way to examine whether infants and young children are sensitive to the animate–inanimate distinction is to see when they distinguish biological from non-biological movement. An ingenious study by Bertenthal, Proffitt, Spetner, and Thomas (1985) suggests that this distinction is already present by 5 months of age. In their study, Bertenthal et al. showed infants displays of "point-light walkers". Point-light walker displays were first created by Johansson (1973), who placed small lights on the major joints and head of a person, dressed them in black, and then filmed them walking in the dark. Johansson found that adults easily recognised these 10–12 points of moving light as a person walking. Adults could also recognise people doing push-ups, people dancing, and people riding a bicycle. Later work showed that the gender of the person could also be determined just from seeing the moving points of light (Cutting, Proffitt, & Kozlowski, 1978).

One of the key cues in recognising the points of light as a human form turns out to be the patterns of occlusion created by the act of walking. Imagine a person walking past you. Each time the lights on the limbs on the far side of his or her body (e.g. wrist, knee, elbow, ankle) pass behind the near-side limbs or torso, they will be briefly occluded. Bertenthal et al. used this occlusion cue as a test of infants' recognition of the point-light displays as human walkers. They created computer displays of points of light, allowing occlusion to be manipulated experimentally, and then showed the babies point-light displays with and without occlusion. Babies were either habituated to an occluded display and then shown the non-occluded version, or vice versa. Additional control groups of babies saw scrambled point-light displays with and without occlusion, which tested their detection of occlusions that did not specify biological motion.

Bertenthal et al. found that the babies dishabituated to the point-light displays that specified biological motion ("canonical" displays), but not to the scrambled displays. This suggested that they were indeed preferentially sensitive to the occlusion information characteristic of biological motion. In a later experiment, Bertenthal et al. demonstrated that the babies' sensitivity was due to their implicit detection of the body of the point-light walker. The babies discriminated the canonical walker from a random occlusion display, but did not show the same discrimination when the walker was presented upside-down. Bertenthal and his colleagues argued that this implied that the detection of biological motion is due to rapid learning on the part of the infants, who detect biological motion only in the familiar upright position (as do adults). Younger babies of 3 months did not restrict dishabituation to the upright canonical point-light walker displays.

Basic movement cues other than occlusion also seem to be used to distinguish biological from non-biological motion. Lamsfuss (1995) suggested that the *predictability* and *regularity* of motion was another useful cue to the animate–inanimate distinction, because although we can usually make fairly accurate predictions about the movement patterns of non-biological kinds such as cars and other machines, we cannot make accurate predictions about the movements of biological kinds such as house flies. In order to test her idea, Lamsfuss showed 4- and 5-year-old children different pairs of "tracks" that had purportedly been left by either an animal or a machine. The tracks were simple dot patterns (see Fig. 3.4), one of which was always more regular than the

FIG. 3.4.
Some of the simple dot patterns used to test children's intuitions about biological and non-biological movement by Lamsfuss (1995). Reprinted with permission.

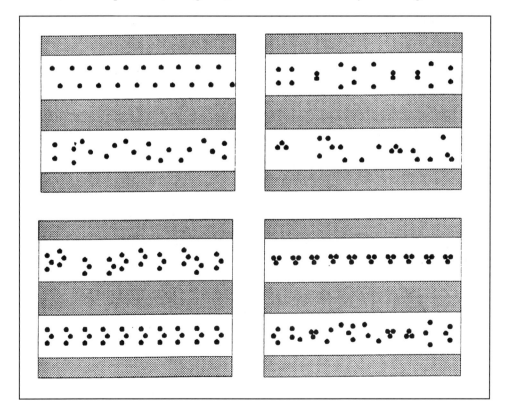

other. Dot patterns were used so that no additional perceptual information about the object that produced the motion would be provided by the displays. Lamsfuss found that, when asked which of the two tracks looked more as if it could have been left by a machine, the children chose the regular track significantly more often than when asked the same question about animals. She argued that this indicated that children expect animals to move in unpredictable ways, regular as well as irregular, whereas they expect machines to produce highly predictable, regular movements. Adults and biology experts who took part in the study showed the same response pattern as the young children. Thus a variety of movement cues seem to be an important source of information about the biological/non-biological distinction.

Evidence from knowledge of self-generated movements

Another way to assess young children's ability to make a conceptual distinction between animate and inanimate entities is to see whether young children recognise that biological entities can move on their own. Massey and R. Gelman (1988) investigated 3- and 4-year-olds' understanding of self-initiated movements by showing them photographs of unfamiliar objects and asking them whether the objects could move up and down a hill on their own. The photographs depicted unfamiliar exemplars of two animate categories—mammals (e.g. tarsier, marmoset) and non-mammals (e.g. tarantula, lizard)—and exemplars of three inanimate categories—statues of animals, wheeled objects (e.g. golf caddy, bicycle), and complex rigid objects (e.g. camera, exercise machine). Notice that the golf caddy and the bicycle can move *down* a hill on their own. This choice of categories was intended to pre-empt responding on the basis of shared perceptual features, such as linear vs. non-linear edges. Only the animate objects could move *uphill* on their own.

Massey and Gelman introduced the children to the task by showing them a picture of a hill, and asking them whether photographs of some practice items (a man, a little girl, a fork, and a chair) could go up and down the hill "all by itself". The target pictures were then shown in a randomised order, and the child was asked to decide whether these objects, too, could go up and down the hill by themselves. Overall, the 3-year-olds made correct decisions about 78% of the photos, and the 4-year-olds made correct decisions about 90% of the photos. Even though the animals were not depicted as moving and feet were seldom evident, the children's comments often focused on the feet and legs. For example, (echidna) "It can move very slowly ... it has these little legs. Where's the legs? Underneath." (Gelman, 1990, p.93) and "It has feet and no shoes" (Gelman,

1980, p.88). [*Experimenter:* Can you point to the feet?] "I can't see them". In contrast, where feet were depicted for inanimate objects (e.g. the statues), the children denied that they were feet, because they were not movement-enabling. Most of the errors made by the 3-year-olds concerned the unfamiliar animate non-mammals, such as the tarantulas and lizards. The younger children who made errors with these pictures nonetheless appeared to be basing their decisions on the animate–inanimate distinction. For example, they would say that "bugs" (the spider) could not go up the hill by themselves because they were too little to go up such a big hill.

Similar results concerning young children's assumptions about self-generated movement have been reported by S. Gelman and Gottfried (1993, discussed in S. Gelman, Coley, & Gottfried, 1994). They showed 4-year-old children videotapes of animals, wind-up toys, and household objects moving across a surface. The animals and toys were deliberately chosen from unfamiliar categories, for example a chinchilla and a wind-up toy sushi (a kind of food). The household objects (e.g. a pepper mill) were all transparent, in order to see whether this would make it more difficult for the children to assume an internal cause for movement. In a control condition, all of the animals, toys, and objects were moved manually, and the hand doing the moving was clearly visible on the video.

The children were asked three critical questions about each animal and object. These were: Did a person make this move? Did something inside this make it move? Did this move by itself? Gelman and Gottfried found a clear distinction between the animals and the toys and objects in the children's responses to these questions. In the manual carrying condition, the children said that the animals moved on their own, whereas the toys and the objects were moved by a person. In the self-generated movement condition, the children attributed movement to internal mechanisms, even for the transparent objects. However, they were unable to explain how this movement occurred. Many children suggested the involvement of a supernatural agent, hidden persons, or invisible natural causes such as electricity. So even children as young as 4 are quite clear that animals are different. Animals can move on their own, whereas toys and objects can only move with the help of an external agent.

Evidence from the assumption of shared core properties

A different cue to animacy vs. inanimacy is similarities and differences in the "insides" and "outsides" of objects. "Insides" are more important than "outsides" for understanding the true nature of an object. For example, biological kinds share key internal properties (dogs and birds both have blood and bones), and these differ from the key internal properties of non-biological kinds (chairs and doors may be wood or metal). In order to examine young children's understanding of the "inside–outside" distinction, S. Gelman and Wellman (1991) asked 3- and 4-year-old children to make a series of judgements about which pictured objects shared insides or outsides.

In their study, the children were asked "Which has the *same kinds of insides* as x?" (insides), or "Which *looks most like* x" (outsides). The pictures were always presented in threes, two of which were similar in their insides, and two in their outsides. For example, in the triad *orange, lemon, orange balloon*, the orange and the lemon had the same insides, while the orange and the balloon had the same outsides (appearance). In the triad *pig, piggy bank, cow*, the pig and the cow had the same insides, and the pig and the piggy bank had the same outsides. Gelman and Wellman found that both the 3-year-olds and the 4-year-olds performed at levels above chance, although the 4-year-olds were correct on more trials than the 3-year-olds (73% correct and 58% correct, respectively). Additional analyses showed that errors were not due to a reliance on similarity of appearance (a perceptual error, such as saying that the pig and the piggy bank had the same insides). Although such errors occurred, an equal number of errors were made on the basis of using insides to assess appearances (saying cows and pigs looked similar). Gelman and Wellman argued that what developed with age was the ability to deal with conflicts between insides and outer appearances (as in the piggy bank), rather than the ability to distinguish insides from outsides.

This conclusion is supported by the results of a study by Rochel Gelman and Meck (cited in Gelman, 1990). Gelman and Meck asked 3-, 4-, and 5-year-old children about the insides and outsides of animate and inanimate objects. The animates were person, elephant, cat, bird, and mouse, and the inanimates were rock, ball, doll, and puppet. The children's answers showed a clear distinction between the animates and the inanimates. The animates were said to have blood, bones, and hearts inside, while the inanimates had hard stuff (rock, ball) or material and cotton inside (dolls and puppets). All the inanimates were said by some children to have "nothing" inside, while none of the animates were ever thought to contain "nothing". The children also tended to say that the animates would have different insides from outsides (the outsides included skin, hair, and eyes), whereas the inanimates were judged to have the same outsides as insides ("hard stuff", "material").

Concrete or abstract knowledge?

Although these responses appear to indicate that young children have fairly concrete ideas about the insides and outsides of animates and inanimates, Simons and Keil (1995) have argued that the basis of young children's judgements about insides and outsides are *abstract expectations* about the sorts of things that should differentiate the two. Simons and Keil argue that, rather than having concrete knowledge about which insides are appropriate for biological vs. non-biological kinds, children have an abstract framework of *causal* expectations about natural kinds and artifacts that guides their search for concrete differences. To test their idea that younger children lack concrete knowledge about these differences, Simons and Keil conducted a series of experiments designed to examine the kinds of things that 3-, 4-, and 5-year-old children expected to be inside biological and non-biological kinds. They argued that their hypothesis was consistent with the findings discussed earlier, as the tasks used by Wellman and Gelman and by Gelman and Meck actually required abstract knowledge about category membership.

In their experiments, Simons and Keil introduced children to a toy alligator, Freddy, who had the ability to "see right through the outsides of things into the inside". The children were told that Freddy had never been to Earth before, so he sometimes got confused about what was inside different sorts of things. The children were asked to help Freddy to decide which of a pair of things had the real insides. For example, in one study the children were shown two pictures of either a natural kind (such as a sheep, a frog, or an elephant) or an artifact (such as a clock, a telephone, or a bus). Each picture had a computer-generated inside depicted in its middle (see Fig. 3.5). One inside was always animal-like, and the other was machine-like. For example, one of the two pictures of a sheep had cogs and gears inside it, and the other had some internal organs. The children were asked to show Freddy which picture showed "a sheep with real sheep insides". In another study, the children were

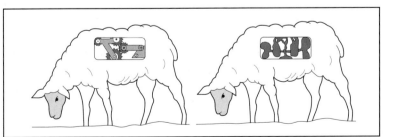

FIG. 3.5.
The sheep with animal vs. machine insides adapted from Simons and Keil (1995). Reproduced by kind permission of Elsevier Science.

just shown a single picture of a sheep without any depicted insides, and had to choose the appropriate insides from a set of three glass jars. One jar contained gears, dials, and wire (machine insides), a second contained the preserved abdominal organs of two cats (biological insides), and the third contained some small white rocks suspended in gelatin (representing a mixture of biological and non-biological insides, or "aggregate insides"). The children were asked to point to the sort of insides that Freddy would see if he looked right through the outside of each animal or machine.

The findings across these different studies were quite consistent. The younger children had more difficulty in selecting the correct insides than the older children, but they did not err randomly. Instead, they showed a clear distinction between the natural kinds and the artifacts. Even the youngest children were highly accurate at selecting the correct insides for the machines, but for the natural kinds they tended to choose the aggregate insides as frequently as the biological insides. Simons and Keil argued that the younger children did not know what insides are like, but they did know that some things are more likely to be inside animals than inside machines, and vice versa. These general ideas about what insides should look like were taken to indicate that even the youngest children had *abstract* expectations about the sorts of things that can be inside animals and machines. However, they lacked experience with *concrete* examples of insides.

Another way of examining children's knowledge about shared core properties is to ask them to make *verbal* judgements about the internal properties of biological and non-biological kinds. Without the aid of pictures, children are forced to reason about categories as abstract wholes. Gelman and O'Reilly (1988) asked 5- and 8-year-old children whether different biological and non-biological kinds, such as dogs, horses, snakes, and tractors, had "the same kinds of stuff inside" (p.882). These comparisons were made sequentially. The children were asked, in a random order, (1) whether all dogs had the same kinds of stuff inside, (2) whether dogs and horses had the same kinds of stuff inside, (3) whether dogs and snakes had the same kinds of stuff inside, and (4) whether dogs and tractors had the same kinds of stuff inside. Gelman and O'Reilly found that the children knew that animals had the same kinds of internal parts, and that they differentiated the animals from the artifacts such as the tractor. For example, they told the experimenters "Every dog has the same stuff unless they're missing a tail or something", and "All chairs aren't the same. Some of 'em have metal, some of 'em have wood. Some of 'em have iron" (p.884).

Structure vs. function in categorising natural kinds and artifacts

The research on children's intuitions about "insides" and "outsides" rests on the assumption that the shared core properties that are important for categorisation are similar for biological and non-biological kinds. However, Keil (1994) has pointed out that, while children may judge shared *structure* (insides and outsides) as important for categorising living kinds, they may judge shared *function* as more important for categorising artifacts. Although shared function in artifacts does not necessitate similarity of appearance, shared structural similarity in animals frequently does. For example, the handles of bags can look quite different. They may be rigid or flexible, thick or thin, and long or short. Nevertheless, we do not categorise bags according to the appearance of their handles as long as these differences have no *functional* implications. Different varieties of rodent, however, may have tails that vary in appearance as much as the handles of bags (thick or thin, bushy or hairless, long or short), and yet these variations in appearance may be very important for classification purposes. Such differences do not necessarily affect the function of tails, but they may indicate important differences between species (e.g. squirrels vs. rats). In the case of animals, differences in the appearance of parts thus often imply other underlying differences, such as differences in specific genetic structure.

In order to test the idea that children judge shared *function* as important for categorising artifacts and shared *structure* (insides and outsides) as important for categorising living kinds, Pauen (1996a) created pictures of pairs of artifacts and pairs of biological kinds which shared a key part. Her idea was that the perceptual similarity of this key part could be manipulated across the pairs. The function of the key part was the same within each biological or non-biological pair, but its appearance differed. For example, a pair of mice had either a wide tail or a narrow tail, and a pair of tape recorders had the same perceptual feature forming either a wide handle or a narrow handle (the two mice or tape recorders were otherwise identical in appearance, see Fig. 3.6).

Children aged 4–5 were shown the different matched quadruples of pictures, and were told a cover story about needing to tidy a room. Tidying required putting the pictures together "that were the same kind of thing", and the experimenter began this by separating the artifacts from the living kinds. An "expert" then appeared, and told the children that this was not the proper way to organise things, as some of the pairs of pictures that had been put together were "not really the same kind of thing". It was necessary to separate one of the two pairs (either the artifacts or the living kinds). The children were then asked which of the experimenter's pairs could be separated. Pauen found that the majority of the children said that the biological kinds could be separated rather than the artifacts. This supports the idea that perceptual dissimilarities are taken to specify different subcategories within biological kinds. The same does not appear to apply to artifacts, at least as long as the function of the dissimilar feature remains the same.

Evidence from studies of growth

Children's understanding of the difference between biological and non-biological kinds can also be examined by studying their understanding of growth. As time goes by, biological kinds change in their appearance. They may grow bigger (a tree), they may change colour (a tomato), and they may even change their appearance (a caterpillar changing into a butterfly). Artifacts do not alter as time goes by. They may become scuffed or worn, but they cannot grow, change their shape, or change their colour.

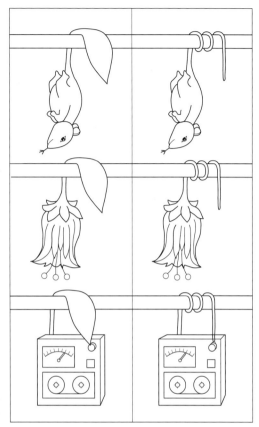

FIG. 3.6.
The same perceptual feature functioning as either a mouse's tail, a plant stem or a tape recorder's handle, from Pauen (1996a). Reprinted with permission.

In a series of studies examining young children's understanding of growth, Rosengren and his colleagues have shown that children as young as 3 are aware of these distinctions. For example, Rosengren, Gelman, Kalish, and McCormick (1991) showed 3- and 5-year-old children pictures of baby animals and brand-new artifacts, and then asked them to choose which of two other pictures showed the animal or the artifact after it had been around for a very long time. In some example pairs the children had to make a choice between a picture showing the target the same size and a picture showing the target as larger (*same-size–bigger* condition), and in others they were given a choice between a picture showing the target the same size and a picture showing the target as smaller (*same-size–smaller* condition, see Fig. 3.7). In the case of the artifacts, the same-size pictures were drawn to show the passing of time, with cracks and scuff marks. The animals depicted included alligators, bears, and squirrels, and the artifacts included

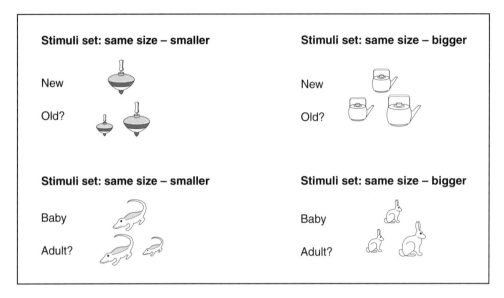

FIG. 3.7.
Examples of the
artifact (top row) and
natural kind (bottom
row) stimuli used to
study children's
understanding of
growth by Rosengren
et al. (1991).
Reprinted with
permission.

mugs, lightbulbs, and televisions. If children understand that animals grow but that artifacts do not, then they should consistently select the picture of the artifact that is the same size in each type of pair, and they should never select the picture of the animal that is smaller.

Rosengren et al. found that the 5-year-olds' performance on the task was at ceiling level for the animals, being 100% correct for the same size–smaller comparison, and 97% correct for the same-size–bigger comparison. The 3-year-olds also performed at high levels in the animal task, at 78% correct for the same-size–smaller comparison, and 89% correct for the same-size–bigger comparison. Performance with the artifacts was at ceiling for the older children. In contrast, the 3-year-olds performed at 78% correct for the artifacts in the same-size–smaller comparison, and were at chance in the same-size–bigger comparison. Both age groups thus expected animals to change in size over time, and knew that they got larger and not smaller. However, the 3-year-olds seemed uncertain as to whether artifacts grew over time, occasionally selecting the larger artifact rather than the aged and scuffed one in the same-size–bigger condition.

Rosengren's work suggests that the principle of growth is understood first in the biological domain. Even young children expect animals to undergo changes over time that do not affect their identity, understanding that biological kinds only grow bigger and not smaller over time. Artifacts are less well understood. Although an emerging understanding of the fact that artifacts do not grow with the passing of time was clear in these studies, the younger children did not seem to have fully grasped the kind of changes that artifacts actually undergo. Nevertheless, by the age of 5 the children were drawing a principled distinction between animate and inanimate patterns of transformations.

Analogy as a mechanism for understanding biological principles

Convergent evidence for the idea that 5- to 6-year-old children have grasped that the principle of growth applies only to biological kinds comes from a study by Inagaki and Hatano (1987). They were interested in how often children base their predictions about biological phenomena on analogies to people. As human beings are the biological kinds best known to young children, and as we already know that analogical mappings can be made quite early in development (see Chapter 2), it seems plausible that children may use their biological knowledge about people to understand biological phenomena in other natural kinds. In order to study this question, Inagaki and Hatano asked 5- to 6-year-olds to make biological predictions about a person, a rabbit, a tulip, and a stone. The growth question was "Suppose someone is given a baby X and wants to keep it forever the same size because it's so small and cute. Can he or she do that?". Inagaki and Hatano found that 89% of the children said that he or she couldn't do that for the person, 90% said that he or she couldn't do that for the rabbit, and 81% said that he or she couldn't do that for the tulip; 80% of the children also said that he or she could keep the stone the same size. The understanding that growth is inevitable for biological kinds thus appears to be present in this age group. Inagaki and Hatano also found that the children had some idea about the biological mechanism underlying inevitable growth. They tended to make statements like "No, we cannot keep the baby the same size forever, because he takes food. If he eats, he will become bigger and bigger and be an adult" (p.1015).

In fact, analogies to people appear to provide an important source of preschoolers' understanding of a variety of biological phenomena. Inagaki and Sugiyama (1988) asked 4-, 5-, 8-, and 10-year-olds a range of questions about various properties of eight target objects, including "Does x breathe?", "Does x have a heart?", "Does x feel pain if we prick it with a needle?", and "Can x think?". The target objects were people, rabbits, pigeons, fish, grasshoppers, trees, tulips, and stones. Prior similarity judgements had established that the target objects differed in their similarity to people in this order, with rabbits being rated as most similar and stones being rated as least similar. The children all showed a decreasing tendency to attribute the physiological properties ("Does x breathe?") to the target objects as the perceived similarity to a person decreased. Apart from the 4-year-olds, very few children attributed physiological attributes to stones, tulips, and trees, and even 4-year-olds only attributed physiological properties to stones 15% of the time. A similar pattern was found for the mental properties ("Can x think?"). This study supports the idea that preschoolers' understanding of biological phenomena arises in part from analogies based on their understanding of people.

Evidence from studies of inheritance

Living things also transmit some of their properties to their offspring. Baby kangaroos have the properties of adult kangaroos, and baby goats have the properties of adult goats. Artifacts are different. They do not reproduce, and so they cannot transmit their properties. A coffee pot cannot transmit its shape or colour to a smaller coffee pot, as coffee pots are created by man. Young children appear to know certain facts about biological inheritance from quite an early age.

One important fact about inheritance is that "genes will out"—if you are a baby kangaroo, you will grow up to be an adult kangaroo, even if you live with goats. Gelman and Wellman (1991) investigated young children's understanding of this essential fact by telling 4-year-olds about baby animals that were raised among members of a different species. For example, the children were shown a picture of a baby kangaroo, which looked like a shapeless blob, and were told that it was taken to a goat farm as a baby and raised with goats. A picture of the goat farm was then shown to the children, and they were asked how the baby kangaroo behaved when she grew up. For example, was she good at hopping or good at climbing? Did she have a pouch? The children were almost all sure that the grown-up kangaroo was good at hopping, and had a pouch.

Another important fact about inheritance is that identity is maintained over transformations in appearance. For example, if a doctor bleaches the hair of a tiger and sews a mane onto its neck, it looks like a lion, but it is still really a tiger. If the same doctor paints the skin of a raccoon so that it resembles a skunk, it is still a raccoon. However, if a doctor saws off the handle and the spout of a coffeepot, seals the top and then attaches a bird's perch, a little window at the side and some birdseed, it not only looks like a birdfeeder, it can function as a birdfeeder (see Fig. 3.8). Keil (1989) has shown that younger children behave as though such transformations in appearance change identity for both the natural kinds (e.g. tiger–lion) and the artifacts (coffee pot—birdfeeder), whereas older children (7- and 9-year-olds) only accept identity changes for the artifacts. His explanation is that the older children are operating on the basis of a biological *theory*, in which natural kinds are identified by underlying essences and deep causal relations. In contrast, artifacts are identified by virtue of the functions that they serve by children of all ages.

For example, when the younger children were asked "After the operation, was the animal a tiger or a lion?" for the bleached tiger with a mane, they would say things like:

> *Child:* "I think he changed it into a real lion."
>
> *Exp:* "OK. Even though it started out as a tiger, you think now it's a lion?"
>
> *Child:* "Um hmm."
>
> *Exp:* "Why do you say that?"
>
> *Child:* "Because a tiger doesn't have long hair on his neck." (p.205)

In a similar paradigm, older children would say things like:

> *Child:* "It looks like a lion, but it's a tiger."
>
> *Exp:* "Why do you think it's a tiger and not a lion?"
>
> *Child:* "Because it was made out of a tiger." (p.190)

In contrast, a typical response to the coffee pot—birdfeeder example at all ages was:

> *Child:* "I think they made it into a birdfeeder because it doesn't have a spout, and coffeepots need spouts, and it doesn't have a handle ... and how are you supposed to hold onto it if it doesn't have a handle?"
>
> *Exp:* "Can it be a birdfeeder even though it came from a coffeepot?"
>
> *Child:* "Yes." (p.192)

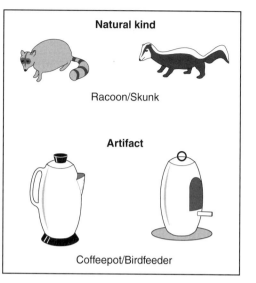

Natural kind

Racoon/Skunk

Artifact

Coffeepot/Birdfeeder

FIG. 3.8.
A racoon transformed to resemble a skunk, and a coffeepot transformed into a birdfeeder, two of the examples used by Keil (1989). Reproduced by kind permission of MIT Press.

However, even the youngest children seemed to realise that transformations that appeared to change an object from one type of natural kind into another were impossible (e.g. porcupine to cactus). This fits with Keil's notion that biological knowledge is theory-driven, with natural kinds being identified on the basis of deeper structural characteristics like being alive and having offspring. For example, the same young child who had argued that a tiger could be changed into a lion denied that a porcupine could be changed into a cactus:

Child: "I think he's still really a porcupine."

Exp: "And why do you say that?"

Child: "Because he started out like a porcupine."

Exp: "Oh, OK. And even though he looks like a cactus plant, you think he's really a porcupine?"

Child: "Um hmm."

Exp: "OK. Can you think of any other reasons why he's still a porcupine? Something you know about him?"

Child: [Shakes head.] (p.206)

However, whereas some bodily characteristics such as eye colour and gender are inherited and so cannot be changed or modified, others such as running speed and body weight can be modified by training or diet. Inagaki and Hatano (1993) investigated whether Japanese children aged 4 and 5 years were aware of such distinctions. For example, the children were told "A boy, Taro, has black eyes. He wants to make his eyes blue like a foreigner's (Caucasian). Can he do that?", and "Taro is a slow runner. He wants to be a fast runner. Can he do that?".

Inagaki and Hatano found that the children were very good at distinguishing between whether Taro could change his eye colour if he wanted to (no), and whether Taro could become a faster runner if he wanted to (yes). For the modifiable characteristics, they gave explanations like "He can run fast if he practises more". Inagaki and Hatano concluded that even rather young children understand biological phenomena like inheritance. Perhaps the younger children studied by Keil demonstrated a poorer understanding of inheritance because his modifications were based on non-natural transformations like surgery, which may not have been well understood.

Evidence from studies of natural cause

Children's understanding of natural cause is not quite the same as inheritance, although it taps the same underlying conception that features can be inborn. For example, a rabbit may not hop at birth, but the ability to hop is inborn. In contrast, the behaviour of artifacts is not a result of natural cause. A ball can bounce, but this is because someone made it that way—the cause is man-made.

S. Gelman and Kremer (1991) asked 4- and 7-year-old children about the behaviours of a variety of natural kinds and artifacts (e.g. rabbits hopping, birds flying, leaves changing colour, salt melting in water, balloons going up into the sky, cars going up hills, telephones ringing, guitars playing music, crayons drawing). For example, the children might be shown a picture of a rabbit, and told "See this? It's a rabbit. It hops". They were then asked "Why does it hop?". This open-ended question was followed by two direct questions, such as "Did a person make it hop?" and "Is there anything inside it that made it hop?". For the balloon, the equivalent questions would be "Did a person make it go up into the sky?" and "Is there anything inside it that made it go up into the sky?".

Gelman and Kremer found that the children tended to over-gener-alise the involvement of man-made causes to the less familiar natural kinds. For example, human influence was attributed to the dissolution of salt in water (42%), but not to the colour change of leaves (0%). However, the children were extremely accurate at identifying man-made causes in the case of the artifacts, knowing for example that guitars couldn't play music on their own. Although natural causes were ascribed to artifacts in some cases, the ascription of internal cause depended on the artifact. Internal causes were largely attributed to *self-sustained* properties of artifacts, such as a telephone ringing, a balloon going up into the sky, or a car going up a hill. Internal causes were seldom attributed to properties that were not self-sustained, such as guitars playing music or crayons drawing.

Gelman and Kremer concluded that children as young as 4 realised that natural causes existed independently of human influences. The chil-dren applied *different causal mechanisms* to natural kinds and to artifacts, and realised the importance of internal causes, which were applied to all of the natural kinds: "The leaf just makes itself change colours", "Rabbits are made to hop", "Flowers open up theirselves", "It grew that way". Gelman and Kremer argued that children can develop a core understanding of natural cause for objects, their properties, and their behaviours before knowing the precise origins of such natural causes. Also, children appreciate that causal mechanisms can be inferred rather than directly observed. As we will see when we discuss theories of conceptual development, the idea that young children can go beyond information that can be directly observed and can grasp the significance of non-obvious properties for surface appearances is becoming increasingly important in explaining conceptual development.

The representation of categorical knowledge

Before we discuss recent theories of conceptual development, however, we need to address the question of how conceptual knowledge is represented in semantic memory. Adults organise semantic memory on the basis of *categorical knowledge*. At one time, it was thought that young children did not share this categorical bias. Instead, it was thought that young children organised conceptual knowledge in terms of *thematic* relationships.

The role of thematic relations in organising conceptual knowledge

The belief that young children organise semantic memory according to thematic associations arose from some experiments which suggested that younger children were more inclined to learn about thematic relationships than about categorical relationships. A thematic relationship is an associative one: dogs go with bones, and bees go with honey. As the young child tends to experience instances of different categories along with associated instances of other categories, the notion that categories are first represented in terms of thematic relations seemed quite plausible.

For example, a picture-sorting study carried out by Smiley and Brown (1979) found a preference for thematic over categorical relations in 4- and 6-year-old children. Only 10-year-olds appeared to prefer categorical relations. In Smiley and Brown's study, children were given a matching-to-sample task using triads of pictures. The triads used included *bee*, honey, butterfly; *dog*, bone, cat; and *bird*, nest, robin (see Table 3.2). The children were asked "Which one goes best with the [bee], the [honey], or the [butterfly]?". Children who chose *honey* were scored as preferring a thematic match, and children who chose *butterfly* were scored as preferring a category match. Smiley and Brown found that the conceptual preferences of the younger children were consistently for the thematic match.

TABLE 3.2

Examples of the stimulus sets used by Smiley and Brown (1979)

Standard	Thematic	Taxonomic
Bee	Honey	Butterfly
Cow	Milk	Pig
Crown	King	Hat
Spider	Web	Grasshopper
Dog	Bone	Cat

However, the instructions used in this task were very open-ended. More recent work has shown that even 1-year-olds are able to sort objects by category relations rather than by thematic relations when they are given more direct sorting instructions. Bauer and Mandler (1989a) used the matching-to-sample task with 16- and 20-month-olds in a paradigm similar to that used by Smiley and Brown, except that triples of real objects were presented rather than triples of pictures. For example, the toddlers were shown a toothbrush, and were asked to select the correct match from another toothbrush (category relation) and some toothpaste (thematic relation). Alternatively, they might be shown a hammer, and asked to make a choice from another hammer (category relation) and a nail (thematic relation). Bauer and Mandler changed the verbal instructions given to the children to "find the other one just like this one". They also checked that the thematic relations were familiar to their young subjects.

Under these circumstances, a preference for thematic selections was shown on only 26% of trials by the 16-month-olds, and 15% of trials by the 20-month-olds. Although it could be argued that the children were matching on the basis of object identity, a follow-up study using slightly older children found similar results, even though this time the triads were at the superordinate level (*monkey*, banana, bear; *hammer*, nail, pliers; *bed*, pillow, cot; this study was discussed earlier). Bauer and Mandler's work suggests that children organise semantic knowledge in the same way as adults do, in other words, on the basis of categorical relations. They only show a preference for thematic relations under the influence of certain task instructions.

Children, like adults, therefore organise conceptual knowledge according to categorical knowledge. The next question is how this categorical knowledge is represented. Work on adult concepts suggests that there are at least two sets of features that can be used to store conceptual information in semantic memory. Concepts can be coded on the basis of their *defining* features, or on the basis of their *characteristic* features.

Representing categories in terms of characteristic vs. defining features

A characteristic feature is a feature that is typically associated with a concept. For example, a characteristic feature of grandmothers is that they are old. A defining feature is a feature that applies to 100% of all the instances of a concept. A defining feature of a grandmother is that she is the mother of your parent. One possibility that has interested developmental psychologists is that children initially represent concepts in terms of *characteristic* features, which tend to be perceptually salient. As they learn more about the world, children pass through a period of conceptual re-organisation, developing conceptual representations that take account of *defining* features. According to this hypothesis, the basis of categorisation changes developmentally from being based on well known characteristic features to being based on more sophisticated defining ones. This hypothesised re-organisation has been called the "characteristic-to-defining shift" (Keil, 1991). Earlier investigators have talked in similar general terms of a "concrete to abstract" shift in conceptual development, a "perceptual to conceptual" shift, and a "holistic to analytic" shift (see Keil, 1987).

One way to examine the possibility that children's conceptual representations pass through a "characteristic-to-defining" shift is to pit characteristic features against defining ones, and then to examine whether younger children prefer characteristic features and older children prefer defining ones. Keil and Batterman (1984) used this technique with 5-, 7-, and 9-year-old children. They told the children pairs of stories about familiar concepts like *uncle, robber,* and *island*. The first of the stories in each pair had no information about the characteristic features of being an uncle, a robber, or an island, but did include a defining feature. The second story in each pair had no information about the defining features of being an uncle, a robber, or an island, but included a number of characteristic features. The children were then asked "Could [x] be an uncle/robber/island?".

Examples of the "defining feature" stories include:

> Suppose your mommy has all sorts of brothers, some very old and some very, very young. One of your mommy's brothers is so young that he's only 2 years old. Could that be an uncle? (p.227)

> This very friendly and cheerful woman came up to you and gave you a hug, but then she disconnected your toilet bowl

and took it away without permission and never returned it. Could she be a robber? (p.226)

Examples of the "characteristic feature" stories include:

This man your daddy's age loves you and your parents and loves to visit and bring presents, but he's not related to your parents at all. He's not your mommy or daddy's brother or sister or anything like that. Could that be an uncle? (p.227)

This smelly, mean old man with a gun in his pocket came to your house one day and took your coloured television set because your parents didn't want it anymore and told him he could have it. Could that be a robber? (p.226)

Keil and Batterman reported that the 5-year-olds relied on characteristic features in making their judgements, whereas the 9-year-olds relied on defining features. Although the children did not shift at the same time for all concepts, the younger children usually said that the "characteristic feature" stories were instances of the concept, while the older children chose the "defining feature" stories. Keil and Batterman concluded that the children seemed to represent the concepts in different ways at different ages. Of course, this could reflect increasing knowledge about the appropriate defining features for different concepts. For example, it is fairly common for parents to use terms such as "uncle" for family friends, and detailed knowledge about kinship relations may only come later in development. As children learn more about defining features, these could replace characteristic features as the basis for representation.

Representing categories in terms of prototypes

A somewhat different question is whether categories are stored in terms of prototypes. Following the influential work of Rosch, discussed earlier, this possibility has received a lot of attention in adult cognitive psychology. A prototype is an exemplar that is highly representative of a given category. Prototypes are either conceived of as the category member with *average* values on the features or attributes associated with the category (Rosch & Mervis, 1975), or as an individual exemplar that is judged as highly typical in terms of the number of other exemplars of the category that it resembles (Medin & Schaffer, 1978). If prototypes depend on the averaging of features, then the extraction of prototypes would depend on the exemplars to which children have been exposed (see Eimas & Quinn, 1994; Younger, 1990, discussed in Chapter 2). If prototypes depend on the selection of typical exemplars, then category boundaries should be determined on the basis of similarity to the prototype. However, although in principle these different conceptions of a prototype imply different paths of conceptual development, in practice the two measures often generate the same prototype: the category member with average values is often the exemplar that is most typical.

Prototype effects in categorising tasks.   Although there is quite a lot of developmental evidence for prototype effects in categorising tasks, most of this evidence comes from studies with infants. If prototype effects do provide direct evidence about the nature of categorisation, then the infancy data only provide evidence for the representation of *perceptual* categories via prototypes (see previous discussion in Chapter 2, and also Lakoff, 1987, for an opposing view). Studies of the representation of *conceptual* categories via prototypes are somewhat sparse, and depend mainly on demonstrations that category abstraction is easier when prototypical category members are provided as category exemplars.

For example, Mervis and Pani (1980) studied category generalisation and category learning in a paradigm using artificial categories that were designed to mimic the structure of natural object categories in the real world. The stimuli were 24 three-dimensional objects, forming six categories with four members each. All category members shared overlapping sets of attributes ("family resemblance"), but some were designed to be better exemplars of the category than others (see Fig. 3.9). The best category exemplars shared a high number of attributes with other category members, and shared very few attributes with members of different categories. Each category had a best exemplar, a good exemplar, a poor exemplar, and a very poor exemplar. The intention was to mimic category abstraction at the basic level, the

FIG. 3.9. Category members of the artifical "*naete*" category (Mervis & Pani, 1980). Reprinted by permission of Academic Press Inc.

level at which the attribute structure of the natural world provides a reasonable basis for the assignment of objects to particular categories.

In Mervis and Pani's experiment, 5-year-olds were taught the name of one object from each of the six categories. They were then asked to point to the sub-set of objects among the 24 that they would call by the same name when the experimenter said the name aloud. They were also asked to name each of the 24 objects. Half of the children were taught the names of the six best exemplars, and half were taught the names of the six poorest exemplars. Mervis and Pani predicted that the children in the "best exemplar" condition would generalise the category name more accurately than the children in the "poor exemplar" condition. This was exactly what they found, for both comprehension (the pointing task) and production (the naming task) of the different categories. Mervis and Pani concluded that children generalise category membership more appropriately if the initial exemplar is a good category member, and suggested that this finding was consistent with categorical representation in terms of prototypes.

Prototype effects in sequential touching tasks. More recently, Bauer and her colleagues have tackled the question of whether prototypicality facilitates category formation by using the sequential touching measure developed by Bauer and Mandler (e.g. Mandler & Bauer, 1988, discussed earlier). Bauer, Dow, and Hertsgaard (1995) tested 13-, 16-, and 20-month-old infants' categorisation of sets of objects that consisted entirely either of prototypical exemplars, or of non-prototypical exemplars. The categories that they used were *animals* and *vehicles*, at either the superordinate or the basic level. For example, a set of prototypical animals at the superordinate level might include a cow, a dog, a pig, and a cat. A set of prototypical vehicles at the superordinate level might include a bus, a motorcycle, a truck, and a car. A set of non-prototypical animals at the superordinate level might include a snail, a rhinoceros, an alligator, and an ostrich, and a set of non-prototypical vehicles at the superordinate level might include a canoe, a tank, a space shuttle, and a battleship. The basic-level sets contrasted prototypical and non-prototypical fish, dogs, cars, and aeroplanes (e.g. trout, salmon, bass, pike; or sunfish, eel, fancy goldfish, nurse shark; see Table 3.3). If prototypicality is important in category formation, then prototypicality should affect sequential touching at both the superordinate and basic levels. For example, children should sequentially touch the cow, pig, dog, and cat as frequently as they sequentially touch the trout, salmon, bass, and pike.

TABLE 3.3
Examples of the stimuli used by Bauer et al. (1995)

Stimulus Type/ Category	Level of Contrast		
	Global level	Basic level	
	Animal vs. Vehicle	Dogs vs. Fish	Cars vs. Aeroplanes
Prototypical			
Category 1	pig	German shepherd	Mercedes-Benz
	house cat	collie	Mustang convertible
	dog	Labrador-retriever	Renault sedan
	cow	brown mongrel	Thunderbird
Category 2	school bus	bass	KLM airliner
	motorcycle	trout	Pan Am airliner
	pick-up truck	walleyed pike	Comanche prop
	4-door sedan	salmon	airforce jet
Nonprototypical			
Category 1	alligator	bulldog	Indy racer
	snail	Chihuahua	drag racer
	rhinoceros	spitz	Lotus
	ostrich	terrier	3-wheeled roadster
Category 2	wooden canoe	sunfish	glider
	armoured tank	eel	stealth bomber
	battleship	fancy goldfish	WWI bomber
	space shuttle	nurse shark	X-wing fighter

Bauer et al. found that the categorisation of the prototypical object sets was indeed superior to that of the non-prototypical object sets. However, for the 13-month-olds, categorisation of the prototypical object sets occurred at the basic level only, whereas for the 16- and 20-month-olds, categorisation of the prototypical objects sets occurred at *both* the basic and the superordinate levels. Categorisation of the non-prototypical object sets was more variable. For the 16-month-olds, categorisation of non-prototypical objects (e.g. sunfish, eel, fancy goldfish, nurse shark) was found only at the basic level. Sequential touching of all the other non-prototypical object sets did not differ from chance. This finding appears to support the cognitive primacy (and perceptual similarity) of the basic level. For the 24-month-olds, categorisation of the non-prototypical object sets was only found at the superordinate level, while for the 28-month-olds categorisation of the non-prototypical object sets was found at both levels (basic and superordinate). Finally, prototypicality accounted for more variance than either age or categorical level (basic vs. superordinate). This finding demonstrates the importance of prototypicality in categorisation. However, it does not tell us whether conceptual categories are *represented* by prototypes.

It is thus difficult to draw any strong conclusions about the representation of categorical knowledge in children. As the nature of the representation of categorical knowledge in adults is still the subject of debate, it is perhaps unsurprising to find that developmental psychology is in a similar state. Furthermore, given the complex and wide-ranging nature of human concepts, it is unlikely that any one means of representation will be primary. Lakoff (1986) has argued that the properties that are relevant for the characterisation of human categories do not exist objectively in any case. Instead, what we *understand* as properties depend on our interactive functioning with our environment. Our theories about the world are important for our decisions about what is categorically similar. This notion has recently been incorporated into developmental psychology by reference to the importance of "essences" for conceptual understanding.

Conceptual development, "essences" and naive theories

Some researchers in adult cognitive psychology have argued that category membership is defined not only in terms of characteristic and defining features, similarity to prototypes etc., but in terms of "essences". One of the major proponents of this view is Medin (1989). His view can be summarised by the following quote (p.1476): "People act as if things (e.g. objects) have essences or underlying natures that make them the thing that they are." In other words, people have implicit assumptions about the structure of the world, and about the underlying nature of categories, and these beliefs are represented in the categories that they develop. This view is sometimes called "psychological essentialism". According to this view, categories are not discovered via the passive observation of correlations between features. Rather, they are created by "carving nature up at its joints".

We can illustrate how category membership can go beyond clusters of characteristic features by returning to our example of birds. It is true that feathers reliably co-occur with wings, with flight, and with light body-weight, and that these co-occurrences help to distinguish the category "bird". But adults also have a "theory" about why these features go together. This theory involves the causal relations necessary to enable flight. Adults believe that low body-weight, feathers, and wings facilitate flight, thereby imposing a degree of *causal necessity* on the covariation of these features in birds. This tendency to create causal explanatory constructs may not be limited to adults. Children, too, may create intuitive theories to understand conceptual structure. These "theories" would correspond to core sets of interconnected beliefs about category membership.

The essentialist bias

Such sets of causal beliefs about the co-occurrence of core properties apply to a great many concepts (although not all). They apply particularly to categories of natural kinds, such as animals, birds, and plants. A number of developmental psychologists have suggested that children's growing understanding of the category of natural kinds is partly governed by their implicit appreciation of the causal/explanatory relations that explain featural clusterings within this category (e.g. Carey & Spelke, 1994; Gelman et al., 1994; Keil, 1994). For example, Gelman et al. suggested that young children have an essentialist bias, and that this bias constrains the ways in which they reason about natural kinds. Their early understanding of living things is theory-like, leading them to search for invisible causal mechanisms to explain an object's actions.

Some of the evidence reviewed in this chapter is consistent with Gelman's idea that even young children go beyond observable features when developing biological concepts. For example, children as young as 4 years appear to assume that living things transmit some of their properties to their offspring. Evidence discussed in previous chapters also supports her idea, as we have seen that children have an inherent tendency to search for causal explanations of phenomena in their everyday worlds, and that they show an early ability to go beyond surface features to focus on structural characteristics (e.g. when reasoning by analogy, see Chapter 2). However, a strong version of the "psychological essentialism" theory argues that the theories and core principles that guide essentialism are *innate*. This innate knowledge is thought to guide cognitive development by setting important limits (or "constraints") on the information that can and cannot be learned (e.g. Carey & Gelman, 1991). Whether such a strong "genetic determinism" is justified is as yet undetermined. Nevertheless, there is clear evidence for similar "constraints on learning" in animals. For example, rats are more likely to learn that being sick is caused by water that tastes funny than that it is caused by a drinking spout that emits flashing lights and sounds (e.g. Garcia & Koelling, 1966), even if the covariation information for the two potential causal variables is identical.

The "causes and effects of changes" model

Even if this strong version of "psychological essentialism" is rejected, however, the idea that children have an inherent tendency to search for causal explanations of everyday phenomena may *in itself* be enough to support the patterns of conceptual development that have been documented in this chapter. A particularly clear version of this position has recently been advanced by Pauen (1996b). Pointing out that infants pay special attention to changes in their environment from the first day of life, Pauen argues that the activity of understanding the causes and effects of such changes may be enough to account for the early learning of ontological distinctions. She calls her model the "Causes and Effects of Changes" or "CEC" model of conceptual development.

Pauen highlights three dimensions of change in everyday objects that carry crucial information. These are whether the causes of a given change are *self-initiated* or *externally induced*, the *functional value* of such changes, and the *predictability* of such changes. For example, for biological kinds, changes in location are self-initiated and not externally induced, changes in location may be made in order to guarantee survival (therefore they have functional value), and any changes in location that are made are usually much harder to predict than for machines. Put simply, some objects behave in mostly unpredictable ways, they perform changes in the absence of external agents, and such changes occur independently of human intentions. These objects tend to be biological kinds. Other objects perform changes that are highly dependent on human intentions, that follow well known rules, and that are comparably easy to predict. These objects tend to be non-biological kinds. The advantage of the CEC model is that it postulates only one innate "constraint" on the information that can be learned: a focus on causal relations. As we will find repeatedly in this book, a focus on causal relations is central to cognitive development in many areas of cognition. The causal focus of Pauen's model of conceptual development is thus a highly appealing one.

Conceptual change in childhood

Although we have reviewed a large amount of evidence indicating that young children have rich conceptual structures that they have abstracted from their everyday experience of the world, this does not mean that they never experience conceptual change. The level of knowledge that can be abstracted from perceptual causal information about different entities has limits. For example, although early conceptual development appears to depend on a process of enrichment of initial core principles derived from the perception of causes (such as that biological entities are capable of self-generated movement whereas non-biological entities are not), at some point children may need to distinguish plants as biological entities that are essentially similar to animals, even though they differ markedly in terms of their capacity for self-generated movement. When conceptual change occurs, then new principles emerge that "carve the world at different joints" (see Carey & Spelke, 1994, for a fuller discussion).

Carey has argued that conceptual change in childhood (and in science) depends on children and scientists making *mappings* between different domains. Such mappings entail relating objects in one system (e.g. people) to objects in another (e.g. plants). If such a mapping is created, then the principles that govern children's understanding of people can be applied to their understanding of plants. We have already seen that children use analogical mappings from people to decide whether animals and plants can be kept small and cute forever or whether they would feel pain if pricked by a needle (see the work of Inagaki and her colleagues discussed earlier in this chapter). Furthermore, there is a growing body of work which demonstrates that analogical mappings are used by children as young as 3 in other areas of cognition such as causal reasoning (Goswami & Brown, 1989), physical reasoning (Pauen & Wilkening, 1997), and reasoning about natural kinds and artifacts (Goswami, 1996). The availability of the mapping mechanism proposed by Carey is thus well documented.

Carey (1985) has herself made a convincing case for her view about the importance of analogical mappings in the domain of biology (although see Kuhn, 1989). Carey has argued that preschool children's understanding of biological phenomena differs radically from that of older children. Her data show that younger children base their understanding of animals on their understanding of people, projecting behavioural and psychological properties onto other animals according to how similar these animals are to human beings. For example, the attribution of the property "breathes" was made to humans by 100% of the 4-year-olds studied by Carey, to aardvarks by 78% of the children, to dodos by 67%, and to stinkbugs by 33%. The property "breathes" was never attributed to plants. Only older children showed a coalescence of the concepts *animal* and *plant* into the new concept, *living thing*. Carey argued that children's understanding of biology emerged *out of* their understanding of people. This tendency to attribute physiological and mental properties to other objects on the basis of their similarity to people has also been termed a "personification analogy" (Inagaki & Hatano, 1987; Inagaki & Sugiyama, 1988).

Not everyone agrees with every aspect of Carey's views, however (e.g. Atran, 1994; Keil, 1989; Kuhn, 1989; see Wellman & Gelman, in press, for a useful review). Perhaps the most inclusive view of the mechanisms of conceptual change has been summarised by Wellman and Gelman (in press). They suggest that young children may be developing several alternative conceptual frameworks *at the same time*. Rather than developing a monolithic understanding of the world, young children may develop distinct conceptual frameworks to describe the "foundational domains" of biology, psychology, and physics, foundational domains that are thought to engender, shape, and constrain other conceptual understandings. Wellman and Gelman point out that many concepts will be represented in *more than one* of these foundational frameworks. For example, persons are psychological entities, biological entities, *and* physical entities. Wellman and Gelman suggest that this necessary *conceptual multiplicity* will fuel the need to compare, share, merge, and create new conceptions. At the same time, children will use at least two levels of analysis within any framework; one that captures surface phenomena (mappings based on attributes) and another that penetrates to deeper levels (mappings based on relations).

Finally, it is worth noting that the kind of merging, sharing, and creation of new concepts that goes on in childhood may differ in cultures with a developed science, like Western cultures, and cultures without a developed science. Within the general frameworks outlined by Wellman and Gelman, children must engage in much culture-specific learning. For example, different cross-domain mappings may be encouraged by the assumptions of the adults around them, by the technology of the culture and by systematic teaching received in school. On a smaller scale, similar factors may lead to individual differences in cognitive development between children growing up in the same culture, who may nevertheless experience qualitatively different input from the adults around them and may benefit to different degrees from the teaching received in school. Finally, individual differences in knowledge structures and mapping abilities may be another source of cognitive differences between children growing up in the same culture.

Summary

The evidence discussed in this chapter has shown that many sources of information contribute to conceptual development in infancy and early childhood. One important source of information is perceptual. The attribute structure of the world provides information about the assignment of objects to particular categories at all hierarchical levels (superordinate, basic, and subordinate), but provides especially rich information about the basic level of categorisation. By noting the co-occurrence of perceptual features such as wings, feathers, and beaks, categories such as bird can be distinguished from other animals.

A second source of information about category structure is linguistic. Conceptual organisation is partly guided by linguistic biases that help to determine conceptual hierarchies. For example, children interpret the introduction of novel nouns as signalling superordinate categories, but the introduction of novel adjectives as signalling subordinate categories. A third source of information is children's inherent tendency to search for causal explanations of everyday phenomena. By noting information such as whether the causes of changes in an object's position are self-initiated or externally induced and whether objects share core properties in structure or in function, children can distinguish biological from non-biological kinds. As these core principles become increasingly enriched with growing world knowledge, children's conceptual structures become more detailed and more finely organised. Finally, children can use analogies to aid conceptual organisation. Using people as their base analogy, children can understand biological phenomena in a range of natural kinds, and can make predictions about whether stones, tulips, and rabbits should feel pain or have a heart. Children can also use analogies to map from one domain to another, enabling conceptual change.

Children's tendency to search for causal explanations of everyday phenomena also contributes in an important way to the naive theories that they develop to distinguish biological and non-biological kinds. It has been argued that children have an abstract framework of causal *expectations* about natural kinds and artifacts, which forms the basis of their naive theories. Conceptual development thus involves the development of beliefs about how the world is organised as well as the development of perceptual and linguistic skills. Furthermore, the properties that are relevant for the characterisation of exemplars as categorically similar depends to some extent on what we *understand* to be properties, which depends in turn on our world knowledge and our interactions with our environment. As we saw, child-basic categories may differ from adult-basic categories, and children may give early priority to characteristic rather than defining features in making their category judgements. Category judgements can also be made on the basis of "essences", the underlying nature that makes things what they are. According to the "psychological essentialism" view of conceptual development, children make implicit assumptions about the structure of the world and about the underlying nature of categories, theory-like assumptions based on core sets of interconnected causal beliefs about category membership. For example, children's understanding of natural kinds may be partly governed by their implicit appreciation of the causal/explanatory relations that explain the clustering of features within the category (e.g. that the relation "capable of self-generated movement" explains the clustering of features like legs and feet in natural kinds).

The view that children's early understanding of natural kinds is theory-driven means that children can be thought of as searching for invisible causal mechanisms to explain an object's actions, going beyond observable features to deeper structural characteristics. At the "basic level" of categorisation, observed features and deeper structural characteristics are most likely to correspond in assigning objects to the same category. This means that at the basic level, perceptual similarity can act as a guide to structural similarity. This is also true at the super-ordinate and subordinate levels of conceptual hierarchies, but to a lesser extent. The basic level has thus been assumed to play the core role in conceptual development.

Development of causal reasoning 4

The notion that the human infant is born with an innate bias to learn about causal relations and to acquire causal explanations should by now be a familiar one. In Chapter 1, we learned that young infants remember events that are causally related and forget events that are arbitrary. In Chapter 2, we learned that infants seek causal explanations for physical events, that they can infer how "impossible" physical events are caused from initial state information, and that they have some understanding of the causal intentions of others. We have also seen from Chapter 3 that this causal bias guides conceptual learning in early childhood, and that the search for causal relations to explain featural clustering in categories generates an enormous amount of conceptual information for the young child. For example, we saw that young children use explanatory relations such as self-caused vs. other-caused motion to divide the world into categories and kinds, and shared core structure vs. shared core function to develop conceptual knowledge about biological kinds and artifacts. Causal reasoning therefore plays an important role in interpreting, representing, and remembering events in the physical world from very early in development.

This early focus on causal information appears to be a critical mechanism in the development of children's cognition. As pointed out by Shultz and Kestenbaum (1985), one reason for children's attention to causal information may be that working out how an event was caused enables them to understand the event itself (a form of "explanation-based learning", see Chapter 7). As well as enlarging the knowledge base and facilitating conceptual development, however, this early focus on causality enables the development of a body of knowledge about causal relations themselves. The development of knowledge about physical causation is sometimes referred to as the development of a "naive" or "intuitive" physics. As well as helping children to understand the physical world, causal reasoning may also enable children to predict and even control causal events within it. This will in turn promote the development of scientific and logical reasoning.

Such cognitive benefits are only possible if children's causal reasoning follows recognised causal principles, however. These include the principle of causal priority, the principle of covariation, and the principle of temporal contiguity, which are discussed in detail later in this chapter. Similarly, children's causal understanding will only promote the development of scientific and logical thinking if they can recognise the relationship between hypotheses and evidence. Logical thought requires the ability to test causal hypotheses in a systematic way, recognising which causal possibilities must be ruled out as well as which can be maintained in the light of the available causal evidence. This requires an appreciation of disconfirmatory as well as confirmatory evidence, and of what is causally relevant in a given situation.

The topic of this chapter is causal reasoning itself. Our focus will be on children's causal reasoning about physical objects and events rather than on their causal reasoning about psychological states and experiences. Although an understanding of psychological causality appears to develop alongside an understanding of physical causality, the two have generally been treated separately. For example, while Wellman and Gelman (in press) argue that both "naive psychology" and "naive physics" are *foundational* domains (bodies of knowledge that engender, shape, and constrain other conceptual understandings) and that causality is a developmental primitive which influences development in both of these domains, they also demonstrate that naive psychological understanding can be *contrasted* with an understanding of physical objects and forces. In fact, some developmental theorists view the two types of causal knowledge as quite distinct. For example, Leslie (1994) has argued that the understanding of psychological causation develops as an independent module in the brain, the "theory of mind" module (e.g. Leslie, 1994), and that this module operates independently of physical causal reasoning, which takes place in a different module (see Chapter 2).

Reasoning about causes and effects

By the age of around 3 years, children have experienced many different physical causes and their effects. For example, they have many experiences of *cutting* (apples, paper, hair), of *melting* (chocolate, snow, butter), of *breaking* (a toy, a cup, a chair), of *wetting* (washing clothes, rain, having a bath), and so on. One way to investigate the development of causal reasoning is thus to ask whether children know that causal agents can produce transformations in objects, changing them from one state to another. For example, if children are shown a picture of a cup and a picture of a shattered cup, do they know that a hammer is a more likely agent of the causal transformation than a knife or scissors?

Reasoning about the causal transformations of familiar objects

Gelman, Bullock, and Meck (1980) used three-picture causal sequences such as *cup, hammer, broken cup* to investigate cause–effect reasoning in 3- and 4-year-old children. They first trained children to read the picture sequences from left to right. Following this training, they showed the children picture sequences that either depicted an object being transformed from its *canonical* form (an intact cup) to its *non-canonical* form (a broken cup), or from its non-canonical form (a broken cup) to its canonical form (an intact cup). The middle picture in the sequence always depicted the causal agent (the correct agents in this example were a hammer or some glue). As well as familiar causal transformations like cups breaking, the children were shown unfamiliar causal transformations like a cut banana being restored to its canonical form using a needle and thread.

In the experiment, the children were shown the picture sequences in an incomplete form, with one of the three pictures missing. Their job was to select the correct picture to fill the empty slot from three alternatives. For example, if the picture of the agent was missing, then pictures of three possible agents were provided as alternatives. If the first or the final picture in the sequence was missing, then the children were shown pictures of the correct object with either a correct or an incorrect causal transformation, and a picture of an incorrect object with the correct causal transformation. Examples of each type of trial are depicted in Fig. 4.1.

Gelman et al. found that 92% of the 3-year-olds and 100% of the 4-year-olds could select the correct causal agent when the middle picture was missing from the canonical stories (e.g. cup to broken cup), and that 75% of the 3-year-olds and 100% of the 4-year-olds could select the correct causal agent when the middle picture was missing from the non-canonical stories (e.g. broken cup to cup). Performance fell slightly for the younger children when the missing picture was the final item (83% and 100% respectively for canonical sequences, 58% and 100% respectively for non-canonical sequences), and fell more markedly when the missing picture was the first item (66% and 92% respectively for canonical sequences, 58% and 100% respectively for non-canonical sequences). Nevertheless, performance was significantly above chance in all cases. Gelman et al. concluded that pre-school children could predict or infer the states of objects changed by a causal transformation,

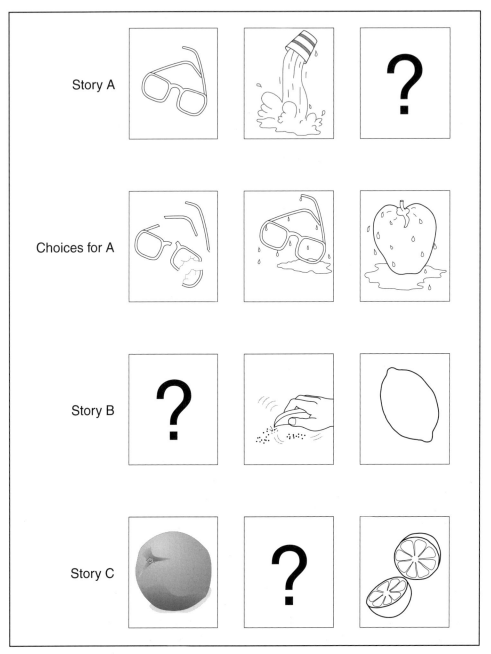

FIG. 4.1.   Examples of the three-picture causal sequences used by Gelman et al. (1980). Story A has the final picture missing, story B the initial picture, and story C the picture of the agent. Reproduced with permission.

and could also infer the kind of transformation that related two object states.

Reversible reasoning about causal transformations of familiar objects

In a second study, the *reversibility* of the same children's causal thinking was investigated. In this study, the missing picture was always the middle picture, and the children were first asked to select a picture of an agent for a *left-to-right* reading of the causal sequence, and then a picture of an agent for a *right-to-left* reading of the causal sequence. This required the children to think about the same object pairs (e.g. cup and broken cup) in two different (reversed) ways. The 3-year-olds found this task quite difficult, and were only correct on 49% of trials. The 4-year-olds succeeded on 75% of trials. Gelman et al. argued that the 3-year-olds scored poorly because they tended to impose their *own* causal ordering onto the task. They preferred canonical to non-canonical readings over non-canonical to canonical readings, and so were scored as being wrong on half of the trials. Overall, however, Gelman et al. claimed that the 3-year-olds' representations of the causal transformations were abstract enough to permit reversibility.

Although Gelman et al.'s work suggests an early understanding of many cause–effect relations and of their reversibility, Das Gupta and Bryant (1989) criticised their studies on methodological grounds. Das Gupta and Bryant argued that it was possible to "solve" the reversible causal sequences by associative rather than by causal reasoning. This was an important criticism, as associative reasoning is a relatively unsophisticated type of reasoning that is also found in animals such as fish and rats. Das Gupta and Bryant argued that, rather than considering *both* the initial and the final states of the object when choosing the causal instrument, the children could simply have focused on the *more salient* non-canonical state of the object (e.g. the broken cup). They could then have selected the instrument associated with that non-canonical state. Thus the children could have solved the picture sequences without taking the object's initial state into consideration at all.

Das Gupta and Bryant argued that a *genuine* causal inference depended on the children being able to work out the *difference* between the initial and final states in a causal chain. To examine whether 3- and 4-year-olds could do this, Das Gupta and Bryant showed them three-picture causal sequences in which the objects *began* as non-canonical in one way (e.g. a broken cup), and ended up as non-canonical in *two* ways (e.g. a wet, broken cup). Trials were paired, so that later in the experiment the children also saw a picture sequence that began with a wet cup and ended with a wet, broken cup. As in Gelman et al.'s procedure, the children's job was to select the missing middle term in the three-picture sequences, which was the causal agent. However, in Das Gupta and Bryant's task, the selection of the agent *most highly associated* with the non-canonical form of the object (a hammer) would be an *incorrect* response in the picture sequence broken cup to wet, broken cup, but the *correct* reponse in the picture sequence wet cup to wet, broken cup (see Table 4.1). Thus if the same causal agent was chosen on a given pair of trials (e.g. the hammer for broken cup to wet, broken cup *and* for wet cup to wet, broken cup) then a genuine causal inference was unlikely to be being made.

TABLE 4.1
One of the pairs of causal sequences used by Das Gupta and Bryant (1989)

| 1. Wet cup | [Blank} | Wet *broken cup* |
| 2. Broken cup | [Blank] | Broken *wet* cup |

Following Gelman et al., the children were again required to choose from three possible causal agents, in this case *hammer, water*, and *feather* (an irrelevant agent). Das Gupta and Bryant found that the 3-year-olds chose the same causal agent (e.g. the hammer) in 49% of trials for the pairs of sequences, whereas the 4-year-olds only chose the same causal agent in 21% of trials. The younger children selected the correct answer to both sequences in a pair on 39% of occasions, and the 4-year-olds on 78% of occasions. Das Gupta and Bryant concluded that 3-year-olds were often distracted by the salience of particular causal effects (such as breaking), which led them to disregard the relation between initial and final states. This made the causal status of their inferences questionable.

The salience of non-canonical states in early causal reasoning

In a second experiment, Das Gupta and Bryant went on to argue that the best test of children's ability to make genuine causal inferences was to use non-canonical (broken cup) to canonical (whole cup) sequences. Such sequences necessitated a causal inference based on the *difference* between the object's initial and final states. In contrast, canonical to non-canonical sequences (cup to broken cup) could be solved on the basis of the departure from canonicality. The salience of the broken cup could lead children to "correctly" select a hammer as an agent in a canonical to non-canonical sequence, but would probably also lead them to choose a hammer in the non-canonical to canonical sequence.

In support of their claim, Das Gupta and Bryant showed that 3-year-olds were significantly poorer at reasoning from a non-canonical initial state to a canonical state (broken cup to cup) than from a canonical initial state to a non-canonical one (cup to broken cup), success rates being 47% correct and 88% correct, respectively. Their conclusion was that the ability to make genuine causal inferences developed between 3 and 4 years, rather than being already present at age 3.

However, recent work reported by Blue (1995) suggests that Das Gupta and Bryant's conclusions may have been too pessimistic. Blue used a video display to present 3-year-olds with a series of object transformations. This enabled him to show the children the initial and final states of each object *sequentially*, rather than at the same time. For example, a presenter first showed the children an object such as a sheet of paper with a drawing on it (non-canonical form), along with two instruments that could mediate a causal transformation, such as a pencil and an eraser. The presenter then disappeared with all of these objects, and returned after a pause with the main object transformed (a clean sheet of paper—canonical form). Each causal agent was then displayed in turn, and the presenter asked whether it had produced the change. In addition to drawing (or erasing) on paper, Blue used the causal transformations of writing on/cleaning a blackboard, and applying or removing make-up to/from a face.

Blue found that the 3-year-olds selected the correct causal agent 82% of the time, whether they received a canonical to non-canonical causal sequence (clean paper to paper with drawing), or a non-canonical to canonical causal sequence (paper with drawing to clean paper). These impressive performance levels suggest that inferring causes for familiar effects is not difficult for young children, even when the causal transformation involves a non-canonical to canonical sequence. Difficulties in reasoning from a non-canonical initial state may thus be limited to tasks in which children are given *representations* of causal sequences, in which the all-important temporal information is omitted. Alternatively, Blue's choice of "canonical" and "non-canonical" forms, which are less clear-cut than those of Das Gupta and Bryant, may explain his data. Nevertheless, picture sequences may be less useful for probing the development of causal understanding than videos, which seem highly suited to use with even younger children.

Reasoning on the basis of causal principles

Having shown that genuine causal inferences appear to be present by 3 years of age, we need to know whether children's causal reasoning follows recognised causal principles. Take the simplest kind of causal contingency, when one event A causes another event B. In order for A to cause B, a number of causal principles must apply. One is that A must either precede B or occur at the same time as B. It cannot occur after B. This assymetry of causal relations is called the *priority* principle (that causes precede or co-occur with their effects). Other important principles in assigning causality are the *covariation* principle (that causes and their effects must systematically covary); the *temporal contiguity* principle (that causes and effects must be contiguous in place and time); and the *similarity* principle (that causes and their effects should have some similarity to each other, for example, that a mechanical effect should have a mechanical cause).

The priority principle

The assumption that causes precede their effects appears to be present by at least age 3. For example, imagine that you see a puppet dropping a marble into an apparatus, and that soon afterwards a jack-in-the-box pops out of the middle of the apparatus. You are likely to attribute the appearance of the jack to the action of the marble. It is unlikely that you will attribute causation to a second marble that is dropped into the apparatus by a second puppet *after* the jack has appeared.

Bullock and Gelman (1979) used this "jack-in-the-box" apparatus to investigate whether 3- to 5-year-old children understand that the jack-in-the-box can only be activated by an event *preceding* the jack's appearance, and not by an event that occurs after his jump. In their task, the children were shown a long black box. This box was divided internally into three sections (see Fig. 4.2; these divisions were not visible to the children). The two outer thirds of the box each had a tunnel for marbles to roll down, with each tunnel running on a sloping path towards the centre of the box. The tunnels were visible through plexiglass windows, so that only their ends (in the middle third of the box) were hidden from view. The central section of the box was opaque, and concealed the ends of the tunnels and the jack-in-the-box. The experimenter could make the jack jump by dropping a marble down either tunnel, although the jack was in fact controlled by a hidden pedal and not by the marbles themselves.

In order to test the children's understanding of the unidirectional order of causes and effects, the experimenter (via two puppets) dropped a marble down one tunnel before the jack jumped, and another marble down the second tunnel after he had jumped. The children's task was to infer which puppet's marble had made the jack jump. Bullock and Gelman found that the majority of children at all

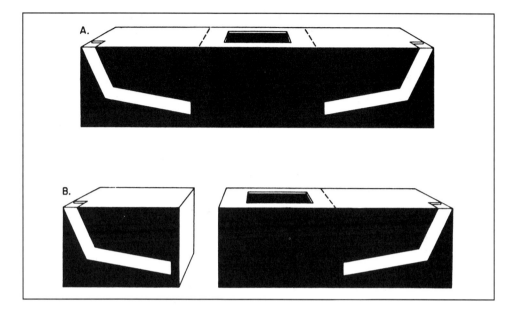

FIG. 4.2.
The apparatus used in
Bullock and Gelman's
(1979) "jack-in-the-
box" study, showing
(a) the complete
apparatus, and (b) its
appearance when the
causally appropriate
runway was separated
from the remaining
two-thirds of the box.
Reproduced with
permission.

ages tested could work out that the first marble had made the jack jump. This was the case for 75% of the 3-year-olds, 88% of the 4-year-olds, and 100% of the 5-year-olds. Bullock and Gelman then made the task more difficult by physically separating the causally appropriate runway from the remaining two-thirds of the box. Following the separation, one tunnel was in apparent contact with the jack, and the other tunnel was not. The experimenter dropped a marble down the detached tunnel before the jack jumped, and a marble down the attached tunnel after he had jumped. Even under these more stringent conditions, causality was attributed to the first marble by 75% of the 3-year-olds, 94% of the 4-year-olds, and 100% of the 5-year-olds. The children in Bullock and Gelman's study appeared to assume that temporal ordering cues were more critical than spatial proximity in determining causality in the jack-in-the-box apparatus. Nevertheless, they were surprised that action-at-a-distance was possible in the detached tunnel condition, and assumed that it needed some explanation ("It's a trick, right?", "It's magic", "When I wasn't looking, the ball slided over").

It is not necessary to assume from this data that the children assigned *more* causal importance to temporal priority than to spatial proximity. The simplest conclusion from Bullock and Gelman's data is that the children were basing their judgements on what was *causally relevant* to the experimental set-up. Consistent with this conclusion,

Shultz (1982) has shown that children will favour spatial factors over temporal ones when spatial factors are more causally relevant to a particular outcome than temporal ordering factors.

Shultz's demonstration was based on an apparatus in which two electric air blowers were directed at a lit candle. The candle flame could be protected from the jets of air by a three-sided plexiglass shield, which could be rotated to field the air emitted by one of the blowers at a time. Shultz showed 5-year-old children this apparatus, and then switched on one of the blowers when the shield was in a position to protect the candle. Five seconds later the second blower was switched on, and at the same time the shield turned to protect the candle from this second blower. The flame immediately went out. The children correctly attributed the flame's extinction to the action of the first blower, even though the onset of the second blower was the event that was temporally contiguous with the candle going out. The particular *mechanisms* of causal transmission, rather than spatial or temporal parameters *per se*, thus appear to determine children's causal attributions.

The covariation principle

Another important principle in establishing causality is the principle of covariation. If an effect has a number of potential causes, then the true cause will be the one that regularly and predictably covaries with the effect. For example, if a child is shown a box with two levers, and has to work out which lever causes a light on the lid of the box to come on, the correct answer is the lever that is always activated when the light is on. If a child is shown a box with two holes in the top, and has to determine which hole a marble must be dropped into in order to make a bell inside the box ring, then the correct answer is the hole that is always associated with the ringing of the bell.

Shultz and Mendelson (1975) gave causal problems such as these to 3- to 4-year-old and older children to determine their ability to use the covariation principle. Covariation information was varied by manipulating the number of times that the cause and the effect were associated with each other. For example, if lever 1 caused the light on the lid of the box to come on, then the children might receive the following pairings of the light and the two levers: lever 1, light; lever 2, no light; lever 1, light; levers 1 and 2, light; lever 2, no light; levers 1 and 2, light. Shultz and Mendelson found that even the 3- to 4-year-olds could use this kind of covariation information to determine causality, with the majority of children choosing the correct cause across all the different kinds of apparatus used. Shultz and Mendelson thus concluded that the ability to make causal attributions on the basis of covariation information for simple physical phenomena was present by at least 3 years of age.

Siegler and Liebert (1974) devised a similar covariation task using a "computer" and a "card programmer". Both were metallic boxes, but the computer had flashing lights and the card programmer had a slot to accommodate IBM program cards. The computer and the card programmer were both attached via cables to a large electric light bulb. All children saw the light illuminated six times, and their job was to decide which causal mechanism made the light bulb come on under different covariation conditions. For some children, the light came on immediately after a card was placed in the card programmer (100% covariation with temporal contiguity). For others, there was always a five-second delay between the insertion of the card into the card programmer and the illumination of the light (100% covariation without temporal contiguity). For a third group, the light went on immediately the card was inserted, but only on 50% of trials (50% covariation with temporal contiguity), and for a fourth group the light came on five seconds after insertion of the card, but only on 50% of trials (50% covariation without temporal contiguity).

Siegler and Liebert found that both 5-year-old and 8-year-old children were more affected by temporal contiguity than by covariation. All of the children were more likely to attribute the light going on to the card programmer when the light came on immediately, but only the older children took the regularity of the pairings into account, attributing causality to the programmer more frequently in the 100% covariation conditions than in the 50% covariation conditions. This does not mean that the younger children were insensitive to the covariation information, however, as the older children only recognised the regularity of the pairings when the sequence of six illuminations was almost over. Siegler and Liebert argued that, with more trials, the younger children may also have shown a sensitivity to covariation information. Shultz and Mendelson's data suggest that this would indeed have been the case.

The temporal contiguity principle

The principle of temporal contiguity, which states that causes and effects must be contiguous in time and place, is intimately related to the covariation principle, as in many causal situations the same cause is implicated by both temporal contiguity and covariation (an example is Bullock and Gelman's jack-in-the-box study, just discussed). It is also intimately related to the priority principle, which states that causes must temporally precede or co-occur with their effects. However, the temporal contiguity principle refers to the fact that, in addition to covarying systematically, causes and effects must be linked to each other by an intervening chain of contiguous events (Sedlak & Kurtz, 1981). If there is a physical rationale for a temporal delay between cause and effect, then the principle of temporal contiguity may still hold.

For example, imagine that you are shown an apparatus consisting of a box painted half green and half orange which sits on top of a wooden stand. The box is linked by a piece of rubber tubing 34" long to another box, which has a bell inside it. The green and orange box has two holes in it, one on the green side and one on the orange side. If a marble is dropped into the hole on the green side, a five-second delay ensues, and then the bell in the second box rings. If a marble is dropped into the hole on the orange side, then the bell in the second box does not ring. If a marble is dropped into the hole on the green side, and then five seconds later another marble is dropped into the hole in the orange side, the bell rings immediately. Which side of the box is responsible for making the bell ring, the orange side or the green side?

On the basis of covariation information, it seems as though the green side is responsible for making the bell ring. However, on the basis of temporal contiguity, the orange side is a more plausible candidate— except that the marble must pass through the rubber tubing before it can reach the second box which contains the bell. Mendelson and Shultz (1975) showed children this apparatus in two conditions. In one condition the rubber tubing was present, and in the second condition the first box sat directly on top of the second. They found that when the tubing was present, most of the children (who were aged 4–7 years) attributed the ringing of the bell to the green side of the box. However, when the tubing was absent, most of the children attributed the ringing of the bell to the orange side of the box, even though they knew that in some cases dropping a marble into the hole in the orange side failed to make the bell ring. Mendelson and Shultz concluded that, in the absence of a physical rationale for a temporal delay, children assigned more causal importance to information about temporal contiguity than to information about covariation. However, when they could see a reason for the temporal delay (the rubber tubing), then they attributed causality to the consistent covariate (the green side), despite the lack of temporal contiguity.

The principle of the similarity of causes and effects

So far, we have seen that young children's causal reasoning follows the principles of priority, covariation, and temporal contiguity. When attempting to reason about causality in the absence of any information about temporal contiguity or covariation, however, the *similarity* of potential causes and effects can be useful. For example, imagine that you are shown a box that is equipped with a heavy lever and a delicate lever, which can either emit a loud electric bell sound or a very gentle sound. The typical assumption in these circumstances is that the delicate lever is the cause of the gentle sound and the heavy lever is the cause of the loud sound. Similarly, if you are shown two small bottles of clear fluid, one with a pink cap and one with a blue cap, and you are also shown a flask of water that is tinged pink, then the typical assumption is that the pink colouring was caused by fluid from the bottle with the pink cap. Of course, if you are then shown that a drop of fluid from the bottle with the blue cap turns the water pink, and a drop of fluid from the bottle with the pink cap has no effect on the colour of the water, then this covariation information is likely to change your causal attribution. Similarly, if you are shown that a drop of fluid from the bottle with the blue cap has no effect on water colour, and then five seconds later that a drop from the bottle with the pink cap immediately turns the water blue, this temporal contiguity information is likely to change your causal attribution as well.

Shultz and Ravinsky (1977) used a number of physical reasoning problems of this type to see whether, in the absence of information about covariation or temporal contiguity, young children would make causal inferences on the basis of the similarity of cause and effect. They were also interested in whether young children would abandon the similarity principle when it conflicted with temporal and covariance information. Shultz and Ravinsky tested children aged 6, 8, 10, and 12 years with a variety of physical problems, presenting a variety of covariation and temporal contiguity information in addition to similarity information. In the *absence* of information about temporal contiguity or covariation, all of the children used similarity information to make their causal attributions. When information about *covariation* conflicted with similarity information, then the older children (10- and 12-year-olds) abandoned the use of similarity information. The younger children appeared confused about which principle to apply, and did not make consistent attributions. A similar pattern was found when information about *temporal contiguity* conflicted with similarity information, although in this case only the 6-year-olds showed the confused pattern of responding. Shultz and Ravinsky concluded that similarity of causes and their effects is a potent principle of causal inference for children at all ages, but that the abandonment of this principle in situations of conflict occurs at an earlier age for conflicting temporal information than for conflicting covariation information.

Does this mean that developmentally, temporal information is recognised to have causal importance prior to covariation information? As Shultz and Ravinsky point out, this would fit Mendelson and Shultz's (1975) data (described earlier) based on the experiment with a marble and some rubber tubing. Here, too, children preferred to attribute causality to a temporally contiguous but inconsistent event rather than to a temporally non-contiguous but consistent event. However, before such a general conclusion can be reached, the comparison of children's use of temporal and covariation information over a wider range of paradigms is probably required. Given more recent data collected by Bullock, Gelman and their co-workers using the jack-in-the-box paradigm and the Fred-the-Rabbit paradigm (see later), it seems most probable that *all* of the causal principles discussed here are available to young children. Their judgements in any particular paradigm will depend on what is *causally relevant* to the experimental set-up. Shultz himself has recently argued for a version of this position, pointing out that an effect is most likely to be attributed to a cause that seems capable of directing the appropriate sort of *transmission* (Shultz, Fisher, Pratt, & Rulf, 1986).

The understanding of causal chains

Children's grasp of causal transmission can be examined by studying their understanding of three-term causal chains. The experiments discussed so far have all involved two-term causal chains. The use of three-term causal chains results in a more complex reasoning task, as the presence of a *mediate cause* requires a transitive inference as well as an understanding of physical causal contingencies (see Shultz, Pardo, & Altmann, 1982). In a three-term causal chain, an event A causes an event B to occur, which in turn results in an event C. For example, a tennis ball (A) can be rolled so that it strikes a golf ball (B), which in turn strikes a light plastic ball (C), dislodging it from its resting position. The golf ball is a *mediate* cause, as to predict whether the tennis ball will set the plastic ball in motion, the child must make a transitive inference based on the relations between the tennis ball and the golf ball and the plastic ball and the golf ball. The golf ball is analogous to the middle term in a transitive inference problem (transitive inference problems are discussed further in Chapter 7). If the child understands that A causes C, then that understanding must involve the knowledge that B functions as a causal mediator. The understanding of causal mediators also necessitates the understanding of the causal principles discussed in the preceding section.

The understanding of mediate transmission

Shultz et al. (1982) gave 3- and 5-year-old children simple causal chains of the type just described in two conditions. In one condition, the mediate causal event (B) was effective, and in the other it was not. For example, to administer the tennis ball problem, Shultz et al. devised an apparatus in which balls of different sizes could roll along converging lanes (see Fig. 4.3). The first pair of lanes was wide enough for tennis balls, the second pair for golf balls, and the lanes then converged onto a single lane for a light plastic ball. The light plastic ball was positioned at the point of convergence, so that following impact from the golf ball, it would roll to the end of the apparatus. On each side of the apparatus an arch was created that separated the tennis ball lane from the golf ball lane. These arches were too narrow for the golf ball to pass through. In order for the golf ball to act as a mediate cause, it therefore had to be on the far side of an arch. In order to create the two conditions, on one side of the apparatus the golf ball was on the near side of the arch (at Y'—ineffective mediate cause), and on the other it was on the far side of the arch (at Y—effective mediate cause).

The children's job was to choose which of the lanes to roll the tennis ball along in order to dislodge the light plastic ball from its position at the point of convergence of the lanes. If the child chose lane Y', then the plastic ball would not be dislodged, whereas if the child chose lane Y then the desired outcome could occur. The sides of the ineffective and effective mediate causes were varied at random over 10 trials. Shultz et al. found that the children were able to select the correct lane for the tennis ball on the majority of trials. The correct lane was chosen on 69% of trials by the 3-year-olds and on 86% of trials by the 5-year-olds. Most of the errors were on the first trial, and also on the third trial for the 3-year-olds. From the fourth trial onwards, children of both ages were consistently correct in choosing the lane with the effective mediate cause.

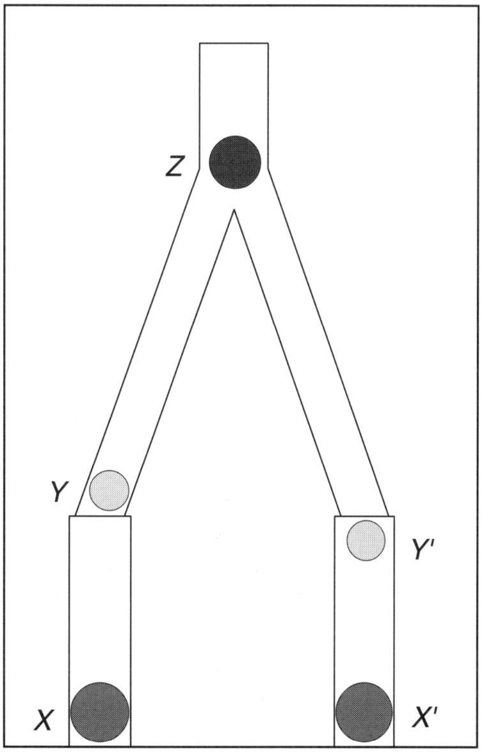

FIG. 4.3.
The runway apparatus used to study children's understanding of mediate causal transmission by Shultz et al. (1982). Reproduced with permission.

Children's understanding of three-term causal chains has also been investigated by Baillargeon and Gelman (1980, described in Bullock et al., 1982). They designed a "Fred-the-Rabbit" apparatus, in which the final step in the causal chain consisted of a rabbit (Fred) falling into his bed (a mat at the end of the apparatus). Fred was first presented to the children standing on a platform above his bed. The mediate cause for getting Fred into his bed was a series of wooden blocks, which were arranged in a row in front of the platform like a series of dominoes (see Fig. 4.4). Each block in turn could fall onto the block in front (in a "domino effect"), thereby causing the final block to fall onto a lever which pushed Fred off his platform and into his bed. The initial cause in the chain was a rod positioned in a post, which could be pushed through the post to activate the first block in the series. The children's task was to explain how to get Fred into his bed.

The children were first shown the entire apparatus during pretest demonstration trials. The mid-portion of the apparatus (the blocks) was then covered, leaving only the rod in its post and Fred on his platform visible to the child. The rod and Fred were separated by a distance of around one metre. The children (4- and 5-year-olds) correctly predicted that Fred could be got into his bed by pushing the rod through the post. The experimenter then introduced two new rods, a short one that was of insufficient length to reach the first block, and a long one that was of sufficient length. Both rods failed to get Fred into his bed (the longer rod was prevented from working by a trick). The children were asked to explain why each rod had failed to get Fred into his bed.

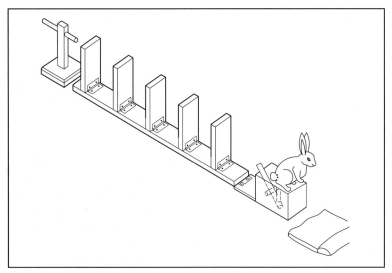

FIG. 4.4.
The "Fred-the-Rabbit" apparatus used by Bullock, Baillargeon and Gelman (1982). Reproduced by permission of Academic Press Inc.

Baillargeon and Gelman found that the children were able to offer causally coherent explanations in both cases, distinguishing between relevant (short rod) and irrelevant (long rod) modifications. For the short rod they said that the rod was too short to reach the first block, and for the long rod they said that the experimenter must have done something to disrupt the mediating event, such as taken some of the blocks away. Baillargeon, Gelman, and Meck (1981, reported in Bullock et al., 1982) then extended the Fred-the-Rabbit task to 3- and 4-year-olds. The children were asked to predict whether Fred would fall into his bed following a variety of modifications to either the initial or the mediate event. Modifications to the initial event included substituting a soft, flexible rod for the wooden rod, and substituting a rod with a stopper on the end that could not pass through the post. Modifications to the mediate event included the experimenter moving Fred's platform away from the final block in the series, and the experimenter moving the platform to one side of the blocks. Children's predictions were highly accurate whether the initial or the mediate event was changed (81% and 78% correct, respectively, for the 3-year-olds, 87% and 85% correct, respectively, for the 4-year-olds).

From this research, it seems that even very young children can use information about three-term causal chains to reason about event sequences. This holds true whether causal reasoning is measured via a prediction task (Baillargeon et al., 1981) or via a problem-solving task (Shultz et al., 1982). As performance in prediction tasks is often inferior to performance in problem-solving tasks (e.g. Goswami & Brown, 1990), Baillargeon et al.'s data provide particularly strong evidence that children understand mediate transmission by 3 years of age.

The understanding of logical search

A different way of measuring children's understanding of the causal constraints on event sequences is to use search tasks. For example, imagine that you are on a visit to the zoo and that you want to photograph the chimpanzees, but you find that you have lost your camera. As the chimpanzees are about the eighth group of animals that you have visited, one strategy for finding the camera is to try to remember the last animals that you photographed. If you clearly remember taking a photo of the lions, but you don't recall taking a photo of the elephants, then you probably lost your camera somewhere after the lion enclosure but before you reached the elephants. If young children can use this kind of causal logic when searching for objects, then this must entail some understanding of causal chains and causal necessity.

In a playground version of the logical search task just described, Wellman, Somerville, and Haake (1979) took children aged 3, 4, and 5 years around eight different locations in a playground (see Fig. 4.5). Each location was visited in turn. Upon arrival in each new location, the experimenter and the child played a distinctive game, such as jumping in the sandbox or hopping in tyres. At location 3, the experimenter took a photograph of the child doing the long jump as this made a good "action shot". At location 7, the experimenter was about to take another photograph when he discovered that his camera was missing. The children's job was to help him to find it. Wellman et al. were interested in whether the children would limit their searching behaviour to the critical area (between locations 3 and 7), or would search all of the areas that had been visited in turn. In a control condition, the experimenter discovered the loss of a calculator that had been in his bag throughout the experiment. The loss was discovered at location 8, and so in this control condition searching at each location in turn was an appropriate search strategy.

The important measure was the number of searches that were in the critical area (between locations 3 and 7) in both conditions. Wellman et al. found that most of the children concentrated their searches in the critical area in the camera condition, but not in the calculator condition. There were no marked age differences. The 3-year-olds seemed as capable of logical searching behaviour as the 5-year-olds. However, closer inspection of the data revealed that half of the searches in the critical target area were actually searches at location 3, the location where

FIG. 4.5.
Schematic depiction of the playground used in the logical search study devised by Wellman et al. (1979), showing the eight locations and their associated games. Copyright © by the American Psychological Association. Reprinted with permission.

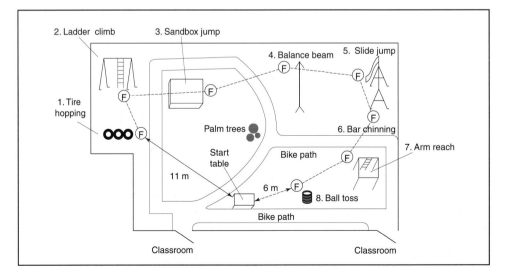

the camera had last been seen. Because of this, it is not clear whether the children in Wellman et al.'s study understood that each of the locations between 3 and 7 was *equally likely* to contain the missing camera.

This point was made by Somerville and Capuani-Shumaker (1984), who set out to investigate more directly the question of whether young children understand the causal implications of a sequence of events. Again using a search task as their critical measure, they devised a hiding and finding task in which two locations were at any one time equally likely to contain a hidden toy. This toy was a small Minnie Mouse doll, which could be concealed at one of four possible locations by the experimenter. However, in some of the hiding and finding trials it was more logical to go *forwards* and search in the next two locations from where the Minnie Mouse doll had last been seen, and in others it was more logical to go *backwards* and search in the previous two locations. Somerville and Capuani-Shumaker were interested in whether young children would recognise that some search sequences were more logical than others.

The experimental set-up consisted of a dark tablecloth with the four possible hiding locations marked by smaller stiff white cloths. Each cloth was pulled up into a peak so that it was unclear whether it concealed a Minnie Mouse doll or not. In a given *hiding* trial, the experimenter showed the children the Minnie Mouse doll in her hand, closed her hand and then moved it beneath the first two cloths, pausing beneath each in turn. She then opened her hand to show the children whether the doll was still present or not, closed her hand again and moved it beneath the second two cloths. If the Minnie Mouse doll was still *present* after cloth 2, then the children were meant to infer that the hiding location had to be cloth 3 or cloth 4. If the Minnie Mouse doll was *absent* after cloth 2, the children were meant to infer that the hiding location had to be cloth 1 or cloth 2.

The *finding* tasks were the inverse of the hiding tasks (see Fig. 4.6). This time the children's job was to find Minnie Mouse's *sister*, who always liked to hide together with Minnie under a cloth. In the finding trials, the adult's hand was always empty to begin with, and then after passing beneath cloth 2 was either shown to be still empty or to now contain Minnie Mouse. The question was whether the children could infer that Minnie's sister must be hiding under cloth 3 or cloth 4 when Minnie Mouse was still absent after cloth 2, but must be hiding under cloth 1 or cloth 2 when Minnie Mouse was present after cloth 2. Both 3- and 4-year-olds were tested.

Somerville and Capuani-Shumaker scored the first location at which the children searched. They found that the children were able to narrow

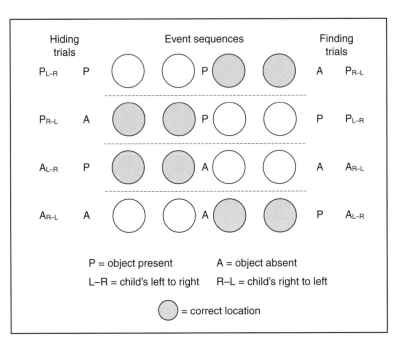

FIG. 4.6. Schematic depiction of the sequences of events in the hiding and finding tasks devised by Somerville and Capuani-Shumaker (1984). Reproduced with permission.

down the potentially correct hiding locations of Minnie and her sister to two out of the possible four, as searching behaviour was above chance at both age levels. Interestingly, first searches were also significantly more likely to be correct when the children had to reason from the continued *presence* of Minnie after location 2 in the hiding task, and from the continued *absence* of Minnie after location 2 in the finding task. This suggests that the causal implications of the event sequences were easier to understand when the cause and the effect were temporally more contiguous. This reflects use of one of the principles of causal reasoning discussed earlier. However, when the experimenters scored the children's second searches, they found that they were by no means always correct. This was surprising given that an incorrect first search in the target area left only one plausible alternative hiding or finding location. Subsequent experiments replicating and extending Somerville and Capuani-Shumaker's basic design have shown that, although even 2-year-olds respond logically on their first searches (Haake & Somerville, 1985), children younger than 4 appear to search by considering only one possibility at a time (Sophian & Somerville, 1988). Having searched in the critical area on their first search, they sometimes search outside the critical area on their second search. Thus the causal implications of the hiding and finding event sequences studied by

Somerville and her colleagues do not seem to be fully understood before the age of 4 years.

Scientific reasoning: The understanding of situations involving multiple causal variables

The research discussed so far has shown that the basic principles of causal reasoning are well established by the age of 4. However, even though the different causal principles appear to be available to young children, related research has shown that difficulties arise when they have to use the different causal principles to *rule out* potential causal variables as the cause of a particular effect. This involves an understanding of the "scientific method". When young children are asked to determine the causes of a particular phenomenon, they may fail to test a hypothesis in a systematic way, omitting to control for confounding variables. They may also fail to seek evidence that could disconfirm their hypotheses, and they may accept causes that account for only part of the available data (Sodian, Zaitchek, & Carey, 1991). In short, younger children appear to have little understanding of the components of *scientific* reasoning.

Most of the evidence supporting the position that young children are poor scientific reasoners has come from the work of Kuhn and her colleagues, who have conducted extensive studies of children's understanding of hypotheses and evidence (e.g. Kuhn, Amsel, & O'Loughlin, 1988; see also discussion of Piaget, Chapter 8). Kuhn's studies have suggested that children have little understanding of how hypotheses are supported or contradicted by causal evidence until around 11 or 12 years of age (e.g. Kuhn, 1989). This has led her to argue that younger children are incapable of "scientific thinking"—the kind of thinking that requires the co-ordination and differentiation of theories and evidence, and the evaluation of hypotheses via evidence and experimentation (see also Klahr, Fay, & Dunbar, 1993). Young children do not seem to know what kind of causal evidence does or could support a particular hypothesis, or what kind of evidence does or would contradict a particular theory.

For example, Kuhn et al. (1988) reported an experiment in which subjects were asked to evaluate evidence about the covariation of the various foods that children ate at a hypothetical boarding school, and their susceptibility to colds. The children, who were aged 11 and 14 years, were given the covariation information about the different foods pictorially (see Fig. 4.7). For example, in the figure, apples and french fries (chips) covary perfectly with colds, and *Special K®* and *Coca-cola®*

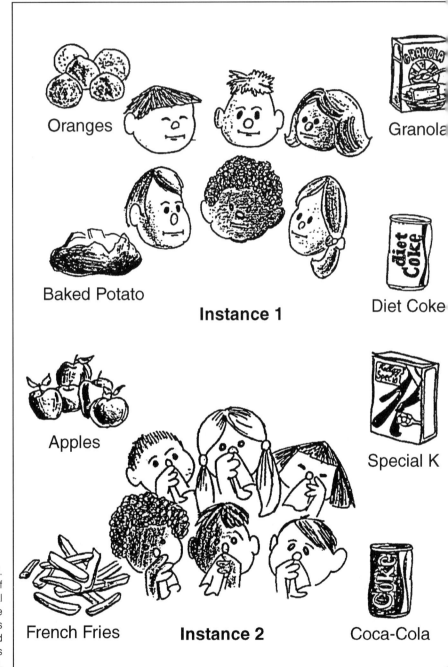

Oranges

Granola

Baked Potato

Instance 1

Diet Coke

Apples

Special K

French Fries

Instance 2

Coca-Cola

FIG. 4.7.
Four examples of
the pictorial
covariation evidence
concerning foods
eaten and
susceptibility to colds
(Kuhn et al., 1988).

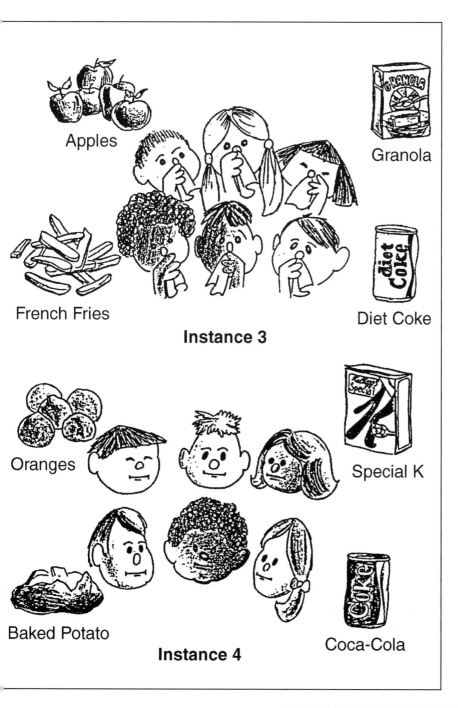

Apples

Granola

French Fries

Diet Coke

Instance 3

Oranges

Special K

Baked Potato

Coca-Cola

Instance 4

do not. The children were then asked questions like "Does the kind of drink the children have make any difference in whether they get lots of colds or very few colds?". Only the older children showed an ability to evaluate the covariation evidence effectively, although their performance was far from perfect. The spontaneous evidence-based responses given by the 11-year-olds constituted 30% of responses, and of the 14-year-olds, 50% of responses. Adults performed at the same level as the 14-year-olds.

Kuhn et al. (1988) also reported that children showed a strong tendency to make incorrect inferences about causality based on "inclusion errors". Inclusion errors involve the attribution of causal status to variables that only covary with the outcome on a single occasion. In our example, the children would accept a single instance of a food covarying with colds as evidence that the food was a cause of susceptibility to colds (e.g. *Granola* in Fig. 4.7). Such incorrect single-instance inclusion inferences were made on 47% of occasions by the 11-year-olds, and on 65% of occasions by the 14-year-olds. Kuhn points out that this is an error-prone strategy for inferring causal relations, because even though inclusion inferences may on occasion be correct, they may also be false. Kuhn et al.'s ongoing investigations (e.g. Kuhn, Garcia-Mila, Zohar, & Andersen, 1995) have suggested that an important source of the persistence of inclusion errors is the prior theories that children hold about the causal status of the variables being investigated. These prior beliefs influence the selection of the instances that are attended to, and are relied upon when justifying conclusions about causality. Adults are more likely to attend to the evidence at hand, even though they may still make inferential errors in interpreting it.

Sodian et al. (1991) were interested in how children would perform in reasoning tasks that were not set in contexts (like "catching a cold") that were probably already the subject of strongly held beliefs. In order to see whether young children have any insights into the relationship between hypotheses and evidence in a novel context, Sodian et al. asked children to choose between a conclusive and an inconclusive test of a hypothesis. They used a simple paradigm in which pre-existing beliefs were unlikely to be evoked, which also involved a single test that was sufficient to draw a causal conclusion. The test concerned how two brothers could decide whether they had a small or a large mouse in their house.

In Sodian et al.'s experiment, 6- and 8-year-old children were told a story about two brothers who knew that they had a mouse in their house, even though they had not actually seen it (because it only came out at night). One brother believed that it was "a big daddy mouse" and the other believed that it was "a little baby mouse". The problem was how they could decide who was right. To test their hypotheses about the size of the mouse, the brothers were planning to put some cheese into a box for the mouse to eat. Two boxes were available, one with a large opening that could take either the large or the small mouse, and the other with a small opening that would only allow the small mouse to enter. The children had to decide which box the brothers should use in order to determine the size of the mouse. The majority of children in both age groups realised that the box with the small opening was required. As one child remarked (Sodian et al., 1991, p.758) "They should take the house with the small opening, and if the food is gone, this tells them that it is a small mouse, and if it's still there it is a big mouse." Sodian et al. concluded that even quite young children understand the goal of testing a hypothesis, and can distinguish between conclusive and inconclusive tests of that hypothesis in simplified circumstances.

More recently, Ruffman, Perner, Olson, and Doherty (1993) devised a "Fake Evidence" task to investigate whether even younger children can work out how a pattern of evidence relates to a hypothesis when only a single cause is involved. The children's task was to work out which kind of food was more likely to lead to tooth loss, green food or red food (the "food" consisted of bits of coloured paper). Both 4- and 5-year-olds were shown consecutive pictures of 10 boys in the act of eating food. Five of them were eating green food and had healthy teeth, and five of them were eating red food and had teeth missing. The children were asked "Which type of food makes kids' teeth fall out?". All of them answered that it was red food (showing use of the covariation principle).

The children were then shown a picture of 10 boys' heads, five with missing teeth and five with intact teeth. Directly in front of each boy's mouth was a piece of red or green food, depicting the covariation information. The experimenter then "faked" the evidence, rearranging the food so that the opposite pattern of tooth loss was suggested (that green food caused tooth loss). A doll, Sally, was introduced, who didn't know that the evidence had been faked. The children were asked "When Sally sees things the way they are now, which food will she say makes kids' teeth fall out?". The majority of the 5-year-olds correctly said that Sally would arrive at a mistaken hypothesis. In a second experiment in which the faked covariation evidence was not perfect (so that the *pattern* of covariation was in favour of a particular hypothesis), 5-year-olds were unsuccessful in realising that Sally would arrive at a mistaken hypothesis, but 6-year-olds were successful (4-year-olds were not tested). Ruffman et al. concluded that, by the age of around 6 years, children understand how simple covariation information forms the basis for a hypothesis.

Despite these positive findings, however, Kuhn's basic proposal appears to hold. When children have to make causal inferences in situations involving *many* potential causal variables, they experience some difficulty, even though their basic causal intuitions are sound. As Kuhn et al. (1995) pointed out, many adults also perform poorly in fully fledged scientific reasoning tasks—tasks that require them to examine a database and draw conclusions. Conducting scientific investigations into the relations between variables in real-world situations is simply not an easy task when many variables are present. Multivariable causal inferences thus remain difficult even *beyond* childhood.

Integrating causal information about different physical dimensions

The need to *integrate* information about different causes is characteristic of causal reasoning in everyday life, however, as we seldom have to reason about causes and their effects in isolation. Instead, we frequently have to reason about more than one cause at a time. Even everyday problems require us to take into account many causal factors and their effects, and some of the causal factors relevant to a particular problem may interact with each other. Causal reasoning is thus *usually* multi-dimensional.

To take a trivial example, imagine that you are trying to decide whether you have enough time to go to the post office during your lunch hour. You need to consider not only how far the post office is, how long your lunch hour is, and how fast you can walk, but also whether it is raining (this could affect speed and time), whether sufficient cashiers will be available to prevent long queues (this could affect time in the post office itself), and whether there are any potential hold-ups en route. In other words, you will need to consider many causal factors and how they may interact with each other before deciding whether it is actually worth trying to go to the post office.

The integration of knowledge about two dimensions

The question of when young children become able to interrelate information about different causal dimensions has been investigated using a variety of paradigms. We will begin by considering experiments that investigate children's ability to interrelate information about two causal dimensions, and we will then consider experiments that investigate children's ability to interrelate information about three causal dimensions. One of the best-known paradigms for investigating children's ability to interrelate information about two causal dimensions is the balance scale task.

The balance scale task.   The balance scale task measures children's ability to interrelate information about weight and distance. A typical apparatus consists of two arms of equal length that extend from a central fulcrum, like a see-saw (see Fig. 4.8). Each arm can have weights attached to it at different distances from the fulcrum. The child's task is to predict which side of the balance scale will go down when different combinations of weights are placed at different distances from the centre. In order to judge this correctly, children must take into account *both* the relative number of weights and their relative distance from the fulcrum, and then combine these variables multiplicatively. For example, if three weights are placed on one arm of the balance scale 20cm from the fulcrum, and six weights are placed on the other arm 10cm from the fulcrum, the scale will balance. However, if both groups of weights are placed 10cm from the fulcrum, then the side with six weights on it will go down.

Siegler (1978) used a balance scale to assess the different *rules* that children use to interrelate information about weight and distance during cognitive development. His method was to ask the children to make judgements about which arm of the balance scale would go down in a choice format that held one variable (weight or distance) constant while varying the other. For example, in *distance* problems, the same number of weights were placed on each arm, but at different distances from the fulcrum. In *weight* problems, different numbers of weights were placed on each arm, but at the same distance from the fulcrum. In *conflict-weight* problems, there were more weights on one arm, but the fewer weights on the other arm were at a greater distance from the fulcrum (e.g. two weights 8cm from the fulcrum vs. three weights 6cm from the fulcrum: weight wins), and so on. Girls aged 5, 9, 13, and 17 were tested.

Siegler's results led him to postulate that the development of physical understanding in the balance scale task proceeded through four different rules. Only the final rule involved the integration of the

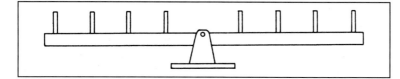

FIG. 4.8.
A balance scale apparatus.

different causal dimensions (see Fig. 4.9). The first three rules depended on considering the dimensions of weight and distance *separately*, without trying to integrate them. Children who used rule 1 always said that the arm with the most weights would go down. Children who used rule 2 took into account distance information, but only when the two arms had equal weights. In all other cases, they ignored distance and made judgements on the basis of relative weight. Children who used rule 3 showed a developmental progression to considering distance information as well as weight information, but only when the two variables did not conflict. When one side had a greater weight and the other side had a greater distance, as in the *conflict-weight* problem given earlier, performance was at chance. Only children who used rule 4 showed an ability to integrate weight and distance information multiplicatively.

FIG. 4.9.
An illustration of the four rules proposed by Siegler (1978) to explain the development of physical understanding in the balance scale task.

Rule 1: Is weight the same?	If **YES**, then **balance** If **NO**, then **greater weight down**	
Rule 2: Is weight the same?	If **YES**, then check distance Is distance the same? ➝ If **NO**, then **greater weight down**	If **YES**, then **balance** If **NO**, then **greater distance down**
Rule 3: Is weight the same?	If **YES**, then check distance Is distance the same? ➝ If **NO**, then check distance Is distance the same? ➝ 	If **YES**, then **balance** If **NO**, then **greater distance down** If **YES**, then **greater weight down** If **NO**, then check — if greater weight is same side as greater distance? If **YES**, then **greater weight and distance down** If **NO**, then **muddle through**
Rule 4: Is weight the same?	If **YES**, then check distance Is distance the same? ➝ If **NO**, then check distance Is distance the same? ➝ 	If **YES**, then **balance** If **NO**, then **greater distance down** If **YES**, then **greater weight down** If **NO**, then check — if greater weight is same side as greater distance? If **YES**, then **greater weight and distance down** If **NO**, then check — are cross products the same? If **YES**, then **balance** If **NO**, then **greater product down**

However, Wilkening and Anderson (1991) argued that Siegler's task could *underestimate* younger children's ability to apply integration rules because of a problem with "false positive" responses. They pointed out that younger children might be using a simpler integration rule of *adding* weight and distance information rather than a more sophisticated rule of multiplying weight and distance. Such children would be scored by Siegler as following a non-integration rule (one of rules 1–3, and therefore show a "false positive"), whereas in fact they were following a *simpler form* of an integrative rule. To test their idea, Wilkening and Anderson asked children to *adjust* the position of a fixed set of weights on one arm of the balance scale in order to balance a set of varying weights on the other.

The adjustment task required the children to adjust either weight or distance. For example, if the fixed set was three weights placed 12cm from the fulcrum and the variable set was one, two, three, or four weights placed at 6, 12, 18, or 24cm from the fulcrum, then the children had to adjust the distance of the fixed set in order to balance the scale. To balance one weight at 6cm, the children would have to move their fixed set to 2cm from the fulcrum; to balance one weight at 12cm the children would have to move their fixed set to 4cm from the fulcrum, and so on. This was the *distance* adjustment task. An analogous *weight* adjustment task was also used, in which a fixed set of two weights at 24cm had to be adjusted by adding more weights to balance either one, two, three, or four weights placed at 8, 16, 24, or 32cm from the fulcrum. Using the adjustment methodology, Wilkening and Anderson found that 9-year-olds, 12-year-olds, and adults all used multiplicative integration rules to combine information about relative weight and distance. The youngest children tested (6-year-olds) tended to focus on either weight or distance, without trying to integrate the two. Nevertheless, Wilkening and Anderson argued that their data showed that children's causal understanding in the balance scale task was seriously underestimated by Siegler's methodology.

Integrating information about the causal effects of forces. Another type of physical information that must be integrated in the real world is information about forces. Consider a tug-of-war. This is a simple force problem. Two teams of men are pulling on the ends of a rope. Both teams hope to move the centre of the rope beyond a certain pre-agreed point. If one team consists of 20 men and the other team of 10 men, then most people would predict that the team of 20 men should win the tug-of-war. The reason is that this team should exert the stronger force. However, if the team of 10 men all weigh 20 stones or more, and the team of 20 men all weigh 8 stones or less, then the prediction might go the other way. Perhaps the combined force of 10 strong men will be greater than the combined force of 20 weak men. Alternatively, if the teams are *equal* in number and in strength, then the centre of the rope may not move at all. The forces may cancel each other out.

Pauen (1996c) gave a version of this force problem to young children. As well as the special case of two forces acting at 180° to each other (the tug-of-war), she used problems in which two forces acted at 45°, 75°, and 105° to each other. The forces, which were represented by weights, were in the ratios 1:2, 1:3, and 1:6 respectively. In order to solve these problems correctly, the children had to combine two force vectors. The problem was presented using a special apparatus called a force table (see Fig. 4.10).

The force table consisted of an object that was fixed at the centre of a round platform. Two forces acted on this object, both represented by plates of weights. The plates of weights hung from cords attached to the central object at either 45°, 75°, or 105° to each other. The children's job was to work out the trajectory of the object once it was released from its fixed position. Although the central object was never actually released, the children had to move a barrier surrounding the platform until an opening in the barrier was in exactly the right position to catch the object. Their predictions were measured and scored in terms of whether the opening in the barrier was positioned closer to one or the other plate of weights, or was equidistant from both.

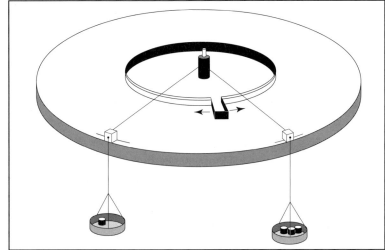

FIG. 4.10.
The force table
used by Pauen
(1996c).

The force table problem was presented to the children in the context of a story about a King (central object) who had got tired of skating on a frozen lake (the platform) and who wanted to be pulled into his royal bed on the shore (a box behind the opening in the barrier). The children were asked to turn the barrier so that the royal bed would be in the right place for the king to slide into it. Different combinations of weights were used, and children aged 6, 7, 8, and 9 years of age were tested. Pauen found that most of the younger children (80–85%) predicted that the king would move in the direction of the stronger force only. For example, if there were three weights on one plate and one weight on the other, these children would move the opening in the barrier so that it was directly below the cord holding the plate with three weights (the "one-force-only" rule).

An ability to consider the two forces simultaneously was shown by some of the 9-year-olds (45%). These children realised that the correct location for the opening in the barrier was near the cord holding the heavier weights, but not exactly below it. However, although they showed this insight on some trials, they reverted to the one-force-only rule on other trials. Pauen thus judged them to be in a transitional stage regarding the integration rule. Very few children (5–10% across all groups) showed pure integration rule behaviour. Such behaviour required the placing of the opening in the barrier between the bisector of the angle and the stronger force. However, such integration rule responses were shown by the majority of the adults tested (63%).

In the special cases when the forces were at 180° to each other (analogous to the tug-of-war situation described earlier), the majority of children at all ages tested gave the correct answer to the force problem. Pauen thus decided to change the situational context of the force problem, to see whether it would be easier for children to use the integration rule if the forces were represented by men pulling on ropes rather than by weights sitting on plates. In a second experiment using the force table, she replaced the plates of weights with teams of toy people pulling on ropes (see Fig. 4.11). The children were told that two groups of cowboys were trying to pull a barrel to the shore in order to take it to their camp.

In this replication, fewer of the younger children used the incorrect one-force-only rule (40–50% instead of 80–85%). However, correct integration solutions did not increase. Furthermore, the solution of the special-case (180°) problems actually *decreased* when Pauen used the cowboys context with the younger children. Pauen speculated that this may have been because the children who received the plates of weights applied a balance scale analogy to the force integration

FIG. 4.11.
The force table
used in Pauen's (in
press) cowboys
paradigm.

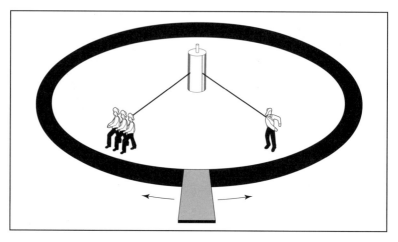

problem. A balance scale analogy gives rise to one-force-only solutions, which are correct in the case of the 180° problems, but not in the cases of the 45°, 75°, or 105° problems.

Erroneous analogies to balance scale problems in reasoning about the causal effects of forces. Pauen's idea about the balance scale analogy was prompted by the comments of the children themselves, who said that the force table reminded them of a balance scale (presumably because of the plates of weights). This led her to propose that the children were using spontaneous analogies in their reasoning about the physical laws underlying the force table, analogies that were in fact misleading. To investigate this idea further, Pauen and Wilkening (1997) decided to give 9-year-old children a training session with a balance scale prior to giving them the force table problem. One group of children received training with a traditional balance scale, in which they learned to apply the one-force-only rule, and a second group of children received training with a modified balance scale that had its centre of gravity below the axis of rotation (a "swing boat" suspension). This modified balance scale provided training in the integration rule, as the swing boat suspension meant that even though the beam rotated towards the stronger force, the degree of deflection depended on the size of *both* forces. These two balance scales are depicted in Fig. 4.12. In each case, the children had to predict the location of a pointer attached to the centre of the beam for different ratios of weights. When the beam was balanced, the pointer pointed straight up.

Following the balance scale training, the children were given the force table task with the plates of weights. A third group of children

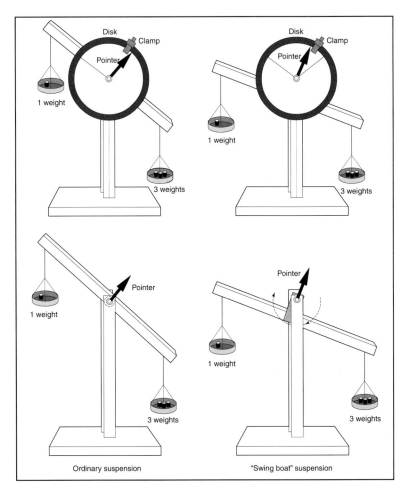

FIG. 4.12.
The balance scale
apparatus used to
provide training in (a)
the "one force only"
rule vs. (b) the
integration rule
(Pauen and
Wilkening, in press).
Reproduced with
permission.

Disk

Clamp

Pointer

1 weight

3 weights

Disk

Clamp

Pointer

1 weight

3 weights

Pointer

1 weight

3 weights

Ordinary suspension

Pointer

1 weight

3 weights

"Swing boat" suspension

received only the force table task, and acted as untrained controls. Pauen and Wilkening argued that an effect of the analogical training would be shown if the children who were trained with the traditional balance scale showed a greater tendency to use the one-force-only rule than the control group children, while the children who were trained with the modified balance scale showed a greater tendency to use the integration rule than the control group children. This was exactly the pattern that they found. The children's responses to the force table problem varied systematically with the solution provided by the analogical model. These results suggest that the children were using spontaneous analogies in their reasoning about physics, just as we have seen them do in their reasoning about biology (children's use of the personification analogy was discussed in Chapter 3). As discussed in more detail in Chapter 7, analogies seem to play an important role in children's everyday reasoning.

The integration of knowledge about three dimensions

Children's ability to interrelate information about three different dimensions has also been studied by Wilkening and his colleagues. In this work, they examined children's ability to interrelate information about time, distance, and velocity (e.g. Wilkening, 1981, 1982). Time, distance, and velocity information is crucial for a decision such as whether to go to the post office in one's lunch hour (discussed earlier). The critical information is "How long is my lunch hour?" (time), "How far is the post office?" (distance), and "How fast can I go?" (velocity). These variables are related by simple physical laws. For example, velocity is equivalent to distance divided by time, and distance is equivalent to time multiplied by velocity. In order to see whether children reason according to these physical laws when integrating information about time, distance, and velocity, Wilkening (1981) devised a task involving a turtle, a guinea pig, and a cat.

In Wilkening's task, children were shown a model of a footbridge with a turtle, a cat and a guinea pig fleeing along it. The animals were all fleeing at their own different speeds, and were running from a fierce barking dog, who was shown at the left side of the apparatus. The children's task was to judge how far each animal could run in a certain period of time. The time period was either 2, 5, or 8 seconds, and was represented in terms of the amount of time that the dog barked. The children made their judgements by moving each animal to the correct location on the footbridge after the dog had stopped barking. This version of the task required the children to integrate information about time and velocity in order to judge distance.

Wilkening also devised versions of the task that required the integration of distance and velocity, and the integration of distance and time. He argued that if the children could integrate these different sources of information successfully, then they should use multiplicative rules to make their judgements. For example, in the barking dog task just described, they should use the rule "distance equals time multiplied by velocity". When 5- and 10-year-old children were given the barking dog task, Wilkening found that both age groups did indeed use a multiplying rule, as did a control group of adults. However, in the other versions of the task the younger children did not always use the correct integration rules. For example, when asked to use information about distance and velocity to make judgements about time (judging how long the dog must have barked when shown the point that the turtle, the cat, or the guinea pig had reached on the footbridge), the youngest children used a subtraction rule. This suggested that they knew that the dog had barked for different amounts of time for each animal, but that they could not estimate these differences proportionally.

Even the adults used the wrong integration rule in some versions of the task, however. When asked to use information about distance and time to make judgements about velocity (deciding which animal would have been able to reach a certain point on the footbridge in the time that the dog barked), adults used a subtracting rule, just like the younger children in the time judgement task. From Wilkening's perspective, however, the fact that children and adults did not always select the correct rules was not critical. The important finding was that even 5-year-olds attempted to apply algebraic rules when trying to reason about different physical dimensions. This meant that they had some conceptual understanding of the separate variables involved, even though they (and the adults) occasionally selected the wrong algebraic rules to integrate these variables. Although the psychological rules used in information integration did not always mirror the physical rules of mechanics, Wilkening argued that his results implied an implicit understanding of dimensional interrelations—a naive or "intuitive" physics. Children were adopting a practical approach to the psychological integration of separate variables in which the procedures chosen did not *violate* the physical rules, but simplified them.

Intuitive physics

The idea of a naive or intuitive physics has now been defined theoretically by a number of developmental psychologists, and given a central role in explaining the development of physical reasoning. For example, according to Wilkening's view, intuitive physics is rooted in the perception of objects and events (see Anderson & Wilkening, 1991). Children's perceptions of the world around them become the basis of mental models that are formed to mimic the structure and action of physical systems, and these mental models are then used in reasoning about the physical world (see Russell, 1996, for a discussion of the role of mental models in children's reasoning). Mental models in Wilkening's sense include many different levels of knowledge all acting together. For example, Anderson and Wilkening suggest that the mental models used in intuitive physics incorporate knowledge about action and cognition as well as knowledge derived from perception. As we saw in Chapter 2, some mental models to explain physical events can be observed operating in infancy (e.g. Baillargeon, 1995; Spelke, 1991). Anderson (1983, p.252) himself once noted: "Learning of intuitive physics starts in the cradle."

Intuitive physics and projectile motion

Despite a growing body of evidence for an "intuitive physics", however, our intuitions about physical causation are not always correct. There are also some deeply held and intuitive *misconceptions* about physical phenomena. One of the best documented of these misconceptions concerns intuitions about projectile motion.

When asked to predict the trajectories of objects, adults as well as children seem to follow a "straight down" rule. They seem to believe that if an object is dropped by a walking person, then it will fall downwards in a straight line. In fact, it will fall forwards in a parabolic arc (e.g. Kaiser, Profitt, & McCloskey, 1985). Similarly, when asked to predict the motion of a ball ejected at speed from a curved tube shaped like the letter "C", adults and children judge that the ball will continue to move in a curvilinear arc, whereas in fact it follows a straight line with respect to the horizontal plane (e.g. Kaiser, McCloskey, & Profitt, 1986; see Fig. 4.13). A number of authors have noted that these misconceptions bear a striking resemblance to medieval physical theories, such as the medieval theory of motion in which the concept of impetus was very important (e.g. Viennot, 1979).

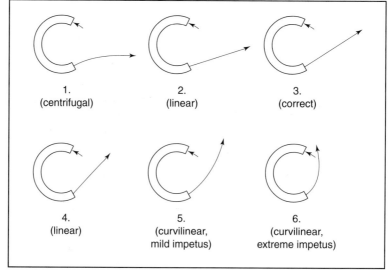

FIG. 4.13.
Schematic depiction of six alternative trajectories for the curved tube problem (Kaiser et al., 1986).

Intuitive but misleading concepts of mechanics may be very difficult to dislodge. For example, the "straight down rule" noted earlier is applied not only to projectile motion, but also in tasks that test children's understanding of the effects of gravity. One example is the "tubes task" invented by Hood (1995). In the tubes task, young children (2- to 4-year-olds) are asked to find a ball that is dropped into one of three tubes. The tubes are all opaque and they can be interwoven to form a visuo-spatial maze. When the tubes are interwoven, a reliance on the "straight down" rule will lead the child to search in the *wrong* location for the ball. The tubes task can be administered at different levels of difficulty by increasing the number of tubes and the complexity of their intertwining (see Fig. 4.14).

Hood found that children who erred in the tubes task consistently searched in the location directly beneath the point at which the ball was dropped. He termed this a "gravity error". Gravity errors were the most frequent kind of error at every difficulty level tested, although the ability to solve the tubes task at different levels was related to age (older children passed the easier levels) and sex (boys showed superior performance to girls). All erroneous search behaviour seemed to be predominantly determined by the straight-down trajectory, irrespective of the trajectory of the tube.

In later experiments using transparent tubes instead of opaque tubes, Hood showed that even the youngest children tested (2-year-olds) were able to search successfully for the ball when they could see its trajectory, and that this success occurred at all difficulty levels. Surprisingly, however, he found no evidence for transfer. Children who searched successfully with the transparent tubes were immediately given problems at the same level of difficulty with the opaque tubes, and promptly failed them. Even extensive training on the tubes task with a single tube failed to dislodge the prepotent gravity error in a group of 2-year-old children. Hood concluded that his task documented a growing understanding of the operation of tubes, and of how they constrain the movements of invisibly falling objects. This explanation suggests that the gravity error is an intuitive one, and

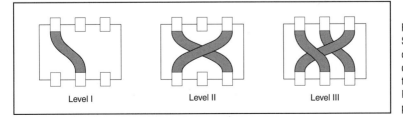

Level I   Level II   Level III

FIG. 4.14. Schematic depiction of different levels of difficulty in the "tubes" task (Hood, 1995). Reproduced with permission.

would recur in children who have become quite sophisticated in the tubes task if they were presented with a very different apparatus.

The distinction between knowledge and action

It is notable that most of the more complex causal reasoning tasks discussed so far have measured knowledge via action. For example, Shultz et al. (1982) asked children to roll tennis balls to measure their understanding of mediate transmission, Wilkening and Anderson (1991) asked children to move weights on a balance beam to measure their understanding of the integration of weight and distance information, and Wilkening (1982) asked children to move toy animals along a bridge to measure their understanding of the integration of three physical variables (time, distance, and velocity). One interesting possibility is that intuitive physical knowledge as measured by action may be *distinct from* intuitive physical knowledge as measured by judgement tasks. Judgement tasks require *reflection* on one's physical knowledge. For example, action-based knowledge about projectile motion may be fairly sophisticated, whereas explicit judgements about the same motions may be naive. Action-based knowledge and verbalisable knowledge may also follow different developmental paths (see Chapter 5, for a discussion of the different developmental paths followed by implicit/procedural and explicit/declarative knowledge). The possibility that intuitive physics is best measured directly, via action, was investigated by Krist, Fieberg, and Wilkening (1993), in a task using projectile motion.

The task used by Krist et al. was a throwing task; 6-year-olds, 10-year-olds, and adults were asked to throw a tennis ball from different heights so that it would hit a target on the floor. The subjects were asked to use a horizontal motion when throwing the tennis ball, which was somewhat awkward to produce as it involved sliding one's arm along a horizontal "throwing" board before releasing the ball. This meant that the speed with which the ball was released was critical if the ball were to reach its target. In addition, the height of the throwing board was varied during the experiment (a lower board requires a faster throw), and so variable throwing speeds were required. As well as requiring the subjects to throw the ball themselves, Krist et al. asked them to make judgements about how fast the ball should be released in order for it to reach the target when the throwing board was raised or lowered. These judgements were either required prior to, or following, the action phase of the experiment.

Krist et al. found that the functional relation between speed and height was present in the *action* data at all age levels tested, whereas it was only present in the *judgement* data for the adult subjects. Whereas the adults judged that a lower throwing table would require a faster speed of release, the 10-year-olds did not differentiate between the speeds required for the different height levels, and some of the 6-year-olds showed an *inverse* pattern, judging that greater heights would require greater speeds. In contrast, mean speeds of actual throwing represented the physical law very closely, across all age groups. Thus whereas performance in the judgement condition reflected a strong age trend towards integrating height and distance in an appropriate way, performance in the action condition showed an intuitive understanding of this relationship. These data fit the "mental models" explanation of naive physics proposed by Anderson and Wilkening (1991—discussed earlier). They imply that such models develop from the acquisition of perceptual-motor knowledge and skills, which in turn lead to the development of intuitive concepts of mechanics.

Causal reasoning and the direction of causality

Another variable thought to affect causal reasoning in adults is whether the direction of reasoning is "forwards", from cause to effect, or "backwards", from effect to cause. For example, Waldmann, Holyoak, and Fratianne (1995) have suggested that adults preferentially learn cause-to-effect relations rather than effect-to-cause relations, as this can reduce cognitive complexity in learning tasks. According to their "causal model" theory of learning, regardless of the temporal order in which causal information is received, the underlying mental representation of the situation will honour the cause-to-effect direction.

The temporal order in which causal information is received has not been seen as a particularly important variable in the development of causal reasoning, although perhaps it should be. For example, there was a suggestion from Blue's work using videos of canonical and non-canonical causal sequences that younger children performed at a high level when they could reason from effect to cause. In their work on infants' memory for events that have a causally necessary temporal order (such as "making a rattle" by putting a small object inside a container, see discussions of Mandler & McDonough in Chapter 2, and Bauer & Shore in Chapter 5), Bauer, Mandler, and their colleagues have found that infants are more successful in making a rattle when they are given information about the end state (the "effect") than when they are not (Bauer, Schwade, Wewerka, & Delaney, submitted). Other data (from 3-year-olds) also suggest that it may be easier to reason "backwards" from an effect to a cause than to reason "forwards" from a cause to an effect (Cutting, 1996). On the other hand, Bauer and her colleagues have found that children are unable to *imitate* reversed "making-a-rattle" sequences (beginning with the end state) until the age of around 36 months.

Cutting's work was based on two tasks devised by Cutting, Charlesworth, and Goswami (1991) to measure children's understanding of the "appearance–reality distinction" or ARD, which refers to the understanding that how things look is not always how they are. One aspect of the ARD is the understanding that objects placed behind coloured filters only *appear* to change colour. In reality, they are the same colour as before. In Cutting et al.'s ARD tasks, 3-year-old children were shown (for example) two crayons, one green and one yellow. Both crayons were then placed under a blue filter, so that they appeared to be identical shades of green. The children were told "We can draw yellow cars with yellow crayons, and green cars with green crayons. What can we draw with these crayons? Can we draw a yellow car and a green car, or can we draw two green cars?". This task involved *forwards* reasoning, from cause to effect (as well as an understanding of the appearance–reality distinction). In the *backwards* version of the appearance–reality task (from effect to cause), the children were asked "Which crayon can I use to draw a green lorry? This one [indicating one crayon] or this one [indicating the other crayon]?".

Children's ARD performance in these tasks showed a curious and consistent discrepancy that seemed best explained by the comparative ease of reasoning "backwards" from an effect to a cause rather than "forwards" from a cause to an effect. The "cars" task was more difficult than the "lorry" task, and similar results were found in a number of related experiments using a variety of materials. As Cutting pointed out, however, children in the forwards reasoning task had to reason about *two* effects (green vs. yellow cars), whereas children in the backwards reasoning task had to reason about a *single* effect (a green lorry). This in itself could have made the backwards reasoning task easier.

Cutting thus designed a new experiment which included an extra backwards reasoning condition. This was the "4-items" backwards reasoning task. In the "4-item" task the children were shown two *pairs* of crayons (green + green, and green + yellow, both then placed under blue filters). The children were told "I want two crayons to draw two green trucks with. Which two crayons can I use to draw two green trucks? These two [indicating one pair] or these two [indicating the other pair]?". Cutting argued that, as both the "2-item" and the "4-item" backwards reasoning tasks required the same kind of reasoning, they should be easier than the (2-item) forwards reasoning task, despite the variation in the number of causes and effects to be considered.

The results showed that only 27% of the answers in the forwards reasoning task were correct, compared to 70% and 78% correct respectively in the 2-item and the 4-item backwards reasoning tasks. Performance in the forwards reasoning task was significantly below chance, while performance in the backwards reasoning tasks was significantly above chance. Cutting argued that young children seem to find reasoning backwards, from effects to causes, easier than reasoning forwards, from causes to effects. However, she cautioned that more tasks involving variations in the number of causes and effects were required to support this conclusion properly. There may also be differences in the causal directions preferred in reasoning and problem-solving paradigms, such as those discussed here, and learning paradigms, such as those discussed by Waldmann et al. (1995). The question of whether children preferentially *learn* cause-to-effect relations rather than effect-to-cause relations, but preferentially *reason* about effect-to-cause relations rather than cause-to-effect relations seems a promising one for future research on the development of causal reasoning.

Summary

We began this chapter by arguing that an early focus on causal information is a critical mechanism in the development of children's cognition. We also noted that a causal focus could only offer impressive cognitive benefits if children's causal reasoning followed recognised causal principles. A variety of evidence has shown that children do indeed reason in accordance with causal principles, and do so from surprisingly early in development. Children follow the principle of causal priority, that causes precede or co-occur with their effects, the principle of covariation, that true causes regularly and predictably covary with their effects, and the principle of temporal contiguity, that causes and their effects must be contiguous in time and space. Furthermore, their application of these principles depends on what is *causally relevant* in a particular experimental paradigm.

Similarly, children seem to have some understanding of the relationship between hypotheses and evidence, although this understanding is less impressive early in development. In situations where there are multiple potential causes, children tend to make inclusion errors, attributing causal status to variables that may only covary with a particular outcome on a single occasion. On the other hand, in simplified contexts even 6-year-olds can distinguish between conclusive and inconclusive tests of a hypothesis. It is also worth noting that even teenagers and adults have difficulties in reasoning about multiple causal variables. They also have difficulties in integrating causal information on a variety of dimensions, as do young children. We saw that the integration of causal information was very difficult before the age of around 10 years. However, younger children did not completely fail to integrate causal information, rather they did so according to simplified integration rules. Furthermore, they could be misled by spontaneous analogies to inappropriate physical systems. Interestingly, when integration was measured in terms of *action* rather than judgement, then even 6-year-olds were very good at information integration. This suggests that it may be the ability to *reflect* on one's physical knowledge that improves with age, rather than the ability to integrate causal information *per se*.

Overall, therefore, the evidence suggests that causal reasoning shows remarkable continuities from childhood to adulthood. Causal inferences that come easily to adults also come easily to children, and causal inferences that are difficult for adults are also difficult for children. Both children and adults also hold some intuitive *misconceptions* about physical phenomena, not all of which decline with age. Nevertheless, a "naive physics" is discernible even in infancy.

Is the development of causal reasoning domain-general?

We noted at the beginning of this chapter that our focus would be on children's causal reasoning about objects and events rather than on children's understanding of psychological causation. Nevertheless, similar logical processes may underlie developments in causal reasoning about physical events and causal reasoning about psychological events, and some parallels can be observed, suggesting that the development of causal reasoning may be domain-general. For example, Sedlak and Kurtz (1981) noted that younger children's tendency to fail to use multiplicative rules when integrating information about physical causes (Wilkening, 1981) could be related to their use of additive rules instead of multiplicative rules when trying to combine psychological causes to predict an effect. Das Gupta and Bryant (1989) speculated that 3- to 4-year-old children's difficulty in working out a cause on the basis of the difference between an object's initial state and its final state could be related to the difficulties shown by this age group in the appearance–reality task (e.g. Flavell, Flavell, & Green, 1983), a task that requires children to work out whether various transformations of objects affect their real state or their apparent state.

More recently, Frye, Zelazo, and Palfai (1995) have argued that developments in the understanding of psychological causation—"theory of mind" developments—may be the consequence of changes in underlying inferential reasoning processes. In particular, they have proposed that the development of the understanding of psychological causality is linked to becoming able to reason with "embedded rules"— that is, to make a judgement from one perspective while ignoring another. Frye et al. have found significant correlations between 3-year-old children's performance on some "theory of mind" tasks and a causal contingency task of the kind used by Shultz and his colleagues that required rule switching. We will discuss such "rule-switching" tasks in more detail in Chapter 5. The possibility that there are connections between general developments in logical thinking and particular developments in reasoning about psychological and physical causality appears to be another promising area for future research on the development of causal reasoning.

The development 5
of memory

Adults have surprisingly few memories of the period before the age of around 3 years. This is surprising given that the first three years are an active period for conceptual development, which involves semantic memory about how the world is, and also for the development of physical knowledge and causal reasoning, which depend on a stable and efficient memory for events and their outcomes. The absence of early memories is often referred to as *infantile amnesia*. One explanation for this phenomenon has been that there is an age-related reorganisation or structural change in the memory system, with the system that supports conscious memories being late developing (e.g. Schacter & Moscovitch, 1984). We will discuss this view in the next section. However, the infancy research discussed in Chapters 1 and 2 suggests that it is unlikely that infants and young children represent and remember events in substantially different ways to adults. As learning, reasoning, and problem solving are all functioning effectively during the period of assumed infantile amnesia, and as these processes rely on memory, the notion of a structural change in the memory system with age is not persuasive.

One important factor that may need to be considered when thinking about the development of memory is that children (and adults) do not record events into their memories verbatim. Even though it may feel as though you can remember "exactly what happened" when you went to visit your friend, your friend is bound to have a somewhat different recollection of events to you. As originally demonstrated by Bartlett (1932), children and adults *construct* memories, and the process of construction depends on prior knowledge and personal interpretation. It also depends on how much sense the memoriser can make of the temporal structure of their experiences. In other words, the development of memory cannot be isolated from the development of other cognitive processes, because remembering is embedded in larger social and cognitive activities. Thus the knowledge structures that young children bring to their experiences may be critical in explaining memory development.

Despite the importance of the larger social and cognitive context in explaining memory processes, it is the usual practice in cognitive psychology to discuss memory as a modular system. Emphasis is placed on the *fractionation* of the developed system, and different types of memory are considered independently of each other. Many studies of these different memory "modules" use tasks that are purposely disembedded from larger social/cognitive activities. The aim is to provide a "pure" measure of the memory system of interest. However, an unintended result may be that the applicability of the research findings from such tasks is limited. According to Neisser (1987, p.1) "Students of human memory ... [ignored] almost everything that people ordinarily remember. Their research did not deal with places or stories or friends or life experiences, but with lists of syllables and words...[leading] to a preference for meaningless materials and unnatural learning tasks..." Wherever possible in this chapter, we will focus on studies of memory development that use more familiar, less artificial memory situations and that are based on memory tasks that have some meaning and relevance to the child—in other words, tasks with greater "ecological validity".

The different sub-types of memory that have been identified by researchers who study the developed adult system include semantic memory, recognition memory, working memory, implicit memory, episodic memory, and procedural memory. We have already discussed the development and organisation of semantic memory in the chapter on conceptual development (Chapter 3), and seen procedural memory at work in the infancy studies discussed in Chapter 1. Studies of the other memory systems identified by adult researchers have also been carried out with children, and following a brief review of early memory development, these studies will be considered in this chapter. In Chapter 6, we will discuss the development of mnemonic strategies, and will consider some recent theories of cognitive development that have been based on the development of processing capacity and representation in memory.

Early memory development

Infantile amnesia: A real phenomenon?

The general absence of memories before the age of about 3 years is a genuine phenomenon (e.g. Howe & Courage, 1993). Even when we feel convinced that we can recall events from our own infancy, these events often turn out to have happened to someone else. For example, the memory researcher David Bjorklund (Bjorklund & Bjorklund, 1992, p.207) reports a vivid memory of having croup (bronchitis) as an infant.

> My crib was covered by a sheet, but I remember looking past the bars into the living room. I can hear the whir of the vaporiser, feel the constriction in my chest, and smell the Vicks Vaporub. To this day the smell of Vicks makes my chest tighten...

However, when he reminded his mother about this memory, it turned out that he had never had croup. She told him "You were such a healthy baby... That was your brother, Dick. You were about 3 years old then..."

The interesting question is why we have so few memories of the earliest period of our lives. One of the first explanations for infantile amnesia came from Freud (1938), who argued that early amnesia was caused by the repression of the emotionally traumatic events of early childhood. Although this idea can account for the active rejection of emotionally troublesome material from consciousness, it does not explain why memories for pleasant events are also later inaccessible. Another possibility is that early memories are coded in terms of physical action or pure sensation. Early memories are thus irretrievable, as they are stored in a different format to later memories, which depend on linguistically based encoding and storage. The finding that females tend to have earlier memories than males appears to be consistent with this explanation, as language development is usually more advanced in girls than in boys. According to this idea, early memories survive intact, but the context in which these memories were laid down is so discrepant from the one in which we seek to retrieve them (during later childhood or adulthood) that it is impossible to make contact with the relevant memory traces (Howe & Courage, 1993).

Alternatively, as noted earlier, it may be the case that the memory systems that support the formation of conscious memories are late developing, because the brain structures that underlie these systems are not functional at birth (e.g. Schacter & Moscovitch, 1984). One speculation is that the subcortical limbic–diencephalic structures are essential for the formation of conscious memories, and that this brain system only begins to function properly at around 2–3 years of age. However, such arguments depend largely on drawing parallels between infant humans and infant monkeys (infant monkeys perform poorly on tasks thought to depend on the limbic–diencephalic system until the age of around 2 years). McKee and Squire (1993) reject this view on the grounds that the limbic–diencephalic structures underlie visual recognition memory, which appears to be functional early in life (see Chapter 1). They argue instead that immaturities in the neocortical areas *served* by the limbic–diencephalic structures (e.g. inferotemporal cortex) may explain the phenomenon of infantile amnesia.

Finally, the development of knowledge structures may be important in explaining infantile amnesia. Fivush and Hammond (1990) argue that infantile amnesia may be due to a combination of the absence of distinctive memory cues and the fact that young children have yet to learn a *framework* for recounting and storing events. Because young children are in the process of trying to understand the world around them, they focus on what is similar about events, namely routines. The *routine* aspects of novel events do not make good retrieval cues for future recall. Similarly, because young children do not possess their own frameworks for constructing memories, early memories are fragmented, also making them more difficult to recall. Childhood amnesia is thus explained as a natural by-product of the development of the constructive process of memory itself.

Fivush and Hammond's argument is appealing, because it places infantile amnesia firmly within the context of memory development in general. According to their argument, the lack of early memories is not the result of basic structural changes in the memory system with development. Instead, it is a result of the absence of abstract knowledge structures for describing the temporal and causal sequences of events. We discuss the development of these abstract knowledge structures in the next section. By adulthood, the routine events that young children prefer to recall have merged into *scripts* (or generic knowledge structures) about specific events like "what happens when we go to a restaurant". Childhood amnesia is therefore due to a combination of script formation and the forgetting of novel events (see also Nelson, 1993)

Understanding symbolic representation as an aid to memory

The development of abstract knowledge structures for describing the temporal and causal sequences of events depends in part on linguistic coding. Language is a symbolic system. Words stand for or represent concepts and events in the everyday world, and we use them as symbols to encode our experiences. However, words are not the only symbols that we use. Children use a number of symbolic systems in addition to language at a young age. For example, they make gestures, they point to things, and they engage in symbolic (pretend) play. These symbolic systems seem to be innately specified in the same way as language (although some children, such as autistic children, may lack innate specification of gestures, pointing, and pretend play).

Other symbols are culturally determined. These include symbols such as maps and models. These symbols also represent or stand for objects or events, and include drawings, photographs, and sculptures. All of these symbols bring to mind something other than themselves. The use of many of these forms of symbolic coding enables children to represent information in memory in a form that will be accessible later on. As symbolic understanding *itself* develops, this may be another factor that helps us to understand why early memories are less accessible than later memories. One of the most intriguing sets of experiments investigating the development of symbolic understanding comes from work on young children's understanding of models (e.g. DeLoache, 1987, 1989, 1991).

The basic paradigm used in DeLoache's model studies is always the same. A 2½- or 3-year-old child is shown a scale model of a room, containing various pieces of furniture such as a couch, a dresser, a chair, and some pillows (see Fig. 5.1). The child is then introduced to two central characters, the stuffed toy animals Little Snoopy and Big Snoopy, who both like hiding. The scale model is introduced as Little Snoopy's room, and an adjacent room, which contains the same furniture as the model in the same spatial layout, is introduced as Big Snoopy's room. The child is told "Look, their rooms are just alike. They both have all the same things in their rooms!" Each correspondence is demonstrated "Look—this is Big Snoopy's big couch, and this is Little Snoopy's little couch. They're just the same".

Following this "orientation phase", the child watches as the experimenter hides one of the Snoopy toys in the appropriate room. For example, Little Snoopy might be hidden under the little couch in the model room. The child is then asked to find Big Snoopy in the real room. The child is told "Remember, Big Snoopy is hiding in the same place as Little Snoopy". Children of 3 go straight to the big couch and find Big Snoopy; 2½-year-old children do not. They search around the big room at random, even though a memory post-test shows that they can remember perfectly well where Little Snoopy is hiding. DeLoache argues that the problem for the younger children is that they do not understand the *correspondence* between the model room and the real room. They do not seem to appreciate that they have a basis for knowing where to search for Big Snoopy.

The most compelling reason for believing that the younger children's problem lies in their lack of awareness of the correspondence between

FIG. 5.1.
Diagram of the
experimental room
used in DeLoache's
(1989) scale model
studies, with the scale
model shown below
(darkened areas in
the model correspond
to the labelled items
of furniture in the
room).
Reproduced with
permission.

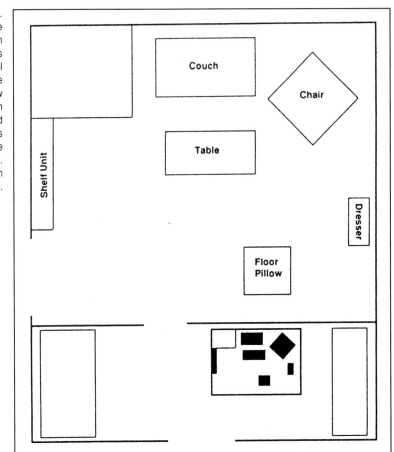

the model and the room comes from DeLoache's "magical shrinking room" studies. In these studies, 2½-year-old children were persuaded that the experimenters had built a "shrinking machine" that could shrink a doll and a room (DeLoache, Miller, & Rosengren, 1996). They were then shown where Big Snoopy was hiding in the big room, and asked to find Little Snoopy in the model room. As the children believed that the model was the shrunken big room, there was no representational relationship between the model and the room to confuse them, and indeed the children were very successful at searching for Little Snoopy in this task. DeLoache has also shown that younger children can find Big Snoopy when they are shown Little Snoopy's hiding place in a picture, which implies that they do understand the representational relation between the *picture* and the room (DeLoache, 1991).

Furthermore, experience with the picture task transfers to the model task. Experience with a symbolic medium that is understood (or partially understood), as pictures are by the age of 2 years, seems to facilitate the use of an unfamiliar symbolic medium (the model). For example, Marzolf and DeLoache (1994) have shown that experience with a model–room relation can help 2½-year-old children to appreciate a map–room relation. DeLoache argues that early experience with symbolic relations helps the development of symbolic sensitivity, which is a basic readiness to recognise that one object or event can stand for another. Thus, in order to use these other symbols in memory and in learning, children may first have to learn what it is to *represent* something.

DeLoache's work shows clearly that symbol–referent relations are not always transparent to young children. However, the ability to represent the higher-order relation between symbol and referent (to adopt a "representational stance") appears to develop fairly rapidly during the first three years of life. As DeLoache has argued, the ability to *map* similarities between symbol and referent is an important component of the developing understanding of symbol–referent relations, and frequently depends on the ability to map *relational* similarities. The importance of relational mappings or analogies in cognitive development has been noted at a number of other points in this book. Given the centrality of symbol use in human cognition, it is interesting to note that DeLoache attributes a key role to the ability to make relational mappings in her model of the development of early symbolic understanding (see DeLoache, in press, for a discussion). The links between early symbolic understanding and memory development in general are not well understood, however.

The development of different memory systems

As noted earlier, a number of different memory systems have been identified by researchers in adult cognitive psychology. All of these memory systems can also be studied in children. A selection of developmental studies of recognition memory, implicit memory, episodic memory, eyewitness memory, and working memory will now be considered.

Recognition memory

Recognition memory is the ability to recognise that something is familiar and has been experienced before. In psychology, *recognition* memory is usually contrasted with *recall* memory, which is the retrieval of a conscious memory of what has been experienced in the past. We have already seen that infants have good visual recognition memories, and that individual differences in visual recognition memory in infancy are a reliable predictor of later individual differences in intelligence (see Chapter 1). It can also be argued that most of the other studies of memory in infancy that were discussed in Chapters 1 and 2 concern recognition memory rather than recall. Habituation, which is a key measure of information processing in infancy, is a recognition measure, and paradigms that use conditioned responses are also based on recognition (such as Rovee-Collier's kick-to-work-a-mobile paradigm, or de Caspar and Fifer's suck-to-hear-your-mother paradigm).

Recognition memory seems to be fairly ubiquitous in animals as well as in humans, and so this early developing memory system is far from unique. For example, pigeons can "remember" 320 pictures for 700 days when tested in a recognition memory paradigm (Vaughan & Greene, 1984). Given its ubiquity, the status of recognition memory as a *cognitive* skill can be questioned. For example, Fagan has argued that recognition memory may actually be a measure of *processing* rather than a measure of cognitive ability *per se* (see Fagan, 1992). It thus seems likely that psychologists will find little development in recognition memory with age. This is in fact the case.

The traditional way of examining recognition memory in young children is to show them a series of pictures, and then to measure the number of pictures that they recognise as familiar after a certain period of time. In a classic study of this type, Brown and Scott (1971) showed children aged from 3–5 years a set of 60 pictures drawn from four familiar categories: people, animals, outdoor scenes/objects, and household scenes/objects. Of the set of pictures, 44 recurred and 12 were seen only once, making a series of 100 pictures in all. The pictures that recurred were seen after a lag of either 0, 5, 10, 25, or 50 items. The children's task was to say "yes" if they had seen a picture before, and "no" if the picture was novel.

Brown and Scott found that the children showed accurate recognition memory on 98% of trials. There was also little difference in recognition accuracy depending on the lag between the items. In fact, the children were equally accurate for lags of 0 and 50 pictures, showing 100% recognition accuracy for each. Accuracy levels for lags of 5 and 25 pictures were around 95%, and for a lag of 10 pictures, 98%. These remarkable levels of performance fell slightly on a long-term retention test which was given after 1, 2, 7, or 28 days. In the long-term retention test, the children were shown the 12 pictures that had been seen only once, 24 of the 44 pictures that had been seen twice, and 36 new pictures. For intervals of up to seven days, recognition memory levels were above 94% for pictures that had been seen twice. The level was somewhat lower for pictures that had been seen only once, falling from 84% after one day to around 70% after seven days. After 28 days, recognition accuracy for pictures that had been seen twice was 78%, and for pictures that had been seen only once, 56%. In a subsequent study, Brown and Scott showed that the superior memory for items seen twice was due to *both* the extra exposure to the items and to the need to make a judgement in the recognition task given in the first phase of the study. The previous requirement of a "yes" judgement seemed *in itself* to act as a retrieval cue for the twice-seen items.

The excellent levels of recognition memory found in young children suggest that there is little for the developmental psychologist of memory to study here. However, interest in children's memory for what is familiar has revived recently through the study of the development of implicit memory.

Implicit memory

Implicit memory is "memory without awareness". In implicit memory tasks, children and adults behave in ways that demonstrate that they have memory for information that they are not consciously aware of having. Although most of us would measure our memories in terms of what we can recall rather than in terms of what we can recognise, the possibility that previous experiences can facilitate performance on a particular memory task even though the subject has no conscious recollection of these previous experiences is a very intriguing one. Implicit memory has also been called "unintentional memory", or "perceptual learning".

Perceptual Learning Tasks.   One of the first studies of implicit memory in children was carried out by Carroll, Byrne, and Kirsner (1985). They measured "perceptual learning" in 5-, 7-, and 10-year-old children using a picture recognition task. In the first phase of the experiment, the children were shown some pictures and either had to say whether each picture contained a cross (crosses had been drawn at random on 33% of the pictures), or to say whether the picture was of something portable. The "cross detection" task was intended to induce "shallow processing" of the pictures at a perceptual level only, and the "portability detection" task was intended to induce "deep processing" at the level of meaning.

Memory for the previously experienced pictures was then studied in an unexpected recognition task. In this task, the children were asked to name a mixture of the pictures that they had already seen along with some new ones. Implicit memory was measured by the difference in the children's reaction times to name the old vs. the new pictures. Half of the children received this *implicit* memory task, and the other half were asked to say whether the old and the new pictures were familiar or not. The latter was the measure of *explicit* memory.

Carroll et al. predicted that implicit memory for the pictures would not vary with depth of encoding, whereas explicit memory would. In other words, deep processing should lead to better explicit memory for the previously experienced pictures than shallow processing, whereas implicit memory levels should be identical for both processing manipulations. This was essentially what they found. Carroll et al. concluded that perceptual learning (implicit memory) does not develop with age.

Fragment-completion tasks. Another way of measuring whether implicit memory develops or not is to use a fragment completion task based on either words or pictures. For example, Naito (1990) devised a word-fragment completion task to measure implicit memory in children aged 5, 8, and 11 years. The children were given some of the letters in a target word, and were asked to complete each fragment into the first meaningful word that came to mind. Although Naito used words written in Japanese characters, her task was equivalent to presenting a fragment like CH–––Y for the target word CHERRY. This is the example given in Naito's paper, and actually the fragment CH–––Y could also be CHEERY or CHUNKY. However, each Japanese fragment was chosen to have only *one* legitimate completion.

Prior to receiving the fragment completion task, the children were given two other tasks based on 67% of the target words. For half of these words, the children were asked to make a *category* judgement in a forced choice task ("Is this a kind of ? – fruit/clothes"), intended to induce "deep" processing. For the other half of the words, they were asked to judge whether the target word contained a certain letter ("shallow" processing). Naito then measured whether more word fragments were completed correctly for the 32 previously experienced target words than for the 16 novel items. She found that the "old" items were completed correctly significantly more frequently than the "new" items at all ages, and that implicit memory did not vary with depth of processing (deep vs. shallow). She also found that implicit memory levels were invariant across age group (even though a group of adults were also included in the study). In a related experiment in which children were asked to recall the target words explicitly, Naito found a strong improvement in recall with age and an effect of depth of processing. Taken together, her results suggest that implicit memory does not develop, but that explicit memory does. Naito argued that her results showed that the two types of memory were developmentally dissociable.

In *picture*-fragment completion tasks, the child is shown an increasing number of fragments of a picture of a familiar object, such as a saucepan or a telephone, until the object is recognised (see Fig. 5.2). If the complete object has been presented in a prior task, such as a picture naming task, then implicit learning should result in faster recognition for fragments of previously experienced objects than for fragments of completely novel objects.

Russo, Nichelli, Gibertoni, and Cornia (1995) used a picture completion paradigm of this type to measure implicit memory in 4- and 6-year-old children. The children were first shown a series of 12 pictures for three seconds each, and were required to name each in turn. After a 10-minute break spent playing with blocks, the children were shown the fragmented versions of the familiar pictures along with fragmented versions of 12 new pictures, in random order. For each set of fragments, they were asked to say as quickly as possible what they thought the fragments were a picture of. The number of fragments that were presented was increased until the child recognised the picture. Performance in this implicit memory condition was contrasted with performance in an explicit version of the task, which was presented without time constraints. In the explicit memory task, the children were asked to use the fragments as cues to try and recall the pictures presented during the naming phase of the experiment.

FIG. 5.2. Examples of the fragmented pictures used by Russo et al. (1995). Reprinted by permission of Academic Press Inc.

Russo et al. found that children of both ages recognised the familiar pictures from fewer fragments than the novel pictures, showing implicit memory. A group of young adults who were given the same picture

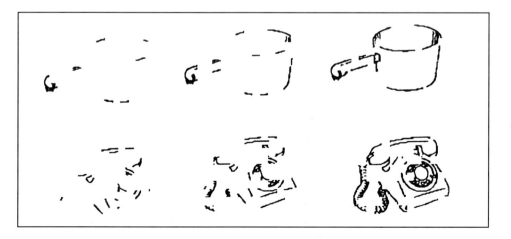

completion task performed at similar levels to the children. Significant age differences were found in the explicit memory task, however, with the 6-year-olds showing better recall than the 4-year-olds. Russo et al. concluded that implicit memory as measured by fragment completion tasks is equivalent in children and in adults, and that the memory processes supporting implicit memory are fully developed by 4 years of age.

A similar study carried out by Bullock Drummey and Newcombe (1995) suggested that even 3-year-olds may have fully fledged implicit memory processes. Their measure of implicit memory was the recognition of blurred pictures after long delays. Bullock Drummey and Newcombe showed 3-year-olds, 5-year-olds, and adults blurred versions of pictures that they had seen three months previously in a reading book. They found that all groups showed comparable levels of implicit memory for the pictures. However, the adults had better *explicit* memory of the pictures than the children.

Memory for faces.   A third measure that can be used to study implicit memory in children is memory for faces. Faces have the advantage of being salient and important stimuli that are not dependent on verbal recall. For example, if the same face is presented to adult subjects on two occasions, the reaction time to recognise the face as familiar on the second occasion is dramatically reduced. This is known as a "priming" effect. Ellis, Ellis, and Hosie (1993) investigated whether young children would also show "priming" effects for faces.

In their experiment, children aged 5, 8, and 11 years were shown pictures of both their classmates and unfamiliar children, and were asked to judge whether the children were smiling or not (half were smiling) and whether the picture was of a boy or of a girl. Following this "priming" stage, the pictures of the children's classmates were presented for a second time, mixed in with previously unseen pictures of other classmates and with pictures of other unfamiliar children. On this second showing, the children were asked to judge whether the children depicted were familiar. Ellis et al. found that children of all ages were quicker to make judgements about the familiarity of the classmates that they had just seen in the priming phase of the experiment than about the familiarity of their non-primed classmates. The amount of implicit memory, as measured by the proportional differences in primed and unprimed reaction times, was the same for the 5- and 8-year-olds, and was slightly *less* for the 11-year-olds, again suggesting that the memory processes supporting implicit memory are fully developed early in childhood.

A different way to measure memory for faces is to study children's implicit memory of their classmates over time. Newcombe and Fox (1994) showed a group of 10-year-old children slides of 3- and 4-year-old children who had been their class-mates in pre-school. These slides were intermixed with slides of other children from the same preschool who had attended the school five years later. In order to see whether the children had implicit memories of their familiar class-mates, galvanic skin response measures were recorded, a measure of autonomic nervous system arousal. The children were then shown the slides again, and were asked to say whether the depicted children were familiar and how much

they liked them. The liking measure was included to see whether the children would show a preference for their previous classmates, even if they could not remember them.

Newcombe and Fox found that the children showed recognition of their former classmates according to *both* the implicit and the explicit measures. Overall recognition rates were fairly low (26% on the implicit measure and 21% on the explicit measure), but there were large individual differences in recognition rates. When the experimenters divided the children into two groups—a "high explicit recognition" group and a "low explicit recognition" group—they found that performance on the *implicit* recognition measure was equivalent in both groups. This is a very interesting result, as it implies that implicit memory for pre-school experiences can be maintained even when explicit memories are lacking. Newcombe and Fox's data thus support Naito's (1990) suggestion that implicit and explicit memories may be developmentally dissociable.

These studies demonstrate that "memory without awareness" is present in children as young as 3–4 years of age. Young children retain sufficient unconscious memories of previously presented pictures or words to facilitate later recognition on the basis of fragments, and their reaction time when judging previously experienced pictures (or children!) is significantly enhanced. However, it is worth noting that the idea that there are two dissociable memory systems in human cognition is currently the subject of dispute (e.g. Shanks & St. John, 1994). Two dissociable memory systems would require two dissociable learning systems, an implicit system that operates independently of awareness and an explicit system that cannot function without a concurrent awareness of what is being learned. Shanks and St. John have argued that most of the implicit learning and memory data do not require learning without awareness at all. Instead, they can be explained on the basis of memorising the instances or fragments of pictures or words that are presented during the training phase that is usual in implicit memory experiments. Whether their argument turns out to be correct or not, however, does not affect the fact that such memory processes are well-established in young children.

Episodic memory

There is no comparable debate concerning episodic memory, which all psychologists assume to be a memory system that involves awareness. Episodic memory usually refers to memory for episodes or events in one's life, and as such involves conscious or explicit recall. In adults, episodic memory tends to be organised around "schemas", or scripts, for routine events. Each script is a generic or abstract knowledge structure that represents the temporal and causal sequences of events in very specific contexts. For example, adults have a "restaurant schema" for representing the usual sequence of events when eating in a restaurant, and a "laundry schema" for representing the usual sequence of events when doing one's laundry. In order to study the development of episodic memory, we need to find out whether children organise episodic information in similar ways to adults. One way to do so is to model familiar event sequences to children, such as "having a bath". To see whether they have represented the temporal and causal sequences of events in this specific context, the children can then be asked to reproduce the modelled event.

Temporal order as an organising principle in children's episodic memories. Bauer and Shore (1987) modelled "having a bath" to young children aged from 17 to 23 months by demonstrating giving a teddy bear a bath. The sequence of events was that the teddy bear's t-shirt was removed, he was put in a toy tub, and he was washed and then dried by the experimenter (in pretend mode!). The teddy bear was then handed to the child, who was asked "Can you give the dirty bear a bath?". The children proved quite capable of reproducing the modelled event sequence when tested for immediate recall. They also remembered the correct sequence of events six weeks later, when they returned to the laboratory and were simply handed the teddy without prior modelling (delayed recall). These data suggest that very young children's representations of events are similar in structure to those of adults. Their event memory is not composed of a series of disorganised snapshots of individual components of the event. Instead, like adults, their representations display temporal ordering and are arranged around a goal.

Event sequences like "having a bath" are very familiar to young children, however, and this familiarity may aid temporally ordered recall. An important question is whether the experimenters would have found similar effects if the temporally ordered events had been novel instead of familiar. To find out, Bauer and Shore invented a novel causal event sequence called "building a rattle". During this event the experimenter modelled putting a plastic ball into a stacking cup, covering it with a slightly smaller stacking cup, and shaking the "rattle" near her ear. The children again showed both immediate and delayed recall for the elements of the sequence, and for their temporal order. Bauer and her colleagues argued that even very young children were sensitive to the causal relations underlying event sequences from their very first experience of them, and that this early causal sensitivity meant that very young children's representations displayed goal-oriented temporal ordering, just like those of adults.

Causal relations as an organising principle in children's episodic memories. To test the idea that causal relations play a special role in organising the temporal order of events for young children, Bauer and Mandler (1989b) carried out a study that used two novel causal event sequences and two familiar sequences. Their subjects were younger children aged either 16 or 20 months. The novel causal event sequences were "build a rattle" and "make the frog jump". "Make the frog jump" involved building a see-saw by putting a wooden board onto a wedge-shaped block, putting a toy frog at one end of the board, and making him "jump" by hitting the other end of the board. The familiar event sequences were "give teddy a bath", and "clean the table". For the "clean the table" event, a wastebasket, paper towel, and empty spray bottle were used. The experimenter mimed spraying the table, wiping it with the towel, and then throwing the towel away. In order to separate temporal from causal information, Bauer and Mandler also included "novel arbitrary" event sequences. An example of a novel event whose temporal ordering was arbitrary was the "train ride" event sequence. For this event, two toy train cars were linked together. A toy driver was then put into one of the cars, and a piece of track was produced for the train to sit on. Although the events were modelled in this order, there was no causal necessity in this ordering, and so these components could be reproduced in any order without affecting the final event.

Bauer and Mandler found that immediate recall for the temporal order of events was indeed significantly lower for the novel arbitrary events than for the novel causal events, even though recall levels for the former were still significant. Furthermore, they found that when an irrelevant component was inserted into each kind of novel event sequence (such as attaching a sticker either to one of the cups making up the rattle or to the toy train driver), then this irrelevant component was far more likely to be displaced in the causal event sequences. Attaching the sticker to the cup was frequently displaced to another position in the "building a rattle" sequence, or was even left out entirely. In contrast, attaching the sticker to the train driver was treated no differently from any of the other components in the "train ride" sequence. This finding suggests that causally related pairs of elements enjoy a privileged organisational status. Bauer and Mandler concluded that causal relations were an important organising principle both for constructing event memories and for aiding recall. The importance of causal relations in structuring *episodic* memory complements the data discussed in Chapter 3, in which we saw the importance of causal information for developing and organising *semantic* memory (e.g. Pauen, 1996b).

The work of Bauer and her colleagues has shown convincingly that even very young children show long-term ordered recall for novel events. Another way to find out whether children organise episodic information in similar ways to adults is to ask them about very familiar events. Bauer's work suggests that, if children are asked questions about familiar routines, then evidence for script-like information should be found.

TRIP/H. ROGERS

The use of scripts to organise episodic memories. Asking questions about familiar routines was exactly the method used by Nelson and her colleagues in their pioneering developmental work on scripts. They examined the episodic memories of 3- to 5-year-old children for events like going grocery shopping, attending birthday parties, and baking cookies. The children were simply asked to tell the experimenters "what happens" during such events. A series of ordered prompts was then used as necessary to encourage elaboration: "I know you know a lot about grocery shopping. Can you tell me what happens when you go grocery shopping? ... Can you tell me anything else about grocery shopping? ... What's the first thing that happens? What happens next?".

Even the youngest children gave ordered and conventionalised reports of what typically occurred during these events. For example, here is a 5-year-old telling the experimenters about going grocery shopping (Nelson, 1986, p. ix):

> Um, we get a cart, uh, and we look for some onions and plums and cookies and tomato sauce, onions and all that kind of stuff, and when we're finished we go to the paying booth, and um, then we, um, then the lady puts all our food in a bag, then we put it in the cart, walk out to our car, put the bags in our trunk, then leave.

Research such as this shows that episodic memory is organised around general event representations from a very early age. Nelson (1993) argues that the basic ways of structuring, representing and interpreting reality are consistent from early childhood into adulthood.

Because of this, as she points out, scripts for routine events may play a very salient role in memory development. Nelson (1988) has suggested that younger children *concentrate* on remembering routines, as routine events such as going to the babysitter are what makes their world a predictable place. The importance of this predictability means that routine events are focused on at the expense of novel and unusual events, which are forgotten.

The relationship between scripts and novel events.   However, more recent studies have shown that younger children can also remember novel and unusual events over long periods of time. In a study by Fivush and Hamond (1990), a 4-year-old recalled that, when he was 2½, "I fed my fish too much food and then it died and my mum dumped him in the toilet". Another 4-year-old told the experimenters that when he was 2½ "Mummy gave me Jonathan's milk and I threw up" (this child was lactose-intolerant). Both of these events were genuine memories. These novel events had obviously made a big impression on the children concerned, as they could remember them accurately 18 months later! Fivush and Hamond agree with Nelson's idea that young children focus largely on routines, but suggest that children's understanding of routine events *also* helps them to understand novel events, events that differ from how the world usually works.

Fivush and Hamond's suggestion that the development of scripts enables the development of memories for novel events is at first sight inconsistent with other evidence showing that young children have a tendency to *include* novel events in their scripts, however. Whereas older children can separate novel events from the routine, tagging them separately in memory as atypical, younger children display a tendency to blur the routine with the unusual. For example, Farrar and Goodman (1990) compared 4- and 7-year-old children's ability to recall novel and repeated ("script") events. In their study, the children visited the laboratory five times during a two-week period in order to play "animal games". These games included making bunny and frog puppets jump fences, and having bears and squirrels hide from each other. Each game took place at a special table, and the games occurred in the same order on each visit. However, during one visit a novel event was inserted into the familiar routine (the event was two new puppets crawling under a bridge).

A week later, the children were interviewed about their experiences using both free recall techniques and specific questions such as "What happens when you play at this table with the puppets?". The younger children frequently reported that the novel event had occurred during the script visits as well as during the single deviational visit. They appeared to be unable to differentiate between a typical "animal game" visit and the novel event that had occurred only once. The older children did not report that the novel event had occurred during both the script visits and the deviational visit. They were more likely to have formed separate and distinct memories for the two types of visit, tagging the novel event as separate and as a departure from the typical script.

Farrar and Goodman suggested that younger children relied on their general event memory when recalling events, and that this general memory had absorbed information from *both* the script visits and the novel visit. They concluded that the ability to establish separate memories of unusual episodes may still be developing at age 4. However, it is also possible that both groups of researchers are correct. Younger children's tendency to merge novel events with their general event memories may depend on the *salience* of the novel event *to the child*. Highly salient novel events such as those documented by Fivush and Hamond (which may be frequently "refreshed" in family contexts) may be accorded a special status in younger children's memories, while less salient events such as the deviation from the game played in Goodman's laboratory may be merged with their scripts.

Parental interaction style and the development of episodic memories.
There is also growing evidence that the ways in which parents interact

with their children influences the development of event memories. Parents tend to ask young children fairly specific questions about shared past events, such as "Where did we go yesterday?", "Who did we see?", and "Who was there with us?" (Hudson, 1990). Repeated experience of such questions may help young children to organise events into the correct temporal and causal order, and to learn which aspects of events are the most important to recall. If this is so, then parents who ask more of these specific questions should have children with better memories. This seems to be the case. For example, in a longitudinal study of mother–child conversations about the past, Reese, Haden, and Fivush (1993) observed mother–child dyads talking about the past when the children were aged 40, 46, 58, and 70 months. The mothers were asked to talk about singular events from the past, like a special visit to a baseball game or a trip to Florida. They were asked to avoid routine events like birthday parties or Christmas, which could invoke a familiar script.

TRIP/H. ROGERS

Reese et al. found that there were two distinct maternal narrative styles, which were related to the ways in which the children became able to recall their own past experiences. Some mothers consistently elaborated on the information that their child recalled and then evaluated it. Other mothers tended to switch topics and to provide less narrative structure, and seldom used elaboration and evaluation. For example, an elaborative mother who was helping her child to remember a trip to the theatre included questions like "Where were our seats?" and "What was the stage set up like?". A non-elaborative mother who was helping her child to recall a trip to Florida asked the same question repeatedly ("What kinds of animals did you see? And what else? And what else?"). The children of the elaborative mothers tended to remember more material at 58 and 70 months. Reese et al. suggested that maternal elaborativeness was a key factor in children's developing memory abilities.

Eye-witness memory

A rather different kind of recall memory is memory for events that may not have appeared significant at the time that they were experienced. This is eye-witness memory. Studies of eye-witness memory in adults have shown that they have remarkably poor memories for the specifics of events that they have seen. For example, adults who have witnessed a car accident in a video film can be misled into "remembering" false details such as a broken headlight simply by the experimenter asking them leading questions like "Did you see the broken headlight?" (Loftus, 1979). If the eye-witness memory of adults is faulty, then presumably the eye-witness memory of *children* is even worse. This is an interesting research question in its own right, but it is also becoming an important legal issue. As more and more children are being called as witnesses in investigations concerning physical and sexual abuse, the status of their testimony has become of paramount importance. In such cases, it is critical to know whether the abuse really occurred, or whether "memories" of abuse have been created as a result of repeated suggestive questioning by adults.

The accuracy of children's eye-witness testimony.   Imagine that an experimenter comes to your school, takes you off to a quiet room to do a puzzle with two friends, and leaves you on your own. While you are working on the puzzle, a strange man comes into the room and messes around, dropping a pencil and fumbling with objects. He claims to be looking for the headmaster. He then steals a hand-bag and walks out. How much do you remember about these events? Ochsner and Zaragoza (1988, cited in Goodman, Rudy, Bottoms, & Aman, 1990) showed that 6-year-old children remembered quite a lot. The children produced more accurate statements about the other events that they had witnessed in the room and fewer incorrect statements than a group of control children who had experienced the same events except that the man had left the room without stealing the bag. The experimental group were also less suggestible, for example being less willing to select suggested misleading alternative events during a forced-choice test. This study suggests that the eye-witness testimony of young children may be no less accurate than that of adults.

The role of leading questions.   Other studies, however, have found that although young children's memory for centrally important events is equivalent to that of adults, younger children are more suggestible than adults. For example, Cassel, Roebers, and Bjorklund (1996) reported a study in which 6- and 8-year-old children and adults watched a video about the theft of a bike. A week later the subjects were asked to recall the events in the video, and were asked a series of increasingly suggestive questions. Cassel et al. found that children and adults showed equivalent levels of recall for items central to the event (e.g. Whose bike was it?). However, when Cassel et al. compared the effect of repeated suggestive questioning on the 6- and 8-year-old children and the adults, they found a greater incidence of false memories in the children. Interestingly, they also found that *unbiased* leading questions such as "Did the bicycle belong to (a) the mother, (b) the boy, or (c) the girl?" were as likely to produce false memories as biased (mis)leading questions such as "The mother owned the bike, didn't she?". This is an important result, as it suggests that the mechanisms that result in false memories may be *general* ones to do with the way that the developing memory system functions, rather than *specific* ones related to false memories of negative events.

As Cassel et al.'s study relied on watching a video, we can hypothesise that leading questions may have an even *greater* effect on the recall of younger children when they actually experience an event themselves. Goodman and her colleagues devised a paradigm based on a visit to a trailer (caravan) to investigate this question (Rudy & Goodman, 1991, see also Goodman et al., 1990). In the "trailer experiment", children aged 4 and 7 years were taken out of their classrooms to a dilapidated old trailer, chosen to be a memorable location. The children went in pairs, and once inside the trailer they played games with a strange man. One child in each pair had the important task of watching (the bystander), and the other child (the participant) played games. This enabled the experimenters to see whether the children would show similar levels of suggestibility when they were participants or bystanders at real events. The games included "Simon Says", dressing up, having your photograph taken, and tickling. During the "Simon Says" game, the children had to perform various actions including touching the experimenter's knees. These games were chosen because child sexual abuse cases frequently involve reports of being photographed, of "tickling", and of other touching.

The children were later interviewed about what had taken place in the trailer. The interview began with the interviewer asking the child to tell him or her about everything that had happened in the trailer. The interview then continued with misleading questions like "He took your clothes off, didn't he?", "How many times did he spank you?", and "He had a beard and a moustache, right?". In fact, the dressing up game did not involve removing the children's clothes, no child was spanked, and the man was clean-shaven. Goodman et al. found that children of both ages recalled largely *correct* information about the games that they had played in the trailer. Neither participants nor bystanders invented information. The children were also largely accurate in their responses to specific questions about abuse, like "How many times did he spank you?", and "Did he put anything in your mouth?". The 7-year-olds answered 93% of the abuse questions correctly, and the 4-year-olds answered 83% correctly.

A related study with 3- and 5-year-olds showed that false reports of abuse did not increase when anatomically detailed dolls were provided to enable the children to *show* as well as tell what had happened (Goodman & Aman, 1990). In this study, however, the younger children *were* more susceptible to leading questions than the older children. Under the influence of misleading questions about abuse, the 3-year-olds tended to make errors of *commission* (that is, they agreed to things that had not happened) 20% of the time. Embroidery of these events was rare. In fact, the majority of commission errors occurred with the leading question "Did he kiss you?", to which the children simply nodded their heads. The 5-year-olds only made commission errors on 2 out of 120 occasions, and both of these errors were on the question "Did he kiss you?". The younger children made very few errors on the potentially more worrying misleading abuse questions such as "He took your clothes off, didn't he?" and "How many times did he spank you?".

The striking thing about Goodman's findings in these very "ecologically valid" studies is that, in the main, the children did *not* invent false reports of abuse. They were also fairly resistant to misleading questioning by the adult, and this resistance remained robust in the face of anatomically detailed dolls, a factor that might have been expected to encourage invention. Nevertheless, as in Cassel et al.'s video study, the younger children in Goodman et al.'s studies were more susceptible to leading questions. Other studies of young children's eye-witness testimony have also found that levels of suggestibility are higher in younger children (see Ceci & Bruck, 1993, for a review). The levels of suggestibility in different studies appears to vary with factors such as the emotional tone of the interview itself, the child's desire to please the interviewer, and whether the child is a participant in the action or not, among others. All studies find *some* age differences in suggestibility, however.

Links between the development of episodic memory and the development of eye-witness memory. Ceci and Bruck (1993) have suggested that the greater susceptibility of younger children to repeated questioning by adults might be related to the findings of Nelson and others concerning event memory. Their idea is that the over-dependency of younger children on scripted knowledge could mean that suggestions made by the experimenter get included into the children's script for an event, and are thereafter reported as having actually taken place. This clearly fits with Farrar and Goodman's finding that, when a novel event occurs in a standard setting, younger children tend to incorporate it into their script rather than tagging it separately (Farrar & Goodman, 1990). As children get older, they seem to become better at establishing separate memories of suggested episodes, and at keeping these suggestions distinct from their scripts. As they get older, they also become less susceptible to leading questions.

Ornstein and his colleagues have made the related point that children cannot provide accurate testimony about events that they cannot remember. In order to examine how much children actually remember about salient, personally experienced events, Ornstein, Gordon, and Larus (1992) investigated 3- and 6-year-old children's memories of a visit to the doctor for a physical examination. Each physical examination lasted about 45 minutes, and included weighing and measuring the child, checking hearing and vision, drawing blood, checking genitalia, and listening to the heart and lungs. Ornstein et al. argued that such visits shared a number of features with instances of sexual abuse. These included physical contact with the child's body by an adult and emotional arousal due to injections and other procedures. Memory for the events in the physical examination was measured immediately after the examination was over, and after intervals of one and three weeks.

Ornstein et al. measured the children's memories by first asking them open-ended questions such as "Tell me what happened during your check-up". More detailed questions were then asked, such as "Did the doctor check any parts of your face? "and "Did he/she check your eyes?" Misleading questions were also asked, involving features of the physical examination that had not been included in an individual child's check-up. Ornstein et al. found that children in both age groups showed good recall of the physical examination immediately after it was over, recalling 82% (3-year-olds) and 92% (6-year-olds) of the features respectively. Both groups showed some forgetting of these features after three weeks had passed, but recall was still highly accurate, being around 71% in the 3-year-olds. Responses to misleading questions were also largely accurate. Children in both age groups were able to correctly reject misleading features most of the time. For the 3-year-olds after a three-week delay, correct denials were made to 60% of the misleading questions, and for the 6-year-olds, to 65% of the misleading questions. Intrusions ("remembering" features that had not in fact occurred) were also at similar levels in the two groups after the three-week delay, being 26% for the 3-year-olds and 32% for the 6-year-olds. Ornstein et al. concluded that young children's recall of a personally experienced event was surprisingly good, supporting the findings obtained by Goodman and her colleagues in their "trailer" paradigm.

A different way of looking at the link between children's knowledge of routine, script-like information and their eye-witness recall is to investigate whether children who have *more* episodic knowledge about a certain class of events are *less* likely to demonstrate susceptibility effects. According to this hypothesis, the possession of prior knowledge about a class of events should result in the formation of more stable memories, and these more stable memories should be less susceptible to the influence of leading questions. This hypothesis can be examined by studying the role of knowledge in children's memories, and the more recent work of Ornstein and his colleagues provides a good example of such research.

Clubb, Nida, Merritt, and Ornstein (1993) looked at whether children's memories of what happens when you visit the doctor were linked to their knowledge and understanding of what happens during routine pediatric examinations. The children, who were 5-year-olds, were interviewed about their knowledge of physical examinations using open-ended questions like "Tell me what happens when you go to the doctor". They were then asked a series of yes–no probe questions such as "Does the doctor check your heart?". Clubb et al. found that the majority of the children remembered highly salient features such as having an injection (64%), having the doctor listen to your heart (64%), and having your mouth checked (55%). Few children remembered features such as having a wrist check (5%). These percentages were then taken as an index of knowledge. A different group of 5-year-olds provided the eye-witness memory scores. This group of children had been interviewed previously about a real visit to the doctor as part of an earlier study. Clubb et al. checked the percentages of these children who had spontaneously recalled the same features (injection, heart check, mouth check etc.) either immediately or one, three, or six weeks following their real examination. These "eye-witness memory" numbers were then correlated with the corresponding knowledge scores obtained from the first group of children.

The researchers found that the correlations between knowledge and memory were highly significant at each delay interval. From this finding, they argued that variability in knowledge in a given domain is associated with corresponding variability in recall. However, the significant correlations obtained by Clubb et al. do not tell us about the *direction* of the relationship between knowledge and memory. It could be that variability in recall determines variability in knowledge, rather than vice versa. The relationship would also be more convincing if it were demonstrated in the *same* children. Nevertheless, the hypothesis that there should be a relationship between episodic knowledge and susceptibility to leading questions seems worth exploring further.

Working memory

Both episodic memory and eye-witness memory are aspects of long-term recall. We also have a memory system for short-term recall, which is called *working* memory. Working memory is a "workspace" that maintains information temporarily, and at the same time processes this information for use in other cognitive tasks such as reasoning, comprehension, and learning (e.g. Baddeley & Hitch, 1974). The information that is being maintained in working memory may either be new information, or it may be information that has been retrieved from the long-term system.

Working memory has at least three sub-components. These are the central executive, the visuo-spatial sketchpad, and the phonological loop (see Fig. 5.3). The central executive is conceived of as a regulatory device which co-ordinates the different working memory activities and allocates resources. The visuo-spatial sketchpad is thought to process and retain visual and spatial information in a visuo-spatial code, and also to hold any verbal information that is being stored as an image. The phonological loop is thought to maintain and process verbal

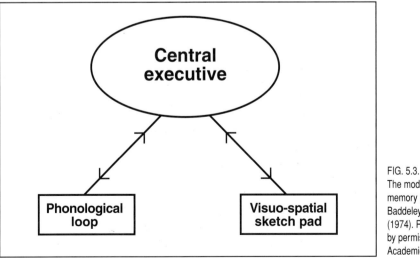

FIG. 5.3.
The model of working memory proposed by Baddeley and Hitch (1974). Reproduced by permission of Academic Press Inc.

information in the form of speech sounds. It can be conceptualised as a kind of tape-loop lasting 1–2 seconds. Decay in the phonological loop is fairly rapid, and so this verbal information may need to be *refreshed* or *rehearsed* by sub-vocal articulation.

Developmental psychologists have mainly been concerned with the development of the two "slave systems" of the central executive, the visuo-spatial sketchpad and the phonological loop. One influential idea has been that children initially rely on visual codes in short-term memory, and then switch to phonological codes at the age of around 5 years (e.g. Conrad, 1971). The age of this switch has been seen as potentially very important, as it is similar to the age at which Piaget proposed that a fundamental shift occurred in children's logical reasoning abilities (see Chapter 8). In fact, a number of information-processing theories of cognitive development, sometimes called "neo-Piagetian" theories, are loosely based on this temporal co-occurrence. As working memory has a central role in reasoning, comprehension and learning, it seems plausible to argue that the development of working memory must somehow be important for cognitive development in general. However, it is also possible that the development of reasoning, comprehension, and learning *in themselves* lead to improvements and developments in working memory. We will explore these neo-Piagetian theories briefly in the next chapter.

The visuo-spatial sketchpad.   Most of the evidence for the idea that children rely on visual memory codes prior to around 5 years of age is indirect. It depends largely on showing that younger children are not susceptible to effects that are related to the use of speech sounds for coding material in working memory. As the presence of these effects is usually taken as evidence for the operation of the phonological loop (see later), the absence of these speech-based effects has been taken to imply that working memory in young children relies on the visuo-spatial sketchpad.

The classic study in this tradition was performed by Conrad (1971). He gave children aged 3–11 years a series of pictures to remember. The pictures had names that either sounded similar (rat, cat, mat, hat, bat, man, bag, tap), or sounded different (girl, bus, train, spoon, fish, horse, clock, hand). The children first learned to play a "matching game" with the pictures. In the matching game, one complete set of pictures was presented face-up in front of the child, and then two or three pictures from a second, duplicate, set were presented for matching. After the children had grasped the idea of matching, the experimental trials began. The experimenter set out the eight cards in the full set (using either the "sounds similar" pictures or the "sounds different" pictures), and then concealed them from view. A sub-set of the duplicate pictures were then presented for matching. The experimenter named each card in the duplicate set, turned the cards face-down, and then re-exposed the full set. The children had to match the face-down cards to the correct pictures.

As adults find names that sound similar more difficult to remember over short periods of time than names that sound different, Conrad expected that the children would find the "sounds similar" picture cards more difficult to match than the "sounds different" picture cards. However, this "phonological confusability" effect in adults arises because adults tend to code the picture names verbally and then to retain them in the phonological loop using rehearsal. Conrad's argument was that if a phonological confusability effect did not occur in children (i.e. if the children found the "sounds different" cards as difficult to remember as the "sounds similar" cards), then they were using a different memory code to support recall, presumably a pictorial one.

Conrad's results showed that only the younger children showed a "no difference" pattern between the two picture sets (the 3- to 5-year-olds). The memory spans of this age group for the phonologically confusable and non-confusable pictures (measured by the number of pictures correctly recalled) were equivalent. Children aged 6 years and above showed longer memory spans for the "sounds different" picture cards than for the "sounds similar" picture cards, suggesting that they were using rehearsal strategies as a basis for recall. The possibility that the youngest subjects were also rehearsing but were idiosyncratically renaming the pictures prior to recall (e.g. "cat" as "pussy" or "Tibby", thereby effectively converting the "sounds similar" set into a "sounds different" set) was ruled out by the children's spontaneous naming behaviour. The youngest children tended to speak aloud as they performed the task, and made comments like "cat goes with cat"or "cat here". This suggested that young, non-rehearsing children use some form of visual storage to remember visually presented materials.

If short-term storage in younger children is visually based, then visually similar objects should be easily confused in short-term memory, just as phonologically similar names are confused when short-term storage is phonological. This prediction is easily tested by using pictures of objects that look like each other in a memory span task, and then seeing whether visually similar objects are more difficult to remember than visually dissimilar objects. Hitch, Halliday, Schaafstal, and Schraagan (1988) devised a picture confusion memory task of this type. Their visually similar set of pictures consisted of pictures of a nail, bat, key, spade, comb, saw, fork, and pen. Their visually dissimilar set of control pictures consisted of pictures of a doll, bath, glove, spoon, belt, cake, leaf, and pig. An additional set of visually dissimilar pictures that had long names was also used in the task. This set comprised an elephant, kangaroo, aeroplane, banana, piano, policeman, butterfly, and umbrella. Examples of stimuli from each set are shown in Fig. 5.4. Hitch et al. then compared 5- and 10-year-old children's memory for these pictures of familiar objects.

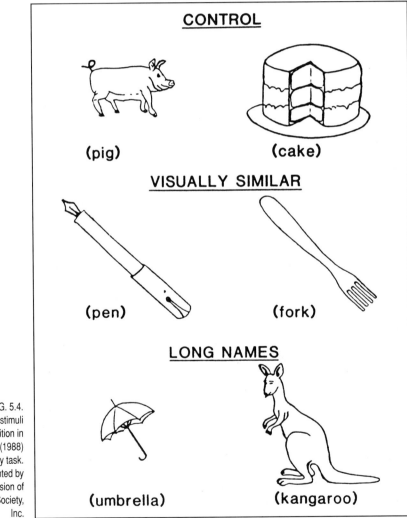

FIG. 5.4. Examples of stimuli from each condition in Hitch et al.'s (1988) picture memory task. Reprinted by permission of Psychonomic Society, Inc.

Hitch et al.'s memory task was similar to Conrad's, except that no matching was required. Instead, the experimenters presented each picture face-up, and then turned it over, telling the child that they would have to repeat the names of the pictures in the order in which they were shown. The 5-year-olds were given sequences of three pictures, and the 10-year-olds were given sequences of five pictures. Hitch et al. argued that, if the children were using rehearsal to remember the order of the pictures, then they should find the pictures with long names more difficult to recall than the visually similar pictures and the control pictures. On the other hand, if the children were using visual memory strategies, then they should find the visually similar pictures the most difficult set to recall. Hitch et al. found that, for the 10-year-olds, the pictures with long names were the most difficult to recall. For the 5-year-olds, the visually similar pictures were the most difficult to recall, although there was a small effect of word length. Hitch et al. concluded that the tendency to use visual working memory becomes less pervasive as memory development proceeds.

All of these experiments, however, have studied the retention of *visually presented* items. Rather than showing that children rely on visual memory codes prior to around 5 years of age, it may be that younger children tend to rely on visual codes in working memory *when they are given visual information to remember*. This means that experimenters may be documenting a tendency in younger children to attempt to retain information in the modality in which it is presented, rather than a tendency to rely on visual memory codes. Older children may translate visually presented material into a speech code. The visual working memory effects observed by Conrad and by Hitch et al. may thus be due to children's failure to select a particular mnemonic strategy, rather than to an early reliance on visuo-spatial memory codes. We will discuss this possibility further in the next section.

Meanwhile, it is interesting to note that deaf children continue to rely heavily on visuo-spatial codes in memory, even for material that hearing children code linguistically. O'Connor and Hermelin (1973) devised a spatial span task to measure short-term recall in the deaf. In this task, three digits were presented successively on a screen, appearing in three different windows in a horizontal visual array (e.g. 5, 2, 7). The left–right order did not always correspond to the temporal–sequential order of presentation. For example, the first digit to appear might be the one in the middle window, the second the one in the right-hand window, and the third the one in the left-hand window, giving a left–right order of 7, 5, 2. O'Connor and Hermelin found that whereas the hearing children tended to recall the digits in their *temporal* order of appearance (5, 2, 7), the deaf children recalled them in the *spatial* order of their (left–right) appearance (7, 5, 2). This suggests that the hearing children were rehearsing the digits verbally in order to remember them, while the deaf children were representing the digits as visual images.

The phonological loop.   Activity in the phonological loop is usually measured by the presence of effects that are related to the use of speech sounds for coding material. For example, it is more difficult to remember words that sound similar over a short period of time (bat, cat, hat, rat, tap, mat) than words that do not. This is called the "phonological confusability" or "phonological similarity" effect. Similarly, long words like "bicycle, umbrella, banana, elephant" take longer to rehearse than short words like "egg, pig, car, boy", and so more short than long words can be retained in working memory. This is called the "word length" effect.

The number of items that can be retained in the phonological loop over a short period of time is used to provide a measure of an individual's "memory span". Memory span gives a measure of working memory capacity, and increases with age. As span length differs with different types of material, however, such as long vs. short words (and with background knowledge, see Schneider & Bjorklund, in press), most measures of memory span are based on the retention of items like digits which are assumed to be equally familiar to all subjects. However, number words vary in length in different languages. This can lead to different estimates of memory span in children of the same age who speak different languages. Chinese children have much longer digit spans than English children, because the Chinese number words are much shorter than the English number words (e.g. Chen & Stevenson, 1988). Welsh children have shorter digit spans than American children, as the Welsh number words are longer than the English number words. As memory span is usually one of the things that is measured in IQ tests, at one time it was wrongly thought that Welsh children had lower IQs than American children! Upon closer investigation, it was found that the IQ difference was an artifact of systematically lower Welsh scores on the digit span component of the test (Ellis & Hennelley, 1980).

Another important component of working memory capacity is speech rate or articulation rate, which also affects memory span. Children who articulate slowly tend to have shorter memory spans than children who can articulate more quickly, presumably because it takes them longer to rehearse individual items. Speech rate also increases with age. Because of this, it has been proposed that the development of memory span with age is entirely accounted for by developmental increases in speech rate. As older children speak more quickly than younger children, they can rehearse more information during the 1–2 seconds available in the phonological loop, and can thus remember more items than the younger children, giving them longer memory spans.

As required by this proposal, speech rate and memory span are highly correlated. This connection was established in a series of studies by Hulme and his colleagues, using a word repetition task (e.g. Hulme, Thomson, Muir, & Lawrence, 1984; Hulme & Tordoff, 1989). For example, in Hulme et al. (1984), children aged 4, 7, and 10 years and adults were given a pair of words, such as "apple, tiger", to repeat as quickly as they could. The number of words produced per second provided the measure of speech rate. The results showed that speech rate was linearly related to memory span: increases in memory span were always accompanied by increases in speech rate across age. Furthermore, the relation between recall and speech rate was constant across different word lengths. When the children's memory spans for long (e.g. helicopter, kangaroo), short (e.g. egg, bus) and medium-length (e.g., rocket, monkey) words was compared, Hulme et al. found that the relationship between recall and speech rate was constant across age. This shows that, at any age, subjects can recall as much as they can say in a fixed time interval (about 1.5 seconds). Hulme et al. argued that individuals with higher speech rates could rehearse information more quickly, and could thus remember it better.

When Hitch, Halliday, Dodd, and Littler (1989) replicated Hulme et al.'s work using pictures instead of words, however, the results were rather different. With *visual* presentation of the names to be remembered, only the 10-year-olds showed a correlation between speech rate and memory span, as only this group appeared to spontaneously rehearse the visual inputs. With auditory presentation, all age groups showed the correlation. Thus speech rate *does* govern the number of items that can be retained in working memory, but only when the items to be remembered are presented in speech form. This is, of course, in keeping with the findings of Conrad (1971) and Hitch et al. (1988) that we discussed earlier. Younger children appear to prefer to maintain visually presented information by using a visuo-spatial code, whereas older children spontaneously translate visual inputs into a speech code.

Henry and Millar (1993) explain this developmental pattern by proposing that rehearsal develops out of naming behaviour. They point out that younger children are frequently called upon to use naming to translate visual or tactile material into a verbal form, particularly as they enter school and rely increasingly on verbal strategies for learning and retaining information. Henry and Millar suggest that children's increasing speed and facility with naming leads to the discovery of rehearsal, and that the development of rehearsal probably explains the development of memory span after the age of about 7 years. The development of memory span prior to this point depends both on naming and on the child's familiarity with the items to be remembered. Items that are highly familiar in long-term (semantic) memory are easier to store and to retrieve. Highly familiar items also have well-specified phonological representations in the mental lexicon, and as the speech output system is used in memory span tasks for both rehearsal and recall, words with better specified representations will require less processing and can be articulated faster (see also Roodenrys, Hulme, & Brown, 1993). According to this view, although speech rate is related to the development of memory span, speech rate is also determined by the quality of a child's phonological representations.

Henry and Millar's proposal is an interesting one, as it suggests that the *development* of working memory is intimately related to the development of long-term or semantic memory. According to their argument, the key variable that affects the capacity of working memory, speech rate, is dependent on the development of well specified phonological representations in semantic memory. As we saw earlier (Chapter 3), the development of semantic memory is linked to conceptual and linguistic development. Items that have well specified phonological representations are those that are highly familiar, easily accessed and often retrieved for speech. Thus Henry and Millar's view implies that the conventional conceptual distinctions between short-term and long-term memory may be only partially applicable as far as the *development* of memory is concerned. Although children do use the phonological loop to maintain information over short periods of time, just like adults, its utilisation appears to be gradual, depending on task features (e.g. verbal vs. pictorial input) as well as the age of the child. Nevertheless, the concept of a short-term "workspace" that enables the active processing of material on a moment-to-moment basis has made an important contribution to recent theories of cognitive development based on the notion of processing capacity, as we will see in Chapter 6.

Executive processes. The third component of working memory hypothesised by Baddeley and Hitch is the central executive, which is said to play a central role in cognition via planning and monitoring cognitive activity. The central executive is said to control the transmission of information among different parts of the cognitive system, to monitor the functioning and co-ordination of the phonological loop and the visuo-spatial sketchpad, and to retrieve information from long-term memory. Although it is difficult to study the central executive directly, it has been suggested that central executive activities are located in the frontal cortex. Tasks that measure frontal cortex involvement may thus also provide an index of "executive function".

We already know from Chapter 2 that the frontal cortex contains primary motor cortex, which is involved in the planning and control of movement. As discussed in that chapter, some of the errors made by infants (such as the A-not-B search error) that were thought to show cognitive confusions actually derive from immaturities in this neural system. These frontal immaturities lead to inappropriate searching behaviour because the infants are unable to inhibit a predominant action tendency to search at A, and not because of any misconceptions about where to look for hidden objects (e.g. Diamond, 1991). Similar arguments can be made about apparent cognitive confusions in young children. As the frontal cortex is also the site of higher thought processes such as planning and monitoring cognitive activity and abstract reasoning, and as young children are not always very good at planning and monitoring their cognitive activities, some developmental psychologists have suggested that this developmental deficiency may reflect the fact that the frontal cortex is still maturing. The idea that young children may have "executive deficits" has been studied by examining whether children make the kind of "executive errors" that are characteristic of adults who have injuries to the frontal cortex.

A typical "executive error" seen in adults with frontal cortex damage is perseverative card sorting. As discussed earlier (Chapter 2), if a frontal patient has been sorting a pack of cards according to a particular rule (e.g. colour) and the sorting rule is changed (e.g. to shape), then the patient finds it very difficult to change his sorting rule, and continues to sort the cards according to colour. However, at the same time as making these consistent sorting errors, the patient tells the experimenter "this is wrong, and this is wrong ..." (Diamond, 1988). It is as though the patient's behaviour is under the control of his previous action (he is unable to inhibit the "prepotent" tendency to search by the old rule), rather than under the control of his conscious intent. Clinical measures of card sorting behaviour, such as the neuropsychological test called the Wisconsin Card Sorting Test, typically require the patients to participate in many sorting trials, with a shift in sorting principle after each block of 10 trials. Patients with frontal lesions are found to make significantly more sorting errors and to achieve significantly fewer shifts than control subjects on the card sorting task. Pennington (1994) has argued that "executive errors" occur when behaviour is controlled by salient features of the environment, including prior actions, rather than by an appropriate rule held in mind.

A growing number of developmental psychologists have argued that some of the logical errors made by children at 3–4 years and at 6–7 years of age may be explained as "executive failures" (e.g. Russell, 1996). The idea is that children have inadequate strategic control over their mental processes. For example, Russell argues that at 3–4 years this inadequate strategic control can lead to failure on "theory of mind" tasks, because children cannot think "explicitly and at will" about mental processes. Similarly, at 6–7 years, this inadequate strategic control can lead to failure on Piagetian "conservation" tasks (see Chapter 8), because children cannot think "explicitly and at will" about certain properties of the objects that are being conserved (Russell, 1996, pp. 215, 222).

Although there is relatively little direct evidence for an "executive deficit" in 3- to 4-year-old children, recent work by Frye and Zelazo and their colleagues has shown that children of this age do experience difficulty in rule shifting, just like frontal patients. For example, Frye, Zelazo, and Palfai (1995) asked children aged 3, 4, and 5 years to sort a set of cards into two trays on the basis of either shape or colour. Each card depicted a single shape, a red triangle, a blue triangle, a red circle or a blue circle. To play the "colour game", the children were told that all the red ones went into one tray, and all the blue ones went into the other. The instructions were quite explicit: "We don't put any red ones in that box. No way! We put all the red ones over here, and only blue ones go over there. This is the colour game...". After training in *both* games (colour and shape), the children were tested for their ability to shift their sorting strategy (e.g. from colour *to* shape) over three sets of five trials. On the first set of five trials, the children were given test cards to sort according to colour. Having sorted this set, they were then told "Okay, now we're going to play a different game, the 'shape game'. You have to pay attention". Five new test cards were then presented to sort by shape. Finally, five consecutive switching trials were administered, during which the children had to sort according to a new rule (shape or colour) on each trial. Again, the instructions were quite explicit: "Okay, now we're going to switch again and play a different game, the colour game. You have to pay attention".

Frye et al. found that the 3- and 4-year-olds in their study experienced great difficulty in shifting their sorting strategy on the second set of five trials despite the explicit instructions from the experimenter. They typically sorted the cards correctly for the first five trials, and then continued to sort by colour (or shape) for the second five trials, perseveratively using the wrong rule. Performance on the final set of five trials, which required consecutive switching, was at chance level. In contrast, the older children (5-year-olds) were able to switch sorting rule in the second set of five trials, and were also able to switch sorting rule on a trial-by-trial basis during the last set of five trials. They did not show the "executive failures" characteristic of the younger children.

In order to make sure that the difficulties of the 3- and 4-year-olds were not due to the use of abstract and perhaps unfamiliar geometric shapes, Frye et al. carried out a similar card sorting experiment using pictures of red and blue boats and red and blue rabbits. The children were again required to sort the cards first according to one rule, then according to a second rule, and finally to alternate between the two rules on the last set of trials. Essentially the same results were found as with the geometric shapes, although the 4-year-olds proved to be better at switching their sorting rule with the more familiar dimensions of boats and rabbits. Frye et al. also checked that the children's difficulties were not due to the use of the dimensions of shape and colour *per se*, by devising card sorting tasks based on rules about number and size. Again, essentially the same results were found, with 3- and 4-year-olds showing difficulties when required to switch their sorting rule.

On the basis of these findings, Frye et al. argued that children become able to make a judgement on one dimension while ignoring another between 3 and 5 years of age. Frye et al.'s results can also be explained within the "executive failure" account, by arguing that children cannot inhibit a prepotent tendency to use the pre-switch rule at will, even though the post-switch rule is known to them. In order to test the "executive failure" interpretation of Frye et al.'s results, we need evidence that the post-switch rules are indeed available to the younger children.

This evidence has been provided in a replication of the original card sorting study using shape and colour rules with pictures of flowers and cars (Zelazo, Frye, & Rapus, 1996). In this replication, Zelazo et al. found that 89% of the 3-year-olds who failed to use the new rule on the post-switch trials could verbally report the new rule. For example, when asked "Where do the cars go in the shape game? Where do the flowers go?" the children would point to the correct boxes, and then immediately sort according to the colour rule when told "Play the shape game. Here's a flower. Where does it go?". Similar results were found even when the children received only one pre-switch trial. These findings suggest that 3-year-olds fail to use post-switch rules despite knowing these rules and despite having insufficient experience with pre-switch rules to build up a habit to sort on one dimension only.

A complementary view of the role of the frontal cortex in cognitive development has been put forward by Dempster (1991). Dempster argues that intelligence cannot be understood without reference to *inhibitory* processes in the frontal cortex, and that individual differences in inhibitory processes show how efficient the frontal cortex is in different individuals. He suggests that the critical aspect of many "frontal" tasks like card sorting is that these tasks require the suppression of task-*irrelevant* information for effective performance. In Frye et al.'s paradigm, this would mean suppressing the colour rule when asked to begin sorting the cards on the basis of the shape rule. Impaired inhibitory functioning could thus be the explanation for the children's susceptibility to interference.

As the frontal cortex is still developing in young children, and as children find clinical versions of card sorting tasks very difficult until the age of around 12 years (with children suffering from attention deficit disorders with hyperactivity showing particular problems), Dempster argues that inhibitory processes are a neglected dimension of cognitive development. According to Dempster's views, individual differences in frontal inhibitory activity should be correlated with individual differences in cognitive development, and with performance on "executive" tasks. This suggestion is consistent with the evidence discussed at the end of Chapter 1 concerning the predictive power of infant habituation and recognition memory for later cognitive development. As noted, McCall and Carriger (1993) argued that this predictive relationship arose because infant habituation and recognition memory measures provided an index of individual differences in the ability to *inhibit* responding to familiar stimuli. Although no-one has yet linked this argument to performance on executive tasks, Dempster's suggestions would seem to be important research questions for future work on the development of "executive functions".

Dempster's views concerning the relative neglect of inhibitory processes are closely related to the views of those who argue that the mechanisms underlying the development of selective attention should also receive greater emphasis in studies of cognitive development (e.g. Lane & Pearson, 1982). The development of selective attention requires the active *inhibition* of irrelevant stimuli as well as habituation to them. Although the habituation mechanisms of attention appear to be functioning as well in children as in adults, the inhibition mechanisms do not (Tipper, Bourque, Anderson, & Brehaut, 1989). However, the remarkable paucity of studies on the development of attention means that it is too early to draw any useful conclusions about individual differences in selective attention and individual differences in cognitive development.

Summary

This survey of some of the different types of memory that can be measured in children has shown that, while some memory systems develop with age, others do not. Little developmental change was found in recognition memory and in implicit memory, while large developmental changes were found to occur in episodic memory, working memory, and semantic memory (see also Chapter 3). The different developmental trajectories of these different memory systems can be explained by the fact that the development of memory cannot be isolated from the development of other cognitive processes. The knowledge structures that young children bring with them to memory tasks play an important role in determining what is remembered, and such knowledge structures are important for organising episodic memory and semantic memory, and for increasing the efficiency of working memory. The memory systems that *develop* are thus characterised by the fact that they benefit from the increasing sophistication of other cognitive processes. In contrast, recognition memory and implicit memory are more automatic perceptual learning systems, and are relatively unaffected by the development of other processes.

The developmental changes in episodic and semantic memory in turn seem to explain some of the developments seen in other memory systems, such as the decrease in suggestibility found in eye-witness memory and the decline in "infantile amnesia". Older children are less likely than younger children to be susceptible to leading questions that cause them to falsely recall events that never took place, and this decline in susceptibilty seems to be related to the development of scripts and to the degree of children's episodic knowledge about the events being remembered. Similarly, the absence of infantile amnesia after the age of around 3 years may be linked to the development of a framework for storing and recounting events. Once abstract knowledge structures are available for describing the causal and temporal sequences of the events that constitute episodic memory, amnesia is no longer found. We also saw that the increase in working memory capacity (memory span) found with age may result in part from the development of semantic memory. The availability of long-term memory representations of items seems to facilitate short-term memory performance. The *development* of short-term and long-term storage systems may thus be intimately linked, even though when measured in adults the two memory systems appear to be distinct. However, the development of the executive component of working memory may depend on quite different factors. Rather than being consequent on the development of other aspects of the memory system, the development of the central executive may depend on neural development and the maturation of the frontal cortex.

Mnemonic strategies, metamemory and cognition 6

The development of an efficient memory does not depend only on the development of different types of memory systems. Perhaps equally important is the development of different mnemonic strategies for retaining and retrieving information from these memory systems, and the development of knowledge about how one's memory works and how to use it most effectively—so-called "metamemory". These are the aspects of memory in which the largest individual differences are found. Consequently, it is in the differential individual use of mnemonic strategies and metamemorial abilities that specific links are sought between individual differences in memory development and individual differences in cognitive development.

The development of strategies for remembering

The most widely used mnemonic strategies are *rehearsal* and *organisation*. Although other strategies such as visualisation can also be used to improve one's memory, these strategies have not been the object of much developmental research. Studies of the development of strategies for remembering have shown that young children are surprisingly confident about their mnemonic abilities. In fact, they do not seem to expect that they will need to use mnemonic strategies to improve their recall at all. In a study conducted by Yussen and Levy (1975) using a standard memory span task, half of a group of 4-year-olds who were presented with 10 unrelated items to recall predicted that they would remember all 10 items. In actual fact, they remembered about three! This experience did not change the children's confidence in their mnemonic abilities, however, and very few of them changed their predictions about their memory capacities. Instead, they said things like "If you gave me a different list like that, I could do it!".

The emergent use of mnemonic strategies

Nevertheless, when given a specific "ecologically valid" memory task to perform, even very young children appear to have some realisation that they will need to use mnemonic strategies to aid their memories. This was demonstrated in a study by Wellman, Ritter, and Flavell (1975), who told a group of 3-year-olds a story about a toy dog. Among the props used in the story were four identical plastic cups. At one point in the procedure, the experimenter put the toy dog under one of these cups, explaining that the dog would go into the doghouse while the experimenter left the room to find more things. The child was asked to remember which cup the dog was under while the experimenter was away.

During the 40 seconds that the experimenter was out of the room, most children used a variety of strategies to help them to remember which cup was the doghouse. They looked at and touched the cup hiding the dog significantly more often than the other cups, they looked at the target cup and nodded to themselves "yes", looked at the other cups and shook their heads "no", they rested their hand on the target cup, and so on. Wellman et al. also found that recall for the dog's location was more successful in the children who used these strategies than in the children who didn't. An attempt to use this procedure with 2-year-olds was thwarted by the restlessness of the children, who wouldn't keep still during the experimenter's absence.

Better success with 2-year-olds has been reported by DeLoache, Cassidy, and Brown (1985). They used a hiding game to investigate children's strategic memory for spatial locations. The children, who were aged from 18–24 months, watched the experimenter hide a favourite toy (e.g. Big Bird) in a natural location (e.g. under a pillow in the child's home). The children were told that Big Bird was going to hide, and that they should remember where he was hiding as they would need to find him later when the bell rang. A timer was then set for four minutes, during which time the child took part in a number of distraction activities with other toys organised by the experimenter. The children frequently checked on Big Bird's hiding location during this distraction period, for example pointing at the pillow, saying "Big Bird!", and peeping underneath it. In a control condition in which Big Bird was put on top of the pillow, similar strategies were not observed. DeLoache et al. argued that this showed that the children's self-reminding behaviours were indeed strategic, as they were adopted as a function of the memory demands of the task.

Somerville, Wellman, and Cultice (1983) also succeeded in measuring strategic recall in 2-year-olds by using a highly motivating task. The task was the need to remember to buy candy at the store at a particular time specified by their mother (e.g. tomorrow morning). Memory for two events was compared—getting candy at a specified future time, and removing the washing from the washing machine at a specified future time (e.g. when Daddy gets home). Children aged from 2 to 4 years all showed better memory for the highly motivating candy event, indicating an ability to plan ahead and to keep a particular event in mind. At short delays (five minutes), even the 2-year-olds achieved a level of 80% unprompted remindings for the highly motivating event. On the low-motivation task (getting the washing out of the machine), overall success with unprompted reminding was much lower, falling to 26% over long delays. Somerville et al. argued that even very young children were capable of adopting a deliberate "set" to remember at an early age.

Evidence for the strategic use of rehearsal

The spontaneous mnemonic strategies observed in these experiments were fairly task-specific, however. One mnemonic strategy that is widely used by adults when they want to remember some information over a short period of time is rehearsal. Saying things to ourselves over and over again can make it easier to remember them. We saw in Chapter 5 that the spontaneous use of rehearsal may not emerge until children are at school, and are having to rely increasingly on verbal strategies for learning and retaining information. This idea of a deficiency in younger children's spontaneous use of rehearsal is supported by the findings of a classic study of children's rehearsal, carried out by Flavell, Beach, and Chinsky (1966).

Flavell et al. asked children aged 5, 7, and 10 years to remember a set of pictures over a short delay of about 15 seconds while wearing a space helmet. The space helmet had a visor that concealed the children's eyes, but left their mouths visible. The short delay period began when the experimenter said "Visor down!", and any spontaneous rehearsal during this delay was measured by a trained lip-reader. While the visor was up, the children were shown up to seven pictures (apple, comb, moon, owl, pipe, flowers, American flag), and were required to remember between two and five of them while the visor was down. Flavell et al. found that only 10% of the 5-year-olds used a rehearsal strategy, whereas 60% of the 7-year-olds and 85% of the 10-year-olds did so. There was also some evidence from the 7-year-olds' data that the children who rehearsed more recalled more pictures. Flavell and his colleagues argued that the majority of the younger children failed to rehearse because they did not realise that they needed to use strategies such as rehearsal to help them to remember. As we saw earlier, younger children are also less likely to convert visually presented information into a verbal code.

Although Flavell et al.'s study did find some evidence for a relationship between the use of rehearsal and the accuracy of recall, later work has shown that the strategic rehearsal of 7-year-old children tends to be piecemeal and not particularly helpful to short-term memory. They tend to rehearse just the currently presented item, or the current item with very few other items. However, small amounts of training can lead to rapid improvement in the strategic use of rehearsal, with accompanying improvements in recall.

For example, Naus, Ornstein, and Aivano (1977) gave 8- and 11-year-old children a list of words to remember. Some of the children were told to practise the words aloud as they normally would do to themselves, and others were told to practise the words aloud by saying the word that had just been presented in a given trial along with two other words. The children who were trained how to rehearse remembered significantly more items at test than the children who were told to practise the words as they normally would to themselves. Naus et al. argued that it was the content of rather than the activity of rehearsal that improved memory in list-learning tasks. The quality of rehearsal was more important than its frequency.

The fact that children can be trained to use rehearsal leaves open the question of whether younger children have the strategy of rehearsal available to them, but simply do not think of using it (a "production deficiency"). One way of finding out whether younger children's lack of rehearsal is due to a "production deficiency" is to offer them an *incentive* to use rehearsal. Kunzinger and Witryol (1984) devised an incentive-based technique that used financial rewards for studying the spontaneous use of rehearsal by 7-year-olds. They told the children that recall of some words on a list would win them 10 cents, whereas recall of others would win them only 1 cent. If children can rehearse without being trained in efficient strategy usage, then they should be more likely to rehearse "10 cent words" than "1 cent words".

Kunzinger and Witryol indeed found that the children in their study allocated more rehearsal to the "10 cent words" than to the "1 cent words". In fact, they were six times as likely to rehearse the former as the latter at the beginning of the list. In a control condition in which every word was worth 5 cents, the children rehearsed less overall. Kunzinger and Witryol argued that this was because the children in the experimental condition generalised the use of rehearsal from the "10 cent words" to the "1 cent words". The extra rehearsal allocated to the "10 cent words" also resulted in better recall. These words were recalled significantly more often than the "1 cent words" or the "5 cent words".

Clearly 7-year-olds can be induced to use rehearsal, and when they do so, their memories improve.

Attractive incentives can also be used to induce memory strategies in 4-year-olds, although without apparent improvement in their memories. O'Sullivan (1993) showed 4-year-old children 15 different toys (doll, horse, ball, aeroplane etc.) and told them that they would win a prize if they could remember all the toys in a recall test. Two prizes were on offer, a pencil and a box of crayons. The crayons were universally judged to be the more appealing prize. In the experiment, the toys were presented in a bag. The experimenter took them out of the bag, allowed the children to study them for three minutes, and then put them back into the bag. The children then spent 25 seconds drawing Xs on a sheet of paper to eliminate short-term memory effects, after which the recall phase of the experiment began.

O'Sullivan found that the children who were playing to win the box of crayons showed more visual examination of the toys than the children who were playing to win the pencil, and also spent less time in "off-task" behaviour. Spontaneous use of rehearsal was not observed. However, although the possibility of winning the better prize elicited significantly more efforts to remember than the possibility of winning the poorer prize, this did not translate into superior recall for the "crayons" group. Recall performance was in fact equivalent across the two incentive groups, and averaged eight items. It should be mentioned that all the children received both prizes at the end of the study!

Many other studies of the development of rehearsal in young children report broadly similar findings to the studies discussed here (see Schneider & Pressley, in press, for a review). Younger children seem disinclined rather than unable to rehearse. Rehearsal first appears when it is encouraged by training or by task-specific factors such as remembering a list of words, or by the use of verbal rather than visual presentation of the items to be remembered. Rehearsal is only used strategically somewhat later in development. The early lack of spontaneous rehearsal can thus be seen as a production deficiency rather than a competence deficiency.

Evidence for the strategic use of organisation by semantic category

Organisational mnemonic strategies, such as sorting required grocery items into related groups and using this clustering to aid recall, show a similar developmental pattern to rehearsal. Early strategic use is largely task-driven, and depends on the items to be recalled. Later strategic use is child-driven, and occurs independently of the materials to be remembered.

For example, Schneider (1986) told 7- and 10-year-old children that they would be shown a set of 24 pictures, and that they should try to do anything that would help them to remember the items in the set. The sets of pictures were either defined as having "high category relat- edness" (e.g. dog, cat, horse, cow, pig, mouse), or "low category relat- edness" (e.g. goat, deer, hippopotamus, buffalo, monkey, lamb). In addition, the sets either had high inter-item associativity according to word association norms (e.g. chair, table, bed, sofa, desk, lamp), or low inter-item associativity (e.g. refrigerator, stool, bookcase, rocking chair, stove, bench). The children were given two minutes to sort the pictures, and an additional two minutes to study them.

Schneider found that only 10% of the 7-year-olds spontaneously grouped the pictures according to their category relationships, whereas about 60% of the 10-year-olds did so. In addition, the younger children, but not the older children, were less likely to group together the items that had low inter-item associativity. Whereas the 10-year-olds used categories like "furniture" to group the pictures of the stove, bench etc., the 7-year-olds did not. Schneider argued that the use of organisational strategies in younger children depended on the degree to which the items were associated. For the 7-year-olds, high associativity *in itself* led to the use of clustering, in a largely involuntary way. In contrast, the 10- year-olds used clustering as a deliberate strategy. The older children were apparently becoming aware of the value of organisational strategies as a mnemonic. In support of his argument, Schneider found that approximately half of the 10-year-olds in his study showed systematic and strategic behaviour that facilitated recall, and were aware of the value of organisational strategies.

Similar results were reported in a memory task devised by Bjorklund and Bjorklund (1985), in which 6-, 8-, and 10-year-old children were asked to recall the names of their current classmates. All of the children found this an easy task, and appeared to be behaving strategically, organising their recall in terms of grouping cues such as the seating arrangements in their classroom, the children's reading groups, or boys vs. girls. However, when the experimenters asked the children how they went about remembering their classmates' names, the children were unable to outline particular strategies, which suggested that their use of clustering was involuntary. Bjorklund and Bjorklund tested this hypothesis by asking the children to use specific retrieval strategies, such as remembering all of the boys first and then all of the girls. They found that recall in this strategic condition was equivalent to recall in the free condition, when no instructions were given. Bjorklund and Bjorklund concluded that semantic associations between highly associated items can be activated with little effort, resulting in retrieval that appears to be organised and strategic when in fact it is simply a by-product of high associativity. High associativity thus *automatically* guides the structure of recall.

However, evidence for more strategic use of semantic associativity can also be found. Schneider and Sodian (1988) asked 4- and 6-year-old children to hide 10 pictures of people (doctor, farmer, policeman) in 10 wooden houses, and then to retrieve them by matching each picture with its "twin" (a duplicate picture provided by the experimenter). The wooden houses all had roofs that could be opened and shut like boxes, and they also had magnetic stickers on the front doors to which a picture cue could be attached. The available picture cues were either functionally related to the people who were hiding (syringe, tractor, police car) or not (key, flower, lamp).

Schneider and Sodian first asked the children to perform the hiding task without the picture cues, and measured the time taken for hiding and retrieval. They then attached a picture cue to each house, and asked the children to perform the hiding and retrieval tasks a second time. Systematic use of the semantic associations between the picture cues and the targets should lead to slower hiding times on the second trial, but more accurate retrieval. This was exactly what happened. Children of both age groups spent longer hiding the people pictures on the second trial, and also remembered more locations on the second trial. Furthermore, the 6-year-olds remembered significantly more locations on the second trial than the 4-year-olds, indicating that they benefited more from the semantic associations in the cue pictures. Indeed, they were more likely to hide people at semantically appropriate locations than the younger children, hiding on average 72% of the possible people appropriately, compared to 40% for the 4-year-olds.

Schneider and Sodian also reported that the older children showed more understanding of the use of retrieval cues. When asked specific questions like "Which of the games I just played with you was easier?", the 6-year-olds displayed greater conscious knowledge of the strategic use of the semantic cues than the 4-year-olds. However, even the 4-year-olds showed some knowledge of cuing as a memory aid. Furthermore, a relationship between conscious awareness of the usefulness of the cues and successful memory performance was found in both groups. Schneider and Sodian argued that the idea that pre-schoolers can only react automatically to highly associated cues without any awareness of their value may be misguided. Even 4-year-olds appear to have some understanding of the utility of cognitive cuing. The fact that this study used a simpler and more meaningful task from the child's point of view may also be important in eradicating the apparent production deficiency in children's spontaneous use of organisation as a mnemonic strategy.

Metamemory

One way of describing the development of the realisation that various strategies can be used to improve memory is to use the concept of "metamemory". Metamemory is knowledge *about* memory. The development of metamemory is the development of the ability to monitor and regulate one's own memory behaviour (Brown, Bransford, Ferrara, & Campione, 1983). As children understand more about how their memories work, they should become more sensitive to the fact that certain memory tasks will benefit from particular strategies, and they should also become more aware of their own strengths and weaknesses in remembering certain types of information (Flavell & Wellman, 1977). As metamemory develops, children should actively begin to use mnemonic strategies to improve their encoding and retrieval of information in memory. So as metamemory improves, production deficiencies in memory tasks should decline.

There are a number of different types of metamemory knowledge that a child can acquire. These include knowledge of oneself as a memoriser, knowledge of the present contents of one's memory, and knowledge of task demands (Wellman, 1978). Wellman argued that in addition to acquiring knowledge about these different metamemory "variables", the child needs to realise that intentional memory behaviour is required ("sensitivity"). In order to examine the development of knowledge about metamemory "variables", Wellman gave 5- and 10-year-old children pictures of different memory situations to assess as easy or difficult. An easy situation was a picture of a boy who had to remember 3 items, whereas a difficult situation was a picture of a boy who had to remember 18 items. In addition, some of the situations measured children's understanding that two different variables could *interact* to determine memory difficulty. For example, a picture of a boy with 18 items to remember and a long walk during which to remember them (long recall time) was intended to be assessed as easier than a picture of a boy with 18 items to remember and a short walk during which to remember them (short recall time).

Wellman found that the 5-year-olds were as good as the 10-year-olds in judging the difficulty of memory tasks involving a single variable (such as 3 vs. 18 items). However, they were significantly worse than the 10-year-olds when the memory tasks involved interactions between variables. For example, the 5-year-olds tended to predict that both boys with 18 items to remember had equally difficult memory tasks, even though one boy had more time to remember the items than the other. The 10-year-olds rarely made such errors. Wellman concluded that the 5-year-olds could only judge memory performance on the basis of one of the relevant variables. He argued that an important aspect of the development of metamemory concerned the ability to *inter relate* the effects of different metamemory variables.

A different question about metamemory is when children first become able to assess the *relative* usefulness of different strategies for remembering. Justice (1985) asked children aged 7, 9, and 11 years to make judgements about the relative effectiveness of four alternative strategic behaviours: rehearsing, categorising (by semantic category), looking, and naming. The children first watched a video of a child, "Lee", performing a memory task requiring the recall of a set of 12 categorisable pictures. The children were told that Lee would try to remember the pictures in different ways. For example, to demonstrate *categorisation*, Lee grouped the pictures by semantic category (e.g. apple, pear, banana), and named each group aloud twice. To demonstrate *rehearsal*, Lee grouped the pictures at random and named each group twice (e.g. truck, apple, hand). For *naming*, Lee simply named each picture twice without rearranging them spatially, and for *looking*, Lee stared hard at each picture twice without rearranging them spatially.

The children were then asked to make a series of judgements about which strategy would "help Lee remember best". Each strategy was paired with all of the others, making 24 paired comparison judgements in all. The 7-year-olds made no distinction between rehearsal and categorisation as the better strategy, but the 9- and 11-year-olds judged categorisation to be more effective than rehearsal (which was the case in Lee's scenario). Justice (1985) suggested that some metacognitive awareness of the usefulness of categorisation was present by at least 9 years of age.

Another aspect of metamemory is "self-monitoring", which is the ability to keep track of where you are with respect to your memory goals. A related aspect is "self-regulation", which is the ability to plan, direct, and evaluate your own memory behaviour. Children's ability to self-monitor and self-regulate their strategic memorial behaviour was investigated by Dufresne and Kobasigawa (1989). They examined whether 6-, 8-, 10-, and 12-year-old children could distribute their study time efficiently between easy and hard material.

In their experiment, children were given two sets of booklets of paired-associate items to study. One set of booklets contained "easy" paired-associates, such as *dog–cat*, *bat–ball*, and *shoe–sock*. The other set of booklets contained "hard" paired-associates, such as *book–frog*, *skate–baby*, and *dress–house*. The younger children were given fewer sets of booklets, to equate task difficulty across age. The children's goal was to remember all of the pairs perfectly, and they were allowed to study the booklets until they were sure that they could remember all of the "partners". The way in which the children allocated their study time was measured by videotaping the study period, and then timing the portions of each period spent in studying either the easy or the hard booklets.

Dufresne and Kobasigawa found that the 6- and 8-year-old children did not differentiate between the easy and the hard booklets, allocating an equivalent amount of study time to each. In contrast, the 10- and 12-year-old children spent significantly longer studying the hard booklets, with the 12-year-olds spending a longer time on the hard pairs than any other group. This suggested that older children were better at self-regulating their memory behaviour. Dufresne and Kobasigawa then divided the children in each age group into those who spent "more time on hard pairs" vs. those who spent "more time on easy pairs". This showed that the 8-year-olds, too, had some ability to allocate study time. More 8-year-olds spent "more time on hard pairs" than "more time on easy pairs", and this pattern was even stronger for the 10- and 12-year-olds. Only the youngest group contained more children who spent "more time on easy" problems than "more time on hard" problems, even though a separate test showed that the 6-year-olds could differentiate between the easy and the hard booklets. Dufresne and Kobasigawa argued that the younger children lacked the *metamemorial* knowledge necessary to enable them to allocate more study time to the hard pairs. Although they were able to monitor problem difficulty, they did not use this knowledge to regulate their study time accordingly.

Finally, an important question about metamemory is whether children with better metamemories perform better in different memory tasks. After all, if the development of the ability to monitor and regulate one's own memory behaviour plays an important role in the development of memory *per se*, then children who are better at self-monitoring and at self-regulation should also remember more. Meta-analyses of the relationship between measures of metamemory and memory behaviour suggest that the relation is indeed a significant one. In a meta-analysis of some of the key empirical studies of this issue

(27 studies and 2231 subjects), Schneider (1985) reported an overall correlation of 0.41 between metamemory and memory performance. Schneider and Pressley (1989) reported an identical correlation in an even larger meta-analysis (of 60 publications and 7079 subjects).

Individual studies suggest the same conclusion. For example, the relationship between metamemory and memory performance is related to achievement. Kurtz and Weinert (1989) showed that German children who scored highly on a general test of cognitive ability had more metacognitive knowledge (e.g. about the usefulness of clustering by semantic category for recall) than children who scored at average levels. The high-ability children also recalled more words in a list memory task in which the words could be clustered according to categories (such as emotions). The relationship between metamemory and memory performance also seems to be bi-directional (see Schneider & Bjorklund, in press). A child's experience of the benefits of using a particular strategy, such as clustering words by semantic category, can add to their task-specific metamemory as well.

The relationship between memory development and cognitive development

Kurtz and Weinert's (1989) study shows that the development of metamemory is intimately linked to cognitive development in general, as children's levels of metacognitive knowledge are highly related to their overall performance on a general test of cognitive ability. This is hardly surprising, as the relationship between memory development and cognitive development is widely recognised. Most of the debate concerns exactly how best to characterise this connection.

We saw earlier that one approach to explaining children's cognition was knowledge-based. According to knowledge-based theorists, a rich and principled understanding of a particular domain is necessary before cognitive processes such as deductive reasoning can operate effectively to develop further understanding within that, and perhaps other, domains (see Foreword). Knowledge-based accounts thus credit the *storage* components of memory with a key role in explaining cognitive development. However, it is equally possible that the *processing* components of memory carry the critical explanatory load. Perhaps children become capable of more sophisticated kinds of information processing with development, and this is the major factor in explaining changes in children's cognition. According to such an account, domain-general changes in the processing components of memory would enable more effective utilisation of the knowledge base, for example by enabling more sophisticated reasoning strategies to be applied to current knowledge. A third alternative is that some kind of *meta knowledge* is the critical factor in cognitive development. Knowledge about one's own cognition may play the key developmental role in enabling advances in children's cognition. Knowledge about one's own cognition is called "metacognition", and this explanatory concept was at one time very popular in explaining cognitive development (see Forrest-Pressley, MacKinnon, & Waller, 1985).

More recently, however, it has been recognised that all three of these possibilities are probably correct. Rather than one component in isolation carrying the major explanatory load, it seems more plausible to argue that the quality of the knowledge base, the sophistication of the processes that operate on that knowledge base, *and* children's own awareness of what they know and of how they might operate on that knowledge *all* play important roles in developing children's cognition. We turn now to a brief consideration of how *all* of these components of memory may play important roles in cognitive development.

The novice–expert distinction

Although the storage components of memory may appear to be an unlikely source of individual differences in cognitive development, it is now recognised that the knowledge base itself can play a role in memory efficiency. Children's prior knowledge can have an important impact on their encoding and storage of incoming information, and also on the efficiency of their recall. One of the most interesting approaches to studying the influence of prior knowledge on cognitive development has been to contrast the performance of *novices* in a domain, who have little prior knowledge, with that of *experts*, who have a lot of prior knowledge. As such comparisons are usually confounded with age (novices are usually younger than experts), the most developmentally informative contrasts are those in which the experts are *younger than* the novices. Such contrasts are usually only possible in quite circumscribed domains, for example chess playing, soccer playing, and expertise in physics.

As Brown and DeLoache (1978) once called young children "universal novices", it may come as a surprise to find that young children occasionally display more expertise in circumscribed domains than older children and adults. This can occur, however, because experts and novices in a particular domain are distinguished by differences in *experience* as well as by differences in age. If you are motivated enough, it is possible to gain a lot of experience in a domain at a relatively young age. For example, some children know an amazing amount about dinosaurs, because they find this domain so interesting that they become veritable experts in dinosaur classification and behaviour. Another such domain is chess. Some young chess players display a remarkable level of expertise, and regularly beat their adult opponents.

If differences in experience distinguish novices and experts, then we can predict that differences in expertise should be correlated with differences in the structure and organisation of domain memory. In a pioneering study of this question, Chi (1978) examined the factors that distinguished the memories of chess experts and chess novices. Her group of experts were children aged from 6 to 10 years, and her group of novices were graduate students who could all play chess. Chi measured the memory of both groups for "middle game" chess positions, which involved on average 22 chess pieces. The chess players were allowed to study the chess board for 10 seconds, and were then expected to re create the middle game position from memory. Chi found that the children positioned 9.3 chess pieces accurately on the first trial, compared to 5.9 chess pieces for the adults. She then measured how long it took both groups to learn the *entire* middle game position. The children took on average 5.6 trials, and the adults 8.4 trials. Expert vs. novice performance was significantly different in each case.

Although it seems plausible that the children were chess experts because they could remember more about the chess board, it is also possible that they could remember more about the chess board because they were experts. Chi argued that her data supported the latter possibility. She proposed that the child experts could see meaningful patterns in the arrays of chess pieces that were not apparent to the less-skilled adults. Schneider and his colleagues tested this proposal in a replication of Chi's study which included additional control tasks (Schneider, Gruber, Gold, & Opwis, 1993, see Fig. 6.1). Schneider et al. found that recall for random as well as meaningful chess positions was better in experts than in novices. In the control task, in which the position of geometrically shaped wooden pieces had to be reconstructed on a board that did not resemble a chess board, the effect of expertise was eliminated. These findings suggest that expertise involves both *qualitative* differences in the way that knowledge is represented and *quantitative* differences in the amount of knowledge available. The latter would in this case include knowledge about the geometrical pattern of the chess board and the form and colour of chess pieces.

FIG. 6.1.
Examples of the chess task (a) and (b), and of the control task used by Schneider et al. (1993). Reproduced by permission of Academic Press Inc.

The data on children's dinosaur expertise also suggest that experts structure their knowledge in qualitatively different ways from novices. Chi, Hutchinson, and Robin (1989) found that experts organised their knowledge about dinosaurs in more integrated and locally coherent ways than novices. Their knowledge was more coherent at a global level, representing superordinate information such as "meat eater" vs. "plant eater", and also at a sub-structural level, representing information about shared attributes such as "has sharp teeth" or "has a duckbill".

Chi et al. used a picture-sorting task to establish these differences. They found that 7-year-old dinosaur experts sorted pictures of dinosaurs on the basis of several related attributes and concepts ("He had webbed feet, so that he could swim, and his nose was shaped like a duck's bill, which gave him his name"). The 7-year-old novices sorted the same pictures on the basis of the depicted features ("He has sharp fingers, sharp toes, a big tail"). Chi and her colleagues pointed out that it was easier to understand the attributes of a dinosaur (sharp teeth, webbed feet etc.) if one knew how they were related in a causal or correlated structure. The importance of causal relations and relational mappings for conceptual development and knowledge acquisition should already be familiar from Chapters 3 and 4.

Expertise may also be *more* important for memory performance than general cognitive ability, at least when a particular domain like chess or soccer is the object of study. In a study of "soccer experts" carried out in Germany, Schneider and his colleagues found that grade 3 soccer experts (boys and girls) recalled more information about a story concerning a soccer game than grade 7 soccer novices, and that expertise was a stronger predictor of performance than general cognitive ability, regardless of age (Schneider, Korkel, & Weinert, 1989). Similar effects have been demonstrated in adults by other researchers. For example, extensive experience of attending horse racing meetings and calculating the odds is a better predictor of who wins money at the races than IQ (Ceci & Liker, 1986). Findings such as these suggest that the old saying "practice makes perfect" does capture something important about the development of expertise. In a longitudinal study of talented young German tennis players (the sample included Boris Becker and Steffi Graf), Schneider, Boes, and Rieder (1993) found that the amount and level of practice was an important predictor of the rankings of the players five years later. So was the level of achievement motivation. Perhaps unsurprisingly, basic ability *per se* was only one important predictor of later tennis excellence.

Overall, studies of novices and experts show that expertise plays a crucial role in the organisation of memory. The idea that knowledge enrichment leads to the re-organisation of memory has some obvious parallels with Carey's ideas about the role of knowledge acquisition and relational mappings in conceptual change (see Chapter 3). It is also comforting to learn that anyone can become an expert in certain domains if they are motivated enough to learn about them. Memory development thus depends on the depth of the knowledge base as well as on the use of explicit strategies such as rehearsal. High levels of expertise can even compensate for low levels of general intelligence in some memory tasks, such as recall tasks. We can conclude that the storage components of memory play a clear role in individual differences in some aspects of cognition.

The development of processing capacity

The processing components of memory have been a more popular source of theories of cognitive development than the storage components. The notion of a short-term "workspace" in which new material or material retrieved from long-term memory could actively be processed was discussed in Chapter 5. The amount of processing *capacity* that is available to the child has been seen as a particularly important variable in the development of children's cognition. In fact, a number of recent "neo-Piagetian" theories of cognitive development are based on variations of the processing capacity idea.

For example, Pascual-Leone (1970) has argued that processing space increases with age, and that as processing space ("central computing space") increases, so does the cognitive stage of the child. A similar notion has been advanced by Case (1985), whose model includes a *trade-off* between "short-term storage space" (a retention component) and "operating space" (a processing component). Overall capacity ("executive processing space") is not thought to change with development, but the amount of available capacity is thought to increase as processing becomes more efficient (e.g. via practice) and consequently takes up less "space". A third neo-Piagetian is Halford (1993), who has proposed a developmental model centred on the capacity of "active" or "primary" memory. Halford defines primary memory as the memory system that holds any information that is currently being processed, and he argues that the capacity of this system increases with development. Finally, a somewhat different neo-Piagetian theorist is Fischer (1980), who has proposed that development is best understood in terms of the control and construction of skills. A skill refers to the ability to carry out a set of actions in a particular context.

The common element central to the neo-Piagetian theories proposed by Pascual-Leone, Case, and Halford is the notion of processing capacity, which is a form of working memory or attentional capacity. These neo-Piagetian theorists suggest that the size of available processing capacity places an upper limit on cognitive performance, and that specifiable biological factors (as yet unknown) regulate the gradual shift in this upper limit with age. Cognitive development is explained by older children having more processing capacity than younger children, and qualitative improvements in cognitive performance are predicted with increasing age (as in Piaget's theory, see

Chapter 8). These qualitative improvements generally arise from the use of more sophisticated information-processing strategies, which become available once increased processing capacity is present. For example, Halford (1993) has argued that increases in processing capacity enable children to use relational mappings of greater complexity.

As processing capacity imposes a theoretical ceiling on children's performance in particular kinds of cognitive tasks, children who have yet to attain sufficient levels of processing capacity should be unable to reach given levels of performance in such tasks. This theoretical assumption of an "upper limit" provides the most usual means of testing neo-Piagetian theories (see Case, 1992). However, neo-Piagetian models can also account for large individual differences between children, as they postulate that some developmental restructuring is more local ("domain-specific") in nature than the restructuring that follows an increase in processing capacity. All neo-Piagetian theories also allow a role for the storage components of memory in cognitive development, as they recognise the quality of the knowledge base as an additional factor in explaining individual differences in cognition. A detailed discussion of the neo-Piagetian theories, which are quite complex, is beyond the scope of this book. However, an illustration of how neo-Piagetian models can account for cognitive development will be provided at the end of Chapter 7, when Halford's (1993) model will be examined in some detail.

Representational redescription as a theory of cognitive development

Finally, we will consider a theoretical account of how insight into the contents of one's memory could affect cognitive development. Such an account has been proposed by Karmiloff-Smith (1992), as part of her theory of representational redescription. Karmiloff-Smith's model makes a critical distinction between information being *in* memory, and being available as explicit information *to* the cognitive system. Her aim is to explain how children's representations become more manipulable and flexible as development proceeds. An important insight is that the *same* behaviour may arise from *different* representations at different points in developmental time, so that the same performance can be generated at different ages by very different representations. Karmiloff-Smith suggests that there are at least three levels at which knowledge is represented and re-represented with development. The levels are called implicit representations, explicit level 1 representations, and explicit level 2 representations. As the child progresses through these three levels, knowledge representation becomes progressively more *explicit*. Although the process of representational redescription is domain-general, it depends on the level of explicitness of the representations supporting particular domain-specific knowledge at any given time, and therefore will occur in different domains at different times.

The first phase in the representational redescription process is "data-driven" learning. During this phase, the child takes in relevant and salient information from the external environment until consistently successful performance in a given domain is achieved— "behavioural mastery". Behavioural mastery depends on implicit representations, and at this level knowledge is wholly inaccessible to consciousness. It is "in the mind", and therefore entirely "procedural". Procedures are activated purely as a response to external stimuli, and so children who are operating on the basis of implicit representations show behaviour that is determined by the particular stimuli that are present in a given task ("bottom-up" behaviour). As the child has no way of halting a procedure in mid-flow, once started she has to "run off" the entire procedure. For example, if the child sets out to draw a picture of a man, she cannot amend her usual "draw-a-man" procedure in order to draw "a man that doesn't exist", even if she had been planning to do so (see Karmiloff-Smith, 1992, for a fuller account of these data).

The second phase of representational redescription is internally driven. Instead of the child's representations depending on external data, the currently available internal representations predominate, and these representations become the focus of change via "system-internal dynamics". These *explicit level 1* representations are accessible to other parts of the mind, although the child herself has *no* explicit awareness of this accessibility. This means that the products of interactions between explicit level 1 representations are not available to conscious awareness. In terms of drawing "a man that doesn't exist", the child may be able to change elements in the procedure, such as body shape or leg size, but cannot introduce re-orderings of the sequential constraints (e.g. by drawing his feet sticking out of his head). This requires a further level of redescription, called *explicit level 2* representations.

The third phase of representational redescription depends on the reconciliation of internal representations and external data, so that a balance is achieved. This gives children *conscious access* to their own knowledge. Explicit level 2 representations are stateable verbally, and can be communicated to others. Level 2 children can "draw a man that doesn't exist" by inserting elements from other conceptual categories, such as giving the man a pair of wings. It is only at this final level of redescription that Karmiloff-Smith credits children with insight into their own conceptual processes. This can be thought of as having metaknowledge about your knowledge ("metacognition").

Karmiloff-Smith suggests that a useful analogy for understanding her theoretical ideas is learning to play the piano (Karmiloff-Smith, 1994). The pathway to becoming an efficient pianist involves a first phase of learning to play a whole piece automatically via paying conscious attention to particular notes and to chunks of several notes which can be played together as blocks. At this point, the sequence has become a "procedure", analogous to an implicit representation. Knowledge is *implicit* at this stage as the fledgling pianist cannot start playing in the middle of the piece, and cannot play variations on a theme. Instead, his or her "knowledge" of the piece is embedded in the motor commands and actions sustaining its execution. Representational redescription must now take place, so that knowledge of the different notes and chords can become explicit and available as manipulable data. Eventually the learner will become able to generate

variations on a theme, to introduce insertions from other pieces of music, and to play creatively. The end result of representational redescription is representational flexibility and control.

Karmiloff-Smith's theory depends on the idea that knowledge can be stored and accessible at *more than one* level. The key idea is that the human mind recursively rerepresents its own internal representations, and that this re-representation is the main process that underlies cognitive development. Furthermore, the redescriptions that

TRIP/H. ROGERS

occur during development remain in the mind. This results in *multiple* representations of similar knowledge at different levels of detail and explicitness. The notion of multiple encoding means that the child's mind as envisaged by Karmiloff-Smith is a storehouse of knowledge and processes, some of which have become redundant. The idea that humans differ from other species because of their unique ability to "appropriate" their own internal representations— to "know about" their knowledge—is a very appealing one. The capacity to enrich knowledge from within, by redescribing

knowledge that is already stored in memory, seems to be a specifically human capacity.

Representational redescription theory differs markedly from the
"neo-Piagetian" theories based on processing capacity that were
described earlier, as it is not a stage theory of cognitive development.
This is because the three kinds of representation postulated by
Karmiloff-Smith can occur at different times in different domains.
However, the neo-Piagetian theories are in some ways easier to test
than Karmiloff-Smith's theory, because they make empirical predictions
about upper limits on cognitive performance. Representational
redescription theory does not, requiring instead careful and detailed
investigation of how representations change progressively over time.
As Karmiloff-Smith (1994) has pointed out, connectionist models
provide one possible avenue for modelling developmental change that
could incorporate a representational redescription format. A research
strategy based on connectionist simulations is already being widely
used in adult cognition, but to date has not featured strongly in
children's cognition. This situation will probably change during the
next decade of progress in cognitive science, and a review of the current
state-of-the-art in developmental cognitive neuroscience is available
from Johnson (1997).

Summary

This chapter has focused on the aspects of memory development that
show marked individual differences—individual differences that may
in turn contribute to individual differences in cognitive development.
One source of individual differences in memory development is
children's spontaneous use of mnemonic strategies such as rehearsal
and organisation. We saw that although even 2-year-olds show some
signs of realising that mnemonic strategies may be useful in enhancing
memory performance, the spontaneous use of rehearsal and organisation appears to emerge during the school years. This relatively late
emergence seems to be due to a production deficiency rather than a
competence deficiency, with younger children seeming disinclined
rather than unable to rehearse and to use organisational strategies.
Children can also be trained to use strategies such as rehearsal, and
such training improves their mnemonic performance. However, it is
notable that many of the experiments examining children's spontaneous use of rehearsal and organisation have little ecological validity,
being based instead on "laboratory" style tasks. These data may
therefore somewhat underestimate children's spontaneous strategic

abilities. At the present time, the best conclusion is that the early utilisation of rehearsal and organisation depends largely on task-related factors, such as the nature of the material to be recalled.

Another source of individual differences in memory development is children's knowledge about their memories. The development of metamemory, or the ability to monitor and regulate one's own memory performance, requires knowledge of the strengths and weaknesses of one's own memory and sensitivity to the fact that certain memory tasks will benefit from particular strategies. This in turn requires sensitivity to the demands made by different memory tasks and knowledge of the current contents of one's memory. The realisation that intentional memory behaviour is required and may be beneficial appears to increase with age. Children become better at interrelating the effects of different task demands, at judging the relative usefulness of different memory strategies for specific memory tasks, at keeping track of where they are with respect to their memory goals, and at self-regulating their strategic behaviour. Furthermore, children with better metamemories remember more information. Individual differences in the use of memory strategies and in metamemory are also linked to individual differences in cognitive achievement.

A third source of individual differences in memory development is the acquisition of expertise. The quality of the knowledge base can play an important role in memory efficiency. Prior knowledge can affect the encoding and storage of incoming information and also the effectiveness of recall. In contrast to the other sources of individual differences in memory development, expertise is not necessarily dependent on age. Even young children can be experts in certain domains such as chess playing or knowledge about dinosaurs, and will outperform adults in memory tasks set in these domains. Such expertise appears to be characterised by both qualitative differences in the way that knowledge is represented, with experts having more integrated and cohesive knowledge structures, and quantitative differences in the amount of knowledge available.

TRIP/J. KING

Finally, we saw that the development of processing capacity is another source of individual differences in memory development. Processing capacity is a form of working memory or attentional capacity. The amount of available processing capacity is hypothesised to place an upper limit on cognitive performance. Although the development of processing capacity is dependent partly on age, it also depends on the quality of the knowledge base and on individual abilities to restructure specific areas of this knowledge base in the light of incoming information. A number of theories of cognitive development are based on improvements in processing capacity with age. A common element in these "neo-Piagetian" theories is the notion that qualitative improvements in cognitive development will accompany the developmental increases in processing capacity. We consider one neo-Piagetian theory in detail at the end of the next chapter, that of Halford (1993).

Logical reasoning in childhood 7

There are a number of different kinds of logical reasoning. Some of these seem to develop early in young children, such as the ability to use deductive logic and the ability to reason by analogy. Others seem to develop somewhat later, such as transitive reasoning, which requires children to make logical inferences about the relationship between two quantities that are not directly compared, and scientific reasoning (see Chapter 4). As we saw in the Foreword, many of these later-developing types of logical reasoning were first investigated by Piaget. Piaget suggested that "concrete operational" reasoning, such as transitive reasoning, developed at the age of around 6 years, and that "formal operational" reasoning, such as scientific reasoning, developed at the age of 11 to 12 years.

In this chapter, we will first examine the development of the forms of logical reasoning that appear early, and then consider the Piagetian "concrete operations". It is notable that research examining the early-developing forms of logical reasoning has found it important to develop paradigms based on materials and settings that are highly familiar to young children. In fact, the use of ecologically valid, child-centred tasks proved an important step in establishing early competence, as the history of research on the development of analogical reasoning makes very clear. Early analogy research tended to be based on unfamiliar materials and relations, and suggested that analogical reasoning was absent in children prior to the age of 11 to 12 years. More recent research using child-friendly tasks has found analogical abilities in children as young as 2 years. Research in the Piagetian tradition has in general not concentrated on developing ecologically valid, child-centred tasks. The possible importance of this will be discussed later.

Early-developing modes of logical reasoning

Reasoning by analogy
Reasoning and learning by analogy are fundamental cognitive processes. Analogies are used whenever we recall familiar past situa-

tions in order to deal with novel ones. As noted previously, when reasoning by analogy "We face a situation, we recall a similar situation, we match them up, we reason, and we learn" (Winston, 1980, p.1). Analogical reasoning is the basis of much everyday problem solving. For example, when we are faced with a novel problem, we frequently solve it by thinking of a similar problem that we have solved successfully on a previous occasion. However, as well as forming the basis of many everyday decisions, analogies can be used to solve novel problems in science, to solve legal problems by appealing to appropriate precedents, and to understand new material in school.

To solve a new problem by using an analogy, we need to find the *correspondences* between the previously encountered problem and the novel one. This enables us to "match up" the two situations. We then need to transfer knowledge from the familiar problem to the novel one. The identification of these correspondences usually requires *relational* reasoning. The solution to one problem can usually be applied to a different problem if similar sets of relations link different sets of objects in the two problems.

This point can be illustrated by thinking about some of the analogies that have led to new discoveries in science. One of the most famous was Kekule's theory about the molecular structure of benzene, which he discovered on the basis of an analogy to a visual image that he had of a snake biting its own tail (Fig. 7.1, see Holyoak & Thagard, 1995, for other examples). The carbon atoms in benzene are arranged in a ring, which shares visual similarity with a snake biting its tail, even though the objects in the analogy bear no resemblance to each other at all. The similarity is purely relational—in this case, arrangement of an object or objects in a ring. Sometimes, however, there are similarities in the objects *as well as* in the relations in an analogy. An example is the invention of Velcro, which was developed in 1948 after Georges de Mestral noticed that burdock burrs stuck to his dog's coat because they were covered with tiny hooks (see Holyoak & Thagard, 1995). Velcro shares "surface" similarity (similarity of appearance) as well as relational similarity (capacity to stick tight) with burdock burrs.

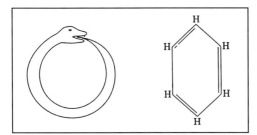

FIG. 7.1. The visual analogy between a snake biting its own tail and the molecular structure of benzene. From Holyoak and Thagard (1995). Reproduced by kind permission of MIT Press.

Most research on the development of analogical reasoning has examined whether children can recognise relational similarities between previously encountered problems and novel ones (i.e. identify correspondences), and whether they can use relational reasoning to solve analogies (transfer appropriate knowledge from the familiar problem to the novel one). Related questions have been how early children are able to make relational mappings, and whether children can map relational similarities in the *absence* of surface similarities (e.g. Gentner, 1989). We will focus here on the issues of the use of relational reasoning and the identification of relational correspondences, as the related questions have been covered to some extent in earlier chapters. For example, research discussed in Chapter 2 showed that even babies can make rudimentary analogies, suggesting that relational mapping abilities are present from very early in life. Similarly, research discussed in Chapters 3 and 4 showed that surface similarities between problems are not necessary for young children to use analogies. The "personification" analogy that children use to help them to develop conceptual knowledge about biological kinds (making analogies from people to dogs and plants) is a good example. More detailed discussion of these points is available in Goswami (1992, 1996).

The use of relational reasoning in childhood. The question of whether children have the cognitive ability to make relational mappings has been investigated through studies using *item* analogies. Item analogies provide a pure measure of relational reasoning. In an item analogy, the relation between two items *A* and *B* must be mapped to a third item *C* in order to complete the analogy with an appropriate *D* term. For example, to complete the item analogy "bird is to nest as dog is to?" (*bird:nest::dog: ?*), children must map the relation *lives in* that links *bird* to *nest* to the item *dog* in order to reason that *doghouse* is the correct solution to the analogy.

   Item analogies can be given to quite young children, as long as they are set in familiar domains (see Goswami, 1991, 1992). For example, a 4-year-old can be given the analogy *bird:nest::dog:doghouse* by presenting the task in the form of a game about constructing sequences of pictures (e.g. Goswami & Brown, 1990). Here is 4-year-old Lucas trying to predict which picture he needs in order to complete the picture sequence *bird:nest::dog: ?*, depicted in Fig. 7.2:

> Bird lays eggs in her nest [the nest in the *B*-term picture contained three eggs]—dog—dogs lay babies, and the babies are—umm—and the name of the babies is puppy! (p.222)

   Lucas used the relation "type of offspring" to solve the analogy. The solution that the experimenters had intended, however, was

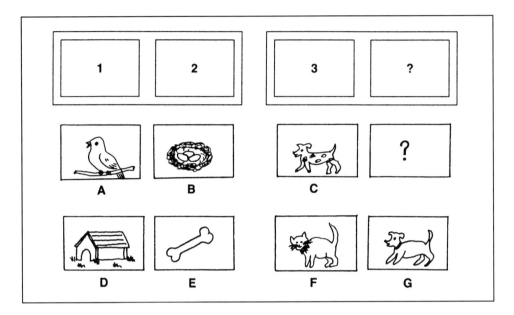

FIG. 7.2.
The gameboard (top row), analogy terms (middle row), correct answer and distractors (bottom row) used for the analogy bird:nest:dog:doghouse by Goswami & Brown (1990). Reprinted with permission.

"doghouse", as they had linked the *A* and *B* terms by the alternative relation "lives in". Following his verbal prediction, Lucas was shown the available completion pictures for the analogy, which did not in fact include a picture of a puppy. Instead, they depicted a *doghouse*, a *bone*, another *dog*, and a *cat*. Lucas was not interested in these pictures, as he was quite certain that his answer was correct:

> I don't have to look [at the distractor pictures]—the name of the baby is puppy!

In the end, when Lucas was persuaded to look at the different solution pictures designed by the experimenters, he decided that the picture of the *doghouse* was the correct response. This shows the strength and flexibility of young children's analogical reasoning skills. Of course, *puppy* was an equally correct solution to the analogy given the *A* and *B* terms in the picture sequence, and Lucas' defence of his solution suggests that he fully understood the relational mapping constraint that determined the correct solution. Nevertheless, he could use this constraint flexibly when faced with alternative solutions to work out another correct answer.

Analogical reasoning as measured by the *A:B::C:D* item analogy format is thus available by at least age 4 (Goswami & Brown, 1990). If the same format is used to explore analogies based on causal relations, such as *cutting* or *melting* (e.g. *apple:cut apple::playdoh:cut playdoh*; *chocolate:melted chocolate::snowman:melted snowman*), then even 3-year-old children succeed in the item analogy task (Goswami & Brown, 1989). It is difficult to use the item analogy format to demonstrate analogical competence in children younger than 3, because of the abstract nature of the task. With children younger than 3, it is necessary to devise ingenious *problem analogies* in order to show analogical reasoning at work.

In problem analogies, a young child is faced with a problem that they need to solve. Let us call this problem B. The use of an analogy from a previously experienced problem, problem A, offers a solution. The measure of analogical reasoning is whether the children can use the solution from problem A to solve problem B. We have already discussed one such problem analogy task, the "reaching-for-a-toy" task devised to study analogical problem-solving in infants and toddlers (e.g. Brown, 1990; Chen et al., 1995). This problem analogy format has also been extended to 2-year-olds.

Freeman (1996) devised a series of analogies for 2-year-olds using real objects and models. Her analogies were based on the simple causal relations of *stretching, fixing, opening, rolling, breaking,* and *attaching*. For example, a child might watch the experimenter *stretching* a loose rubber band between two plexiglass poles in order to make a "bridge" that she could roll an orange across ("Look what I'm going to do, I'm going to use this stuff to roll the orange! Stretch it out, put it on—wow, that's how I roll the orange!"). Following an opportunity to roll the orange by themselves, the children were given a transfer problem involving a loose piece of elastic, a toy bird, and a model with a tree at one end and a rock at the other. They were asked "Can you use this stuff to help the bird fly?". The intended solution was to stretch the elastic from the tree to the rock, and to "fly" the bird along it. In a third analogy problem, the children were asked to "give the doll a ride" by stretching some ribbon between two towers of different heights that were fixed to a base board. Children in a control condition were simply asked to "help the bird fly" and "give the doll a ride" without first seeing the base analogy of rolling the orange.

Freeman found that whereas only 6% of the children in the control condition thought of the *stretching* solution to the transfer problem, 28% of 30-month-olds in the analogy condition did so, and this figure rose to 48% following hints to use an analogy ("You know what? To help the bird fly, we have to change this", said while pointing to the elastic). When the same hint was given to the children in the control condition, only 14% thought of the *stretching* solution. Although these performance levels may appear modest, they are comparable to the spontaneous levels of analogical transfer found in adults. Problem analogy studies conducted with adults typically find spontaneous transfer levels of around 30%, at least in unfamiliar problem scenarios (e.g. Gick & Holyoak, 1980).

The identification of relational correspondences. Of course, in problem analogy tasks children have to *notice* the analogy as well as to perform the relational mapping correctly. This means that our second question about analogical development, which was whether children can recognise relational similarities or correspondences between previously encountered problems and novel ones, can also be investigated via problem analogy tasks. The factors that influence whether young children notice relational similarities between problems have been most extensively examined by Brown and her colleagues (e.g. Brown & Kane, 1988; Brown, Kane, & Echols, 1986; Brown, Kane, & Long, 1989). For example, Brown et al. (1986) gave 4- and 5-year-old children the "Genie" problem invented by Holyoak, Junn, and Billman (1984) to try to solve, and when they failed, demonstrated the solution. The children's ability to notice the correspondences between the Genie problem and a series of analogous problems was then measured in a variety of different conditions.

In the "Genie" problem, a genie is about to move from one location to another. He needs to take some precious jewels with him, and his problem is how to move them from the old location to the new location without damaging them in any way. His solution is to roll his magic carpet into a tube, and then to roll the jewels through this tube. The children in Brown et al.'s study were shown the Genie problem via a toy scenario with toy props. They then enacted the solution with the experimenter, rolling up a piece of paper that represented the magic carpet, and rolling the jewels through the paper tube. In order to help the children to extract the *goal structure* of the problem, a series of questions were asked including "Who has a problem?", "What did the genie need to do?", and "How does he solve his problem?". The children were then shown another problem intended to be analogous to the genie's, which also involved toy props. This was the "Easter Bunny" problem. An Easter Bunny needed to deliver a lot of eggs to children in time for Easter, but had left things a bit late. A friend had offered to help him, but the friend was on the other side of a river, and so the eggs had to be transported across the river to this friend without getting wet. The idea was that the Easter Bunny could use an analogous solution to the genie by rolling his blanket (a piece of paper) into a tube and rolling the eggs across the river through this tube.

Brown et al. found that 70% of the children in the experimental group noticed this analogy spontaneously. However, only 20% of children in a control group noticed the analogy by themselves. This control group had also experienced the Genie's problem, but had not been questioned about the goal structure of the story. Brown's conclusion from this and a series of similar studies was that children found it easy to recognise relational similarities between previously encountered problems and novel ones as long as they had represented the relational structure of the previously encountered problem in memory. Questioning by the experimenter facilitated this representational process, as it encouraged the children to represent the important relations that enabled the character to achieve his goal. Brown's research also showed that relational representation could be enhanced by experiencing a *series* of analogies, and by being *taught* to look for analogies during problem solving ("learning-to-learn"). These findings have clear implications for teaching in school, as they highlight the need for teachers to present a series of examples of a particular concept within an explicit framework that emphasises relational similarity.

Many other studies could have been chosen to show that the ability to reason by analogy is available from early in development (see Goswami, 1992, 1996, for more examples). The early age at which analogies appear suggest that they provide a powerful logical tool for explaining and learning about the world. Analogies also contribute to both the acquisition and the restructuring of knowledge. As children's knowledge about the world becomes richer, the structure of their knowledge becomes deeper, and more complex relationships are represented, enabling deeper or more complex analogies. This means that, as children learn more about the world, the type of analogies that they make will change. For example, as we saw in the chapter on conceptual development (Chapter 3), conceptual change does not depend simply on the enrichment of knowledge. It also depends on making analogical mappings between domains (Carey & Spelke, 1994). Research studies on the role of analogies in knowledge acquisition and restructuring are almost non-existent. Nevertheless, analogical reasoning and relational mappings are widely acknowledged to play an important role in cognitive development (e.g. Carey, 1985), and one theory of how to conceptualise the role of analogy is discussed at the end of this chapter (Halford, 1993).

Deductive logic and deductive reasoning

Another early-developing mode of logical reasoning is deductive reasoning. Problems that can be solved by deductive reasoning have only one right answer. The problem solver deduces this answer on the basis of the logical combination of the premises presented in the problem. For example, we use deductive logic to solve *syllogisms*, which are problems like the following:

All cats bark.
Rex is a cat.
Does Rex bark?

Given these premises, the only possible answer is that yes, Rex does bark. Although the premises in this example are obviously contrary to fact, as in the real world cats cannot bark, the plausibility or potential truth of the premises does not matter as far as the logical deduction is concerned. When children are given syllogisms to solve, the test of deductive reasoning is not whether the premises are counter factual or not, but whether the child can draw the correct deductive inference. The critical test is whether the children can recognise that the premises, whatever they may be, *logically imply* the conclusions.

Syllogistic Reasoning. Experimental research has shown that even quite young children can make deductive inferences about counter-factual premises. The problem about whether Rex barks or not was posed to 5- and 6-year-olds in an experiment by Dias and Harris (1988, see Table 7.1). In addition to "contrary facts" problems such as whether Rex barks, Dias and Harris gave children a selection of "known facts" problems ("All cats miaow. Rex is a cat. Does Rex miaow?"), and "unknown facts" problems ("All hyenas laugh. Rex is a hyena. Does Rex laugh?"). One group of children in their experiment were given the reasoning problems in a "play" mode. In this condition, toy cats, dogs, and hyenas were presented, and the experimenter made them miaow, bark, and laugh. A second group were simply told the premises in the problems without any toys or demonstrations, and asked to judge the conclusion.

Dias and Harris found that the children in the "play" group performed at or close to ceiling on all the different problem types. They were able to reason deductively whether the problems were contrary to fact, used known facts, or used unknown facts. In contrast, the children in the verbal group only showed high levels of responding in the "known facts" problems ("All cats miaow. Rex is a cat. Does Rex miaow?"). These problems could have been solved by using real-world knowledge rather than by using deductive logic.

In a follow-up experiment using only the "contrary facts" problems, Dias and Harris tried presenting the premises verbally to *both* groups of

TABLE 7.1

Examples of the counterfactual syllogisms used by Dias and Harris (1988)

"Yes" answers	"No" answers
(What noise do cats make?)	(Where do fishes live?)
All cats bark.	All fishes live in trees.
Rex is a cat.	Tot is a fish.
Does Rex bark?	Does Tot live in water?
(What are books made of?)	(What colour is milk?)
All books are made of grass	All milk is black.
Andrew is looking at a book	Jane is drinking some milk.
Is it made of grass?	Is her drink white?
(What colour is snow?)	(What colour is blood?)
All snow is black.	All blood is blue.
Tom touches some snow.	Sue has blood on her hand.
Is it black?	Is it red?
(How do birds move?)	(What is the temperature of ice?)
All birds swim.	All ice is hot.
Pepi is a bird.	Ann has some ice.
Does Pepi swim?	Is it cold?

children. Their aim was to rule out the possibility that the presence of the toy animals had been acting as a memory prompt for the children in the "play" group. This time, the children in the "play" group were told that they should pretend that the experimenter was on another planet, and that everything on that planet was different. For example, the experimenter would say "All cats bark. On that planet I saw that all cats bark", using a "make-believe" intonation, and would then verbally present the syllogism. In these "make-believe" conditions, the levels of reasoning shown by the "play" group remained close to ceiling. In a later study (Dias & Harris, 1990), children as young as 4 were found to be capable of syllogistic reasoning. This effect was robust whether the premises were presented as referring to another planet, were presented using a make-believe intonation, or were presented using visual imagery. Dias and Harris concluded that young children were capable of deductive reasoning, even about counterfactual premises, as long as logical problems were presented in the context of play.

Leevers and Harris (1997, unpublished manuscript) went on to show that the play context was not critical to children's capacity for deductive logic, however. Leevers and Harris gave 4-year-old children counterfactual syllogisms similar to those used by Dias and Harris, but whereas some of the children in their study received play context (imagination) instructions, others were simply told to *think* about the problems (e.g. "I want you to *think about* what things would be like if it was true ... are you *thinking about* x?"). Examples of the problems used by Leevers and Harris included "All snow is black. Tom sees some snow. Is it black?", and "All ladybirds have stripes on their backs. Daisy sees a ladybird. Is it spotty?". No significant differences in syllogistic reasoning were found between the "play context" and "thinking" groups. Leevers and Harris argued that their manipulations may have improved counterfactual reasoning because they encouraged the children to *process* the premises mentally instead of dismissing them as absurd. This idea was supported by the types of justifications given by the successful children. These were largely theoretical in nature. For example, one 4-year-old girl commented "All ladybirds have stripes on their back. But they don't" before reasoning that Daisy's ladybird was not spotty. Syllogistic reasoning thus appears to be present by at least 4 years of age.

Permission schemas and the selection task. Another widely used measure of deductive reasoning is the *selection* task, developed by Wason (1966). In the selection task, the subject is told about a certain state of affairs "if *p* then *q*". For example, the subject might be told "If a letter is sealed, then it has a 5p stamp on it". The task for the subject is to decide on the minimum number of pieces of evidence that are needed to validate the rule. The pieces of evidence available are usually *p* (e.g. a sealed letter, shown face-down); *q* (e.g. a letter with a 5p stamp, shown face-up), *not-p* (e.g. an unsealed letter, shown face-down); and *not-q* (e.g. a letter with a 4p stamp, shown face-up, see Fig. 7.3). Most adult subjects can solve the selection task when the problem is presented in a familiar context such as sorting letters in the post office (Johnson-Laird, Legrenzi, & Sonino-Legrenzi, 1972). The correct answer is that the minimum pieces of evidence required are *p* and *not-q*. This answer is given by the majority of adult subjects in tasks using familiar contexts, but in more formal versions of the same task performance can be as low as 10% correct. A typical formal version of the selection task is "If there is a vowel on one side of a card, there is an even number on the other side" (see Wason & Johnson-Laird, 1972).

Cheng and Holyoak (1985) have argued that this huge discrepancy in adults' ability to use deductive logic in the selection task depends on whether the selection task taps into familiar knowledge structures called *pragmatic reasoning schemas*. The pragmatic reasoning schemas relevant to the selection task usually describe permission scenarios in real life. For example, adults frequently encounter permission rules such as "If you want this letter to arrive tomorrow, it must go first

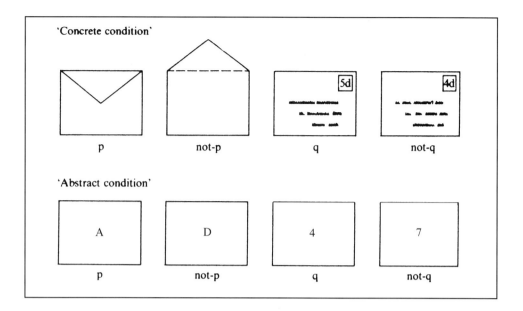

'Concrete condition'

p   not-p   q   not-q

'Abstract condition'

A   D   4   7

p   not-p   q   not-q

class", "If you are 18, you can drink alcohol in a pub", and "If you are 17, you can legally drive a car". Children probably encounter even more permission rules than adults. These may include "If it is 9 o'clock, you must be in bed", "If you are wearing your school blazer, you must wear your school cap", and "If the whistle has gone, you are not allowed to stay in the playground". Following Cheng and Holyoak's logic, we can predict that children should also show successful deductive reasoning in the selection task if it taps into a familiar type of permission schema.

This idea was tested by Light, Blaye, Gilly, and Girotto (1989), who devised permission rules that would be interpretable to 6- and 7-year-old children. They used two rules: "In this town, the police have made a rule which says that all the lorries must be outside of the centre", and "In this game, all the mushrooms must be outside of the centre of the board". The first rule, which was designed to have underlying pragmatic force, was demonstrated by showing the children a game board with a brown centre and a white surround. Pictures of lorries and cars were shown inside and outside the centre area. The second rule, which was designed to be arbitrary, was demonstrated using the same board but with pictures of flowers and mushrooms inside and outside the centre area instead of lorries and cars. Two lorries (or mushrooms) and one car (or flower) were always shown in the brown centre of the board, and one lorry (or mushroom) and three cars (or flowers) were always shown in the white surround (see Fig. 7.4).

FIG. 7.3.
Two versions of the selection task, using concrete and abstract stimuli. From Johnson-Laird and Wason (1977). Reprinted with permission.

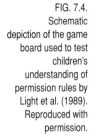
FIG. 7.4.
Schematic
depiction of the game
board used to test
children's
understanding of
permission rules by
Light et al. (1989).
Reproduced with
permission.

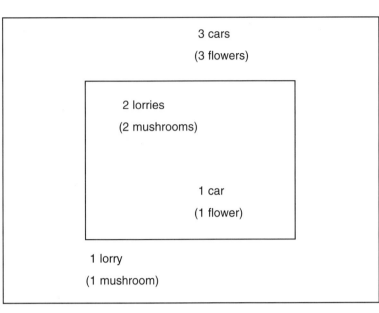

The children's first job was to rearrange the pictures on the game board so that they obeyed the rule (e.g. moving the two offending lorries out of the town centre). The experimenter then tested the children's understanding of the rule by carrying out a potential violation. The violation was moving a picture of a car or a flower outside the centre and asking if that disobeyed the rule (this was permissible). Next, the children themselves were asked to move a picture so that it *did* disobey the rule. Finally, a version of the selection task was given. The children were shown the game board with two pictures on it, both upside-down, one in the brown area and one in the white area. The children were asked (a) which picture they would need to turn over to check whether the rule had been disobeyed, (b) whether the picture that they had turned over disobeyed the rule, and (c) whether the other picture disobeyed the rule. Light et al. found that 45% of the 6-year-olds and 77% of the 7-year-olds succeeded in answering these three components of the selection task correctly in the lorry condition when the rules had pragmatic force. However, only 5% of the 6-year-olds and 23% of the 7-year-olds succeeded in the mushroom condition when the rules were arbitrary.

These results suggest that 6- and 7-year-old children, like adults, can use deductive logic in the selection task as long as an appropriate permission schema has been activated. Furthermore, Light et al. showed that activation of a permission schema in a *pragmatic* context could transfer to an *abstract* context. Some of the children who were successful in the lorry task were given an abstract version of the selection task involving squares and triangles ("all the triangles must be in the centre"). A total of 59% of the successful 7-year-olds and 30% of the successful 6-year-olds showed transfer from the lorry task to the triangles. Light et al. argued that this showed that the children understood the logic behind their correct choices in the lorry version of the selection task. The children were using their grasp of the pragmatics of permission and inhibition to help them to solve the task, and this understanding was then transferred to the triangles.

More recently, Harris and Nunez (1996) have shown that even 3- and 4-year-olds are sensitive to the pragmatics of permission and inhibition in the selection task. Harris and Nunez used a variety of story formats to present different permission rules, and then asked the children to select the correct picture from a set of four that depicted a breach of the rule. For example, in one study using familiar permission rules, the children were told "This is a story about Sally. One day Sally wants to play outside. Her Mum says that if she plays outside, she must put her coat on". The children were then shown four pictures, a picture of Sally outside with her coat on, a picture of Sally outside without her coat on, a picture of Sally inside with her coat on, and a picture of Sally inside without her coat on (see Fig. 7.5). The children were asked to select the picture in which the protagonist was breaking the permission rule ("Show me the picture of where Sally is being naughty and not doing what her mum told her"). This required them to select the picture that depicted the combination of *p* and *not-q*.

FIG. 7.5
The set of choice pictures used to test children's understanding of the permission rule "If Sally wants to play outside, she must put her coat on", Harris and Nunez (1996). Reprinted with permission.

The majority of children in both age groups chose the picture of Sally outside without her coat on. Similar results were found when the children were asked about novel rules ("Carol's Mum says if she does some painting she should put her helmet on"). Obviously, Harris and Nunez's paradigm is less demanding than the traditional selection task paradigm, as they required their subjects to select the picture that depicted the combination of *p* and *not-q* rather than to make an independent identification of *p* and *not-q*. Nevertheless, their conclusion that 3- and 4-year-old children are quite capable of identifying breaches of a permission rule seems a convincing one. Furthermore, they argued that children's grasp of permission rules was not restricted to *familiar* rules, as the link between condition and action could be quite arbitrary. Even so, the actions and conditions used by Harris and Nunez in their unfamiliar condition (painting, wearing a cycling helmet) were in themselves familiar to the children. The links were not quite as arbitrary as in the formal versions of the selection task used with adults ("if there is a vowel on one side of a card, there is an even number on the other side"). How well children would perform with completely arbitrary rules remains to be established.

Later-developing modes of logical reasoning

The later-developing modes of logical reasoning are those first identified by Piaget as requiring "concrete operational" thought. Concrete operational thought is said to be marked in part by an ability to consider multiple aspects of a situation simultaneously. An example would be comparing two numerically equivalent rows of counters. A child who is capable of concrete operational reasoning would be able to consider *both* the size of the gaps between the counters and the overall length of the rows in judging whether the two rows were the same or not. Concrete operational thought is also marked by an ability to understand that any operation on an object simultaneously implies its inverse. In the example of the two rows of counters, this would mean understanding that any increase in the size of the gaps between the counters can be reversed by pushing the counters closer together again (see also Chapter 8). Although more recent research has suggested that concrete operational forms of reasoning may be present at earlier ages than those postulated by Piaget, successful performance in concrete operational tasks by children younger than around 5 years of age is seldom found. When substantially younger children appear to succeed in Piagetian tasks, we must ask whether the experimenters have provided a "true test" of Piaget's theory.

Transitive inferences

One key logical concept identified by Piaget is the transitive inference. Transitive relations hold between any entities that can be organised into an ordinal series, and are fundamental to basic mathematical concepts such as measuring. For example, there is usually a transitive size relation between members of the same family, at least before the children become teenagers. The tallest family member is usually the father, the next tallest is the mother, and then the children usually follow in size in order of their age. If there are three children, aged 10 (Conrad), 6 (David), and 2 (Emma), then we can represent the size relations in the family as follows: $F > M > C > D > E$. We can then make transitive inferences about the size relations between individual family members. For example, if we are told that Conrad is taller than David ($C > D$), and that David is taller than Emma ($D > E$), we can make the logical inference that Conrad is taller than Emma ($C > E$).

Children's ability to make these kinds of transitive inferences has been the subject of some dispute. Much of the debate has focused on an experiment carried out by Bryant and Trabasso (1971), which showed that even 4-year-olds could make transitive inferences as long as they were *trained* to remember the premises. If the children could retain the premises successfully, then the logical ability to make a transitive inference seemed to be present in even the youngest children tested. Bryant and Trabasso pointed out that training the children to remember the premises in a transitive inference problem required the use of a five-term series ($A > B > C > D > E$). This was necessary in order to provide a true test of inferential ability.

In a five-term series, two components will be both "larger" and "smaller". These components are B and D ($B > C$, $A > B$; $D > E$, $C > D$). In a three-term series, in contrast, A is always large and C is always small ($A > B > C$). If children are trained to remember the premises A $> B$ and B $> C$ in a three-term series, then in theory they could work out the relationship between A and C without using a transitive inference. They could remember that A is large and that C is small. However, when children are trained to remember the premises in a five-term series, a memory strategy will not work, at least not for an inference about the relationship between B and D. In order to work out the relationship between B and D, a genuine transitive inference is required, as B and D have been *both* large and small.

Bryant and Trabasso (1971) tested 4-, 5-, and 6-year-old childrens' ability to use transitive inferences in a five-term series task based on coloured wooden rods. In their experiment, the children were shown five rods (red, white, yellow, blue, and green), each of which was a different length (3, 4, 5, 6, and 7 inches long). The particular colour–length combinations used differed from child to child. The rods were always presented in pairs. For example, the child might learn that blue was larger than red, and that red was larger than green. The rods were presented via a container box that had holes of different depths bored into it, so that only one inch of each rod was seen in any training trial. During this training phase of the experiment, the child was asked which rod was taller (or shorter). After making a choice, the two rods were removed from the container and shown to the child, providing direct visual feedback about their relative length.

During the testing phase of the experiment, the same procedure of presenting pairs of rods in the box was used, except that the children were not shown the true length of the rods after being asked to make a comparison. As well as the four direct comparisons on which they had been trained (A>B, B>C, C>D, D>E), the children were asked about the six possible inferential comparisons (A?C, A?D, A?E, B?D, B?E, C?E). These transitive comparisons were presented in a random order. Bryant and Trabasso found that all of the children performed at levels that were significantly above chance on all of the transitive comparisons, including the critical B?D comparison. Although the B?D scores were lower than the other inferential comparisons, they were still impressively high, with 78% of the 4-year-olds knowing that B > D, 88% of the 5-year-olds, and 92% of the 6-year-olds. Bryant and Trabasso concluded that children at all three age levels were able to make genuine transitive inferences very well.

One possible objection to their finding, however, was that the visual feedback provided during the training phase of the experiment had enabled the children to succeed by remembering the *absolute* length of the rods (e.g. remembering that B was 6 inches long and D was 4 inches long, and thus knowing that B was longer than D). Bryant and Trabasso carried out a follow-up study to test this possibility, in which they eliminated the visual feedback previously provided during the training. Exactly the same results were found. Nevertheless, Bryant and Trabasso's conclusion that young children can make transitive inferences extremely effectively has not gone undisputed (see Breslow, 1981, for a useful review). As pointed out by a number of critics, another problem with their rods task was that the container used during the comparisons provided children with a visual *reminder* of which were the "long" rods and which were the "short" rods. This visual reminder was unavoidable, as all of the inferential comparisons (including the B?D comparison) were presented by showing the children the rods protruding from the container box. For the critical B?D comparison, this meant that rod B was near the "long" end of the box and rod D was near the "short" end of the box. This spatial cue might *in itself* have enabled the children to solve the comparison correctly. Such a solution could be arrived at without making a transitive inference, as the children could say that B > D simply by associating the respective rods with the large or the small end points of the box.

A different approach to testing young children's ability to make transitive inferences has relied on providing symbolic *"aides-memoires"* of the premises. This has the advantage of avoiding the fairly extensive memory training necessary to ensure that the children remember the premises, training that also requires the use of a five-term series. For example, Halford (1984) has used coloured pegs as a memory cue to investigate the development of transitive reasoning. His task required children to make transitive inferences about the length of clear perspex rods.

In Halford's experiment, pairs of pegs on a pegboard represented the length relations between the pairs of rods, which were concealed in tubes of different colours. For example, if a red peg was to the left of a blue peg (R_LB), this signified that the perspex rod in the red tube was longer than the perspex rod in the blue tube (R>B). If a blue peg was to the left of a green peg (B_LG), this signified that the perspex rod in the blue tube was longer than the perspex rod in the green tube (B>G). The children's task was to map the spatial relation "left of" to the relation "longer than" in order to work out the relative lengths of the coloured rods. Halford's idea was that integration of the two spatial relations R_LB and B_LG would give the ordered triple R_LB_LG, and so the children would be able to work out that the answer to the rod problem was that R>B>G—as long as they could make a transitive inference. Most children under 7 years of age could not solve the problem about the relative lengths of the perspex rods in these circumstances. Halford argued that this showed a lack of inferential ability, as these children *could* map single relations between the pegs and the rods. Yet the same children did not appear to be able to make a transitive inference about the visible pegs, and also appeared to be unable to make a relational mapping from the pegs to the rods.

Pears and Bryant (1990) devised a different way of removing the heavy memory load necessitated by a premise training task. Their solution was to eliminate the memory load completely, by using *visible* premises. This enabled them to continue to use a five-term series transitive inference task. The premises used by Pears and Bryant were pairs of coloured bricks, and the bricks were presented in little "towers" one on top of the other. The child's task was to build a complete tower of bricks from single bricks of the appropriate colours, using the premise pairs as a guide. Three kinds of tower had to be constructed during the experiment: four-brick towers (involving three premises), five-brick towers (involving four premises), and six-brick towers (involving five premises). To take a five-brick tower as an example, if the little towers showed red on top and blue beneath (R_TB), blue on top and green beneath (B$_T$G), green on top and yellow beneath (G$_T$Y), and yellow on top and white beneath (Y$_T$W), then the target tower was (R$_T$B$_T$G$_T$Y$_T$W). The different kinds of problems used are shown in Fig. 7.6

Prior to being allowed to build the target towers, the children were asked a series of inferential questions such as "Which will be the higher in the tower that you are going to build, the yellow brick or the blue

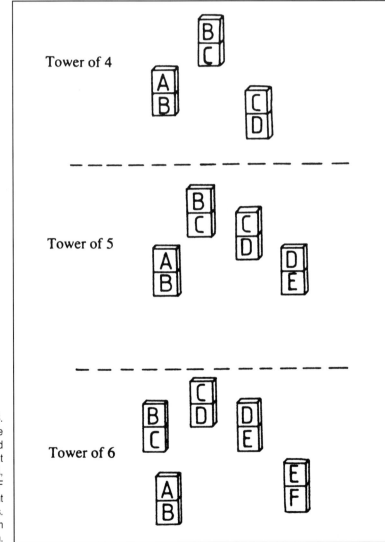

FIG. 7.6.
Examples of the premise towers used by Pears and Bryant (1990). The letters A, B, C, D, E, and F denote different colours. Reprinted with permission.

one?". In order to answer these inferential questions correctly, the children had to combine the information from two premises ($B_T G, G_T Y$) using a transitive inference. Note that this question about the relationship between the yellow and the blue bricks was formally equivalent to the critical B?D comparison in the five-term series task devised by Bryant and Trabasso (the yellow and the blue bricks had been *both* higher and lower). Other critical inferential questions concerned the B?D and C?E comparisons in the "tower of six" problems. All of these critical questions involved a comparison based on bricks that appeared *twice* in the towers and hence had two values, high and low.

Pears and Bryant found that the children were significantly above chance in their performance on two-thirds of the critical inferential questions. From this finding, they argued that 4-year-olds do possess the ability to make transitive inferences, at least about the continuum of space. Pears and Bryant's conclusion thus differs markedly from that reached by Halford (1984), who had argued that children of this age group lacked inferential ability. There are at least two possible explanations for these rather different findings. One is that Halford's critical test required a transitive inference in a different domain (length) from that in which the premise information had been presented (spatial left–right ordering). Pears and Bryant's critical test was in the *same* domain as the premise information. A second possibility is that Halford's choice of left–right ordering premises as the *aides-memoires* for the rods task was at the root of the children's difficulties with relative length. Ding (1995) has shown that spatial ordering problems can cause difficulties for children as old as 9 years if they are asked to integrate left–right premise information.

Ding's (1995) work was closely based on the Pears and Bryant task. She also showed children a series of visual premises that had to be combined, but her binary premises involved left–right rather than up–down ordering information. The children's job was to determine the order of the people in a bus queue. The premises were pictures of pairs of the people in the queue, all facing to the left, and the children were asked to use these premises to work out the order of the complete queue. Three premise pairs were presented, one at a time, in random order. For example, if the order of the people in the queue was ABCD, then the children might receive the three premise pairs in the order AB, CD, and BC. Their task was to re-order them as AB, BC, and CD, enabling them to infer that the order of the people in the queue was ABCD. Children aged 5, 7, and 9 were tested. The bus queue task is depicted in Fig. 7.7.

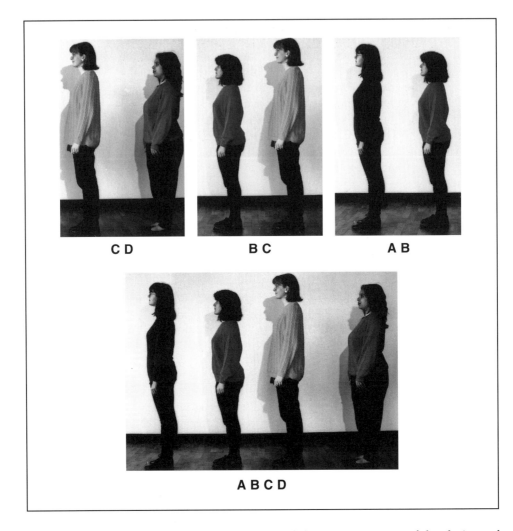

CD   BC   AB

ABCD

FIG. 7.7.
Example of a set of premise pictures used in the bus queue task devised by Ding (1995), with the correctly re-ordered array shown beneath. Used with permission.

Ding found that children's ability to create successful orderings of the whole bus queue depended critically on the order in which the premise information had been presented. Even 9-year-olds found the bus queue task extremely difficult when certain premise orderings were presented, such as CD, AB, BC. In this premise ordering, *no* common elements are present in the first two premises. Children's difficulties with the left–right ordering task remained robust when drawings of real people were used instead of photographs, and when toy train trucks were used instead of a bus queue. Despite the fact that premise presentation was serial and thus enabled *sequential* relational integration, children found Ding's left–right ordering task extremely difficult. In contrast, Pears and Bryant found no effect of presenting the "tower" premises in a randomised order in their up–down ordering task. Left–right spatial relations may thus be particularly difficult relations for young children to integrate. If this is true, then it seems likely that the children in Halford's (1984) experiment could not benefit from the left–right pairings of coloured pegs as *aides-memoires* to the relative lengths of the rods inside the coloured tubes. This would then explain their failure to make transitive inferences.

The understanding of invariance

Another logical concept investigated by Piaget was *conservation*, which is the ability to *conserve* quantity across changes in appearance. This logical operation underpins the understanding of *invariance*, an important logical insight that in turn underpins the number system. Invariance also gives stability to the physical world. Children who understand the principle of invariance understand that quantities do not alter unless something is added to them or taken away from them (*addition–subtraction*). They also understand that simply changing the appearance of a quantity does not affect the amount that is present, as the change in appearance is *reversible*. They are aware that changes in one dimension are *compensated for* by changes in another. All of these insights are involved in a true logical understanding of conservation.

The conservation task. Piaget designed the conservation task as a measure of children's understanding of the principle of invariance. In the conservation task, children's understanding of invariance was assessed by asking them to compare *two* initially identical quantities, one of which was then transformed. For example, a child could be shown two rows of five beads arranged in 1:1 correspondence, or two glasses of liquid filled to exactly the same level (see Fig. 7.8). An adult experimenter would then alter the appearance of one of these quantities while the child was watching. For example, the adult could pour the liquid in one of the glasses into a shorter, shallower beaker, or could spread out the beads in one of the rows so that the row looked longer. Piaget's experimental question was whether children understood that quantity remained invariant *despite* these changes in perceptual appearance. The answer to this question appeared to be "no". Most children below the age of around 7 who were given the conservation task told the experimenter that there was now less water in the shallower beaker, or that there were more beads in the spread-out row.

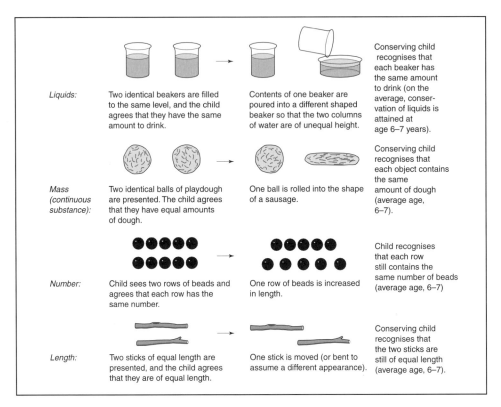

Liquids:	Two identical beakers are filled to the same level, and the child agrees that they have the same amount to drink.	Contents of one beaker are poured into a different shaped beaker so that the two columns of water are of unequal height.	Conserving child recognises that each beaker has the same amount to drink (on the average, conservation of liquids is attained at age 6–7 years).

Liquids: Two identical beakers are filled to the same level, and the child agrees that they have the same amount to drink. Contents of one beaker are poured into a different shaped beaker so that the two columns of water are of unequal height. Conserving child recognises that each beaker has the same amount to drink (on the average, conservation of liquids is attained at age 6–7 years).

Mass (continuous substance): Two identical balls of playdough are presented. The child agrees that they have equal amounts of dough. One ball is rolled into the shape of a sausage. Conserving child recognises that each object contains the same amount of dough (average age, 6–7).

Number: Child sees two rows of beads and agrees that each row has the same number. One row of beads is increased in length. Child recognises that each row still contains the same number of beads (average age, 6–7)

Length: Two sticks of equal length are presented, and the child agrees that they are of equal length. One stick is moved (or bent to assume a different appearance). Conserving child recognises that the two sticks are still of equal length (average age, 6–7).

FIG. 7.8. Examples of different versions of the conservation task. From Schaffer (1985). Adapted from *Developmental Psychology: Childhood and Adolescence*, by D.R. Schaffer. Copyright © 1996, 1993, 1989, 1985 Brooks/Cole Publishing Company, Pacific Grove, CA 93950, a division of International Thompson Publishing Inc. Adapted by permission of the publisher.

The simplest way to test children's understanding of invariance, however, would have been to show them a *single* quantity, such as a glass of liquid or a row of pennies, and then to transform the appearance of this single quantity. For example, the liquid in a single glass can be transferred into a tall narrow beaker without affecting its quantity, and similarly a single row of pennies can be spread out so that the row becomes much longer. Children can then be asked the same "conservation question", which is whether there are (for example) "more, less, or the same number of pennies" as before. Elkind and Schoenfeld (1972) used a "conservation of identity" task of this type in their studies of children's understanding of invariance. They argued that performance in the conservation of identity task might demonstrate an understanding of invariance in children who were much younger than those who were able to pass the traditional conservation task. Elkind and Schoenfeld's argument was that the traditional task was not a *pure* test of the understanding of invariance, as the traditional conservation task involved a hidden transitive inference.

The hidden transitive inference in the traditional conservation task is easily demonstrated (see Fig. 7.2). In the traditional task, the child is shown two identical quantities, Q1 and Q2, and is asked to make a judgement about their relative quantities following a transformation of the appearance of one of them (e.g. Q1 to Q1A). The child is usually asked "Is there more, less, or the same as before?". To answer correctly, the child must reason that (a) quantity 1 = quantity 2 (Q1 = Q2); (b) quantity 1 has changed to quantity 1A, but the two are still equivalent (Q1 = Q1A); and therefore (c) that quantity 1A = quantity 2 (Q1A = Q2). Unless the child can perform all three steps in this transitive reasoning task, the child will fail to solve Piaget's conservation task.

Elkind and Schoenfeld argued that the proof that a transitive inference was required in the conservation task came from a consideration of how an adult would make a judgement about relative quantity in the same circumstances. If shown only Q1A and Q2, such an adult would have no way of knowing whether the two quantities were equivalent or not. Without seeing the initial events Q1 = Q2 and Q1 = Q1A, the adult would have no basis for a judgement of quantitative equivalence. Elkind and Schoenfeld (1972) thus argued that Piaget's conservation task measured the conservation of *equivalence* rather than the conservation of identity, which was measured by their simpler one-quantity task.

In their experiment, Elkind and Schoenfeld decided to contrast the conservation of identity and the conservation of equivalence in 4- and 6-year-old children. The children were given the pennies task (conservation of number), the beaker task (conservation of liquid), a task comparing two pencils (conservation of length—the pencils were initially aligned, and then one pencil was moved so that the 1:1 length correspondence was destroyed), and a task comparing two balls of modelling clay (conservation of mass—the balls of clay were initially identical, and one ball of clay was then transformed into a long sausage). Elkind and Schoenfeld found that, whereas both groups of children had little difficulty in judging the invariance of a single

TABLE 7.2
The hidden transitive inference in the
traditional conservation task

Step (A):	Q1	=	Q2
Step (B):	Q1	=	Q1A
(therefore, via transitive inference)			
Step (C):	Q1A	=	Q2

Based on Elkind and Schoenfeld, 1972.

quantity, the 4-year-olds were poor at judging quantitative equivalence. Elkind and Schoenfeld concluded that the two types of conservation required different mental processes. Although both were measures of the understanding of invariance, the conservation of identity provided a relatively pure measure of this understanding whereas the conservation of equivalence required in addition an understanding of transitivity.

The finding that children below the age of around 5–6 years tend to fail to conserve equivalence is a very robust one (see Field, 1987; McEvoy & OMoore, 1991, for recent reviews). Most investigators who have used the conservation task have replicated Piaget's finding that the conservation of quantity is absent before this age, and most have accepted his explanation of this result, which was that younger children make mistakes because they tend to focus on one dimension of the transformed quantity and ignore the compensating dimension. For example, the children may focus on the fact that the water level is *higher* in the narrower beaker, ignoring the fact that the beaker is not as wide as the original glass in which the water reached a lower level. Similarly, they may focus on the *length* of the transformed row of pennies, ignoring the fact that the gap between each penny is much larger in the transformed row than in the untransformed row.

Intriguingly, children make similar conservation errors when they are reasoning about natural transformations, even natural transformations that involve highly familiar "stimuli" such as their friends. For example, if children are told to watch their classmates playing a game of "Simon Says", and Simon Says "spread out" or "bunch together", the children making the conservation judgements claim that there are more children when the group is spread out, and fewer children when the group is bunched together. If children are shown two rows of toy boats floating in a pool, and then one row is allowed to drift apart so that it appears longer than the other row, the children claim that there are more boats in the longer row (Miller, 1982).

Task pragmatics in the conservation task   Not all investigators agree that the conservation of equivalence is beyond the logical abilities of children younger than 5–6 years of age, however. One productive line of research into children's conservation failures has focused on the *pragmatics* of the traditional Piagetian conservation task. In the standard conservation task, the child is faced with an adult who asks them a question about two quantities ("Are there more, less or the same?"), carries out a transformation, and then asks them the same question again. If someone asks you the same question twice, it usually means that you should change your answer. This is especially true when the other person is older than you, and has just done something that looked to you as though it was meant to be highly salient! In pragmatic terms, therefore, the adult's action in transforming the array may well lead children to infer that he or she plans to talk about the transformation that has just occurred. The children may then answer the question that they *think* the tester plans to ask, rather than attending to the precise question that is *in fact* asked. Donaldson (1978), Rose and Blank (1974), and Siegal (1991) have all argued that different aspects of the pragmatics of the conservation task may mislead children into giving non-conserving responses.

Donaldson's main concern was with the communicative intent of the adult experimenter. To test the idea that adult's actions towards the conservation materials led the children to answer the conservation question on the basis of the attribute that they *thought* the adult intended to ask about, rather than the actual attribute specified linguistically, she devised the ingenious "naughty teddy" paradigm (McGarrigle & Donaldson, 1975). The children were told that they would play a special game with the experimenter. Prior to the start of the game, the children were shown a cardboard box containing a teddy bear, and were told that the teddy was very naughty and was liable to escape from his box from time to time and try to "mess up the toys" and "spoil the game". The conservation materials were then brought out (e.g. two rows of counters in one-to-one correspondence). The child was asked "Are there more here or more here or are they both the same number?". All of a sudden, the naughty teddy appeared and altered the length of one of the rows by shoving the counters together. The teddy received the appropriate scolding, and the children were then asked again "Are there more here or more here or are they both the same number?". Under these conditions of an *accidental* transformation of the arrays, the majority of 4- and 5-year-old children in the experiment gave conserving responses. McGarrigle and Donaldson argued that this supported their hypothesis that the intentional structure of the experimenter's non-linguistic behaviour was affecting the child's interpretation of the question that was asked.

Light et al. devised a different type of accidental transformation of the conservation task, which they called an *incidental* transformation (Light, Buckingham, & Robbins, 1979). In their task, pairs of 6-year-old children were invited to play a game that involved putting pasta shells onto a game board marked into squares. The first player to use up all of their shells was the winner, and so it was important that each child began with the same amount of shells in order to make the game fair.

The children were each given a small beaker to hold their shells. Prior to beginning the game, the pasta shells were poured to and fro between the beakers until the children agreed that the amount of shells in each beaker was equal. It was then discovered that one of the beakers was cracked. For safety reasons, this child's pasta shells had to be moved into a larger beaker. The children were then asked whether the two amounts of pasta shells were still the same (the conservation question). In this incidental version of the conservation task, 70% of the children gave conserving responses. In contrast, the standard version of the conservation task using the same materials produced only 5% conserving responses. Light et al. argued that the crucial feature of their task, and of McGarrigle and Donaldson's accidental paradigm, was that the transformation of the materials seemed incidental to the main purpose of the interaction.

However, given the findings of Miller (1982) concerning natural transformations, it must be asked whether children who experience incidental or accidental versions of the conservation task are receiving a proper test of the conservation of equivalence. Piaget's idea that younger children make mistakes because they tend to focus on one dimension of the transformed quantity and ignore the compensating dimension may not be tested by incidental or accidental paradigms. The reason is that the children may not actually *look* at the transformed arrays (see Bryant, 1982). Although both Light et al. and McGarrigle and Donaldson took care to ensure that the perceptual aspects of their arrays were similar in their incidental/accidental and standard conditions, it is possible that the children did not *notice* the perceptual appearance of the arrays in the incidental/accidental tasks precisely *because* this was incidental to the main purpose of the interaction. If they ignored the perceptual appearance of the arrays in the incidental/accidental tasks, then they could not be misled by a tendency to focus on one dimension of the transformed quantity. Light et al. make this point in a different way, pointing out that in pragmatic terms the tester's actions signal to the child that "this transformation is irrelevant". Conserving judgements in the accidental/incidental versions of the conservation task may thus be examples of "false positives", with children succeeding for reasons other than possession of the requisite logical skill.

A different pragmatic concern is that the standard conservation task involves asking children the *same question twice*. This pragmatic aspect of the conservation task may in itself be enough to convince children that they should change their answer. Pragmatically, we usually only repeat a question when we are looking for a different answer to the one actually given. Teachers often use this conversational device to signal to students that they are incorrect without actually telling them so. Similarly, in the normal course of events one would never ask the same question twice about some materials unless a significant change had occurred as the materials were being observed. The way to test this pragmatic concern is simply to ask the children the conservation question *once* instead of twice.

Rose and Blank (1974) carried out such an experiment using the conservation of number paradigm (with rows of counters) They compared a group of 6-year-old childrens' performance in the standard two-judgement conservation task with the performance of a second group in a one-judgement version of the same task. In the one-judgement version, the children were only asked the "more, less or the same?" question *after* watching the experimenter transform one of the arrays. A third (control) group of children were never shown the original arrays, and were simply asked to make a single judgement about the transformed array (the "fixed-array" condition). The fixed array task was included to show that any improvement in the one-judgement condition was not due to the asking of a single question *per se*, but to the asking of a single question in the pragmatic context of the conservation task.

Rose and Blank found that requiring two judgements did indeed affect the children's conservation behaviour. The 6-year-olds in their study were significantly better in the one-judgement version of the conservation task than in the standard two-judgement version. Performance in the fixed array task was equivalent to performance in the standard conservation task. Rose and Blank argued that the superiority of the one-judgement task supported their hypothesis that when the child has just declared the rows of counters equal (in the standard conservation task), then they interpret the request for a second judgement as a signal to change their response. The positive effect of requiring only one judgement was replicated by Samuel and Bryant (1984), who studied the conservation of mass, length, and liquid as well as the conservation of number.

However, it is fair to say that the overall levels of improvement found in the one-judgement paradigm are fairly modest. The repetition of the conservation question may thus have less pragmatic force than the apparent communicative intent of the experimenter. One way to test this possibility would be to use the natural transformation paradigms devised by Miller (which were designed to avoid the observed transformations of the arrays having any intentional aspect) in conjunction with the one-judgement paradigm devised by Rose and Blank. If a key factor in children's conservation failures is the repetition of the conservation question, then not repeating the question should have a more dramatic effect on conservation performance in these more ecologically valid paradigms.

Current perspectives on the conservation task. Although these demonstrations of conservation success show us that the pragmatics of the conservation task do have an effect on the judgements that children make, it remains true that when asked a direct question involving the comparison of two quantities, one of which they have observed being transformed, children younger than 6 years of age give non-conserving responses. This happens even when the transformations occur naturally, without the intentional intervention of an important adult experimenter (Miller, 1982).

In order to examine how cognitive change occurs in the conservation task, Siegler (1995) used a "microgenetic" method to study the mastery of number conservation in 5-year-olds. The microgenetic method involves the detailed and fine-grained observational study of individual children as they undergo cognitive change. In Siegler's conservation work, change is induced by giving the children different types of feedback in a conservation training paradigm. As these different types of training gradually lead individual children to the understanding of conservation, the experimenter uses the observations made during the training period as a basis for understanding the qualitative and quantitative properties of the processes that give rise to the cognitive change itself.

Siegler's (1995) study investigated the effects of three types of training on performance in a standard number conservation paradigm (using rows of buttons). In order to take part in the study, children first had to fail a pre-test that included the standard Piagetian number conservation task. All of the children were then given further conservation problems during four successive training sessions. Some of the 5-year-olds in the study were simply told whether their answers to different problems were correct or incorrect (the "feedback" training group). Others were asked to *explain* their reasoning, and were then given feedback concerning the correctness of their answers to the problems (the "explanation" training group). Still others received feedback about their answers, and were then asked by the experimenter "How do you think *I* knew that?". This last type of training required the children to explain the *experimenter's* reasoning. This condition was expected to encourage the children to search for the *causes* of the observed events.

Siegler found that the third condition had the largest effect on conservation performance. Learning in this condition was found to involve two distinct realisations: that relative length did not predict which row had the greatest number of objects, and that the type of quantitatively relevant transformation did (i.e. whether buttons were added to or subtracted from the rows, or whether the appearance of the rows was altered by lengthening or shortening). Interestingly, understanding of the importance of the type of transformation did not lead to the immediate rejection of the less advanced forms of reasoning, even when the same problem was presented several times during the experiment. Instead, children's understanding of conservation occurred gradually rather than suddenly. Siegler also found large individual differences in children's ability to benefit from having to explain the experimenter's reasoning. The children who benefited most tended to be those who had displayed greater variability of reasoning in the pre-test.

Siegler concluded that, in mastering number conservation, children do not progress through a series of discrete knowledge states in which they consistently think of a given phenomenon in a single way at a given time. Instead, they know and use several types of reasoning before as well as during transitional periods of cognitive development. Siegler argued that the microgenetic method suggested that Piaget's assumption of the standard concept of a developmental sequence may be misplaced. Rather than conceptualising cognitive development as involving step-wise transitions from one level of reasoning to another, Siegler suggests that a model in which some ways of thinking are prevalent at an early time and then decrease in frequency while others rise and remain frequent, or rise and fall in their frequency of use (an "overlapping waves" model) may be more appropriate. However, Piaget's position may be closer to Siegler's overlapping waves model than it appears from this interpretation of his theory (see Chapter 8).

Class inclusion

The third major logical operation among Piaget's concrete operations was *class inclusion*. The logical concept of class inclusion involves understanding that a set of items can be *simultaneously* part of a combined set and part of an embedded set. For example, imagine a bunch of six flowers, four of which are red, and two of which are white. The *combined set* is the six flowers, and the *embedded sets* are the white flowers and the red flowers. To see whether young children understand the logical concept of class inclusion, Piaget devised the class inclusion task.

In Piaget's task, the child was shown a combined set, such as the flowers, and was then asked "Are there more red flowers or more flowers here?". Children younger than approximately 6 years of age usually responded that there were more red flowers. They appeared to be unable to think about the parts and the whole simultaneously. As in the conservation task, Piaget argued that part of the problem was the failure to understand *reversibility*, namely that the parts and the whole were the same entity. Prior to acquiring the logical concept of class inclusion, Piaget suggested that children could only deal with the parts or with the whole *separately*. They could not think about the flowers in two ways simultaneously, just as they could not simultaneously think about total length and gap size when trying to judge the quantity in a row of pennies.

This class inclusion task with its question about whether there "are more red flowers or more flowers here?" is the "standard" class inclusion paradigm used in experimental studies of the concrete operations. However, Piaget's class inclusion question sounds a bit strange, even to the adult ear. In natural speech, we do not usually contrast a whole and a part by asking "Are there more red flowers or more flowers here?". If we wanted a comparison between two parts, we would typically ask "Are there more red flowers or more white flowers?". If we wanted a comparison between a part and the whole, we would say "Are there more red flowers, or are there more flowers in the bunch?". The use of the term "bunch" is a natural linguistic device for referring to a *collection* of objects. Collection terms such as "bunch" alert the child to the fact that a comparison between a part and a whole is required. In contrast, Piaget's class inclusion question relies on the repeated use of the *class* term "flower", which does not alert the listener to the required part–whole comparison. This means that the language used in Piaget's class inclusion paradigm may *in itself* predispose children to think that a comparison between a part and a part is required.

This argument was made by Markman and Seibert (1976), who pointed out that the collection terms in natural language are usually singular nouns. We say "*a* bunch of flowers", or "*a* pile of bricks". They argued that the psychological integrity of collections may be greater than the psychological integrity of classes, as collections have some degree of internal organisation and form natural units which are marked in the spoken language. Markman and Seibert predicted that part–whole comparisons involving collections should be easier for young children than part–whole comparisons involving classes. To test their idea, they contrasted 5- to 6-year-old children's class inclusion performance in two different versions of the class inclusion task. In one version, the standard class inclusion question was asked using Piaget's class-term format, which was expected to bias the children towards making a part–part comparison. In the second version, the class inclusion question was asked using the collection terms found in natural language. This was expected to facilitate the required part–whole comparison.

The children in the collection version of the experiment were asked about four different types of collection; a *bunch* of grapes, a *class* of children, a *pile* of blocks, and a *family* of frogs. For example, the children were shown some grapes and told:

> Here is a bunch of grapes, there are green grapes and there are purple grapes, and this is the bunch. Who would have more to eat, someone who ate the green grapes or someone who ate the bunch?.

The children in the standard version of the experiment were asked about the same stimuli (grapes, children etc.), but were told:

> Here are some grapes, there are green grapes and there are purple grapes. Who would have more to eat, someone who ate the green grapes or someone who ate the grapes?.

Markman and Seibert found that the children performed at a significantly higher level when the collection term was used to pose the class inclusion question (70% correct) than when the class term was used (45% correct). They argued that this showed that the psychological coherence of collections was greater than that of classes, as collections are more readily conceptualised as wholes.

Markman and Seibert's results were replicated by Fuson et al. (1988) with 5- and 6-year-olds, and also by Hodges and French (1988) with younger children (3- and 4-year-olds). The children in Fuson et al.'s study were additionally asked to *justify* their responses. For example, the children were asked to compare ten blue and five red building blocks. If they gave the correct response to a collection term question like "Who would have more toys to play with, someone who owned the blue blocks or someone who owned the pile?", they were asked "How do you know?". Around 40% of the children were able to give adequate justifications that described the combined structure of the embedded sets. These included "All of them are more", "Because all of them together makes more than one of them", and "The boys and girls are more than the boys" (to a problem about the number of boys and girls in a class).

Fuson et al. also found that experience with the collection terms *transferred* to classic Piagetian class inclusion problems employing class terms. When children who had been asked about the pile of blocks were later asked "Who would have more toys to play with, someone who owned the blue blocks or someone who owned the blocks?", they were more likely to answer the target question correctly than a control group of children who had received the class terms first. The children's justifications suggested that this was because they were continuing to think of the stimulus materials in collection terms (e.g. "The pile would be more toys"). Finally, Fuson et al. showed that 5- and 6-year-olds could succeed with class terms as well as collection terms if the word "all" was inserted into the standard Piagetian question. For example, if they were asked "Who would have more to eat, someone who ate all the grapes or someone who ate the green grapes?", then they were able to answer correctly that the person who ate all the grapes would have more. Fuson et al. argued that collection terms and "combine" descriptions like "all" helped the child to represent the objects as a single labelled combined set, rather than as separate objects. The natural language also helped to disambiguate the class inclusion question for them. This research suggests that the logical concept of class inclusion may be present by at least 5 years.

However, Dean, Chabaud, and Bridges (1981) argued that collection terms could facilitate performance in the class inclusion task simply because collection terms imply large numbers. They pointed out that if children interpret collection nouns as synonymous with "a lot", then their performance on the class inclusion question would improve simply because of the connotation of a large number of objects, and not because collection terms help children to represent objects as a single combined set. In order to test this hypothesis, Dean et al. gave 5- and 6-year-old children part–whole problems in which the collection term was used to describe the *part* rather than the whole. For example, Dean et al. told the children:

> Here are some ducks, some yellow ducks and some brown ducks. Suppose the yellow ducks were a family, but the brown ducks were not a family. Do you think there are more in the family of yellow ducks, or more ducks?.

As there were more brown ducks than yellow ducks in the display shown to the children, the usual class inclusion error would have been to say that there were more brown ducks than ducks. However, as the children could *see* that there were fewer yellow ducks than brown ducks, Dean et al. argued that any tendency to err by choosing the yellow ducks over the brown ducks would show the influence of the "large number" connotation of collection terms. Their results provided some support for this hypothesis. None of the children who received the "class term" version of the class inclusion problem ("Do you think there are more ducks or more yellow ducks?") said that there were more yellow ducks. However, a sizeable minority of the children who received the "collection term" version of the class inclusion problem said that there were more yellow ducks (25%). In a similar problem involving the collection term "army", this minority rose to 45% ("Here are some ants, some red ants and some brown ants. Suppose the red ants were an army, but the brown ants were not an army. Do you think there are more in the army of red ants, or more ants?").

Despite Dean et al.'s findings, however, the "large number" implication of collection terms cannot be the only reason for the children's success in the collection term paradigm. Converging evidence for Markman and Seibert's interpretation that the use of collection terms helps children to impose a more cohesive structural organisation on the whole comes from a recent study carried out by Goswami, Pauen, and Wilkening (1996). They were interested in the possibility that structural organisation facilitates class inclusion reasoning because it enables children to use analogies to natural models of combined and embedded sets, such as the model of the family. Goswami et al. suggested that the collection term "family" might be a particularly useful one for young children's class inclusion reasoning, as the structural organisation of the family is a highly familiar example of an inclusive set (see Halford, 1993). Most young children know that a family is made up of parents and children. The combined set of the family thus has two natural embedded sets, adults and children. These embedded sets also have their own natural language labels ("parents", "children"). Goswami et al. investigated whether family structure could provide a useful analogy for facilitating reasoning in more traditional class inclusion problems involving piles of blocks and bunches of balloons.

The children in Goswami et al.'s study (4- to 5-year-olds) had all failed the traditional Piagetian class inclusion task, which was given as a pretest ("Are there more red flowers or more flowers?"). They were then shown a toy family, for example a family of toy mice (two large mice as parents, three small mice as children) or a family of yo-yos (two large yo-yos as parents, three small yo-yos as children). Their job was to create analogous families (two parents and three children) from an assorted pile of toy animals (such as fluffy toy bears, ladybirds, ducks, and crocodiles) or from a pile of other toys (such as toy cars, spinning tops, balls, and helicopters). After the children had correctly created four families that were analogous to the mice/yo-yo families (having two parents and three children), they were given four class inclusion problems involving toy frogs, sheep, building blocks, and balloons. The class inclusion problems were posed using collection terms ("group", "herd", "pile", "bunch"). A control group of children received the same class inclusion problems using collection terms, but did not receive an analogy training session in which they learned to create families. Goswami et al. predicted that the children in the "create-a-family" condition would solve more of the class inclusion problems involving frogs, sheep, building blocks, and balloons than the children in the control condition, as the former group could use analogies to family structure.

The results showed that 50% of the children in the create-a-family condition were able to solve at least three of the four new class inclusion problems, compared to only 20% of children in the control condition. It should be remembered that all of the children had previously failed Piagetian class inclusion tasks, and that the children in the control group received the collection term wording. This positive result fits nicely with the other evidence discussed in this chapter concerning the facilitatory effects of accessing familiar relational or organisational structures on children's performance in reasoning tasks. For example, in deductive reasoning, Harris and Nunez (1996) and Light et al. (1989) found that the activation of an appropriate permission schema helped children to reason successfully in the selection task.

The idea that familiar relational or organisational structures play a very important role in the development of logical reasoning has been proposed by Halford (1993) within the context of his capacity-driven "structure mapping" theory of cognitive development (see Chapter 6). According to Halford's structure-mapping theory, analogies from familiar mental structures are the basis of solutions to a variety of logical reasoning problems, particularly problems requiring Piagetian concrete operations. We will now consider Halford's "neo-Piagetian" theory of cognitive development in more detail.

Halford's structure-mapping theory of logical development

Halford's structure-mapping theory of logical development (Halford, 1993) can help us to explain why some kinds of logical reasoning, such as analogical reasoning, deductive reasoning, and conditional reasoning, appear fairly early in development, while other kinds of reasoning, notably the Piagetian logical operations, appear rather later.

According to Halford's theory, logical abilities like class inclusion and transitive inference depend on making the appropriate analogical mappings from real-world relational structures. However, although simple analogical reasoning emerges early in development, limitations in processing capacity prevent children from using more complex relational mappings before the age of around 5 years. As logical abilities like class inclusion and transitive inference require more complex relational mappings, these abilities emerge later in development, when sufficient processing capacity has developed to enable the requisite mappings to be carried out. What changes with development is the complexity of the analogies that children can make.

For example, a child can use an analogy from the mental representation of familiar height relations in the world, such as Daddy > Mummy > Baby, as a basis for a mapping to a transitive inference problem such as "Tom is happier than Bill, Bill is happier than Mike, who is happiest?." The correct solution involves mapping Tom to Daddy, Bill to Mummy, and Mike to Baby. As Daddy is the tallest, the answer to the transitive inference problem must be that Tom is the happiest. This relational mapping is complex because it depends on an *ordered pair* of relations. A correct mapping involves the *concurrent* mapping of the relation Daddy > Mummy to Tom "happier than" Bill, and of the relation Mummy > Baby to the relation Bill "happier than" Mike. An example of a similar mapping based on spatial position (top, middle, bottom) is shown in Fig. 7.9.

Halford argues that the usual age at which mappings based on ordered pairs of relations become possible is around $4\frac{1}{2}$ to 5 years. Prior to this age, children's analogies are more limited, because they depend on mappings based on single relations (e.g. *chocolate:melting chocolate::snowman:melting snowman*, see Goswami & Brown, 1989). Halford claims that analogical mappings based on ordered pairs of relations require a greater amount of mental processing capacity, and that the capacity required for such mappings is not present until around age 5. This capacity limitation assumption means that Piagetian tasks should not be solved by children younger than around 5 years.

As we have seen, Halford is not the only "neo-Piagetian" theorist to argue that increases in processing capacity are the basic engine of cognitive development (see Chapter 6). He is also not the only "neo-Piagetian" to argue that increases in processing capacity underlie the emergence of the Piagetian logical operations. Both Case (1985) and Pascual-Leone (1987) have put forward related views. Halford is also not unique in linking increases in processing capacity to increases in the relational complexity of the information that young children can handle

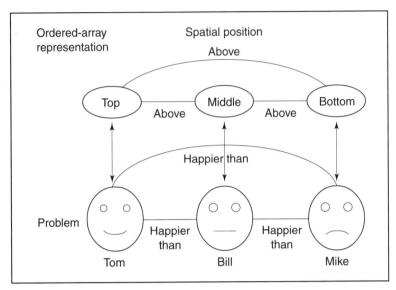

FIG. 7.9. An analogical mapping from the mental representation of spatial position to a transitive inference problem (Halford, 1993).

mentally (see Pascual-Leone, 1987). However, he is unique in linking his theory to the use of analogies in logical reasoning.

Some of the evidence from the analogy literature suggests that Halford's approach may be very useful in explaining the development of children's cognition. We have already observed the spontaneous use of analogies in a number of logical reasoning tasks, such as Pauen's force-table task (see Chapter 4). We have also seen that children use analogies in conceptual development, for example using a "personification" analogy to support learning in the biological domain (see Chapter 3). There is even some evidence that children can use analogies based on the mental representation of familiar structural relations in the real world in Piagetian-type reasoning problems such as class inclusion (Goswami et al., 1996). However, at the time of writing, such evidence is still relatively sparse. There is probably too little detailed work on the development of analogical reasoning available to enable us to decide whether Halford's ideas about the Piagetian logical operations are correct or not. Nevertheless, Halford's theory is a very interesting one, as it extends the notion of analogical reasoning as a very basic mechanism in cognitive development in a potentially extremely fruitful way.

Summary

The research discussed in the first part of this chapter concerned early-developing modes of logical reasoning. The early-developing modes of logical reasoning—analogical reasoning and deductive reasoning—can be observed at work in many areas of cognitive development, as we saw in the chapters on conceptual development and the development of causal reasoning. Furthermore, analogical reasoning, syllogistic reasoning, and deductive logic in the selection task show an impressive continuity from childhood to adulthood. The same factors seem to govern successful reasoning in both children and adults, and similar levels of spontaneous performance are found in both age groups when unfamiliar versions of the different experimental paradigms are administered. This is consistent with some of the evidence discussed in Chapter 5, where we saw that similar effects have been observed in studies of memory. There is remarkable continuity from childhood to adulthood in certain kinds of memory (such as implicit memory), and the effects of using unfamiliar stimuli and paradigms on particular memory systems can be very similar in children and in adults. This is probably a general cognitive phenomenon. Attempts to design "pure" measures of reasoning or memory, in which the reasoning or memory process is measured *independently* of the context in which it is required, are generally counter-productive to performance in both children and adults. A critical aspect of most of the research on early-developing modes of logical reasoning is the use of familiar, "child-centred" paradigms set in familiar contexts.

The same is not true of most of the research examining the later-developing modes of logical reasoning identified by Piaget, however. The research on concrete operational reasoning has tended to stick to the paradigms that were first developed by Piaget. This means that most of the studies of concrete operational modes of reasoning rely on problem contexts that are fairly unfamiliar to young children. Although some natural "pragmatic reasoning schemas" or "mental models" of these logical operations exist (one example would be social dominance hierarchies as a natural example of a transitive system), these natural models have tended to be ignored in most current research. In contrast to analogical reasoning and deductive reasoning, the later-developing modes of logical reasoning identified by Piaget are less easily observed outside the laboratory.

Nevertheless, a number of studies have found evidence that the concrete operational modes of logical reasoning are available considerably earlier than the age of 6 to 7 years suggested by Piaget. For example, if children are asked to use transitive inferences to decide the sequence of colours in a tower that is to be built from pairs of coloured bricks that are visible to the child, then 4- and 5-year-olds can complete the task successfully. If a "naughty teddy" rearranges a row of counters in the conservation paradigm, then 4- and 5-year-olds can successfully conserve number. If children learn a family analogy for the class inclusion task, then 4- and 5-year-olds can answer class inclusion questions successfully. The key issue for Piagetians is whether these successes mean that pre-schoolers are using the *same form of logic* as older children, or whether they are succeeding on the basis of other task factors that in fact alter the logic tested by the concrete operational tasks. For example, the successful children in the "naughty teddy" paradigm may not be looking at the perceptual appearance of the row altered by naughty teddy, which they may consider to be incidental to the main purpose of the conservation "game". The issue of what constitutes a "true test" of Piaget's theory is discussed further in Chapter 8.

Piaget's theory of logical development 8

Piaget's theory of logical development in childhood has been a seminal one. He was the first developmental psychologist to provide a comprehensive theory of child development covering birth to adolescence, and many of the topics that are central to our understanding of children's

cognition were first investigated by Piaget. This is true of most of the topics included in this book, such as cognition in infancy, causal reasoning, categorisation, and logic. This chapter will provide a brief outline of the major aspects of Piaget's theory (more detailed treatments can be found in Beilin & Pufall, 1992; Butterworth & Harris, 1994; Chapman, 1988; Gallagher & Reid, 1981; and Inhelder, de Caprona & Cornu-Wells, 1987; to name just a few). We will then assess key aspects of the theory in the light of some of the recent evidence about children's cognition presented in this book.

Overview of the theory

The mechanisms of cognitive change

Jean Piaget, circa 1978. From J.J. Ducret (1990) *Jean Piaget: Biographie et Parcours Intellectual*, published by Editions Dalachaux et Niestlé, Lausanne.

Piaget was originally a biologist. This led him to translate the notion that organisms adapt themselves to their environments to the study of children's thinking. Piaget's fundamental interest was in the origins of knowledge, just as biologists are interested in the origins of life. He suggested that cognitive development was caused by two processes. These were *accommodation* and *assimilation*. Accommodation is the process of adapting cognitive *schemes* for viewing the world (general concepts) to fit reality. Assimilation is the complementary process of interpreting experience (individual instances of general concepts) in terms of current cognitive schemes. The goal of the organism is cognitive equilibrium. However, as every cognitive equilibrium is only partial, every existing equilibrium must evolve towards a higher form of equilibrium—towards a more adequate form of knowing. This process of evolution drives cognitive development. When one cognitive scheme becomes inadequate for making sense of the world, it is replaced by another.

Stages in cognitive development

In fact, during the passage from infancy to adolescence, the major overhaul of current cognitive schemes was thought to occur three times. Piaget suggested that there were three major cognitive *stages* in logical development, corresponding to three successive forms of knowledge or systems of thought. During each of these stages, children were hypothesised to think and reason in a different way. These stages, and their approximate ages of occurrence, were:

1. The sensory-motor period: 0–2 years.
2. The period of concrete operations: 7–11 years.
3. The period of formal operations: 11–12 years on.

The period from 2 to 7 years was that of pre-operations, or prepa-ration for concrete operational thought. Sensory-motor cognition was action-based, depending on physical interaction with the world. Action-based knowledge was then gradually organised into represen-tation-based or symbolic knowledge, and pre-operational thinking marked the beginning of the internalisation of action on the symbolic plane. Representations or symbols were the basis of the second system of thought, concrete operational reasoning, and they took a long time to be organised according to logical groupings or operations such as transitivity. Once this was achieved, the period of concrete operations had been reached. During concrete operational cognition, the results of internalised actions (called compositions) became reversible, marking the beginning of mental operations. Finally, during formal operational cognition, certain concrete operations became linked together, marking the onset of scientific thought.

The attainment of each cognitive stage was thought to require fundamental cognitive restructuring on the part of the child. However, Piaget recognised that the acquisition of each new way of thinking would not necessarily be synchronous across all the different domains of thought (see Chapman, 1988). Instead, he argued that the chronology of the stages might be extremely variable, and that such variability might also occur *within* a given stage. For example, he suggested that the concrete operations of class inclusion and seriation might pursue slightly different developmental courses, the former being related to linguistic development and the latter to perceptual development. According to this view, these different concrete operations would not necessarily emerge at the same point in developmental time. Thus the ages of attainment that Piaget gave for the different cognitive stages are only approximations.

The sensory-motor stage

A fundamental notion in Piaget's theory of cognitive development was that thought developed from action. In his view, a "logic of action" existed prior to, and in addition to, the logic of thought. A practical logic of relations and classes in terms of sensory-motor action was the precursor of the representational logic of relations and classes that emerged at the concrete operational stage. Piaget pointed out that babies were born with many means of interacting with their environment. Their sensory systems are functioning at birth, as we saw in Chapter 1. They also have a number of motor responses that are ready for use, such as sucking and grasping. Piaget argued that the presence of these reflexes meant that babies were born with the potential to know everything about their worlds, even though at birth they knew almost nothing. These basic responses allowed infants to gain knowledge of the world and to build up hypotheses about it. Piaget's baby was conceptualised as busily interpreting and re-interpreting perceptual information in the light of its hypotheses, hypotheses that were drawn from its sensory-motor experiences in the everyday world.

The six stages of sensory-motor cognition

Within the sensory-motor stage, Piaget identified six sub-stages of development. The first was the *modification of reflexes*. For example, the baby could learn to modify its sucking reflex in order to fit the contours of its mother's nipple (*accommodation*). At the same time, the baby *assimilated* the sucking response to an increasing range of objects, and gradually became able to distinguish between objects that would satisfy hunger and objects that would not. The second stage was called *primary circular reactions*. A circular reaction is a repetitive behaviour. Babies seem to enjoy engaging in repetitive behaviours, and Piaget proposed that this repetition had cognitive value. The first repetitive behaviours were concerned with the self, and thus Piaget labelled them "primary". Primary circular reactions involved the re-creation of sensory experiences. A good example is thumb sucking.

The third stage was called *secondary circular reactions*. Secondary repetitive behaviours involve the outside world. For example, a baby

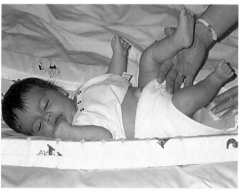

might seek to recreate interesting events in its environment, such as dropping an object. The circular reaction would be to repeatedly drop the object without getting bored—a behaviour that also requires repetitive behaviour on the part of the baby's caretaker, who has to repeatedly pick the object up! The fourth stage was called the *co-ordination of circular reactions*. At this point, the baby became able to co-ordinate a series of behaviours in order to attain a goal. Piaget called this goal-oriented

TRIP/H. ROGERS

behaviour "means–ends" behaviour. An example is pulling on a blanket so that a desired toy at the edge of the blanket moves to a location within the baby's reach.

The fifth stage was called *tertiary circular reactions*. By this stage, babies' ability to recreate events in the outside world has become more sophisticated. Stage 5 infants conduct different trial-and-error explorations in order to determine the results of certain actions. For example, a baby may repeatedly drop an object in a variety of ways in order to examine the different trajectories that the object will take. The focus of interest is now the variation of these trajectories, rather than the repetition of the action of dropping (as in secondary circular reactions). Such actions can be viewed as hypothesis-testing behaviour, and Piaget argued that tertiary circular reactions led to the discovery of the spatial and causal relations between the objects involved.

The final stage of sensory-motor cognition was called the *interiorisation of schemes*. At this point, the baby became able to anticipate the consequences of certain actions, and thus to work out the sequence of actions required to attain a desired goal *prior to* performing the actions themselves. This anticipation occurred via *mental combination* of the actions and their consequences, without the need for trial-and-error exploration. The interiorisation of schemes hence marked the *cognitive* representation of actions and their consequences. These representations were detached from immediate action and were liberated from direct perception—they were fully symbolic. According to Piaget, stage 6 of sensory-motor cognition marked the beginning of conceptual thought.

Sensory-motor cognition in different domains

Piaget went on to demonstrate that the different stages of sensory-motor development could be observed in different domains of sensory-motor cognition, such as spatial relations, time, causality, and the conception of a permanent object. We will only consider two of these examples here, the development of the object concept and the development of causal understanding.

Object permanence. The development of the object concept, or the concept of "object permanence", refers to the understanding that objects continue to exist even when they are hidden from view. Piaget measured the emerging conception of the permanence of objects by studying the development of babies' *searching* behaviour. He had noticed that when he hid a desired object from his own infants, for example if he hid one of their toys under a cushion, they gradually became more capable of retrieving it, and that this capacity to find objects when they were hidden developed in a sequence of stages. The different stages of search that Piaget documented in his own infants have now been replicated many times, by researchers in countries all around the world. There is no question that Piaget was right about the sequential emergence of the different stages of search.

During the first two stages of object permanence, which occur between the ages of 0–4 months, the infant does not show any search behaviour at all. During these first two stages, Piaget argued that objects were not differentiated from the infant's own actions. The disappearance of an object was only registered by the infant continuing to make the "accommodatory movements" being made when the object disappeared. For example, if the infant had been following the trajectory of an object with her eyes, she would continue to look in the direction in which the object was last visible, even if it had by now disappeared.

During the third stage of object permanence, infants began to search for partially-hidden objects. This behaviour suggested a rudimentary recognition of their continued existence. For example, if a favourite toy was partially visible beneath a cushion, the infant would try and retrieve it. However, if the toy was fully hidden from view, no attempt was made to look for it. This behaviour lasted until around 6 months of age.

During the fourth stage of object permanence, the infant became able to search for fully hidden objects. For example, even if a toy was completely concealed beneath a cushion, the infant persisted in trying to retrieve it. However, the act of retrieval was still thought to be tied to spatial location, as although the infant would happily retrieve the toy from the same hiding location again and again, this was the *only* location of search. Even if the toy was hidden under a different cushion, in full view of the infant, the infant would search for the toy under the first cushion. This surprising behaviour is called the "A-not-B" error, and as we saw in Chapter 2 it occurs between 8 and 12 months of age. Piaget suggested that the infant believes that the object is associated with the first location, location A, and that it can recreate the object at A simply by deciding to look there.

The fifth stage of object permanence was characterised by the disappearance of the A-not-B error. As long as the infants could *watch* the object being moved to a new hiding location, they were able to retrieve it over multiple hidings, even when the location was changed from A to B. This marked the onset of the ability to cope with "visible displacement", indicating an understanding of the object itself and of its relation to other objects. The fifth stage of search lasted from around 12–15 months. However, in conditions of "invisible displacement", when the object was moved to a new hiding location *without* the infant observing the action of hiding, search difficulties remained. It was only once invisible displacements were solved and the infant could find objects wherever they were hidden that full object permanence was thought to have been achieved (stage 6). Infants who have attained stage 6 of object permanence search for objects systematically until they find them, indicating the ability to represent object locations even when some of the movements of the object have not been observed. This complete understanding of object permanence emerged between 15 and 18 months, and marked the attainment of a *cognitive representation* of the object.

Causality. According to Piaget's observations, the development of causal understanding also passed through the six stages of sensory-motor cognition. In the first two stages, the modification of reflexes and primary circular reactions, infants had no understanding of cause and effect *per se*. The development of causality occurred at a purely practical level. Thus although behaviours like thumb sucking might appear to show some appreciation of cause and effect ("If I suck my thumb, I will feel comforted"), Piaget argued that there was no reason to suppose that cause and effect were in fact distinguished. The *sensation* of thumb sucking was not necessarily distinguished from the *action* of thumb sucking itself.

The beginning of the understanding that causes are different from their effects was thought to begin to emerge during stage 3 (secondary circular reactions). For example, an infant who repeatedly drops an object in order to recreate the action of dropping must at some level be aware that the object is different from the causal action. However, this does not mean that the infant is aware of the causal *relation* between the action of dropping and its effect. Piaget suggested that infants were not aware of causal relations at this point in development. They had a vague understanding of the temporal sequence involved in causal situations (the sequence *action precedes consequence*), but not of the means by which the action of dropping led to the object pursuing its observed trajectory.

Piaget argued that, even during stage 4 (the co-ordination of circular reactions), infants do not really understand causal relations. Instead, he proposed that stage 4 infants believed that objects were capable of autonomous activity, and at the same time that the behaviour of objects depended on their own actions. Piaget inferred these beliefs from the infants' sensory-motor behaviour towards objects. Perhaps the best example is the A-not-B search error. Recall that part of Piaget's explanation of this error was that the infant believed that a desired object could be recreated at location A simply because the infant decided to look there. At the same time, Piaget argued that the infant associated the object with location A, and that the sensory-motor memory of the action of finding being linked to location A tended to override any memory for the sequence of actions that had resulted in the object being hidden at location B. This motor memory for the object's position led the infant to search erroneously at location A.

Piaget argued that it was only during stage 5 that infants came to realise that objects could behave independently of their own actions. However, even at this point (12–15 months), infants still attributed a degree of autonomy to the behaviour of objects. Although they could recognise that their (the infants') actions were only a single cause of the displacement of objects, they believed that an equally valid cause of such displacements was some kind of spontaneous activity on the part of the objects themselves. Again, these beliefs were inferred from their sensory-motor behaviour. In Piaget's search task, infants who had not observed the displacement of an object did not search for it (invisible displacement). On the other hand, the same infants could cope with visible displacements of the object, suggesting the development of the ability to reconstruct a series of causal actions.

A representational understanding of causality was only thought to develop at stage 6, when infants were aged around 18 months. At this point, cause–effect action schemes were interiorised, enabling the *cogni-*

tive representation of actions and their consequences. As noted earlier, Piaget argued that the representations that developed at stage 6 were fully symbolic, being detached from immediate action and from direct perception. This meant that infants were now able to work out the causes of observed effects, and the likely effects of observed causes. Piaget explained causality as "an organisation of the universe caused by the totality of relations established by action and then by representation between objects as well as between subject and object" (Piaget, 1971, cited in Chapman, 1988, p. 357). Knowledge of causal relations was thus thought to emerge out of the actions that the baby performed on objects in the physical world, and the observed effects of those actions.

Evaluation of Piaget's sensory-motor stage in the light of recent research

Consistent evidence. Piaget's notion of sensory-motor cognition is appealing on a number of levels. Babies must begin to learn about the world via the means that they have available to them, and these means are initially sensory and motor. In fact, most of the evidence that we discussed in Chapters 1 and 2 supports Piaget's view that sensory-motor responses are a primary source of information for infants, and that sensory-motor behaviours play an important role in knowledge acquisition. However, Piaget's proposal goes much further than this. He argued that sensory-motor responses were foundational because a "logic of action" existed prior to, and in addition to, the representational logic of thought. In Piaget's theory, sensory-motor behaviours *became* thought. This idea is less easily assimilated with some of the evidence discussed earlier, as we will see.

Piaget's explanation of how sensory-motor behaviours might become thought does fit well with some of the research discussed in this book, however. His idea was that sensory-motor behaviours became representational via a process of interiorisation, and that this interiorisation occurred via a process of analogy. The analogies that Piaget had in mind were "motor analogies". He had noticed that his own children imitated certain spatial relations that they had observed in the physical world with their own bodies. For example, they imitated the opening and closing of a matchbox by opening and closing their hands and mouths. Piaget suggested that this behaviour showed that the infants were trying to understand the mechanism of the matchbox through a motor analogy, reproducing a kinesthetic image of opening and closing. Mental imagery was then argued to develop out of kinesthetic imitations as a result of progressive interiorisation.

Analogies were also thought to play a role in the generalisation of sensory-motor schemes to new objects. In fact, Piaget argued that analogical transfer was rapid once a new physical concept had been understood. Commenting on the acquisition of the "pull" schema (the ability to use string-like objects as a "means for bringing"), Piaget (1952, p. 297, cited by Brown, 1990) wrote: "Let us note that once the new schema is acquired, it is applied from the outset to analogous situations. The behaviour pattern of the string is without any difficulty applied to the watch chain. Thus, at each acquisition we fall back on the application of familiar means to new situations." As discussed in Chapter 2, recent experiments have supported Piaget's view, showing that simple relational mappings are available to infants as young as 10 months (see Chen et al., 1995), and are readily transferred to new objects by infants of 13 months.

Finally, on a purely theoretical level, we can note that Piaget's idea that a "logic of action" existed prior to, and in addition to, the representational logic of thought, is very similar to the ideas proposed more recently by psychologists interested in the development of "naive" or "intuitive" physics. The idea that physical concepts are first understood at the "intuitive" level of action and only later at the reflective or representational level is remarkably similar to Piaget's idea that representational understanding develops from sensory-motor knowledge. For example, Anderson and Wilkening's view (see Chapter 4) was that intuitive physics was rooted in the perception of objects and events (see Anderson & Wilkening, 1991). Children's perceptions of the world around them became the basis of mental models that were formed to mimic the structure and action of physical systems, and these mental models were then used in reasoning about the physical world. Although some of the experimental evidence discussed in Chapter 4 suggested that action provided a separate and autonomous source of knowledge from representational or reflective understanding, the similarity between current notions of naive physics and Piaget's notion of sensory-motor cognition is clear.

Inconsistent evidence. In other crucial respects, however, Piaget's notion of sensory-motor cognition has been increasingly challenged. Perhaps the most controversial aspect of Piaget's theory has been the idea that cognitive representations do not emerge until the final stage of sensory-motor cognition (stage 6). If this were true, then babies would have to wait a long time before they could engage in any meaningful cognitive activity. Learning, memory, reasoning, and problem-solving abilities would be seriously constrained. However, as we have seen from the evidence discussed in Chapters 1 and 2, learning, memory, reasoning, and problem-solving can all be observed in infants as young as 6 months. Similarly, the studies of infant memory, infant prototypes, and infant categorisation discussed in these chapters imply that representational ability is present much earlier than Piaget supposed. So the idea that the capacity for symbolic mental representation only emerges at the age of around 18 months appears to be wrong. It seems that the behaviours that Piaget took to mark the cognitive representation of objects, actions, and their consequences (namely full object permanence and the interiorisation of schemes) provided too *conservative* a measure of representation.

In fact, some of the evidence discussed earlier, such as the evidence for neonate imitation discussed in Chapter 2 (Meltzoff & Moore, 1983), suggests that the ability to form cognitive representations may be innate. If this ability is not innate, then the imitation data suggests that it emerges rather early, as Meltzoff has argued that imitating a gesture requires representational capacity (although see Anisfield, 1991). Piaget's view was that imitation preceded representation rather than vice versa, with mental images being interiorised imitations. Furthermore, he argued that the ability to imitate motor actions such as tongue protrusion only emerged at stage 4 (at around 9 months). Meltzoff finds this ability in 1- to 3-day-old infants. Thus while Piaget believed that imitation plays an important role in the onset of cognitive representation, Meltzoff argues the opposite, that cognitive representation enables the onset of imitation.

Piaget's view of the development of causal understanding also appears to be too pessimistic, at least given some of the studies discussed in Chapter 2. As we have seen repeatedly throughout this book, the human infant seems to be born with an innate bias to learn about causal relations and to acquire causal explanations. This innate bias appears to play a powerful role in explaining the development of children's cognition. Even by 4 months, infants appreciate rudimentary cause–effect relations, such as launching events (Leslie & Keeble, 1987). Many of Baillargeon's experiments suggest that infants of a similar age can *predict* effects from causes. For example, they expect a rotating screen to collide with a box in its path, even though the collision itself occurs out of view. They expect a tall rabbit passing behind a high wall to be exposed once the central section of the wall is lowered to (the rabbit's) waist height. They expect a box that is suspended in mid-air with no visible means of support to fall. Thus a representational understanding of causality based on the *cognitive* representation of actions and their consequences appears to be available much earlier than 18 months of age.

Finally, we can question Piaget's claims concerning the development of object permanence. His assumption that a full understanding of object permanence was not present until around 18 months of age appears to be too conservative. Again, it seems that Piaget was misled by his focus on sensory-motor behaviour. As infants cannot reach reliably for objects until around 4 months of age, any emergent understanding of the object concept cannot be measured by the study of searching behaviour. Similarly, the development of motor behaviour such as guided reaching depends to some extent on the development of the frontal cortex, which we now know to be immature in young babies. Thus Piaget's experimental method of inferring conceptual understanding from the observation of how and when babies search is fraught with difficulty.

In fact, the habituation experiments discussed in Chapter 2 concerning the "drawbridge" paradigm invented by Baillargeon et al. (1985) suggest that an understanding of object permanence is present in babies as young as 3 months. Converging evidence from the dishabituation effects found in Baillargeon's (1986) "rolling car" paradigm supports this conclusion. Diamond's (1991) analysis of frontal immaturities in non-human species enables an alternative explanation of the A-not-B error in terms of inhibitory failures rather than cognitive confusions about the parameters underlying the existence of objects. The data from the "perseverative crawling" paradigm used by Rieser et al. (1982) and by McKenzie and Bigelow (1986) supports Diamond's view that an inability to inhibit a predominant action tendency is at the root of the A-not-B error.

Piaget's inferences about the understanding of object permanence were thus based on misleading data, and his inferences concerning causal understanding suffered from the same problem. Piaget used the A-not-B error as evidence that stage 4 infants believed that objects were capable of autonomous activity and that the behaviour of objects depended on their own actions. If the A-not-B error can instead be explained by neural immaturities, then the serious limitations that Piaget believed were characteristic of 9-month-olds' causal understanding must also be discounted.

The pre-operational and concrete operational stages

In order to document cognitive changes beyond stage 6 of sensory-motor cognition, Piaget investigated children's symbolic understanding of the properties of concrete objects and the relations between those objects. For example, as we saw in Chapter 7, he investigated children's understanding of classes of objects such as flowers and their part–whole relations, he investigated children's understanding of transitive relations between objects of different lengths or heights, and he investigated children's understanding of addition, subtraction, and equivalence by using stimuli such as rows of pennies and beakers of liquid. His expectation was that the schemes or concepts of sensory-motor thought would be redeveloped in the mental realm.

The set of logical concepts that described classes of objects and their relations were called the "concrete operations". Again, these operations were thought to develop from interiorised actions. For example, the interiorisation of operations such as addition and subtraction on concrete objects led to the symbolic representation of the formal properties of whole numbers, such as that $2 + 2 = 4$ simultaneously implies that $4–2 = 2$. The recognition of the "reversibility" of this operation was a critical feature of concrete operational cognition. Piaget (1952, p.252) argued that an understanding of logical and mathematical relations were interdependent: "The child can grasp a certain operation only if he is capable, at the same time, of correlating operations by modifying them in different, well-determined ways—for instance, by inverting them ... the operations always represent reversible structures which depend on a total system..." In other words, the functional units of thought were not isolated concepts and judgements, but the total system that was formed by particular acts of seriation, classification, and so on.

Pre-operational thought

Piaget's investigations led him to propose that a full symbolic understanding of the properties and relations of concrete objects developed only gradually, between the ages of around 2 and 7 years. During this period, children's solution of problems concerning objects and their relations (e.g. class inclusion problems, conservation problems) displayed "pre-operational" thought. The main characteristics of pre-operational thought were that it was *egocentric*, in that the child perceived and interpreted the symbolic world in terms of the self; that it displayed *centration*, in that the child tended to fix on one aspect of a situation or object and ignore other aspects; and that it displayed a *lack of reversibility*, in that the child was unable to mentally reverse a series of events or steps of reasoning, using symbols or representations in an irreversible fashion. The pre-operational child was thus seen as pre-logical, having a subjective and self-centred grasp of the world.

Concrete operational thought

The acquisition of the concrete operations was marked by the gradual waning of egocentricity, by the ability to "decentre" or consider multiple aspects of a situation simultaneously, and by "reversibility" or the ability to understand that any operation on an object simultaneously implied its inverse. The child's growing logical insights concerning the symbolic understanding of objects were thought to lead to the development of the concrete operational "structures", such as classification, seriation and conservation. Piaget argued that the system of thought based on the organisation of the concrete operations could be described to some extent in terms of mathematical groupings. These mathematical groupings described concrete operations like class inclusion $(A + A' = B)$ and transitivity $(A > B, B > C$, therefore $A > C)$. Piaget's idea was that mathematical logic could be used to describe the psychological reality of the logical structures developed by the child, and the reversibility of those structures. Most subsequent research on pre-operational and concrete operational thought has neglected Piaget's focus on mathematical groupings, however. Instead, it has focused on whether logical concepts like conservation, transitivity, and class inclusion are present at an earlier age than Piaget supposed.

Evaluation of recent research on the concrete operations

As we saw in Chapter 7, a number of researchers have demonstrated very successfully that logical concepts like conservation and transitivity are indeed available to children much earlier than would be predicted by Piaget's theory. For example, 4-year-olds can conserve number successfully in the "naughty teddy" paradigm invented by McGarrigle and Donaldson (1975), 4-year-olds can solve transitive inference problems in the tower building task invented by Pears and Bryant (1990), and 5-year-olds can solve class inclusion problems when collection rather than class terms are used to pose the class inclusion question (Markman & Seibert, 1976). These and many other studies have led to the notion that preschoolers are capable of using the same forms of logic on Piagetian tasks as older children, but that task requirements which are *extraneous* to the assessment of their logic have prevented these capabilities from being demonstrated. However, a number of authors have pointed out that demonstrations such as these may not constitute a true test of Piaget's position. The key point is whether the modified paradigms used in these studies leave the original logical requirements of Piaget's standard tasks intact.

Piaget himself argued that the stage of concrete operations should be defined in terms of the fact that reversibility becomes *simultaneous* rather than successive, and not in terms of the fact that the child can answer some of the experimenter's questions successfully. Pre-operational children were thought to be capable of *successive* reversibility, such as imagining the act of collecting some objects together according to class-type relations (e.g. grouping together flowers of different colours), and then separating them according to their differences (e.g. sorting the different flowers by colour). However, only concrete operational children could think of the flowers as *at the same time* belonging to the common whole and to a set of sub-groups.

Smith (1982) has argued that recent experimental studies have neglected this aspect of Piaget's account. According to Piaget, a child should only be credited with a concrete operational structure like class inclusion once that child understands the *necessity* of the reversibility, that A = B−A′ *and* A′ = B−A. For example, if B is the total class of flowers, and A is the subclass of red flowers, then flowers of other colours are the flowers left over when all flowers that are *not* red are subtracted from the class of flowers, and all the flowers that are colours other than red are the class of flowers minus the subclass of red flowers. Most recent experimental studies have only examined whether children understand the *correctness* of class relationships (e.g. that there are more red flowers than white flowers in a bunch containing six red flowers and four white flowers). They have not examined the necessary corollary of this, that the white flowers are not members of the class of red flowers, even though both are members of the class of flowers.

A similar argument concerning transitivity has been made by Chapman (1988). He pointed out that in Piaget's transitivity tasks, the objects to be compared were always presented successively, preventing a simultaneous perceptual comparison. For example, Piaget showed children first that stick A was longer than stick B (A > B), and then that stick B was longer than stick C (B > C). The child was then asked to infer the relation between A and C, the two sticks that had not been seen together. In more recent experiments, children have often been shown all the comparison objects at once (this was true of most of the transitivity studies discussed in Chapter 7). Chapman argued that the logical structure of these two versions of the transitive reasoning task were different. Piaget's version required children to use an *operational* composition of premise relations in order to draw the correct inference (a mental logic). More recent versions of the transitive inference task only require children to use functional reasoning based on the spatial relations that are visible between the objects. This means that the correct answer can be inferred as a function of these visible relationships, without taking the individual premise relations into account. Even though this functional reasoning also requires a transitive inference, it is not a transitive inference in Piaget's sense of a *mental* inference.

Overall, then, it seems that the conclusion that pre-schoolers are capable of using the same forms of logic on Piagetian tasks as older children is not the right conclusion to draw on the basis of recent experimental work using concrete operational tasks. This is because the *necessity* of the reversibility of concrete operational structures is not usually tested by the experimental tasks given to younger children. On the other hand, these experiments demonstrate that pre-operational children can recognise the *correctness* of class relations, transitive relations, and equivalence relations, and these are important demonstrations. Such demonstrations suggest that the logical concepts required to recognise correctness are indeed present at earlier ages than predicted by Piaget. What is absent at these earlier ages is the full understanding of the reversibility of these relations. Although full reversibility was required by Piaget in order to credit children with a *true* understanding of these logical concepts, modern developmental psychologists may feel that the understanding demonstrated by correctness is sufficient grounds for crediting children younger than 7 years with the capacity for these forms of logical thought.

Formal operational thought

According to Piaget, cognitive change beyond the concrete operational period depended on the emerging ability to take the results of concrete operations and to generate hypotheses about their logical relationships. This "formal operational" reasoning became available at the age of approximately 11 or 12 years. Piaget described this level of reasoning as "operating on operations", or "second-order" reasoning: "This notion of second-order operations also expresses the general characteristic of formal thought—it goes beyond the framework of transformations bearing directly on empirical reality (concrete operations) and subordinates it to a system of hypothetico-deductive operations, i.e., operations which are *possible*" (Inhelder & Piaget, 1958, p.254). Piaget characterised formal operational reasoning in terms of the ability to apply a formal system such as propositional logic to the elementary operations concerning classes of objects and their relations.

Piaget described the basis of this propositional logic in terms of the combinatorial system describing all 16 possible binary relations between the entities *p, q, not-p*, and *not-q* (such as the conditional rule *if p then q* discussed in Chapter 7). He also described the sub-system of transformations that could operate on these relations (such as finding the *inverse* relation or the *reciprocal* relation). This latter analysis has been called the INRC grouping (I for identity of the relation, N for negation or inverse, R for reciprocity, and C for correlation). The presence of these binary combinatorial relations and of the INRC operations were thought to be the hallmarks of formal operational thought. As with concrete operational thought, however, most subsequent research has neglected Piaget's focus on mathematical groupings, and has focused instead on younger children's performance in the *tasks* that Piaget used to demonstrate the presence of the formal operations.

Formal operational tasks

Formal operational thought was scientific thought, as Piaget believed that the attainment of the formal operations allowed the child to represent alternative hypotheses and their deductive implications. Indeed, many of Piaget's tests for the presence of formal operational structures involved scientific tasks, such as discovering the rule that determines whether material bodies will float or sink in water, discovering the rule between weight and distance that will enable a balance beam to balance, and discovering the rule that governs the oscillation of a pendulum. All of these rules are part of the combinatorial or INRC groupings. For example, the rule governing the behaviour of the balance beam is an inverse proportional relation between weight and distance (that simultaneously increasing the weight and distance on one arm of the balance is equivalent to decreasing the weight and increasing the distance on the other arm). Discovery of this proportionality was thought to be a key feature of formal operational reasoning.

Piaget's experimental method was to allow children to manipulate the independent variables in the scientific task (e.g. the length of the string and the weight of the bob in the pendulum task), and then to see whether they could arrive at the correct rule governing the behaviour of these variables. Most children did not manage to discover the appropriate rules before the age of around 11 years. For example, in the pendulum task, children needed to use strings of different lengths and bobs of different weights in order to discover that the period of a pendulum is a function of its length. As children usually began the task by believing that the weight of the bob must be an important factor in determining the oscillation of the pendulum, they needed to hold the length of the string constant while experimenting with a variety of weights in order to conclude that weight alone does not affect the pendulum's period. Children younger than 11 to 12 years usually failed to see the necessity for holding other variables such as string length constant, and thus failed to reason according to Piaget's combinatorial system (use of the system can be expressed as follows: If p is "increases in the period of oscillation", and q is "decreases in the length of the string", then p implies q and vice versa). Piaget argued that children who manipulated the two variables correctly showed an awareness of this combination, and also of all the other possible combinations in the group, as the other combinations were discarded as being irrelevant to the problem at hand.

The emphasis on the discovery of proportionality as a key factor in formal operational reasoning also led Piaget to include reasoning by analogy among his formal operational tasks. His logic was simple. As a full appreciation of the possible relations between objects was a concrete operational skill, the construction of relations *between* those relations must be a formal operational skill. Analogical reasoning was higher-order reasoning in the sense that the simple relations in an analogy ("lower-order relations") had to be linked by a relation at a higher level in order to make the analogy valid. Analogies also involved proportional reasoning, as an analogy like "Rome is to Italy as Paris is to France" (*Rome:Italy:Paris:France*) was logically equivalent to a proportional expression like $3:4 = 15:20$.

Piaget, Montangero, and Billeter (1977) devised an experimental task to measure analogical development that involved the pairing of pictures. Children were simply given a set of pictures all jumbled together, and were asked to pair them appropriately. This pairing measured their understanding of class-type relations (hypothesised to require concrete operational reasoning). Following this, the children were asked to put the pairs of pictures together to make foursomes. This second pairing measured their understanding of higher-order or analogical relations (hypothesised to require formal operational reasoning). For example, if given the pictures dog, feather, car, vacuum cleaner, dog hair, bird, ship (among others), the children were first meant to pair the bird with the feather, and the dog with the dog hair. They were then meant to construct the foursome *bird:feather::dog:hair*.

Piaget et al. found that the children could not reliably construct analogies of this type until the age of around 11–12 years. Children aged 5–6 years (pre-operational) used completely idiosyncratic relations to pair the pictures, for example putting the vacuum cleaner with the feather "because it hoovers up the feather", or with the ship "because it looks like a ship". Children of 7 years and older (concrete-operational) could successfully construct the initial pairings (*bird:feather* etc.) and could even form analogies by trial and error, but did not understand the logical necessity of the analogical pairings, being willing to accept countersuggestions made by the experimenter that destroyed the analogy (e.g. agreeing that the picture of a radio in the analogy *eyes:television::ears:radio* could be replaced by a picture of a plug). Piaget et al. argued that distraction by countersuggestions showed a successive understanding of the relations in the analogy rather than an understanding based on higher-order relations. The ability to construct analogies without any concrete feedback and to resist the countersuggestions made by the experimenter only emerged in formal operational children.

Evaluation of recent research on the formal operations

Evidence concerning children's performance on some formal operational tasks has been presented in Chapters 4 and 7. In Chapter 4, we saw that 9-year-olds could use the multiplicative integration rule linking weight and distance in the balance scale task devised by Wilkening and Anderson (1991). When the ability to combine information about different dimensions was tested using the barking dog and fleeing animals task (requiring the integration of time and velocity to judge distance), even 5-year-olds showed an ability to use multiplicative rules (Wilkening, 1982). Wilkening noted that this finding completely contradicted Piaget's notion that time had to be derived from information about speed and distance, and that the operations for deriving time required formal operational reasoning. In Chapter 7, we discussed a series of experiments on analogical reasoning which suggested that the ability to reason by analogy was present in children as young as 2 years of age. Children as young as 3 could complete pictorial analogies of the kind used by Piaget et al. (1977), and children of 4 could reject misleading countersuggestions in a multiple choice analogy task (Goswami & Brown, 1989, 1990). Thus a number of formal operational competencies appear to be present far earlier than Piaget's theory would suggest.

On the other hand, research on the development of the ability to represent alternative hypotheses and their deductive implications is supportive of Piaget's ideas about the difficulty of hypothesis testing prior to adolescence. For example, we saw from Kuhn's work that children have a rather poor understanding of how hypotheses are supported or contradicted by causal evidence until around 11 or 12 years of age (e.g. Kuhn, 1989). Younger children tend to fail to test hypotheses in a systematic way, omitting to control for confounding variables, and also fail to seek evidence that could disconfirm their hypotheses, accepting causes that account for only part of the available data. The simplified paradigms adopted by Sodian et al. (1991— whether the brothers had a large or small mouse in their house) and

Ruffman et al. (1993—whether green or red food led to tooth decay) showed that even 6-year-olds understood the goal of testing a hypothesis, could distinguish between conclusive and inconclusive tests of that hypothesis, and understood how simple covariation information formed the basis for a hypothesis. Nevertheless, more complicated problems involving more than one causal variable were only solved by older children (Kuhn et al., 1988). Recent research into scientific reasoning thus supports Piaget's view that only older children can represent alternative hypotheses and their deductive implications.

How can we interpret the finding that some formal operational competencies are present as young as age 3 while others are absent until adolescence? One solution is the position adopted by Lunzer (1965). He argued that Piaget's experiments on formal operations fell into two distinct groups. The first group consisted of situations in which the child was required to provide the proofs of hypotheses by the experimental manipulation of variables, varying each while holding the others constant, and noting the effects. An example of this kind of experiment is the problem concerning the motion of the pendulum (Kuhn's experiments would fall into the same category). The second group consisted of experiments in which the child was required to discover relations, usually of inverse proportionality, or was required to understand the reciprocity of physical systems. Examples of such experiments include the balance beam task and reasoning by analogy.

Lunzer's argument was that the *psychological* relationship between these two types of experimental problem was by no means clear. Piaget had sought to demonstrate a logical relationship between them by interpreting the hypothesis-testing experiments as direct applications of propositional logic (in terms of the binary combinatorial relations and the INRC operations), and interpreting the problems of proportionality and reciprocity in terms of the same propositional logic. However, Lunzer suggested that, from a psychological point of view, there was nothing to justify this connection. In particular, there was no need to express the physical relations involved in reciprocity (e.g. weight and distance on the balance beam) or the proportional relations involved in analogies in terms of propositional logic. In fact, he proposed that concrete operational children *should* be able to solve problems involving proportionality and reciprocity—as seems to be the case.

Summary

As the brief survey provided in this chapter makes clear, Piaget's theory of logical development provided some very precise answers to the traditional developmental questions of "what develops" and "why". His experimental paradigms for discovering "what develops" (such as the A-not-B search task, the tasks involving the manipulation of concrete objects, and the balance scale task) were ingenious, and are still used in current investigations. Some of his answers to the "why" of development—that sensory-motor behaviour is the foundation of cognitive development, that imitation and analogy play key roles in cognitive development, and that understanding at the level of action precedes understanding at the representational or reflective level—are still widespread in current theorising, for example in the domain of naive physics. Others, such as the focus on mathematical groupings and on the mechanisms of accommodation and assimilation, have been abandoned by most current researchers. Nevertheless, the degree of continuity between Piaget's ideas and those current in modern developmental psychology is notable.

Piaget's theory also fits well with the explanatory systems that have been developed by current theorists to account for changes in children's cognition. Piaget's was both a domain-general and a domain-specific theory. Although it is popularly believed that Piaget's stage model approach made his theory decidedly domain-general, Piaget himself noted that the chronology of the different stages might be extremely variable, and that variability would occur within as well as between stages. It is true that Piaget does not talk in specific terms about the importance of the knowledge base in children's cognition, but as Chapman (1988) has made clear, he did not believe in general stages that would immediately apply to all domains. Chapman cites the following passage from Piaget (1960, pp.14–15):

> There are no general stages. Just as, in connection with physical growth ... there is an absence of close relationship between the skeletal age, the dental age etc., similarly in the various neurological, mental and social fields we see an intermingling of processes of development which are evidently interrelated, but to different extents or according to multiple temporal rhythms, there being no reason why these processes should constitute a unique structural whole at each level.

Our conclusion must be that Piaget's theory of logical development still has much to offer current students of children's cognition. However, his comparative neglect of the development of conceptual knowledge, of memory development, and of the development of learning and the transfer of learning (to name but a few), and recent developments in cognitive neuroscience which were not available in Piaget's time, mean that the subject matter of children's cognition has expanded far beyond the experimental content of Piaget's work. Research into children's cognition is now much more closely aligned with research into adult cognition. The familiar questions of "what develops" and "why" now apply to the development of cognition *across the lifespan*.

The "what" and "why" of children's cognition 9

At the beginning of this book, we noted that the study of cognition in children has traditionally focused on two major developmental questions, the question of *what develops*, and the question of *why*. We are now in a position to provide a fairly comprehensive answer to the question of "what develops", and at least a partial answer to the question of "why".

What develops?

In terms of "what develops", we have seen that the knowledge that children have about objects and events in their worlds, and the knowledge that they have about the causal and explanatory structures underlying relations between these objects and events, expands at a terrific rate from the very first months of infancy. The depth of the knowledge base by the age of 5, when children usually begin formal schooling, is quite remarkable. Infants and young children gain a lot of their knowledge by observing and interacting with the world around them. However, equally importantly, they seek to *explain* their everyday worlds to themselves. The result is that the knowledge base is continually restructured and revised in the light of experience. This process of revision and restructuring is aided by the development of abstract knowledge structures

TRIP/H. ROGERS

(schemas and scripts) for representing the temporal and causal frameworks of events, frameworks that facilitate the storage and organisation of incoming information. As noted in Chapter 5, the development of memory and the development of other cognitive processes are intimately linked.

The knowledge base can be divided into a number of different "domains" or sets of representations sustaining different areas of knowledge, such as the domain of physical knowledge, the domain of biological knowledge, and the domain of psychological knowledge. Although the domain of psychological knowledge has not been covered in this book, the research discussed in Chapters 1 and 2 showed that infants gain detailed and principled knowledge about the physical domain during the first year of life, and the research discussed in Chapter 3 showed that by 3 years of age detailed and principled knowledge about categories and kinds (deriving from the animate–inanimate distinction) is also available. Both physical knowledge and emergent biological knowledge continue to develop, of course. We saw in Chapter 4 that young children become capable of learning more about the physical domain as they develop the ability to relate hypotheses and evidence and to integrate different causal variables, and we saw at the end of Chapter 3 that the domain of biology undergoes conceptual change as more and more knowledge about categories and kinds is acquired.

The importance of the developing knowledge base means that the other main aspect of "what develops", namely children's cognitive abilities, skills, and strategies, cannot be studied in isolation. As noted in Chapter 7, attempts to measure "pure" reasoning or "pure" memory abilities by using context-free tasks are fatally flawed. If measures of cognitive skills do not tap into the familiar situations in which these skills are normally required, then such measures tend to seriously underestimate children's cognitive abilities. Many apparent changes in children's cognition are in reality changes in the knowledge that children have available as a basis for exercising a particular skill. For example, when syllogistic reasoning is tested using familiar premises, then 4-year-olds can draw logical conclusions on the basis of these premises, even when the premises are counterfactual (e.g. cats barking; see Chapter 7). Similar effects of context can be demonstrated in adults, as when the selection task is presented in a "post office" context the majority of adults reason logically, whereas when it is presented in an abstract context the majority reason illogically (also Chapter 7).

Because of such effects, we cannot assume that by defining a particular principle of logical thought and then tracking its development over time via sensitive experimental tests we are measuring "what develops". We might be measuring the development of the knowledge base rather than the development of the cognitive skill *per se*. A good example is the development of analogical reasoning. Early research concluded that analogical reasoning was absent until early adolescence, but this conclusion was based on misleading data. It depended on experimental tasks using analogical relations that were unfamiliar to younger children. Analogical reasoning skills were found to develop in early adolescence only because knowledge about these relations developed in early adolescence too. However, it is important to note that the nature of a cognitive skill measured at time 1 may differ completely from the nature of a cognitive skill measured at time 2. This point has recently been made about analogical reasoning (Strauss, in press). In Chapter 2, we saw that infants appeared to be able to reason by analogy in certain contexts. Strauss has argued that the kind of analogies made by infants may be completely different from the kind of analogies made by older children. He suggests that the kind of analogies made by young infants are *perceptual* in nature, whereas those made by young children use *conceptual* knowledge. Such questions about the continuity of cognitive skills are important ones for answering the question of "what develops".

Why does development pursue its observed course?

When we turn to the question of *why* development pursues its observed course, we are seeking to organise all the information about "what develops" into an explanatory framework. This framework needs to account for new findings in the area of "what develops" as well as for findings that already exist. In other words, a good answer to the question of why development pursues its observed course will constitute a *theory* about children's cognition that can make *predictions* about the development of cognitive skills or types of knowledge as well as explain existing observations about cognitive skills or areas of knowledge.

In the Foreword, we noted that there are at least three explanatory systems that have had a major impact on theorising in developmental psychology. These are domain-general vs. domain-specific accounts of cognitive development, innate vs. acquired accounts, and qualitative vs. quantitative change accounts. We can examine the power of each of these explanatory systems in relation to the evidence about "what develops" that has been considered in this book.

Domain-general vs. domain-specific accounts of cognition in children

Domain-general accounts of changes in children's cognition are based on the idea that key logical developments apply across all cognitive domains. Such accounts of cognitive development are those traditionally found in the developmental literature. For example, Piaget's theory is basically domain-general in nature (see Chapter 8), and the neo-Piagetian processing capacity limitation theories of cognitive development are similar in spirit (see Chapter 6). Although none of these theories is completely domain-general, more recent domain-specific accounts of children's cognition have been seen as a major alternative to such traditional theorising.

Domain-specific accounts of cognitive development argue that many cognitive abilities are specialised to handle specific types of information. These accounts begin from the idea that children could not have the wealth of knowledge that they do at such young ages in the absence of specialisation (e.g. Hirschfeld & Gelman, 1994). An associated idea is that there are *constraints on learning* that lead children to attend to certain inputs over others, thereby supporting the development of domain-specific knowledge (e.g. Gelman, 1990). Such accounts define a "domain" in a number of different ways. Some theorists see domains as large "chunks" of cognition, such as the physical and biological worlds discussed earlier, and others talk in terms of more circumscribed areas of knowledge, such as expertise about chess or dinosaurs. Domain-specific accounts assume that the development of cognition depends on certain internal mechanisms (perhaps naive "theories") that guide what is learned from experience in rather precise and restricted ways. Different internal mechanisms are assumed to operate in, or be available for, different domains.

The evidence reviewed in this book suggests that *both* domain-general and domain-specific accounts have explanatory power in the field of children's cognition. A good example of the power of a domain-specific account is conceptual development, which was discussed in detail in Chapter 3. Recent research in this domain has shown that what children learn about animate and inanimate kinds is determined in part by their naive "theories". These theories are based on core principles such as self-caused vs. other-caused motion, similarity of key internal properties, and inheritance. A core principle such as "cause of motion" leads children to assume that an unfamiliar animal such as an echidna has "little legs" even when such legs are invisible in a picture, and to assume that a statue cannot move on its own even if it is depicted as having feet. Some researchers have gone so far as to suggest that these theories and core principles are innate, and they can certainly be observed fairly early in development: Even infants attend to properties such as cause of motion, and 5-month-olds can distinguish biological from non-biological motion on the basis of a stimulus as sparse as 10–12 moving points of light.

However, it can also be argued that the privileged attention to particular inputs demonstrated by so much of this research is actually the result of a domain-general process. This domain-general process is the innate bias to search for causal explanations of the everyday world. The attempt to develop explanatory constructs to understand conceptual structure may be part and parcel of the "constraint" of attending to inputs that inform the infant and young child about the causes of different motions. This alternative domain-general explanation of the same data can be illustrated by Pauen's "Causes and Effects of Changes" or CEC model of conceptual development. In her model, Pauen argues that infants are biased to attend to the causes of changes in their environment from the very first day of life. These changes may carry crucial information about animacy and inanimacy, but they may equally well carry crucial information about quite different matters such as whether a surface can provide support or whether certain noises mean that a feed is imminent. According to Pauen, the activity of understanding the causes and effects of changes in the environment may be enough to account for the early learning of the animate–inanimate distinction when the dimensions of change concern particular aspects of the behaviour of objects (see Chapter 3).

Innate vs. acquired accounts of cognition in children

Another way of organising information about "what develops" in children's cognition has been to try to establish whether a given cognitive skill is innate or acquired. If a skill is innate, it is assumed that the skill is "in the genes". If the skill is acquired during development, it is assumed that experience is necessary for the skill to develop, and the particular kind of experience necessary for this development then becomes the object of enquiry. As discussed in the Foreword, neither account alone can provide a satisfactory description of development, as genes and environment always *interact* in the development of any skill. However, given that innate and acquired processes are fused in development, it is important to recognise the corollary of this, which is that describing a skill as innate is not an explanation of its development at all. Claiming that a "naive theory" of biology is innate, or claiming that infants have an innate bias to learn about causal relations and acquire causal explanations, does not mean that there is nothing further for a developmentalist to find out.

This point has been made clearly by Turkewitz (1995). He points out that the early appearance of, say, the bias to learn about causal relations and acquire causal explanations is a *starting* point for investigation rather than an answer to the question of why development pursues its observed course. In fact, an early appearance actually *complicates* a developmental analysis, as we now have to search for the source of the skill or process at an even earlier point in developmental time. As noted in Chapter 6, developmental cognitive neuroscience is beginning to provide some ways of thinking about how such searches may be attempted, as it adds molecular, genetic, and neurological perspectives on the development of the brain to the perspective of cognitive developmental psychology. However, at the time of writing it is too early to suggest ways of investigating how the causal bias in information processing that has been observed at work so frequently throughout this book might originate.

Although it is too early to say much about how "innate" skills develop, it is not too early to try to answer the related theoretical question posed by Turkewitz, which is how the characteristics and limitations of infant motor, sensory, perceptual, and cognitive functioning shape the development of adult cognitive functions. Turkewitz pinpointed three infant characteristics that may be worthy of further study. These are infants' preference for novelty, and the processes of habituation and dishabituation. To these we can add infants' preference for attending to changes in the environment, the processes of inhibition and imitation, the ability to process correlational information present in the environment, and the bias to learn about causal relations and to acquire causal explanations.

The evidence discussed in earlier chapters has already demonstrated the contribution of some of these characteristics to later cognitive functioning. For example, the ability to *process correlational information* appears to lead initially to the development of perceptual prototypes. It leads eventually to the development of conceptual prototypes that help the infant and then the young child to construct and organise the world into the categories and kinds familiar to adults, and thereby also underpins the development of semantic memory. The ability to process correlations also contributes to the ability to learn about causal relations, as correlational information is one basis for attributing causality (when such information follows the causal principles discussed in Chapter 4). The principled use of correlational information thus eventually underpins the ability to reason scientifically and to undertake effective hypothesis testing (see Chapters 4 and 8).

The other characteristics just outlined have been discussed in less detail in preceding chapters (with the exception of the bias to learn about causal relations and to acquire causal explanations, which will be discussed later in this chapter). Nevertheless, a few conclusions about the contribution of these other characteristics to later cognitive function can be offered. The *preference for novelty* (which can be measured by visual recognition memory) and the processes of *habituation* and *dishabituation* are all related to later intelligence. Infants who are "fast habituators" or who demonstrate a strong novelty preference score more highly on cognitive measures taken in childhood and adolescence than infants who are "slow habituators" or who show a smaller novelty preference (see Chapter 1). This is probably because these measures are picking up aspects of basic information processing that play a role in the general efficiency of cognitive functioning, aspects such as depth and speed of stimulus encoding. The ability to *imitate* is important for later cognitive function on a number of levels. It plays a key role in learning and perhaps also in representation, it contributes to the understanding of psychological causation, and it may also function as an early form of reasoning by analogy. The contribution of the process of *inhibition* to later cognitive function is not well understood. However, recent research suggests that it must be important for the development of executive processes such as planning and monitoring one's own cognitive activity, and for the development and efficiency of selective attention.

Finally, in assessing the explanatory power of an innate/acquired perspective on development, we can examine the "interaction" position by asking whether there is any evidence that the experience of *specific* aspects of a rich environment have an effect on *specific* cognitive abilities. Although the general experience of a rich environment has long been known to be important for general cognitive development following research with children brought up in particularly impoverished environments (e.g. Clarke & Clarke, 1976), evidence that there may be more specific connections between children's cognition and their environment has also been discussed in this book. Two examples will suffice, both drawn from the development of memory.

In Chapter 5, we saw that maternal interaction styles have an effect on the development of episodic memory. All children develop episodic memories, which are memories for personal experiences that are organised around generic or abstract knowledge structures that provide frameworks for storing this information in a causally and temporally coherent way. However, children with "elaborative" mothers tend to have better episodic memories than children with "non-elaborative" mothers. Mothers who embellish and extend the information provided by their children about shared events, and who evaluate this information, provide a better environment for the development of episodic memory than mothers who provide less narrative structure and who jump from one topic to another.

Another example of the effects of enriched experience on memory development comes from eye-witness memory. Research in eye-witness memory has suggested that the testimony of children is less reliable than the testimony of adults, as children are more susceptible to misleading questions that produce false memories for events that never actually occurred. However, we now know that there is a relationship between degree of susceptibility and the richness of the knowledge base. Children who have a rich knowledge of a certain class of events, such as going to the doctor, are less susceptible to misleading questions than children with a less rich experience of the same events. Again, therefore, a specific kind of enrichment has a specific cognitive pay-off.

However, the general point is not that an enriched environment explains the observed differences in cognitive abilities. In both of these examples, it is impossible to separate the genetic contribution from the environmental. For example, it could be argued that elaborative mothers have a narrative style that stems from certain characteristics of their own enhanced episodic memories, aspects that are under genetic control and that they pass on to their own children. Similarly, it could be argued that children who are less susceptible to leading questions may be inherently more likely to develop richer memories when experiencing certain events. However, such arguments miss the point of adopting the "interactionist" position, according to which there can never be a pure genetic component that can be isolated from a pure environmental one. The developmental question should rather be *how* an enriched environment plays a role in the development of a specific cognitive skill.

Qualitative vs. quantitative accounts of developmental change

The third explanatory framework that has proved useful in organising information about "what develops" is the delineation of some cognitive changes as qualitative in nature and others as quantitative. Qualitative changes involve radically new modes of thinking, whereas quantitative changes involve the gradual acquisition of a new cognitive strategy or ability. However, just as it has proved impossible to consider domain-specific and domain-general explanations of children's cognition (or acquired and innate explanations) as truly distinct from each other, so it is impossible to separate qualitative from quantitative explanations of development in any sensible way.

A clear illustration of this is provided by infantile amnesia, discussed in Chapter 5. At one time infantile amnesia was thought to show that early memory was qualitatively distinct from later memory.

The assumption was that a structural change in the memory system itself occurred at around the third year. Early memories were considered to be coded in terms of physical action or pure sensation, whereas later memories were coded linguistically. More recently, it has been argued that infantile amnesia is merely a natural consequence of quantitative developments in episodic memory. Very young children do not yet possess a framework for storing memories of events, and in order to develop such a framework they need to focus on what is *similar* about events. A focus on the similarity of experienced events does not provide the young child with good retrieval cues for later recall, resulting in an apparent amnesia for early experiences.

The difficulty of distinguishing between qualitative and quantitative explanations of observed cognitive changes can also be illustrated by considering the development of any cognitive skill that is affected by the development of the knowledge base. As we saw earlier in this chapter, logical abilities (such as reasoning by analogy) have frequently been assumed to show qualitative changes with development, but these changes turned out to depend on the acquisition of certain kinds of knowledge—and thus to be quantitative in nature. We also saw that an important question when considering the development of such cognitive skills is whether a cognitive skill measured at time 1 is the *same* cognitive skill as an apparently identical ability measured at time 2. For example, categorisation abilities in infancy are perceptual skills, based on the processing of correlations between object features. Categorisation skills in childhood also involve perceptual analyses of objects, but in addition are based on naive theories about category membership and knowledge about characteristic or defining category features. The key point is whether we should interpret this to mean that categorisation in infancy is *qualitatively different* from categorisation in childhood. Our interpretation of the data will then determine whether we explain the development of an ability like categorisation in qualitative or quantitative terms.

Finally, developmental theories can themselves be seen as either qualitative or quantitative in nature. We have not discussed any developmental theories in great depth in this book. However, Piaget's stage theory of logical development, Halford's capacity limitation theory of logical development, and Karmiloff-Smith's representational redescription theory of children's cognition have all been considered to some degree, and can be used for illustrative purposes.

All three of these theories can be seen at one level as qualitative theories about developmental change. In Piaget's theory, children's cognition undergoes three major revolutions during development, resulting in three distinct stages, during each of which children are hypothesised to think and reason in a different way. In Halford's theory, children become capable of increasingly complex kinds of analogical mapping with development, each of which depends on an increase in processing capacity and each of which is hypothesised to be too complex for the processing capacity that is available at an earlier stage. In Karmiloff-Smith's theory, children represent information in three distinct formats, formats that are hypothesised to become increasingly explicit with development. At the lowest level of representation knowledge is procedural and inaccessible to consciousness, whereas at the highest level children have insight into their own conceptual processes.

From a different perspective, the same three theories can be described as quantitative theories about developmental change. In Piaget's theory, the mechanisms of change are the processes of accommodation and assimilation—processes that operate at the level of small and incremental change. Accommodation is the process of adapting one's cognitive schemes for viewing the world, and assimilation is the complementary process of interpreting experience in terms of current cognitive schemes. Even at the global level, Piaget's theory has a quantitative aspect. Piaget recognised that the acquisition of the new way of thinking characteristic of each of his major cognitive stages would not be applied to all the different domains of thought at the same time. If changes in the knowledge base determine the adoption of a particular mode of thinking in a given domain at a given time, then Piaget's theory has a quantitative aspect. For example we noted in Chapter 8 that Piaget suggested that the concrete operation of class inclusion might be related to linguistic development, while the concrete operation of seriation might be related to perceptual development. The acquisition of sufficient knowledge in these two separate domains might thus be the factor that determines the acquisition of these two concrete operations.

Karmiloff-Smith makes a similar knowledge-based point about her representational redescription theory. Although her three levels of representation are hypothesised to be domain-general, local change depends on the level of explicitness of the representations supporting particular domain-specific knowledge at any given time. Thus although the representations underpinning all domains become increasingly explicit with development, the domain-general sequence of representational change will occur in different domains at different times. Halford also gives the developing knowledge base a role to play in his theory. He argues that the relational complexity of different analogical mappings may be affected by changes in knowledge. Although the developments in processing capacity that enable more complex relational mappings are age-related, children's ability to "chunk" various relations together can reduce the relational complexity of a particular mapping. This ability makes it possible for some children to carry out the mapping at an earlier developmental time point using *available* processing capacity. The possibility of chunking means that Halford's theory, too, is not simply a qualitative one. Thus most developmental theories can be seen from both a qualitative and a quantitative change perspective.

The causal bias

A large part of this book has been concerned with the contribution made by the causal bias to children's cognition. The bias to learn about causal relations and to acquire causal explanations can be shown to make a contribution to *both* of the major questions in developmental psychology. The causal bias helps us to *organise* the information about "what develops" in all the different areas of cognition considered in this book, thereby providing a partial theoretical framework. It also helps us to decide where to *look* for changes in children's cognition over time, thereby helping us to decide what kind of behaviour it might be important to observe next.

In terms of the "what" of children's cognition, the evidence discussed in preceding chapters has shown that the causal bias helps children to develop appropriate frameworks for organising their memories, and to pick out relations such as "occlude", "contain", "support", and "collide" which are the key to understanding the physical world. It helps them to focus on the relations such as "self-caused" vs. "other-caused" motion which are the key to understanding the biological world, and to reason logically according to causal principles. The causal bias is also important for developing an understanding of agency and adopting an intentional stance (see Chapter 2). Although the design of innovative experimental research paradigms, particularly in infancy research, has been partly responsible for revealing the cognitive richness afforded by the causal bias, children's relentless causal questioning in itself gives us an indication of the importance of causal information to the developing child.

In terms of the "why" of children's cognition, the causal bias enables us to offer a nicely comprehensive explanation of why development pursues its observed course. The reason why children absorb so much information so quickly about their everyday worlds is simply that they want to understand how the world works. In order to do so, the knowledge that they acquire must be causally coherent. As noted in Chapter 4, working out how an event was caused can enable us to understand the event itself, and as any event in the world must also be understood in relation to other

events, the causal bias will result in knowledge structures that are organised in terms of deep causal principles that provide coherence. We also noted in Chapter 4 that causal reasoning can enable children to predict and even to control causal events within the world. As cognition can be defined as the set of processes that enable us to gain information about our environment with the ultimate goal of manipulating and controlling it to serve our needs and desires (see Chapter 1), a "causal bias" explanation appears to provide a rather satisfactory explanatory account

of the "why" of children's cognition.

At a different theoretical level, however, the "explanation" provided by the "causal bias" account is rather unsatisfactory. The developmental question of where this causal focus comes from is a difficult one to answer. In this book, the bias to learn about causal relations and to acquire causal explanations has been described as "innate". This description is dissatisfying in developmental terms, because we are still left wondering why the human infant should be born with such a bias, and how this bias can be created and transmitted in the DNA. Studies of comparative cognition suggest that the causal bias may not be restricted to humans. Some investigators credit rats with causal knowledge (e.g. Dickinson & Shanks, 1995), although not necessarily with an ability to reason according to recognised causal principles. In terms of natural selection, we could argue that early humans who were better at causal reasoning had a survival advantage that led to the bias to seek causal information becoming universal in human cognition. Yet even this "explanation" is simply a redescription of the available data.

Nevertheless, the importance of the causal bias to children's cognition cannot be doubted. Perhaps the best way to conclude is with a quote adapted from White (1993, p.1):

...our every waking moment is filled with things happening. We are constantly perceiving, judging, interpreting, and constructing events and behaviour, their nature and causes, their place in the ordered dynamism of the world. It is hard to imagine anything more important to psychology than this.

References

References

Anderson, J.R. (1980). *Cognitive psychology and its implications*. San Francisco: W.H. Freeman.

Anderson, N.H. (1983). Intuitive physics: Understanding and learning of physical relations. In J. Tighe & B.E. Shepp (Eds.), *Perception, cognition and development* (pp.231–265). Hillsdale, NJ: Lawrence Erlbaum Associates Inc.

Anderson, N.H. (1991). *Contributions to information integration theory: Vol. III. Developmental*. Hillsdale, NJ: Lawrence Erlbaum Associates Inc.

Anderson, N.H., & Wilkening, F. (1991). Adaptive thinking in intuitive physics. In N.H. Anderson (Ed.), *Contributions to information integration theory: Vol. III. Developmental* (pp.1–42). Hillsdale, NJ: Lawrence Erlbaum Associates Inc.

Anisfeld, M. (1991). Neonatal imitation. *Developmental Review, 11*, 60–97.

Atkinson, J., & Braddick, O. (1989). Development of basic visual functions. In A.M. Slater & G. Bremner (Eds.), *Infant development*, (pp.7–41). Hove, UK: Lawrence Erlbaum Associates Ltd.

Atran, S. (1994). Core foundations vs. scientific theories. In L.A. Hirschfeld & S.A. Gelman (Eds.), *Mapping the mind*, (pp.316–340). New York: Cambridge.

Baddeley, A.D., & Hitch, G. (1974). Working memory. In G.H. Bower (Ed.), *The psychology of learning and motivation, Vol. 8* (pp.47–90). London: Academic Press.

Baillargeon, R. (1986). Representing the existence and location of hidden objects: Object permanence in 6- and 8-month-old infants. *Cognition, 23*, 21–41.

Baillargeon, R. (1987a). Object permanence in 3.5- and 4.5-month-old infants. *Developmental Psychology, 23*, 655–664.

Baillargeon, R. (1987b). Young infants' reasoning about the physical and spatial properties of a hidden object. *Cognitive Development, 2*, 179–200.

Baillargeon, R. (1994). Physical reasoning in young infants: Seeking explanations for impossible events. *British Journal of Developmental Psychology, 12*, 9–33.

Baillargeon, R. (1995). A model of physical reasoning in infancy. In C. Rovee-Collier & L. Lipsitt (Eds.), *Advances in infancy research, Vol. 9* (pp.305–371). Norwood, NJ: Ablex.

Baillargeon, R., & DeVos, J. (1991). Object permanence in young infants: Further evidence. *Child Development, 62*, 1227–1246.

Baillargeon, R., & DeVos, J. (1994). *Qualitative and quantitative reasoning about unveiling events in 12.5- and 13.5-month-old infants*. Unpublished manuscript, University of Illinois.

Baillargeon, R., DeVos, J., & Graber, M. (1989). Location memory in 8-month-old infants in a non-search AB task: Further evidence. *Cognitive Development, 4*, 345–367.

Baillargeon, R., & Gelman, R. (1980). *Young children's understanding of simple causal sequences: Predictions and explanations*. Paper presented to the meeting of the American Psychological Society, Montreal.

Baillargeon, R., & Graber, M. (1987). Where is the rabbit? 5.5-month-old infants' representation of the height of a hidden object. *Cognitive Development, 2*, 375–392.

Baillargeon, R., & Graber, M. (1988). Evidence of location memory in 8-month-old infants in a non-search AB task. *Developmental Psychology, 24*, 502–511.

Baillargeon, R., Graber, M., De Vos, J., & Black, J. (1990). Why do young infants fail to search for hidden objects? *Cognition, 36*, 255–284.

Baillargeon, R., Needham, A., & De Vos, J. (1992). The development of young infants' intuitions about support. *Early Development & Parenting, 1*, 69–78.

Baillargeon, R., Spelke, E.S., & Wasserman, S. (1985). Object permanence in 5-month-old infants. *Cognition, 20*, 191–208.

Bartlett, F.C. (1932). *Remembering.* Cambridge: Cambridge University Press.

Bauer, P.J., Dow, G.A., & Hertsgaard, L.A. (1995). Effects of prototypicality on categorisation in 1- to 2-year-olds: Getting down to basic. *Cognitive Development, 10*, 43–68.

Bauer, P.J., & Mandler, J.M. (1989a). Taxonomies and triads: Conceptual organisation in one- to two-year-olds. *Cognitive Psychology, 21*, 156–184.

Bauer, P.J., & Mandler, J.M. (1989b). One thing follows another: Effects of temporal structure on 1- to 2-year-olds' recall of events. *Developmental Psychology, 25*, 197–206.

Bauer, P.J., Schwade, J.A., Wewerka, S.S., & Delaney, K. (submitted). *Planning ahead: Goal-directed problem solving by 2-year-olds.*

Bauer, P.J., & Shore, C.M. (1987). Making a memorable event: Effects of familiarity and organisation on young children's recall of action sequences. *Cognitive Development, 2*, 327–338;

Beilin, H., & Pufall, P.B. (1992). *Piaget's theory: Prospects and possibilities.* Hillsdale, NJ: Lawrence Erlbaum Associates Inc.

Bertenthal, B.I., Proffitt, D.R., Spetner, N.B., & Thomas, M.A. (1985). The development of infant sensitivity to biomechanical motions. *Child Development, 56*, 531–543.

Bjorklund, D.F., & Bjorklund, B.R. (1985). Organisation vs. item effects of an elaborated knowledge base on children's memory. *Developmental Psychology, 21*, 1120–1131.

Bjorklund, D.F., & Bjorklund, B.R. (1992). *Looking at children: An introduction to child development.* Pacific Grove, CA: Brooks/Cole Publishing Co.

Blue, N. (1995, September). *What causes causality? The development of causal reasoning in young children.* Poster presented at the British Psychology Society Developmental Section Conference, Glasgow.

Bornstein, M.H., & Sigman, M.D. (1986). Continuity in mental development from infancy. *Child Development, 57*, 251–274.

Bremner, J.G. (1988). *Infancy.* Oxford: Basil Blackwell

Breslow, L. (1981). Re-evaluation of the literature on the development of transitive inferences. *Psychological Bulletin, 89*, 325–351.

Brown, A.L. (1990). Domain-specific principles affect learning and transfer in children. *Cognitive Science, 14*, 107–133.

Brown, A.L., Bransford, J.D., Ferrara, R.A., & Campione, J.C. (1983). Learning, remembering and understanding. In J.H. Flavell & E.M. Markman (Eds.), *Handbook of child psychology, Vol. 3.* New York: Wiley.

Brown, A. L., & DeLoache, J.S. (1978). Skills, plans and self-regulation. In R.S. Siegler (Ed.), *Children's thinking: what develops?* Hillsdale, NJ: Lawrence Erlbaum Associates Inc.

Brown, A. L., & Kane, M. J. (1988). Preschool children can learn to transfer: Learning to learn and learning by example. *Cognitive Psychology, 20,* 493–523.

Brown, A. L., Kane, M. J., & Echols, C.H. (1986). Young children's mental models determine analogical transfer across problems with a common goal structure. *Cognitive Development, 1,* 103–121.

Brown, A. L., Kane, M. J., & Long, C. (1989). Analogical transfer in young children: Analogies as tools for communication and exposition. *Applied Cognitive Psychology, 3,* 275–293.

Brown, A.L., & Scott, M.S. (1971). Recognition memory for pictures in preschool children. *Journal of Experimental Child Psychology, 11,* 401–412.

Bryant, P.E. (1982). *Piaget: Issues and experiments.* Leicester, UK: The British Psychological Society.

Bryant, P.E., & Trabasso, T. (1971). Transitive inferences and memory in young children. *Nature, 232,* 456–458.

Bullock Drummey, A., & Newcombe, N. (1995). Remembering vs. knowing the past: Children's implicit and explicit memory for pictures. *Journal of Experimental Child Psychology, 59,* 549–565.

Bullock, M., & Gelman, R. (1979). Preschool children's assumptions about cause and effect: Temporal ordering. *Child Development, 50,* 89–96.

Bullock, M., Gelman, R., & Baillargeon, R. (1982). The development of causal reasoning. In W.J. Friedman (Ed.), *The developmental psychology of time* (pp.209–254). New York: Academic Press.

Bushnell, I.W.R., McCutcheon, E., Sinclair, J., & Tweedie, M.E. (1984). Infants' delayed recognition memory for colour and form. *British Journal of Developmental Psychology, 2,* 11–17.

Butterworth, G. (1977). Object disappearance and error in Piaget's stage 4 task. *Journal of Experimental Child Psychology, 23,* 391–401.

Butterworth, G., & Harris, M. (1994). *Principles of developmental psychology.* Hove, UK: Lawrence Erlbaum Associates Ltd.

Callanan, M., & Oakes, L.M. (1992). Preschoolers' questions and parents' explanations: Causal thinking in everyday activity. *Cognitive Development, 7,* 213–233.

Carey, S. (1985). *Conceptual change in childhood.* Cambridge, MA: MIT Press.

Carey, S., & Gelman, R. (1991). *The epigenesis of mind: Essays on biology and cognition.* Hillsdale, NJ: Lawrence Erlbaum Associates Inc.

Carey, S., & Spelke, E. (1994). Domain-specific knowledge and conceptual change. In L.A. Hirschfeld & S.A. Gelman (Eds.), *Mapping the mind* (pp.169–200). New York: Cambridge.

Carroll, M., Byrne, B., & Kirsner, K. (1985). Autobiographical memory and perceptual learning: A developmental study using picture recognition, naming latency and perceptual identification. *Memory & Cognition, 13,* 273–279.

Case, R. (1985). *Intellectual development: Birth to adulthood.* New York: Academic Press.

Case, R. (1992). Neo-Piagetian theories of child development. In R.J. Sternberg & C.J. Berg (Eds.), *Intellectual development* (pp.161–196). Cambridge, UK: Cambridge University Press.

Cassell, W.S., Roebers, C.E.M., & Bjorklund, D.F. (1996). Developmental patterns of eyewitness responses to repeated and increasingly suggestive questions. *Journal of Experimental Child Psychology, 61,* 116–133.

Ceci, S.J., & Bruck, M. (1993). The suggestibility of the child witness: A historical review and synthesis. *Psychological Bulletin, 113*, 403–439.

Ceci, S.J., & Liker, J. (1986). A day at the races: A study of IQ, expertise and cognitive complexity. *Journal of Experimental Psychology: General, 115*, 255–266.

Chapman, M. (1988). *Constructive evolution: Origins and development of Piaget's thought*. Cambridge: Cambridge University Press.

Chen, C., & Stevenson, H.W. (1988). Cross-linguistic differences in digit span of preschool children. *Journal of Experimental Child Psychology, 46*, 150–158.

Chen, Z., Campbell, T., & Polley, R. (1995, March). *From beyond to within their grasp: The rudiments of analogical problem solving in 10- and 13-month-old infants*. Poster presented at the Biennial Meeting of the Society for Research in Child Development, Indianapolis.

Chen, Z., Sanchez, R.P, & Campbell, T. (1997). From beyond to within their grasp: Analogical problem solving in 10- and 13-month-olds. *Developmental Psychology, 33*, 790–801.

Cheng, P.W., & Holyoak, K.J. (1985). Pragmatic reasoning schemas. *Cognitive Psychology, 17*, 391–416.

Chi, M.T.H. (1978). Knowledge structure and memory development. In R.S. Siegler (Ed.), *Children's thinking: What develops?* (pp.73–96). Hillsdale, NJ: Lawrence Erlbaum Associates Inc.

Chi, M.T.H., Hutchinson, J., & Robin, A. (1989). How inferences about novel domain-related concepts can be constrained by structured knowledge. *Merrill-Palmer Quarterly, 35*, 27–62.

Clarke, A.M., & Clarke, A.D.B. (1976). *Early experience: Myth and evidence*. London: Open Books.

Clarkson, M.G., Clifton, R.K., & Morrongiello, B.A. (1985). The effects of sound duration on newborn's head orientation. *Journal of Experimental Child Psychology, 39*, 20–36.

Clubb, P.A., Nida, R.E., Merritt, K., & Ornstein, P.A. (1993). Visiting the doctor: Children's knowledge and memory. *Cognitive Development, 8*, 361–372.

Cohen, L.B. (1988). An information processing approach to infant development. In L. Weiskrantz (Ed.), *Thought without language* (pp.211–228). Oxford: Oxford University Press.

Cohen, L.B., & Caputo, N.F. (1978). *Instructing infants to respond to perceptual categories*. Paper presented at the Midwestern Psychological Association Convention, Chicago, IL.

Conrad, R. (1971). The chronology of the development of covert speech in children. *Developmental Psychology, 5*, 398–405.

Cooper, R.G. (1984). Early number development: Discovering number space with addition and subtraction. In C. Sophian (Ed.), *The origins of cognitive skills* (pp.157–192). Hillsdale, NJ: Lawrence Erlbaum Associates Inc.

Cornell, E.H. (1979). Infants' recognition memory, forgetting and savings. *Journal of Experimental Child Psychology, 28*, 359–374.

Cutting, A.L. (1996). *Young children's understanding of representation: A problem solving approach to the appearance–reality distinction*. Unpublished PhD dissertation, University of Cambridge, UK.

Cutting, A.L., Charlesworth, G.M., & Goswami, U.C. (1991, September). *Three-year-olds can distinguish appearance from reality: Evidence from a problem-solving task*. Poster presented at the British Psychology Society Developmental Section meeting, Cambridge.

Cutting, J.E., Proffitt, D.R., & Kozlowski, L.T. (1978). A biomechanical invariant for gait perception. *Journal of Experimental Psychology: Human Perception & Performance, 4,* 357–372.

Das Gupta, P., & Bryant, P.E. (1989). Young children's causal inferences. *Child Development, 60,* 1138–1146.

Dean, A.L., Chabaud, S., & Bridges, E. (1981). Classes, collections and distinctive features: Alternative strategies for solving inclusion problems. *Cognitive Psychology, 13,* 84–112.

DeCaspar, A.J., & Fifer, W.P. (1980). Of human bonding: Newborns prefer their mother's voices. *Science, 208,* 1174–1176.

DeCaspar, A.J., & Spence, M.J. (1986). Prenatal maternal speech influences newborns' perception of speech sounds. *Infant Behaviour & Development, 9,* 133–150.

DeLoache, J.S. (1987). Rapid change in the symbolic functioning of very young children. *Science, 238,* 1556–1557.

DeLoache, J.S. (1989). Young children's understanding of the correspondence between a scale model and a larger space. *Cognitive Development, 4,* 121–139.

DeLoache, J.S. (1991). Symbolic functioning in very young children: Understanding of pictures and models. *Child Development, 62,* 736–752.

DeLoache, J.S., Cassidy, D.J., & Brown, A.L. (1985). Precursors of mnemonic strategies in very young children's memory. *Child Development, 56,* 125–137.

DeLoache, J.S., Miller, K., & Rosengren, K. (1996). *Shrinking a room reveals obstacles to early symbolic reasoning.* Unpublished manuscript, University of Illinois.

DeLoache, J.S. (in press). Early symbol understanding and use. To appear in D. Medin (Ed.) *The psychology of learning and motivation,* Vol. 32. New York: Academic Press.

Dempster, F.N. (1991). Inhibitory processes: A neglected dimension of intelligence. *Intelligence, 15,* 157–173.

DeVries, J.I.P., Visser, G.H.A., & Prechtl, H.F.R. (1984). Fetal mobility in the first half of pregnancy. In H.F.R. Prechtl (Ed.), *Continuity of Neural Functions from Prenatal to Postnatal Life,* pp. 46–64. Oxford: Blackwell Scientific Publications.

Diamond, A. (1985). The development of the ability to use recall to guide action, as indicated by infants' performance on A-not-B. *Child Development, 56,* 868–883.

Diamond, A. (1988). Differences between adult and infant cognition: Is the crucial variable presence or absence of language? In L. Weiskrantz (Ed.), *Thought without language* (pp.337–370). Oxford: Clarendon Press.

Diamond, A. (1991). Neuro-psychological insights into the meaning of object concept development. In S. Carey & R. Gelman (Eds.), *The epigenesis of mind: Essays on biology & cognition* (pp.67–110). Hillsdale, NJ: Lawrence Erlbaum Associates Inc.

Dias, M.G., & Harris, P.L. (1988). The effect of make-believe play on deductive reasoning. *British Journal of Developmental Psychology, 6,* 207–221.

Dias, M.G., & Harris, P.L. (1990). The influence of the imagination on reasoning by young children. *British Journal of Developmental Psychology, 8,* 305–318.

Dickinson, A., & Shanks, D. (1995). Instrumental action and causal representation. In D. Sperber, D. Premack & A.J. Premack (Eds.), *Causal cognition: A multidisciplinary debate* (pp.1–25). Oxford: Oxford University Press.

DiLalla, L.F., Plomin, R., Fagan, J.F., Thompson, L.A., Phillips, K., Haith, M.M., Cyphers, L.H., & Fulker, D.W. (1990). Infant predictors of preschool and adult IQ: A study of infant twins and their parents. *Developmental Psychology, 25,* 759–769.

Ding, S. (1995). *Developing structural representations: Their role in analogical reasoning.* Unpublished PhD dissertation, University of Nottingham.

Dodd, B. (1979). Lipreading in infancy: Attention to speech in and out of synchrony. *Cognitive Psychology, 11,* 478–484.

Donaldson, M. (1978). *Children's minds.* Glasgow: William Collins.

Dufresne, A., & Kobasigawa, A. (1989). Children's spontaneous allocation of study time: Differential and sufficient aspects. *Journal of Experimental Child Psychology, 47,* 274–296.

Eimas, P.D., & Quinn, P.C. (1994). Studies on the formation of perceptually-based basic-level categories in young infants. *Child Development, 65,* 903–917.

Ellis, H.D., Ellis, D.M., & Hosie, J.A. (1993). Priming effects in children's face recognition. *British Journal of Psychology, 84,* 101–110.

Ellis, N.C., & Hennelly, R.A. (1980). A bilingual word-length effect: Implications for intelligence testing and the relative ease of mental calculation in Welsh and English. *British Journal of Psychology, 71,* 43–51.

Fagan, J.F. III (1984). The relationship of novelty preferences during infancy to later intelligence and later recognition smemory. *Intelligence, 8,* 339–346.

Fagan, J.F. III (1992). Intelligence: A theoretical viewpoint. *Current Directions in Psychological Science, 1,* 82–86.

Farrar, M.J., & Goodman, G.S. (1990). Developmental differences in the relation between script and episodic memory: Do they exist? In R. Fivush & J. Hudson (Eds.), *Knowing and remembering in young children* (pp.30–64). New York: Cambridge University Press.

Fantz, R.L. (1961). The origin of form perception. *Scientific American, 204,* 66–72.

Field, D. (1987). A review of preschool conservation training: An analysis of analyses. *Developmental Review, 7,* 210–251.

Fischer, K.W. (1980). A theory of cognitive development: The control and construction of hierarchies of skills. *Psychological Review, 87,* 477–531.

Fivush, R., & Hammond, N.R. (1990). Autobiographical memory across the preschool years: Toward reconceptualising childhood amnesia. In R. Fivush & J. Hudson (Eds.), *Knowing and remembering in young children* (pp.223–248). New York: Cambridge University Press.

Flavell, J.H., Beach, D.R., & Chinsky, J.H. (1966). Spontaneous verbal rehearsal in a memory task as a function of age. *Child Development, 37,* 283–299.

Flavell, J.H., Flavell, E.R., & Green, F.I. (1983). Development of appearance-reality distinction. *Cognitive Psychology, 15,* 95–120.

Flavell, J.H., & Wellman, H.M. (1977). Metamemory. In R. Kail & J. Hagen (Eds.), *Perspectives on the development of memory and cognition.* Hillsdale, NJ: Lawrence Erlbaum Associates Inc.

Forrest-Pressley, D.L., MacKinnon, G.E., & Waller, T.G. (1985). *Cognition, metacognition and human performance* (Vol. 1). New York: Academic Press.

Freeman, K.E. (1996). *Analogical reasoning in 2-year-olds: A comparison of formal and problem-solving paradigms.* Unpublished PhD thesis, University of Minnesota.

Freud, S. (1938). The psychopathology of everyday life. In A.A. Brill (Ed.), *The writings of Sigmund Freud* (pp.317–385). New York: Modern Library.

Frye, D., Zelazo, P.D., & Palfai, T. (1995). Theory of mind and rule-based reasoning. *Cognitive Development, 10,* 483–527.

Fuson, K.C., Lyons, B.G., Pergament, G.G., Hall, J.W., & Youngshim, K. (1988). Effects of collection terms on class inclusion and on number tasks. *Cognitive Psychology, 20*, 96–120.

Gallagher, J.M., & Reid, D.K. (1981). *The learning theory of Piaget and Inhelder*. Monterey, CA: Brooks/Cole.

Garcia, J., & Koelling, R.A. (1966). The relation of cue to consequence in avoidance learning. *Psychonomic Science, 4*, 123–124.

Gelman, R. (1990). First principles organise attention to and learning about relevant data: Number and the animate-inanimate distinction as examples. *Cognitive Science, 14*, 79–106.

Gelman, R., Bullock, M., & Meck, E. (1980). Preschooler's understanding of simple object transformations. *Child Development, 51*, 691–699.

Gelman, S.A., & Coley, J.D. (1990). The importance of knowing a dodo is a bird: Categories and inferences in 2-year-old children. *Developmental Psychology, 26*, 796–804.

Gelman, S.A., Coley, J.D., & Gottfried, G.M. (1994). Essentialist beliefs in children: The acquisition of concepts and theories. In L.A. Hirschfeld & S.A. Gelman (Eds.), *Mapping the mind: Domain specificity in cognition and culture* (pp.341–365). Cambridge: Cambridge University Press.

Gelman, S.A., & Gottfried, G.M. (1993). *Causal explanations of animate and inanimate motion*. Unpublished manuscript.

Gelman, S.A., & Kremer, K.E. (1991). Understanding natural cause: Children's explanations of how objects and their properties originate. *Child Development, 62*, 396–414.

Gelman, S.A., & Markman, E.M. (1986). Categories and induction in young children. *Cognition, 23*, 183–209.

Gelman, S.A., & Markman, E.M. (1987). Young children's inductions from natural kinds: The role of categories and appearances. *Child Development, 58*, 1532–1541.

Gelman, S.A., & O'Reilly, A.W. (1988). Children's inductive inferences within superordinate categories: The role of language and category structure. *Child Development, 59*, 876–887.

Gelman, S.A., & Wellman, H.M. (1991). Insides and essences: Early understandings of the non-obvious. *Cognition, 38*, 213–244.

Gentner, D. (1989). The mechanisms of analogical learning. In S. Vosniadou & A. Ortony (Eds.), *Similarity and analogical reasoning* (pp.199–241). Cambridge: Cambridge University Press.

Gergely, G., Nadasdy, Z., Csibra, G., & Biro, S. (1995). Taking the intentional stance at 12 months of age. *Cognition, 56*, 165–193.

Gick, M.L., & Holyoak, K.J. (1980). Analogical problem solving. *Cognitive Psychology, 12*, 306–355.

Gillan, D.J., Premack, D., & Woodruff, G. (1981). Reasoning in the Chimpanzee I: Analogical reasoning. *Journal of Experimental Psychology: Animal Behaviour Processes, 7*, 1–17.

Gilmore, R.O., & Johnson, M.H. (1995). Working memory in infancy: Six-month-olds' performance on two versions of the oculomotor delayed response task. *Journal of Experimental Child Psychology, 59*, 397–418.

Goodman, G.S., & Aman, C. (1990). Children's use of anatomically detailed dolls to recount an event. *Child Development, 61*, 1859–1871.

Goodman, G.S., Rudy, L., Bottoms, B.L., & Aman, C. (1990). Children's concerns and memory: Issues of ecological validity in the study of children's eyewitness testimony. In R. Fivush & J. Hudson (Eds.), *Knowing and remembering in young children* (pp.331–346). New York: Cambridge University Press.

Goswami, U. (1991). Analogical reasoning: What develops? A review of research and theory. *Child Development, 62*, 1–22.

Goswami, U. (1992) *Analogical reasoning in children.* [Part of series Developmental essays in psychology"]. London: Lawrence Erlbaum Associates Ltd.

Goswami, U. (1996). Analogical reasoning and cognitive development. *Advances in Child Development and Behaviour, 26*, 91–138. San Diego, CA: Academic Press.

Goswami, U. & Brown, A. (1989) Melting chocolate and melting snowmen: Analogical reasoning and causal relations. *Cognition, 35*, 69–95.

Goswami, U. & Brown, A.L. (1990). Higher-order structure and relational reasoning: Contrasting analogical and thematic relations. *Cognition, 36*, 207–226.

Goswami, U., Pauen, S., & Wilkening, F. (1996). *The effects of a "family' analogy in class inclusion tasks.* Manuscript in preparation, Department of Experimental Psychology, University of Cambridge.

Haake, R.J., & Somerville, S.C. (1985). The development of logical search skills in infancy. *Developmental Psychology, 21*, 176–186.

Haith, M.M., Hazan, C., & Goodman, G.S. (1988). Expectation and anticipation of dynamic visual events by 3.5-month-old babies. *Child Development, 59*, 467–479.

Halford, G.S. (1984). Can young children integrate premises in transitivity and serial order tasks? *Cognitive Psychology, 16*, 65–93.

Halford, G.S. (1987). A structure-mapping approach to cognitive development. *International Journal of Psychology, 22*, 609–642.

Halford, G.S. (1993). *Children's understanding: The development of mental models.* Hillsdale, NJ: Lawrence Erlbaum Associates Inc.

Harris, P.L., & Nunez, M. (1996). Understanding of permission rules by preschool children. *Child Development, 67*, 1572–1591.

Hayes, L.A., & Watson, J.S. (1981). Neonatal imitation: Fact or artifact? *Developmental Psychology, 17*, 655–660.

Henry, L.A., & Millar, S. (1993). Why does memory span improve with age? A review of the evidence for two current hypotheses. *European Journal of Cognitive Psychology, 5*, 241–287.

Hepper, P.G. (1988). Foetal "soap' addiction. *The Lancet* (11 June), 1347–1348.

Hepper, P.G. (1992). Fetal psychology: An embryonic science. In J.G. Nijhuis (Ed.), *Fetal behaviour: Developmental and perinatal aspects* (pp.129–156). Oxford: Oxford University Press.

Hirschfeld, L.A., & Gelman, S.A. (1994). Toward a topography of mind: An introduction to domain specificity. In L.A. Hirschfeld & S.A. Gelman (Eds.), *Mapping the mind: Domain specificity in cognition and culture* (pp.3–35). Cambridge: Cambridge University Press.

Hitch, G.J., Halliday, S., Dodd, A., & Littler, J.E. (1989). Development of rehearsal in short–term memory: Differences between pictorial and spoken stimuli. *British Journal of Developmental Psychology, 7*, 347–362.

Hitch, G.J., Halliday, S., Schaafstal, A.M., & Schraagen, J.M. (1988). Visual working memory in young children. *Memory & Cognition, 16*, 120–132.

Hodges, R.M., & French, L.A. (1988). The effect of class and collection labels on cardinality, class-inclusion and number conservation tasks. *Child Development, 59*, 1387–1396.

Holyoak, K.J., Junn, E.N., & Billman, D.O. (1984). Development of analogical problem-solving skill. *Child Development, 55*, 2042–2055.

Holyoak, K.J., & Thagard, P. (1995). *Mental leaps*. Cambridge, MA: MIT Press.

Hood, B.M. (1995). Gravity rules for 2- to 4-year-olds? *Cognitive Development, 10,* 577–598.

Hood, L., & Bloom, L. (1979). What, when, and how about why: A longitudinal study of the early expressions of causality. *Monographs of the Society for Research in Child Development, 44* (6, serial no. 181).

Howe, M.L., & Courage, M.L. (1993). On resolving the enigma of infantile autism. *Psychological Bulletin, 113,* 305–326.

Hudson, J.A. (1990). The emergence of autobiographical memory in mother–child conversation. In R. Fivush & J. Hudson (Eds.), *Knowing and remembering in young children*. New York: Cambridge University Press.

Hulme, C., Thomson, N., Muir, C., & Lawrence, A. (1984). Speech rate and the development of short-term memory span. *Journal of Experimental Child Psychology, 38,* 241–253.

Hulme, C., & Tordoff, V. (1989). Working memory development: The effects of speech rate, word length, and acoustic similarity on serial recall. *Journal of Experimental Child Psychology, 47,* 72–87.

Inagaki, K., & Hatano, G. (1987). Young children's spontaneous personification as analogy. *Child Development, 58,* 1013–1020.

Inagaki, K., & Hatano, G. (1993). Young children's understanding of the mind-body distinction. *Child Development, 64,* 1534–1549.

Inagaki, K., & Sugiyama, K. (1988). Attributing human characteristics: Developmental changes in over- and under-attribution. *Cognitive Development, 3,* 55–70.

Inhelder, B., de Caprona, D., & Cornu-Wells, A. (1987). *Piaget today*. Hillsdale, NJ: Lawrence Erlbaum Associates Inc.

Inhelder, B., & Piaget, J. (1958). *The growth of logical thinking from childhood to adolescence*. New York: Basic Books.

Johansson, G. (1973). Visual perception of biological motion and a model for its analysis. *Perception & Psychophysics, 14,* 201–211.

Johnson, M. (1997). *Developmental cognitive neuroscience*. Oxford: Blackwell.

Johnson-Laird, P.N., Legrenzi, P., & Sonino-Legrenzi, M. (1972). Reasoning and a sense of reality. *British Journal of Psychology, 63,* 395–400.

Johnson-Laird, P.N. & Wason, P.C. (1977). A theoretical analysis of insight into a reasoning task. In P.N. Johnson-Laird & P.C. Wason (Eds.), *Thinking: Readings in cognitive science*. Cambridge: Cambridge University Press.

Jones, S.S., & Smith, L.B. (1993). The place of perception in children's concepts. *Cognitive Development, 8,* 113–139.

Justice, E.M. (1985). Categorisation as a preferred memory strategy: Developmental changes during elementary school. *Developmental Psychology, 6,* 1105–1110.

Kaiser, M.K., McCloskey, M., & Profitt, D.R. (1986). Development of intuitive theories of motion: Curvilinear motion in the absence of external forces. *Developmental Psychology, 22,* 67–71.

Kaiser, M.K., Profitt, D.R. & McCloskey, M. (1985). The development of beliefs about falling objects. *Perception & Psychophysics, 38,* 533–539.

Karmiloff-Smith, A. (1992). *Beyond modularity: A developmental perspective on cognitive science*. Cambridge, MA: MIT Press/Bradford Books.

Karmiloff-Smith, A. (1994). *Precis of "Beyond modularity: A developmental perspective on cognitive science"*. *Behavioural and Brain Sciences, 17,* 693–745.

Keane, M.K. (1988). *Analogical problem solving*. Chichester, UK: Ellis Horwood.

Keil, F.C. (1987). Conceptual development and category structure. In U. Neisser, (Ed.) *Concepts and conceptual development: Ecological and intellectual factors in categorisation* (pp.175–200). Cambridge: Cambridge University Press.

Keil, F.C. (1989). *Concepts, kinds and cognitive development*. Cambridge, MA: MIT Press.

Keil, F.C. (1991). The emergence of theoretical beliefs as constraints on concepts. In S. Carey & R. Gelman (Eds.), *The epigenesis of mind: Essays on biology & cognition* (pp.237–256). Hillsdale, NJ: Lawrence Erlbaum Associates Inc.

Keil, F.C. (1994). The birth and nurturance of concepts of domains: The origins of concepts of living things. In L.A. Hirschfeld & S.A. Gelman (Eds.), *Mapping the mind* (pp.234–254). New York: Cambridge.

Keil, F.C., & Batterman, N. (1984). A characteristic-to-defining shift in the development of word meaning. *Journal of Verbal Learning & Verbal Behaviour, 23,* 221–236.

Klahr, D., Fay, A.L., & Dunbar, K. (1993). Heuristics for scientific experimentation: A developmental study. *Cognitive Psychology, 25,* 111–146.

Krist, H., Fieberg, E.L., & Wilkening, F. (1993). Intuitive physics in action and judgement: The development of knowledge about projectile motion. *Journal of Experimental Psychology: Learning, Memory & Cognition, 19,* 952–966.

Kuhn, D. (1989). Children and adults as intuitive scientists. *Psychological Review, 96,* 674–689.

Kuhn, D., Amsel, E., & O'Loughlin, M. (1988). *The development of scientific thinking skills*. San Diego: Academic Press.

Kuhn, D., Garcia-Mila, M., Zohar, A., & Andersen, C. (1995). Strategies of knowledge acquisition. *Monographs of the Society for Research in Child Development, 60,* No. 4.

Kunzinger, E.L., & Witryol, S.L. (1984). The effects of differential incentives on second-grade rehearsal and free recall. *Journal of Genetic Psychology, 144,* 19–30.

Kurtz, B.E., & Weinert, F.E. (1989). Metamemory, memory performance and causal attributions in gifted and average children. *Journal of Experimental Child Psychology, 48,* 45–61.

Lakoff, G. (1986). *Women, Fire and Dangerous Things: What categories tell us about the nature of thought*. Chicago: University of Chicago Press.

Lakoff, G. (1987). Cognitive models and prototype theory. In U. Neisser (Ed.). *Concepts and conceptual development: Ecological and intellectual factors in categorisation* (pp.63–100). Cambridge: Cambridge University Press.

Lamsfuss, S. (1995, March). *Regularity of movement and the animate-inanimate distinction*. Poster presented at the Biennial Meeting of the Society for Research in Child Development, Indianapolis, IN.

Lane, D.M., & Pearson, D.A. (1982). The development of selective attention. *Merrill-Palmer Quarterly, 28,* 317–337.

Leavers, H.J., & Harris, P.L. (1997). Persisting effects of instruction on young children's syllogistic reasoning. Unpublished manuscript, University of Oxford, U.K.

Leslie, A.M. (1994). ToMM, ToBY and Agency: Core architecture and domain specificity. In L.A. Hirschfeld & S.A. Gelman (Eds.), *Mapping the mind* (pp.119–148). New York: Cambridge.

Leslie, A.M., & Keeble, S. (1987). Do six-month-old infants perceive causality? *Cognition, 25,* 265–88.

Light, P., Blaye, A., Gilly, M., & Girotto, V. (1989). Pragmatic schemas and logical reasoning in 6- to 8-year-old children. *Cognitive Development, 4*, 49–64.

Light, P., Buckingham, N., & Robbins, A.H. (1979). The conservation task as an interactional setting. *British Journal of Educational Psychology, 49*, 304–310.

Loftus, E.F. (1979). *Eyewitness testimony.* Cambridge: Harvard University Press.

Lunzer, E.A. (1965). Problems of formal reasoning in test situations. In P.H. Mussen (Ed.), European Research in Child Development. *Monographs of the Society for Research in Child Development, 30*, No. 2, pp. 19–46.

Massey, C.M., & Gelman, R. (1988). Preschooler's ability to decide whether a photographed object can move itself. *Developmental Psychology, 24*, 307–317.

Mandler, J.M. (1988). How to build a baby: On the development of an accessible representational system. *Cognitive Development, 3*, 113–136.

Mandler, J.M. (1990). Recall and its verbal expression. In R. Fivush & J. Hudson (Eds.), *Knowing and Remembering in Young Children*, pp. 317–330. New York: Cambridge University Press.

Mandler, J.M. (1992). How to build a baby II: Conceptual primitives. *Psychological Review, 99*, 587–604.

Mandler, J.M., & Bauer, P.J. (1988). The cradle of categorisation: Is the basic level basic? *Cognitive Development, 3*, 247–264.

Mandler, J.M., Bauer, P.J., & McDonough, L. (1991). Separating the sheep from the goats: Differentiating global categories. *Cognitive Psychology, 23*, 263–298.

Mandler, J.M., & McDonough, L. (1993). Concept formation in infancy. *Cognitive Development, 8*, 291–318.

Mandler, J.M., & McDonough, L. (1995). Long-term recall of event sequences in infancy. *Journal of Experimental Child Psychology, 59*, 457–474.

Markman, E.M., & Seibert, K.J. (1976). Classes and collections: Internal organisation and resulting holistic properties. *Cognitive Psychology, 8*, 561–577.

Marzolf, D.P., & DeLoache, J.S. (1994). Transfer in young children's understanding of Spatial Representations. *Child Development, 65*, 1–15.

McCall, R.B., & Carriger, M.S. (1993). A meta-analysis of infant habituation and recognition memory performance as predictors of later I.Q. *Child Development, 64*, 57–79.

McEvoy, J., & O'Moore, A.M. (1991). Number conservation: A fair assessment of numerical understanding? *Irish Journal of Psychology, 12*, 325–337.

McGarrigle, J., & Donaldson, M. (1975). Conservation accidents. *Cognition, 3*, 341–350.

McKee, R.D., & Squire, L.R. (1993). On the development of declarative memory. *Journal of Experimental Psychology: Learning, Memory & Cognition, 19*, 397–404.

McKenzie, B.E., & Bigelow, E. (1986). Detour behaviour in young human infants. *British Journal of Developmental Psychology, 4*, 139–148.

McKenzie, B.E., Day, R.H., & Ihsen, E. (1984). Localisation of events in space: Young infants are not always egocentric. *British Journal of Developmental Psychology, 2*, 1–10.

McKenzie, B., & Over, R. (1983). Young infants fail to imitate facial and manual gestures. *Infant Behaviour & Development, 6*, 85–95.

Medin, D.L. (1989). Concepts and conceptual structure. *American Psychologist, 44*, 1469–1481.

Medin, D.L., & Schaffer, M.M. (1978). Context theory of classification learning. *Psychological Review, 85*, 207–238.

Mehler, J., & Bertoncini, J. (1979). Infant's perception of speech and other acoustic stimuli. In J. Morton & J. Marshall (Eds.), *Psycholinguistic Series II*. London: Elek Books.

Meltzoff, A.N. (1985). Immediate and deferred imitation in 14– and 24–month-old infants. *Child Development, 56*, 62–72.

Meltzoff, A.N. (1988a). Infant imitation after a 1-week delay: Long-term memory for novel acts and multiple stimuli. *Developmental Psychology, 24*, 470–476.

Meltzoff, A.N. (1988b). Infant imitation and memory: Nine-month-olds in immediate and deferred tests. *Child Development, 59*, 217–225.

Meltzoff, A.N. (1988c). Imitation of televised models by infants. *Child Development, 59*, 1221–1229.

Meltzoff, A.N. (1995). Understanding the intentions of others: Re-enactment of intended acts by 18-month-old children. *Developmental Psychology, 31*, 838–850.

Meltzoff, A.N., & Borton, R.W. (1979). Intermodal matching by human neonates. *Nature, 282*, 403–4.

Meltzoff, A.N. & Moore, M.K. (1977). Imitation of facial and manual gestures by human neonates. *Science, 198*, 75–78.

Meltzoff, A.N., & Moore, M.K. (1983). Newborn infants imitate adult facial gestures. *Child Development, 54*, 702–709.

Mendelson, R., & Shultz, T.R. (1975). Covariation and temporal contiguity as principles of causal inference in young children. *Journal of Experimental Child Psychology, 22*, 408–12.

Mervis, C.B. (1987). Child-basic object categories and early lexical development. In U. Neisser (Ed.). *Concepts and conceptual development: Ecological and intellectual factors in categorisation* (pp.201–233). Cambridge: Cambridge University Press.

Mervis, C.B., & Pani, J.R. (1980). Acquisition of basic object categories. *Cognitive Psychology, 12*, 496–522.

Michotte, A. (1963). *The Perception of causality*. Andover, UK: Methuen.

Miller, P.H. (1989). *Theories of developmental psychology* (2nd Edition). New York: Freeman.

Miller, S.A. (1982). On the generalisability of conservation: A comparison of different kinds of transformation. *British Journal of Psychology, 73*, 221–230.

Milner, B. (1963). Effects of brain lesions on card sorting. *Archives of Neurology, 9*, 90–100.

Moore, D., Benenson, J., Reznick, S.J., Peterson, M., & Kagan, J. (1987). Effect of auditory numerical information infants" looking behaviour: Contradictory evidence. *Developmental Psychology, 23*, 665–670.

Murphy, G.L. (1982). Cue validity and levels of categorisation. *Psychological Bulletin, 91*, 174–177.

Myers, N.A., Clifton, R.K., & Clarkson, M.G. (1987). When they were very young: Almost-threes remember two years ago. *Infant Behaviour & Development, 10*, 128–132.

Naito, M. (1990). Repetition priming in children and adults: Age-related dissociation between implicit and explicit memory. *Journal of Experimental Child Psychology, 50*, 462–484.

Naus, M.J., Ornstein, P.A., & Aviano, S. (1977). Developmental changes in memory: The effects of processing time and rehearsal instructions. *Journal of Experimental Child Psychology, 23*, 237–251.

Neisser, U. (1987). *Concepts and conceptual development: Ecological and intellectual factors in categorisation*. Cambridge: Cambridge University Press.

Nelson, K. (1986). *Event knowledge: Structure and function in development.* Hillsdale, NJ: Lawrence Erlbaum Associates Inc.

Nelson, K. (1988). The ontogeny of memory for real events. In U. Neisser & E. Winograd (Eds.), *Remembering reconsidered: Ecological and traditional approaches to the study of memory* (pp.244–276). New York: Cambridge University Press.

Nelson, K. (1993). The psychological and social origins of autobiographical memory. *Psychological Science, 4,* 7–14.

Newcombe, N. & Fox, N.A. (1994). Infantile amnesia: Through a glass darkly. *Child Development, 65,* 31–40.

O'Connor, N., & Hermelin, B. (1973). Spatial or temporal organisation of short-term memory. *Quarterly Journal of Experimental Psychology, 25,* 335–343.

Ornstein, P.A., Gordon, B.N., & Larus, D.M. (1992). Children's memory for a personally-experienced event: Implications for testimony. *Applied Developmental Psychology, 6,* 49–60.

O'Sullivan, J.T. (1993). Preschoolers' beliefs about effort, incentives and recall. *Journal of Experimental Child Psychology, 55,* 396–414.

Pascual-Leone, J. (1970). A mathematical model for the transition rule in Piaget's developmental stages. *Acta Psychologica, 32,* 301–345.

Pascual-Leone, J. (1987). Organismic processes for neo-Piagetian theories: A dialectical causal account of cognitive development. *International Journal of Psychology, 22,* 531–570.

Pauen, S. (1996a). *Wie klassifizieren Kinder Lebeweesen und Artefakte? Zur Rolle des Aussehens und der Funktion von Komponenten. Zeitschrift für Entwicklungspsychologie und Pädagogische Psychologie, 28,* 280–32.

Pauen, S. (1996b). *The development of ontological categories: Stable dimensions and changing concepts.* Unpublished manuscript, University of Tuebingen, Germany.

Pauen, S. (1996c). Children's reasoning about the interaction of forces. *Child Development, 67,* 2728–2742.

Pauen, S. (in press). Children's reasoning about the interaction of forces. *Child Development.*

Pauen, S., & Wilkening, F. (in press). Children's analogical reasoning about natural phenomena. *Journal of Experimental Child Psychology.* Unpublished manuscript, University of Tuebingen, Germany.

Pears, R., & Bryant, P. (1990). Transitive inferences by young children about spatial position. *British Journal of Psychology, 81,* 497–510.

Pennington, B.F. (1994). The working memory function of the prefrontal cortices: Implications for developmental and individual differences in cognition. In M.M. Haith, J. Benson, R. Roberts, & B.F. Pennington (Eds.), *The development of future oriented processes* (pp.243–289). Chicago: University of Chicago Press.

Perris, E.E., Myers, N.A., & Clifton, R.K. (1990). Long-term memory for a single infancy experience. *Child Development, 61,* 1796–1807.

Piaget, J. (1952). *The Child's conception of number.* London: Routledge & Kegan Paul.

Piaget, J. (1960). The general problems of the psychobiological development of the child. In J.M. Tanner & B. Inhelder (Eds.), *Discussions on child development* (Vol. 4, pp.3–27). London: Tavistock.

Piaget, J., & Inhelder, B.A. (1956). *The child's conception of space.* London: Routledge & Kegan Paul.

Piaget, J., Montangero, J., & Billeter, J. (1977). Les correlats. In J. Piaget (Ed.), *L'Abstraction réfléchissante.* Paris: Presses Universitaires de France.

Quinn, P.C. (1994). The categorisation of above and below spatial relations by young infants. *Child Development, 65,* 58–69.

Reese, E., Haden, C.A., & Fivush, R. (1993). Mother–child conversations about the past: Relationships of style and memory over time. *Cognitive Development, 8*, 403–430.

Rieser, J.J., Doxey, P.A., McCarrell, N.J., & Brooks, P.H. (1982). Wayfinding and toddlers' use of information from an aerial view of a maze. *Developmental Psychology, 18*, 714–720.

Roodenrys, S., Hulme, C., & Brown, G. (1993). The development of short-term memory span: Separable effects of speech rate and long-term memory. *Journal of Experimental Child Psychology, 56*, 431–442.

Rosch, E. (1978). Principles of categorisation. In E. Rosch & B.B. Lloyd (Eds.), *Cognition and categorisation.* Hillsdale, NJ: Lawrence Erlbaum Associates Inc.

Rosch, E., & Mervis, C.B. (1975). Family resemblances: Studies in the internal structure of categories. *Cognitive Psychology, 7*, 573–605.

Rosch, E., Mervis, C.B., Gray, W.D., Johnson, M.D., & Boyes-Braem, P. (1976). Basic objects in natural categories. *Cognitive Psychology, 8*, 382–439.

Rose, S., & Blank, N. (1974). The potency of context in children's cognition: An illustration through conservation. *Child Development, 45*, 499–502.

Rose, S.A., & Feldman, J.F. (1995). Prediction of I.Q. and specific cognitive abilities at 11 years from infancy measures. *Developmental Psychology, 31*, 685–696.

Rosengren, K.S., Gelman, S.A., Kalish, C.W., & McCormick, M. (1991). As time goes by: Children's early understanding of growth in animals. *Child Development, 62*, 1302–1320.

Rovee-Collier, C. K. (1993). The capacity for long-term memory in infancy. *Current Directions in Psychological Science, 2*, 130–135.

Rovee-Collier, C., & Hayne, H. (1987). Reactivation of infant memory: Implications for cognitive development. *Advances in Child Development and Behaviour, 20*, 185–238.

Rovee-Collier, C., Schechter, A., Shyi, G.C.W., & Shields, P. (1992). Perceptual identification of contextual attributes and infant memory retrieval. *Developmental Psychology, 28*, 307–318.

Rovee-Collier, C.K., Sullivan, M.W., Enright, M., Lucas, D., & Fagen, J.W. (1980). Reactivation of infant memory. *Science, 208*, 1159–1161

Rudy, L., & Goodman, G.S. (1991). Effects of participation on children's reports: Implications for children's testimony. *Developmental Psychology, 27*, 527–538.

Ruffman, T., Perner, J., Olson, D., & Doherty, M. (1993). Reflecting on scientific thinking: Children's understanding of the hypothesis–evidence relation. *Child Development, 64*, 1617–1636.

Rumelhart, D.E., & Abramson, A.A. (1983). A model for analogical reasoning. *Cognitive Psychology, 5*, 1–28.

Russell, J. (1996). *Agency: Its role in mental development.* Hove, UK: Psychology Press.

Russo, R., Nichelli, P., Gibertoni, M., & Cornia, C. (1995). Developmental trends in implicit and explicit memory: A picture completion study. *Journal of Experimental Child Psychology, 59*, 566–578.

Samuel, J. & Bryant, P.E. (1984). Asking only one question in the conservation experiment. *Journal of Child Psychology and Psychiatry, 25*, 315–318.

Schachter, D.L., & Moscovitch, M. (1984). Infants, amnesics and dissociable memory systems. In M. Moscovitch (Ed.), *Infant memory: Its relation to normal and pathological memory in humans and other animals* (pp.173–216). New York: Plenum Press.

Schaffer, D.R. (1985). *Developmental psychology: Theory, research and applications.* Belmont, CA: Wadsworth Inc.

Schneider, W. (1985). Developmental trends in the metamemory–memory behaviour relationship: An integrative review. In D.L. Forrest-Pressley, G.E. MacKinnon & T.G. Waller (Eds.), *Cognition, metacognition and human performance* (Vol. 1, pp.57–109). Orlando, FL: Academic Press.

Schneider, W. (1986). The role of conceptual knowledge and metamemory in the development of organisational processes in memory. *Journal of Experimental Child Psychology, 42,* 218–236.

Schneider, W., & Bjorklund, D.F. (in press). Memory. To appear in K. Kuhn & R. Siegler, (Eds.), *Handbook of child psychology,* 5th Ed., Vol. 2, *Cognition, perception and language.*

Schneider, W., Boes, K., & Rieder, H. (1993). Performance prediction in adolescent top tennis players. In J. Beckmann, H. Strang & E. Hahn (Eds.), *Aufmerksamkeit und Energetisierung.* Goettingen: Hogrefe.

Schneider, W., Gruber, H., Gold, A., & Opwis, K. (1993). Chess expertise and memory for chess positions in children and adults. *Journal of Experimental Child Psychology, 56,* 328–349.

Schneider, W., Korkel, J., & Weinert, F.E. (1989). Domain-specific knowledge and memory performance: A comparison of high- and low-aptitude children. *Journal of Educational Psychology, 81,* 306–312.

Schneider, W., & Pressley, M. (1989). *Memory development between 2 and 20.* New York: Springer.

Schneider, W., & Sodian, B. (1988). Metamemory-memory behaviour relationships in young children: Evidence from a memory-for-location task. *Journal of Experimental Child Psychology, 45,* 209–233.

Sedlak, A.J., & Kurtz, S.T. (1981). A review of children's use of causal inference principles. *Child Development, 52,* 759–784.

Shanks, D.R. & St. John, M.F. (1994). Characteristics of dissociable human learning systems. *Behavioural and Brain Sciences, 17,* 367–447.

Shultz, T.R. (1982). Rules of causal attribution. *Monographs of the Society for Research in Child Development, 47* (1, Serial No. 194).

Shultz, T.R., Fisher, G.W., Pratt, C.C., & Rulf, S. (1986). Selection of causal rules. *Child Development, 57,* 143–152.

Shultz, T.R., & Kestenbaum, N.R. (1985). Causal reasoning in children. *Annals of Child Development, 2,* 195–249.

Shultz, T.R., & Mendelson, R. (1975). The use of covariation as a principle of causal analysis. *Child Development, 46,* 394–399.

Shultz, T.R., Pardo, S., & Altmann, E. (1982). Young children's use of transitive inference in causal chains. *British Journal of Psychology, 73,* 235–241.

Shultz, T.R., & Ravinsky, F.B. (1977). Similarity as a principle of causal inference. *Child Development, 48,* 1552–1558.

Siegal, M. (1991). *Knowing children: Experiments in conversation and cognition.* Hillsdale, NJ: Lawrence Erlbaum Associates Inc.

Siegler, R.S. (1978). *Children's thinking: What develops?* Hillsdale, NJ: Lawrence Erlbaum Associates Inc.

Siegler, R.S. (1995). How does change occur: A microgenetic study of number conservation. *Cognitive Psychology, 28,* 225–273.

Siegler, R.S., & Liebert, R.M. (1974). Effects of contiguity, regularity and age on children's causal inferences. *Developmental Psychology, 10,* 574–579.

Sigman, M., Cohen, S.E., Beckwith, L., Asarnow, R., & Parmelee, A.H. (1991). Continuity in cognitive abilities from infancy to 12 years of age. *Cognitive Development, 6*, 47–57.

Sigman, M., Cohen, S.E., Beckwith, L., & Parmelee, A.H. (1986). Infant attention in relation to intellectual abilities in childhood. *Developmental Psychology, 22*, 788–792.

Simon, T.J., Hespos, S.J., & Rochat, P. (1995). Do infants understand simple arithmetic? A replication of Wynn (1992). *Cognitive Development, 10*, 253–269.

Simons, D.J., & Keil, F.C. (1995). An abstract to concrete shift in the development of biological thought: The *insides* story. *Cognition, 56*, 129–163.

Slater, A.M. (1989). Visual memory and perception in early infancy. In A.M. Slater & G. Bremner (Eds.), *Infant development* (pp.43–71). Hove, UK: Lawrence Erlbaum Associates Ltd.

Slater, A.M., Morison, V., & Rose, D. (1983). Perception of shape by the new-born baby. *British Journal of Developmental Psychology, 1*, 135–142.

Smiley, S., & Brown, A.L. (1979). Conceptual preferences for thematic or taxonomic relations: A nonmonotonic age trend from preschool to old age. *Journal of Experimental Child Psychology, 28*, 249–257.

Smith, L. (1982). Class inclusion and conclusions about Piagets theory. *British Journal of Psychology, 73*, 267–276.

Sodian, B., Zaitchek, D., & Carey, S. (1991). Young children's differentiation of hypothetical beliefs from evidence. *Child Development, 62*, 753–766.

Somerville, S.C., & Capuani-Shumaker, A. (1984). Logical searches of young children in hiding and finding tasks. *British Journal of Developmental Psychology, 2*, 315–328.

Somerville, S.C., Wellman, H.M., & Cultice, J.C. (1983). Young children's deliberate reminding. *Journal of Genetic Psychology, 143*, 87–96.

Sophian, C., & Somerville, S.C. (1988). Early developments in logical reasoning: Considering alternative possibilities. *Cognitive Development, 3*, 183–222.

Spelke, E.S. (1976). Infants' intermodal perception of events. *Cognitive Psychology, 8*, 553–560.

Spelke, E.S. (1991). Physical knowledge in infancy: Reflections on Piaget's theory. In S. Carey & R. Gelman (Eds.). *The epigenesis of mind: Essays on biology and cognition* (pp.133–169). Hillsdale, NJ: Lawrence Erlbaum Associates Inc.

Spelke, E.S., Phillips, A., & Woodward, A.L. (1995). Infants' knowledge of object motion and human action. In D. Sperber, D. Premack, & A. Premack (Eds.), *Causal cognition: A multidisciplinary debate* (pp. 44–78). Oxford: Oxford University Press.

Starkey, P., & Cooper, R.G. (1980). Perception of number by human infants. *Science, 210*, 1033–1035.

Starkey, P., Spelke, E.S., & Gelman, R. (1983). Detection of intermodal numerical correspondences by human infants. *Science, 222*, 179–181.

Stechler, G., & Latz, E. (1966). Some observations on attention and arousal in the human infant. *Journal of the American Academy of Child Psychology, 5*, 517–525.

Strauss, S. (in press). Review of Goswami, U.: Analogical reasoning in children. *Cognition & Pragmatics.*

Tipper, S.P., Bourque, T.A., Anderson, S.H., & Brehaut, J.C. (1989). Mechanisms of attention: A developmental study. *Journal of Experimental Child Psychology, 48*, 353–378.

Tomasello, M. (1990). Cultural transmission in the tool use and communicatory signalling of chimpanzees? In S. Parker & K. Gibson (Eds.), *Language and intelligence in monkeys and apes: Comparative developmental perspectives* (pp.274–311). Cambridge: Cambridge University Press.

Turkewitz, G. (1995). The what and why of infancy and cognitive development. *Cognitive Development, 10,* 459–465.

Vaughan, Jr. W., & Greene, S.L. (1984). Pigeon visual memory capacity. *Journal of Experimental Psychotherapy: Animal Behaviour Processes, 10,* 265–271.

Viennot, L. (1979). Spontaneous reasoning in elementary dynamics. *European Journal of Science Education, 1,* 205–221.

Vintner, A. (1986). The role of movement in eliciting early imitations. *Child Development, 57,* 66–71.

Visalberghi, E., & Fragaszy, D. (1990). Do monkeys ape? In S. Parker & K. Gibson (Eds.), *Language and intelligence in monkeys and apes: Comparative developmental perspectives* (pp. 247–273). Cambridge: Cambridge University Press.

Waldmann, M.R., Holyoak, K.J., & Fratianne, A. (1995). Causal models and the acquisition of category structure. *Journal of Experimental Psychology: General, 124,* 181–206.

Wason, P.C. (1966). Reasoning. In B. Foss (Ed.), *New horizons in psychology.* Harmondsworth, UK: Penguin Books.

Wason, P.C., & Johnson-Laird, P.N. (1972). *Psychology of reasoning: Structure and content.* Cambridge, MA: Harvard University Press.

Waxman, S.R. (1990). Linguistic biases and the establishment of conceptual hierarchies: Evidence from preschool children. *Cognitive Development, 5,* 123–150.

Wellman, H.M. (1978). Knowledge of the interaction of memory variables: A developmental study of metamemory. *Developmental Psychology, 14,* 24–29.

Wellman, H.M., & Gelman, S.A. (in press). Knowledge acquisition in foundational domains. In D. Kuhn & R. Siegler (Eds.), *Cognition, perception and language. Volume 2 of the Handbook of Child Psychology* (5th edition). [Editor in Chief: William Damon.] New York: Wiley.

Wellman, H.M., Ritter, K., & Flavell, J. (1975). Deliberate memory development in the delayed reactions of very young children. *Developmental Psychology, 11,* 780–787.

Wellman, H.M., Somerville, S.C., & Haake, R.J. (1979). Development of search procedures in real-life spatial environments. *Developmental Psychology, 15,* 530–542.

White, P.A. (1993). *The understanding of causation and the production of action: From infancy to adulthood.* Hove, UK: Lawrence Erlbaum Associates Ltd.

Whiten, A., & Ham, R. (1992). On the nature and evolution of imitation in the animal kingdom: Reappraisal of a century of research. In P.B. Slater, J.S. Rosenblatt, C. Beer, & M. Milinski (Eds.), *Advances in the study of behaviour* (pp.239–283). San Diego, CA: Academic Press.

Wilkening, F. (1981). Integrating velocity, time and distance information: A developmental study. *Cognitive Psychology, 13,* 231–247.

Wilkening, F. (1982). Children's knowledge about time, distance and velocity interrelations. In W.J. Friedman (Ed.), *The developmental psychology of time* (pp.87–112). New York: Academic Press.

Wilkening, F., & Anderson, N.H. (1991). Representation and diagnosis of knowledge structures in developmental psychology. In N.H. Anderson (Ed.), *Contributions to information integration theory: Vol. III. Developmental* (pp.43–80). Hillsdale, NJ: Lawrence Erlbaum Associates Inc.

Winston, P.H. (1980, December). Learning and reasoning by analogy. In *Communications of the ACM, 23* (12).

Wynn, K. (1992). Addition and subtraction by human infants. *Nature, 358,* 749–750.

Xu, F., & Carey, S. (1996). Infants' metaphysics: The case of numerical identity. *Cognitive Psychology, 30,* 111–153.

Younger, B.A. (1985). The segregation of items into categories by 10-month-old infants. *Child Development, 56,* 1574–1583.

Younger, B.A. (1990). Infants' detection of correlations among feature categories. *Child Development, 61,* 614–620.

Younger, B.A., & Cohen, L.B. (1983). Infant perception of correlations among attributes. *Child Development, 54,* 858–867.

Yussen, S.R., & Levy, V.M. (1975). Developmental changes in predicting one's own span of short-term memory. *Journal of Experimental Child Psychology, 19,* 502–508.

Zelazo, P.D., Frye, D., & Rapus, T. (1996). An age-related dissociation between knowing rules and using them. *Cognitive Development, 11,* 37–63.

Indices

Author index

Abramson, A.A. 56
Altmann, E. 130, 133, 154
Aman, C. 180, 181, 182
Amsel, E. 137
Andersen, C. 140, 142, 277
Anderson, J.R. 53, 56, 60, 66
Anderson, N.H. 145, 151–152, 154, 155, 267, 276
Anderson, S.H. 196
Anisfeld, M. 268
Asarnow, R. 20, 66
Atran, S. 112
Atkinson, J. 1
Aviano, S. 202

Baddeley, A.D. 185
Baillargeon, R. 32–33, 33–34, 35–37, 38–39, 47–48, 56, 57–58, 59, 60, 70–71, 132–133, 152, 155, 268, 269
Bartlett, F.C. 161
Batterman, N. 104–105
Bauer, P.J. 75–76, 77, 78–79, 103, 107–8, 155, 174–176
Beach, D.R. 201–202
Beckwith, L. 19, 20, 66
Beilin, H. 259
Benenson, J. 45
Bertenthal, B.I. 87–88

Bertoncini, J. 10
Bigelow, E. 69–70, 269
Billeter, J. 275
Billman, D.O. 226
Biro, S. 51–53, 71
Bjorklund, B.R. 163, 204–205
Bjorklund, D.F. 163, 180–181, 190, 204–205, 209
Black, J. 57–58
Blank, N. 245, 247–248
Blaye, A. 231
Bloom, L. xvii
Blue, N. 123, 155
Boes, K. 213
Bornstein, M.H. 19
Borton, R.W. 15
Bottoms, B.L. 180, 181
Bourque, T.A. 196
Boyes-Braem, P. 26, 27, 74
Braddick, O. 1
Bransford, J.D. 206
Brehaut, J.C. 196
Breslow, L. 236
Bridges, E. 252–253
Brooks, P.H. 69, 269
Brown, A.L. 64, 102, 112, 133, 168–169, 200, 206, 210, 223–225, 226–227, 255, 267, 276

Hulme, C. 191, 192
Hutchinson, J. 212–213

Ihsen, E. 34–35
Inagaki, K. 97–98, 100, 112
Inhelder, B. 259, 273

Johansson, G. 87
Johnson, M.D. 26, 27, 74
Johnson, M.H. 10, 11–12, 72, 218
Johnson-Laird, P.N. 230
Jones, S.S. 80, 84
Junn, E.N. 226
Justice, E.M. 207

Kagan, J. 45
Kaiser, M.K. 152
Kalish, C.W. 95–96
Kane, M.J. 226–227
Karmiloff-Smith, A. xvi, 215–218,
    289–290
Keane, M.K. 64
Keeble, S. 46, 268
Keil, F.C. 92–93, 94, 98–100, 104–105,
    110, 112
Kestenbaum, N.R. 117
Kirsner, K. 169–170
Klahr, D. 137
Kobasigawa, A. 207–208
Koelling, R.A. 110
Korkel, J. 213
Kozlowski, L.T. 87
Kremer, K.E. 101–102
Krist, H. 154–155
Kuhn, D. 112, 137, 140, 142, 276, 277
Kunzinger, E.L. 202–203
Kurtz, B.E. 209
Kurtz, S.T. 158

Lakoff, G. 106, 109
Lamsfuss, S. 88–89
Lane, D.M. 196

Larus, D.M. 183–184
Latz, E. 10
Lawrence, A. 191
Leevers, H.J. 229–230
Legrenzi, P. 230
Leslie, A.M. 46, 48, 54, 55–56, 71, 118,
    268
Levy, V.M. 199
Liebert, R.M. 127
Light, P. 231, 245–246, 254
Liker, J. 213
Littler, J.E. 191
Loftus, E. 180
Long, C. 226
Lucas, D. 6
Lunzer, E.A. 277
Lyons, B.G. 251–252

MacKinnon, G.E. 210
Mandler, J.M. 8, 9, 54, 62, 70, 75–76, 77,
    78–79, 103, 107, 155, 175–176
Markman, E.M. 82, 83–84,
    250–251, 271
Marzolf, D.P. 167
Massey, C.M. 89–90
McCall, R.B. 21–22, 196
McCarrell, N.J. 69, 269
McCloskey, M. 152
McCormick, M. 95–96
McCutcheon, E. 3
McDonough, L. 8, 9, 155
McEvoy, J. 244
McGarrigle, J. 245, 271
McKee, R.D. 163
McKenzie, B.E. 17, 34–35, 69–70, 269
Meck, E. 119–123
Medin, D.L. 105, 109
Mehler, J. 10
Meltzoff, A.N. 8, 15, 16–18, 50–51,
    61–64, 268
Mendelson, R. 126–127, 128
Merritt, K. 184–185

Mervis, C.B. 26, 27, 74, 80, 105, 106–107
Michotte, A. 46
Millar, S. 191–192
Miller, K. 166
Miller, S.A. 244, 246, 248
Milner, B. 67
Montangero, J. 275
Moore, D. 45
Moore, M.K. 16–18, 268
Morison, V. 14
Morrongiello, B.A. 10
Moscovitch, M. 161, 163
Muir, C. 191
Murphy, G.L. 77
Myers, N.A. 5
Myers, N.A. 6

Nadasdy, Z. 51–53, 71
Naito, M. 170–171, 173
Naus, M.J. 202
Needham, A. 47–48, 60
Neisser, U. 74, 162
Nelson, K. 164, 177
Newcombe, N. 172, 173
Nichelli, P. 171–172
Nida, R.E. 184–185
Nunez, M. 233–234, 254

Oakes, L.M. xvii
O'Connor, N. 189–190
O'Loughlin, M. 137
Olson, D. 141–142, 277
O'Moore, A.M. 244
Opwis, K. 211
O'Reilly, A.W. 93
Ornstein, P.A. 183–185, 202
O'Sullivan, J.T. 203
Over, R. 17

Palfai, T. 159, 194–195
Pani, J.R. 74, 106–107

Pardo, S. 130, 133, 154
Parmelee, A.H. 19, 20, 66
Pascual-Leone, J. 214, 255–256
Pauen, S. 94–95, 111, 112, 146–149, 176, 253–254, 256
Pears, R. 237–239, 271
Pearson, D.A. 196
Pennington, B.F. 194
Pergament, G.G. 251–252
Perner, J. 141–142, 277
Perris, E.E. 5
Peterson, M. 45
Phillips, A. 49–50
Phillips, K. 21
Piaget, J. xix–xxi, 66, 137, 186, 214, 221, 234, 241, 249–250, 259–279, 289–290
Plomin, R. 21
Polley, R. 64–65, 225
Pratt, C.C. 130
Prechtl, H.F.R. xv
Premack, D. 64
Pressley, M. 203, 209
Proffitt, D.R. 87–88, 152
Pufall, P.B. 259

Quinn, P.C. 30, 31–32, 75, 106

Rapus, T. 195–196
Ravinsky, F.B. 129–130
Reese, E. 179
Reid, D.K. 259
Reznick, S.J. 45
Rieder, H. 213
Rieser, J.J. 69, 269
Ritter, K. 200
Robbins, A.H. 245–246, 254
Robin, A. 212–213
Rochat, P. 40–45
Roebers, C.E.M. 180–181
Roodenrys, S. 192
Rosch, E. 26, 27, 74, 77, 85, 105

Wilkening, F. 112, 145, 148–149, 150–152, 154–155, 158, 253–254, 256, 267, 276
Winston, P.H. 64, 222
Witryol, S.L. 202–203
Woodruff, G. 64
Woodward, A.L. 49–50
Wynn, K. 40

Xu, F. 39–40

Younger, B.A. 27–30, 40, 75, 106
Youngshim, K. 251–252
Yussen, S.R. 199

Zaitchek, D. 137, 140–141, 276
Zelazo, P.D. 159, 194–196
Zohar, A. 140, 142, 277

Subject index

A-not-B error 66–68, 193, 269
Accommodation 259–260
Agency 46, 48–53
Analogical reasoning xx, 64–66, 97–98,
    112–113, 148–150, 167, 221–227,
    253–256, 266–267, 275–276, 282–283,
    291
Animacy 86–97, 285
Articulation rate 190–192
Assimilation 259–260
Association in memory 205, 208
Attention
    in childhood 196–197
    in infancy 10–18

Balance scale tasks 143–145, 148–150
Biological knowledge 86–113

Canonicality 119–123, 155
Categorisation 14, 25–30, 53–56,
    73–113, 289
Causal bias xvii, 110–111, 117–118, 268,
    291–293
Causal principles 118, 123–130
Causal relations
    and agency 48–53
    and analogy 65–66, 224–225
    and animacy 101–102

and memory 6–9, 175–176
and representation 31, 45–48,
    264–266
knowledge about 118–123
Central executive 185, 192–196
Characteristic-to-defining shift
    104–105
Class inclusion 249–254, 261, 271–272
Collision events 45–46, 49–50
Conceptual development *see*
    Categorisation
Conceptual change 111–113, 213
Concrete operations 221, 234–254, 260,
    269–273
Conservation 241–249, 271
Cross modal
    perception 15–16
    understanding 45
Cueing 7, 11, 205–206, 236

Deafness
    and memory 189–190
Deductive logic 227–234
Depth of processing 169–171
Domains xvi, 55, 113, 118, 209, 282,
    283–285

Ecological validity 182, 199, 218, 244

Egocentricity 35, 270
Elaboration
    and memory 179, 287
Essentialism 110
Executive function 192–196
Eyewitness memory 179–185

False memories 180–185
Fragment completion tasks 170–172
Formal operations 273–277
Frontal cortex 66–68, 193–196, 269
Growth 95–98

Habituation
    speed of 18–20
    visual 18, 26, 287
High amplitude sucking 2
Hypothesis testing 137–142, 273–275,
    276–277

Image schemas 54–55
Imitation
    and representation 266, 268
    delayed 8, 61–64
    learning by 61–64
    neonate 16
    of intentions 50–51
Infantile amnesia 161, 162–164
Inhibition 22, 68–70, 196–197, 269, 287
INRC grouping 274, 277
Integration rules 142–151, 276
Intelligence 18–22, 190, 209, 213–214,
    287
Intentional stance 51–53
Intuitive physics 151–155, 267

Knowledge base xvi, 161, 184–185,
    209–210, 213, 215–218, 227, 281–283,
    288

Language
    and conceptual development 84–86

and conservation 250–253
and memory 163, 164
Leading questions 180–184
Learning
    by analogy 64–66
    by imitation 61–64
    from TV 63–64
    in infancy 2–9, 60–66
    conditional 6
    explanation-based 117, 248–249,
        281
    Matching-to-sample 77-78, 102–103

Memory
    episodic
    explicit 9, 173–174
    eyewitness 179–185
    for novel events 177–178
    implicit 9, 169–174
    in infancy 1–9
    recognition 3, 20, 164, 167–169
    spatial 33–35
    working 185–197
Mental models 151–152
Metamemory 199, 206–210
Mnemonic strategies 199–206
Modules 55–56, 162
Motion 87–90

Naming 191–192, 207
Natural kinds 30, 92–95, 98–102
Nature/nurture xviii
Neo–Piagetian theories 186, 214–215,
    284
Novelty preference 4
Novice–expert distinction 210–214
Number
    conservation 241–242
    in infancy 40–45, 55

Object permanence xx, 35–39, 263–264,
    269